Inner Experience and Neuroscience

Inner Experience and Neuroscience

Merging Both Perspectives

Donald D. Price and James J. Barrell

A Bradford Book

The MIT Press
Cambridge, Massachusetts
London, England

MIT Press books may be purchased at special quantity discounts for business or sales promotional use. For information, please email special_sales@mitpress.mit.edu or write to Special Sales Department, The MIT Press, 55 Hayward Street, Cambridge, MA 02142.

This book was set in Stone Sans and Stone Serif by Toppan Best-set Premedia Limited. Printed and bound in the United States of America.

Library of Congress Cataloging-in-Publication Data

Price, Donald D.
Inner experience and neuroscience : merging both perspectives / Donald D. Price and James J. Barrell.
   p. cm.
"A Bradford Book."
Includes bibliographical references and index.
ISBN 978-0-262-01765-7
1. Phenomenological psychology. 2. Experience—Psychological aspects.
3. Consciousness. 4. Neuropsychology. I. Barrell, James J. II. Title.
BF204.5.P75 2012
153—dc23
2011048196

10 9 8 7 6 5 4 3 2 1

Contents

Preface

This book is the result of two careers that have been dedicated to the development of a science of human experience and its integration with neuroscience and psychology. The first career began with research in neuroscience. Early on, Don Price did research on spinal dorsal horn circuitry and later incorporated the tools of psychophysics. Adding a psychophysical foundation to this line of research extended the insights gained by recording from neurons—it became more obvious why certain experiments were done and what they meant. It led to the idea of relating human sensory experience to neural responses, an idea that has independently arisen in the minds of many sensory neuroscientists. However, the realization that pain is much more than just a sensory experience led him to explore the dimensions of emotions and meanings as well as the sources of variability in the pain experience. Then two major influences shaped the remainder of his career. The first was a longstanding interest in both the science and the philosophy of human experience, an interest fostered by Jim Barrell, coauthor of this book. The second was an explosive growth in neuroscience and its technologies (e.g., neural imaging).

The second career, that of Jim Barrell, focused more explicitly on the development of a science of human experience and was based on several disciplines, including phenomenology, cognitive psychology, Eastern philosophy, psychophysiology, and neuroscience. The key ideas in this book that are about developing a qualitative method for the study of human experience are his. Jim successfully applied experiential methods for performance enhancement of college and professional sports teams (San Francisco Giants, San Francisco Forty-niners, Orlando Magic, University of Florida Gators, Virginia Commonwealth University Rams). Based on these two careers and considerable dialogue and collaboration between the two authors, this book represents a combined vision of how to merge a science of human experience with neuroscience and the rest of psychology.

The organization of this book follows a natural progression. The first chapter opens with questions. Why do we need a science of human experience? Can we construct a science of consciousness? Are there preexisting foundations for a science of meaning and experience?

We then go on to explain that understanding human meanings is essential for explanations of human experience, behavior, and psychophysiological responses and that even understanding results of neuroscience research could greatly benefit from an experiential perspective and methods. In particular, the accuracy of results of both sciences would be improved. We briefly describe preexisting paradigms for investigating phenomenal experience, including classic introspection, phenomenology, the descriptive experiential sampling method (designed by Russell T. Hurlburt and his colleagues), and the experiential–phenomenological method developed by us. The last part of this chapter focuses on issues of philosophy and feasibility in applying experiential methods in neuroscience.

The second and third chapters are about lessons to be learned from psychophysical methods. We think such methods are critical for integrating experiential and natural sciences. They also provide groundwork for training and instructing participants in how to observe and report on simple experiences. At this point in the book, specifically in chapter 3, there is an exploratory exercise designed for the reader. *We think that it is critical that the reader participate in this exercise*, which should be fairly easy and enjoyable. This experiential exploration may be critical for appreciating a key theme of this book: Understanding interrelationships between fundamental dimensions of human emotional feelings helps us to understand how emotions, choosing, and motivation are related within experience. The exercise may help the reader see that these relationships can be directly verified in his or her own experience. We provide several similar opportunities throughout the book.

Chapter 4 describes and explains qualitative paradigms, some of which can be merged with the quantitative methods described in preceding chapters. Some paradigms, such as the descriptive experiential sampling method, simply attempt to describe inner experience of people. This method explores similarities and differences in how people experience moments of everyday life. The results turn out to be very interesting and often surprising. Our experiential–phenomenological method, on the other hand, seeks to arrive at the common factors of different types of experiences, particularly emotions. These common factors then become the basis for hypotheses that can be tested with quantitative methods, as discussed in chapters 5 and 6. As we explain, the results of this approach dovetail in interesting ways with an existing neuroscience literature on emotions and choice behavior.

Chapters 7 and 8 explain how an experiential perspective and some experiential methods help provide a more accurate formulation of the phenomenology of human pain and suffering.

A definition of pain that is directly based on how pain is experienced has clear advantages over attempts to define pain in terms of stimuli that evoke it or behavior that is observed from an external viewpoint. The experiential definition is supported by vast numbers of studies that have taken place in laboratories and health-care settings. As with other topics of this book, many studies show that results from a first-person perspective and from neuroscience can be integrated. This integration extends to relationships between the immediate unpleasantness of pain and emotions based on extended meanings—suffering. In this sense, relationships between immediate feelings and extended ones are like the organization of consciousness itself, as suggested by Antonio Damasio's concepts of core and extended consciousness.

Chapter 9 helps us understand how pain and suffering, as well as other medical conditions, can be dynamically modified by what one is experiencing at the moment. This dynamic modulation occurs during placebo responses (reduction of symptoms as a result of changes in desires and expectations) as well as during nocebo responses. This modulation is accompanied by corresponding changes in the brain, suggesting that placebo responses are real psychological and biological events (as opposed to statistical artifacts or regression to the mean).

Chapter 10 illustrates how characterization of a background state of consciousness, such as a hypnotic state, can begin with a qualitative experiential study, followed by a quantitative study, and finally neuroimaging studies that are informed by results of experiential science. The hypnotic state is comprised of several dimensions that support a background state of consciousness. An interesting implication of this progression is that a similar approach could be used to characterize any background state of consciousness.

The final chapter is a discussion of how merging experiential science with other sciences can extend the efforts of science to address and help solve difficult issues and problems. It begins with an explanation of the types of causation demonstrated by science and shows the necessity of including *mind–mind, mind*–brain, and brain–*mind* causes. This necessity is particularly relevant to the question of "free will" or volition. We end with a discussion of how experiential science can be applied to problems posed by complex negative emotions and states of consciousness that support them.

The book contains several topics discussed from the perspectives of different disciplines, including philosophy, psychophysics, neuroscience, and psychology. We have attempted to simplify discussion within each perspective because we realize that readers will have different levels of knowledge pertaining to these areas and some may even be impatient with one or more of the disciplines. We recommend patience, of course, but we also recommend efforts to relate each topic to experience. That is a reason why exploratory exercises are included. Some background knowledge in philosophy, psychology, and neuroscience would also be helpful.

We have many people to acknowledge and thank for their influence on this book. First, our teachers, both formal and informal ones, have stimulated our imagination and caused us to continuously ponder and question everything. Their influence can be seen within the pages of this book and in the citations. They include scientists and philosophers throughout the world and our colleagues at the University of Florida (U.S.), University of West Georgia (U.S.), and Aarhus University in Denmark. We would like to specifically mention those who influenced the main ideas covered in this book, including Max Velmans, Murat Aydede, Antonio Damasio, Pierre Rainville, James E. Barrell, Donald Medieros, Jeffrey M. Schwartz, and Robert Neimeyer. Then, of course, there are people who gave us personal support, including our wives (Suzanne Sindledecker for JJB and Elizabeth Price for DDP) and adult children (Amy for DDP, Jim and Denise for JJB). We thank Tom Stone, former senior book editor at MIT Press, whose enthusiasm and support for this project inspired confidence that we could complete it. Finally, we are grateful to Art Maynor, now deceased, who supplied cartoons for chapters 4 and 5.

1 Developing a Science of Human Meanings and Consciousness

Within the last two decades there has been an enormous acceleration in work on consciousness within the disciplines of neuroscience, psychology, and philosophy. If enough integration takes place between these fields of inquiry, we might expect a golden age for the science of consciousness and, more importantly, an understanding that could greatly facilitate human progress. We may be very close to some critical answers. Yet despite the progress made so far, it is still partly unclear how to develop paradigms for understanding human experience and how to integrate knowledge obtained from them with the rest of the sciences. The overarching aim of this book is to explain how these problems are being solved and to propose an agenda that could be helpful in understanding consciousness.

1.1 Why Do We Need a Science of Human Experience?

Few would disagree with the need to know the nature of conscious experience. It is the sea in which we live, yet it remains one of the most mysterious of phenomena. Beyond this obvious need, understanding consciousness appears necessary for us to understand anything, even the nature of understanding itself. When we claim to have verified a hypothesis or to know a fact, our method inevitably relies on how we experience ourselves in relation to this fact or hypothesis. In a very critical respect, attaining understanding partly depends on our personal experience of certainty and our desire to know what is true. Let us take a simple hypothetical example from brain science. When a neuroscientist electrically stimulates a site within an area of the human brain that registers body sensations and the person whose brain is being stimulated immediately reports a tingling sensation in his left hand, the neuroscientist might tentatively conclude that neural activity in this location of the brain causes tactile body sensations. The neuroscientist might feel *certain* and even *good* about this conclusion. Since our method of understanding partly depends on these dimensions of experience, we need to know their nature in order to see how they influence our knowledge. After all, we could be deluded, biased, or simply engaging in a belief system when we arrive at our conclusions.

That a critical component of scientific verification relies on subjective dimensions such as certainty and positive regard for a conclusion is not easy to reconcile with a predominant focus of Western scientific practice that implicitly assumes that the conclusions of science exist in a disembodied viewpoint—a view from nowhere. This assumption is understandable because science is largely directed toward the outside world. For example, psychology has been dominated by questions concerning the relationship of environmental factors to behavior. This is so despite our immediate sense of both an outside world in which we live and a subjective life in ourselves (Ouspensky, 1971).

1.1.1   Third-Person Data and First-Person Data

Our sense of the outside world and an inner subjective life relate to two key classes of scientific data: third-person data that are about objects and events that are considered to be external (i.e., in the world) and first-person data that are about how we *experience* phenomena of the world as well as our innermost thoughts, feelings, and meanings (Chalmers, 2004). At the most fundamental level, however, the distinction between first- and third-person data breaks down because even our observations of behavior, brain activity, and events in the world belong to a human perspective and are within at least someone's experience. As Merleau-Ponty has put it, "One must take experience as everything or nothing" (Merleau-Ponty, 1962). For the purposes of this book, the distinction between third- and first-person data is still helpful because science and philosophy strongly and commonly distinguish between the two viewpoints and their related types of data.

1.1.2   Should We Eliminate or Integrate the First-Person Viewpoint?

Western philosophical and scientific practice has largely ignored human subjective life, something that is always potentially available in direct phenomenal experience. Our sense of the "outer" world and our inner life are there, implicitly or explicitly, in our moment-to-moment experience. The natural sciences have placed an enormous emphasis on the world in which we live whereas the arts, religion, and philosophy are concerned with both the outer world and subjective life. Current Western philosophical and scientific practice is predominantly materialistic and inspired by the progress of natural sciences in explaining the material world. Yet there is a crucial sense in which knowledge of the material world and of phenomenal experience has not been integrated within science, much to the detriment of human understanding. Even understanding the material world requires that we look inwardly into the nature of our experience. We are certainly not the first to point this out. This book is an attempt to demonstrate how methods for studying human experience are being developed and integrated with the rest of science, particularly neuroscience and psychology. It focuses on paradigms for investigating human experience and how results of these paradigms are being interfaced with neuroscience studies, such as those using brain imaging. Both the experiential studies and neuroscience experiments that followed them are leading to accelerated understanding of emotions, decision making, pain, placebo responses, and the nature of background states of consciousness.

But why should we even do this? Wherever any science goes, whether it is neuroscience, biological science, social science, or physics, it is first of all a science carried out by human beings having human experiences. There can be no rational denial of this state of affairs. Although human experience is always present and available, at least during the waking state, it is so much a part of us that we often find it difficult to separate it out as an object for study. It is often a "blind spot" in traditional scientific paradigms. There is a crucial sense in which self-observation and much of scientific explanation about human experience are lacking in scientific reports, reviews, and books. For example, studies of pain reduction by hypnosis almost always combine hypnotic inductions with suggestions for pain relief. In the vast majority of such studies, it is the hypnotic procedures and the suggestions that are implicitly or explicitly considered to be the independent variables. Yet controversies have persisted for decades as to whether the hypnotic inductions are even necessary to evoke hypnotic analgesia, whether an altered state of consciousness is necessary for pain reduction, and whether an alteration in conscious state even *occurs* during hypnotic analgesia (see references in Price, 1996). Thus, in experiments that are about hypnosis or hypnotic phenomena, we often ask questions at the end of the project: "What was the experience of hypnosis like for the participants? Were they truly hypnotized?" Similarly, psychologists often study personality constructs and their interactions with psychological phenomena, such as emotions or pain. After all the multiple and complex statistical analyses are conducted and after the results are discussed in relationship to previous literature, we often wonder *how* participants actually *experience* the psychological mediators of the study, and for that matter, the dependent variables such as emotions.

Even within cognitive science, the immersed phenomenology of experience is almost always absent. As pointed out by Marcel,

> [i]ntrinsically first-person forms of awareness are a problem for naturalistic approaches, including cognitive science, and are often dismissed as unscientific. But since such forms of awareness have a role in science and in testing theories about the nature of such awareness, dismissing them as subjective or mere "folk psychology" to be displaced by greater rigor is not an option. That is, science not only needs to take subjectivity as a topic, it needs to somehow to incorporate subjectivity as a method. (Marcel, 2003)

Consistent with Marcel's view, we think that greater rigor requires integrating experiential science with the rest of natural sciences, not eliminating it.

1.1.3   Can We Construct a Science of Consciousness?

Since human experience occurs and influences all of the sciences, it is time that we attempt to remove this "blind spot" and treat human phenomenal experience as a legitimate area for study. This position is similar to Varela's (1996) claim that consciousness is an explanandum (the phenomenon to be explained) in its own right. This claim has received increasing support in recent years. Beyond this general view, there have been considerable attempts to justify or negate specific types of scientific paradigms aimed at understanding consciousness or phenomenal experience (Varela, Thompson, and Rosch, 1991; Dennett, 1991; Velmans, 2009; Hurlburt and Schwitzgebel, 2007). We intend to show how a science of human experience can be developed through a strategy whereby experiential paradigms are interfaced with methods of the natural sciences (e.g., neuroscience). However, even some of the past work on human consciousness could benefit from reexamination from an experiential perspective. Our main claim is that experiential paradigms can be developed, validated, and then expanded through integration with quantitative methods (e.g., psychophysical methods) and with other sciences, particularly neuroscience. Some of this is not new at all. The integration of neuroscience and psychology is developing rapidly, partly through the advances of technologies such as neuroimaging. We think a unique contribution would be that of showing how the integration of experiential science and natural sciences can actually work and presenting an explicit strategy. For example, we show that experiential studies can be interfaced with brain imaging experiments that are about conscious phenomena, such as pain and placebo responses, and about specific background states of consciousness, such as associative thinking and hypnotic states. We maintain that valuable experiential methodologies exist already and that they can continue to be improved. They negate nothing in other scientific paradigms, and they may add depth and accuracy to current explanations of the nature of the brain and mind and how they function. They may provide more transparent explanations for nonscientists. Finally, we think this effort may be essential for finding viable solutions that are at the heart of so many significant problems in the world, including political, social, and health problems.

1.1.4 What Do We Mean by Human Experience?

We use the word "experience" in this book to refer to immediate phenomenal experience. As you are reading these words, ask yourself this question: What is it like to experience this reading? It could be that you are saying the words in inner speech, or it could be that you are associating the words with images, feelings, or meanings. Perhaps you are experiencing a combination of the above. Our use of the term "phenomenal experience" comes close to the term "consciousness" as used by Velmans (2009). He starts with the phenomenology of consciousness itself, picking out the *phenomena* to which the term refers:

In everyday life there are two contrasting situations which inform our understanding of the term "consciousness." We have knowledge of what it is like to be conscious (when we are awake) as opposed to not being conscious (when in dreamless sleep). We also understand what it is like to be conscious *of* something (when awake or dreaming) as opposed to not being conscious of that thing. (Velmans, 2009)

Both terms, "consciousness" and "phenomenal experience," describe something that normally occurs when phenomenal content is present and does not occur when such content is absent. Phenomenal content usually includes a vast array of perceptions, feelings, and meanings. The intrinsic properties of this content are in their appearances (Chalmers, 2003). Philosophers of the mind use the term "qualia" to refer to these experiences. Qualia are simply those properties that characterize conscious states according to what it is like to experience them (Chalmers, 1996). There is something it is like to see a green lawn, to feel a dull aching pain, to visualize the Golden Gate Bridge, to feel a deep disappointment, and to feel that one has found a meaningful answer. Many philosophers and scientists are interested in phenomenal experiences (qualia), if sometimes only indirectly. For well over a century, various people have proposed a special science or a discipline for understanding human experience, particularly experience as it relates to meanings (see Giorgi, 1970, and references contained therein).

1.1.5 Understanding Human Meanings Is Essential for Explanations of Human Experience, Behavior, and Psychophysiological Responses

Understanding qualia is intimately related to understanding human meanings. Human meaning is ubiquitous and underpins how we experience emotions, behave, and even respond physiologically. One example comes from an experience one of us had when he (JJB) was in a glass-enclosed elevator with two students at a psychology conference in Atlanta. Both students were taking a psychology class from JJB and were learning a method of experiential reporting described in chapter 4. The two students appeared anxious when the elevator ascended several floors. Although they both appeared anxious, they reported quite different experiences when they stepped off the elevator. Is it possible that there are two forms of "glass elevator phobia"? One person had a "fear of heights" and the other "claustrophobia" (fear of being in a closed or confined space). During the ride, each person could focus attention on either the glass enclosure or the sights of the city below. For the person with the fear of heights, the meaning of the glass enclosure was security and a protective barrier while, for the person with claustrophobia, the glass enclosure was associated with a meaning of feeling trapped or suffocated. For the person who feared heights, looking through the glass at the city below suggested falling and the absence of physical security. For the claustrophobic person, it meant freedom and breathing space. These different meanings and experiences could not be discerned simply by watching the two people in the elevator. The differences in meanings were clarified using their first-person experiential reports immediately obtained after the elevator experience. Notice that the two forms of anxiety are based on diametrically opposed lived meanings. They might even entail different coping strategies, such as standing close to the elevator door (fear of heights) or looking out at the city below (claustrophobic). We don't think anything in their history of positive or negative reinforcement either inside or outside elevators could account for the two experiential orientations, even if that could be known. Emotions and their associated behavior can be known when their underlying meanings are known.

Positive and negative reinforcement have long been considered powerful determinants of human behavior. However, we cannot know with certainty whether an experience is positively or negatively reinforcing unless the underlying meanings of the experiences are understood. Imagine rafting down a swift river. Suddenly you lose control of the raft and are heading for some large sharp rocks. You are being tossed and turned by the rapids and are gripped by fear. You continue to fight for control. Finally, through what appears to be a miracle, you find yourself washed safely on the bank of the river. At the end of this harrowing adventure, it is possible to have two very different types of experiences. You can look back on the experience and compare it with your safe result, now knowing that you can get through this exciting type of challenge. You might then say to yourself "That was incredible! I want to do it again!" Alternatively you might initially feel relieved and then "relive" the experience, saying to yourself "Never again!" When one remembers by looking back, knowing that the *result* is completely safe, one might think, "If I got through this, I can get through anything." Focusing on the *result* of experience, you might feel less vulnerable and more likely to participate in similar experiences in the future. In contrast, you might remember through reexperiencing the situation as if it were happening again with the result still in question. In the reliving, the future is still open-ended rather than known. Through focusing on the *process* of the experience, you may feel more vulnerable and be less likely to participate in similar experiences. According to opponent process theory (Solomon and Corbit, 1974), feelings of relief and even exhilaration often follow fearful events (e.g., skydiving, roller coasters, and hang gliding). However, there is considerable variability in the magnitude of positive emotions that follow fearful events. Some people never ride roller coasters after their first ride, and others can't be stopped from repeating them. Perhaps an important source of this variability is related to human meanings.

Finally, the results of an actual experiment illustrate how meanings can relate to large differences in psychophysiological responses to the same stressor. In an experiment conducted at the Medical College of Virginia, 22 students from a university campus were presented with a stress condition consisting of "waiting out" the possibility of a painful electric shock delivered to any one of several electrodes placed on the body (Barrell and Price, 1975). Both heart rate and trapezius muscle electromyogram (EMG) activity were monitored in the stress condition and in the control nonstress condition. A previous pilot study, using the experiential method to be described in chapter 4, revealed two diametrically opposed experiential orientations. "Avoiders" were passive and felt restricted by the stress situation. Their attention was focused primarily on a nonstressful situation and their intent was to keep the stressor away as long as possible. They coped by not thinking about the stressor. "Confronters," on the other hand, were active, trying to figure out the situation and prepare for it. Their attention was focused on the coming stressor and their intent was to hurry up and experience the stressor in order to get it over with. Based on this qualitative experiential study, questionnaires were developed for the descriptive statements just given and used with a second group of participants exposed to the same experimental conditions.

For example, one question was My *preference* was to (a) think about the stressor and be prepared for it; (b) not think about the stressor and just let it happen; (c) other. Similar to the pilot study, in this study participants divided sharply along the lines of an "avoiding" or "confronting" orientation. Thus, based on six questionnaire responses, 10 participants were found to be confronting, 11 avoiding, and only 1 mixed during the stress condition. The psychophysiological responses also were sharply divided according to these two orientations. Avoiders had significantly elevated heart rates in the stress condition as compared to the nonstress condition but no elevations in EMG activity. Confronters, on the other hand, had the reverse pattern, significant elevations in EMG activity but not heart rate during the stress condition. The two patterns of psychophysiological response relate to experiential differences in coping strategy, intent, and ways of attending. Whereas the avoider remains passive and copes by not considering possible negative events, the confronter searches for and attempts to deal with threatening cues. The avoiding orientation is accompanied by passive anxiety and increased heart rate, whereas the confronting orientation is accompanied by increased somatomotor activity related to active coping. The two orientations could not be predicted by the stimulus conditions or anything in the environment because they were the same across all participants. The differences in psychophysiological responses between "avoiders" and "confronters" could only be understood when the meanings were identified.

Therefore, understanding human meanings may be essential for understanding emotional experience, behavior, and psychophysiological responses. In later chapters, we show how the common factors within specific types of experiences, such as the example of performance anxiety, are often specific meanings that are common across persons. This approach also works for understanding human differences, as just illustrated by the stress experiment on avoiders and confronters. Given the possibility of precise analyses of human meanings, one has to wonder if they can be integrated with observations from other sciences, such as neuroscience. Suppose, for example, different types of anxiety or coping orientations could be experientially characterized and then related to specific types of neural patterns of activity in the brain and specific brain mechanisms. Certainly there are some neuroscientists, particularly those who conduct brain imaging, who are beginning to ask these types of questions.

The idea that human meanings underpin psychological responses is not one that has guided psychology throughout the twentieth century. For behaviorists, experimental conditions and overall context have been construed operationally from an external perspective. The use of the simple Skinner box with a lever for reinforcement understandably gives little attention as to how different rats construe their situation. Yet even modern pain testing in rats has recently shown that the factor that generates the largest amount of variability in responses to noxious stimulation is the human experimenter! Groups of rats display systematically different results depending on which experimenter conducts the tests (Mogil, 2009). Rats, like humans, must be very sensitive to contextual factors, and it is conceivable, though perhaps not directly testable, that they develop meanings in relation to their physical and social contexts. In constructing a science of human experience, we need to come to grips with how different persons (and perhaps even rats!) develop meanings in response to their physical and psychosocial contexts and not simply assume the viewpoint of an "external observer."

1.2   Are There Preexisting Foundations for a Science of Meaning and Experience?

Interest in understanding human experiences and their underlying meanings has existed for centuries. However, beginning in the nineteenth century and continuing to the present, there has existed much tension and debate concerning how well the subjective lives of persons can be studied by careful scientific observation and analysis. At one end of this debate are those who claim that a "first-person" science of human experience is impossible, unnecessary, or meaningless. The subjective structures of thoughts, emotional meanings, and even sensations appear outside the reach of scientific investigation for those who make this claim (Dennett, 1991; Rakover, 2002; Skinner, 1957). They would settle for studying behavior, physiology, and environments to better understand people. As a consequence, *meanings* behind behavioral, physiological, and perceptual responses were missing from scientific explanations in much of the psychological research of the twentieth century. Meanings and the structures of direct experience have become the blind spots in human psychological research. David Bakan (1967) pointed to the need to develop methodologies to address this problem within science. With the advent of the recent development of consciousness studies and advances in other sciences, such as brain imaging in neuroscience, those at the other end of this continuing debate claim that it is possible to integrate the study of human meanings and direct experience with neuroscience and the rest of psychology. In this section we provide a brief historical overview of four paradigms for the study of human experience in order to set the context for our description and explanation of scientific paradigms presented in detail in the remaining chapters. These four paradigms, which are by no means inclusive of all available ones, include classic introspectionism, phenomenology, Hurlburt's descriptive experience sampling method, termed DES (Hurlburt and Schwitzgebel, 2007), and an experiential approach and method that we developed in the 1970s and 1980s.

1.2.1 Classic Introspectionism

Introspection is a process by which human observers come to be aware of the mental states that they are currently in and are able to represent those states in some way. For example, you can ask someone to gently tap you on the shoulder within the next hour (at some preselected but undisclosed time) and you might be able to report what was just present in your experience. Thus, as suggested by the etymology of the word (from the Latin *spicere* "look" and *intra* "within"), introspection involves representation of what is noticed *within* phenomenal experience. This content could include thoughts, feelings, images, sensations, and combinations thereof. Some people claim that introspection involves higher order mental representations of introspected states and thereby is seen as a kind of conscious metarepresentation or metacognition (Dretske, 1999). Our use of the term "introspection" refers to directly noticing what is in inner or outer experience and reporting on the contents of experience in a verbal or other type of representational manner (e.g., rating some aspect of experience such as pain intensity). Wilhelm Wundt (1911/1912, discussed by Boring, 1960) maintained the view that introspection provides an experimental method for psychology and set up a laboratory in Leipzig in 1879. It was in fact the first experimental psychology laboratory. Wundt and other introspectionists such as Fechner, Ebbinghaus, and Titchener were interested in discovering laws that characterize the "generalized, normal, human, adult mind" (Titchener, 1908; Titchener, 1924; Boring, 1957). The introspective method achieved some degree of success. One successful outcome was the development of psychophysics, a discipline that is an integral component of psychology, neuroscience, and medicine to this day (see chapter 2).

Nonetheless, introspectionism ran into some problems that formed the basis for its claimed demise. One problem was that attempts to observe thoughts often seemed to fail. A major reason for this appearance of failure was in the nature of the observation. Participants of such experiments were instructed to *actively* attend to their thoughts (Titchener, 1908; 1924). When they *actively* attempted to do, they suddenly were aware that there were no thoughts to observe. You can replicate this negative result by trying to vigorously and actively observe your thoughts. Thus, *active* attending tends to eliminate the very experience one is attempting to observe.

Another problem was the well-known dispute between the Wurzberg School in Germany (Kulpe, Wundt) and American introspectionists (Titchener, 1924) concerning the existence of imageless thoughts. Titchener claimed that thinking without images is impossible whereas Wundt and his colleagues claimed that some ideas could be experienced without images, which they labeled "imageless thought." Titchener disagreed, maintaining that cores of images exist for all ideas, even if those ideas are dim and difficult to apprehend. Both groups of investigators continued to experiment and continued to debate this issue with neither side claiming unequivocal victory. The failure to resolve this issue and the negative influence of active attention on thoughts became reasons for the apparent demise of classic introspectionism, along with the rise of behaviorism.

We consider this demise as apparent and not real for two reasons. The foremost is that there currently exist introspective methods in philosophy and psychology that retain many of the same aims and even methods of classic introspection. In fact, these methods are closely related to several topics to be covered in this book. The second reason is that, when examined carefully, the controversy between the German and American introspection groups was not about the introspected observations, that is, the results of their experiments, but rather their interpretations. This kind of controversy often occurs in other sciences, so it seems hardly a reason for dismissal of a branch of science. Monson and Hurlburt showed that the two groups "did in fact agree with each other's reports of the phenomenon which was called imageless thought" (Monson and Hurlburt, 1993). Both groups reported very similar observations, namely, the existence of "vague and elusive processes, which carry as if in a nutshell the entire meaning of a situation…, such as 'a realization that the division can be carried out without a remainde (Hurlbut and Heavey, 2001). Thus, the two sides basically obtained similar results but disagreed about their theoretical interpretations. As Hurlburt and Heavey point out, "Therefore the imageless thought debate should be understood as contributing to knowledge about how to explore inner experience: psychological science should discriminate strictly between the description of inner phenomena and the use of those descriptions in psychological theorizing."

The list of critics of introspection continues to get longer, yet by continuing to denigrate introspection the critics themselves become suspect. As Vermersch points out, "After all, if any one of these criticisms were conclusive, the rest would become unnecessary!" (Vermersch, 1999). Contrary to what one might believe from reading some historical accounts of the demise of introspectionism, the methodologies of the classic introspectionists became more rigorous in the beginning of the twentieth century. For example, introspective data were collected by groups of observers, so that the contributing observations of the primary researcher remained just one among other inputs (Vermersch, 1999). Similar to modern experimental designs in psychology, the tasks and control conditions were the same for all participants and direct introspected observations were clearly distinguished from second-order commentaries and reflections. These principles are retained in modern paradigms of phenomenology and psychological research that involve introspection. Examples include the next two paradigms to be discussed.

1.2.2 Phenomenology

Phenomenology is the study of phenomena, including lived experience or things in the everyday world (Husserl, 1952; Lyons, 1973; Merleau-Ponty, 1962). The aim of phenomenology is to understand human life experiences as they are immediately experienced prereflectively as opposed to how they are understood theoretically. The purpose of phenomenological research is provided by Husserl (1952), whose famous dictum was "To the things themselves." He emphasized the importance of having our subject matter anchored in the "life-world," the world of everyday experiences. This life-world includes both reflective and prereflective experiences. The proposed subject matter is not only our thoughts and beliefs but also our feelings, sensations, movements, and perceptions. The subject matter is from the perspective of immediate embodied experience. It is the *direct experience in the moment* that is the main interest of the phenomenologist.

Phenomenology removes the reliance upon constructs that attempt to explain phenomena. Constructs can be unreliable since they can have multiple meanings. For example, being stressed can mean anxiety, excitement, frustration, anger, or worry. Instead, phenomenology emphasizes describing phenomena as they appear in the immediate experience of the person who lives them. Thus, for phenomenology, description has priority over explanation. On the other hand, phenomenological description does not negate explanation and, as we hope to show, can be integrated with it. For example, a phenomenologist poses questions about experience such as "What is it like to experience a state of anger?" The answers are often provided by observing instances of anger in oneself or in reports of others and noticing the common meanings across different angry experiences. Thus, one may find that anger can entails a sense of unfairness or injustice (blame) and a desire to remove that unfairness. Once the common meanings are identified, they can be studied as psychological factors in conventional psychological experiments.

More than anything, phenomenological research aims to understand the meaningfulness of human experience as it is lived. What phenomenology seeks is an essential description of the experience. This essential *description* is equivalent to an essential *understanding* of the experience. This description includes general meanings that represent a shared core of an experience being researched. Therefore, understanding the meanings that underpin experiences is the goal of the phenomenological method. An example is that three meanings seem to be consistently present during ordinary love toward someone: We like, care about, and feel a significant positive connection with that person.

Because of its subject matter, phenomenologists felt the need to develop a separate approach that would part ways with the traditional natural scientific method. What was needed was a truly human science that would not simply include the outer perspective on the lives of human beings but would replace this with an inner perspective from the viewpoint of the actual direct lived experiences of human beings. And what this would yield is a science that would emphasize understanding direct experience as opposed to explanations that include only external objects, external causation, and computational interactions. The aim of developing a human science based on experience and meaning has a long history. This aim gave impetus to the human science organization in the 1980s, comprised of different groups of psychologists that supported different paradigms for a science of human experience (see Giorgi, 1970, and references therein).

Phenomenologists offer reflections on direct experiences that are nearly totally missing in mainstream psychology (Husserl, 1952; Buytendyck, 1961; Merleau Ponty, 1962). For example, there is relatively little emphasis within mainstream psychology on understanding the experiential structures of emotions, such as satisfaction, joy, anger, jealousy, and anxiety, that are intrinsic to the human condition. Consequently, there is often no direct search for underlying meanings that constitute different types of experiences, such as these emotions. For much of the twentieth century, emotional "feelings" were often considered irreducible and discussed only in relation to their possible external influences (Bakan, 1967; Boring, 1957; Giorgi, 1970). As a consequence, there was no search for the experiential dimensions that underlie emotions. Phenomenology opens up this search with in-depth reflections of how emotional feelings may be experienced, yet it has stopped short of identifying actual causes imbedded in these experiences, partly because phenomenological analysis has not been interfaced with the methods and practices of natural science (Giorgi, 1970; Price, 1999).

Scientifically and practically, human problems related to emotions demand an understanding of causes as well as the intrinsic nature of meanings. Causes include environmental, psychosocial, and physiological factors and are found using natural science paradigms. Meanings and causes from a first-person perspective are found using experiential and phenomenological approaches and yet can be integrated with knowledge generated from the natural sciences. This is a major claim that we intend to support.

The phenomenological method represented the first significant attempt to address the issue of a science of meaning. There was recognition of the relevance of phenomenology to psychology's foundational theorizing. This was important because the vast majority of psychological research never entered the arena of direct human experiences. Instead, it emphasized theories and observations of behaviors. Phenomenology provided the first attempt to understand human meanings, the basic blind spot of psychological science. Unfortunately, a shortcoming of phenomenology is that it has not provided an explicit empirical strategy that is agreed upon by those who "practice" it. It remains in a gray area between philosophy and science. Nevertheless, there are experiential methods that are grounded in the ideas of phenomenology.

1.2.3 The Descriptive Experience Sampling Method

A science of experience and meaning would require a skilled ability to notice the content of experience and to be able to accurately report it. Participants of experiential studies would also need to be able to carefully take into account the potential influences of preconceptions and biases. Hurlburt and Heavey (2006) and Hurlburt and Akhter (2006) have provided a useful method, DES, designed to facilitate noticing and describing inner experience. DES uses a random beeper in the participant's natural environments to signal the participant to notice his or her experience that was ongoing just prior to the beep. The participant then take notes about that experience. After about a half dozen such beeped experiences, the participant meets with the investigator within twenty-four hours for an interview to clarify and describe the experiences. This entire process is repeated over 3 to 10 sampling days. The iterative nature of this method allows the participant's observational and reporting skills to improve over the course of the sampling days. The characteristics of the beep are carefully constructed to be as unobtrusive as possible and yet easily detectable.

The purpose of the interview with the investigator is to provide a simple answer to one question posed for each beeped experience, "What were you experiencing at the moment of the beep?" A complete and detailed answer is sought for that question, while avoiding interpretations, explanations, and confabulations on the part of the participant. To achieve this purpose, the interview technique is critical. The role of the participant in the interview is to provide a description of the experience that is as accurate and faithful to the experience as possible. This requires that the participant neither hide nor add to the content but just simply report what was present in the experience. The role of the interviewer is to help the participant accomplish this aim, and this role requires several skills and guidelines. The interviewer tries to grasp the subject's experience, as experienced by the participant. This requires careful listening, not intruding upon or leading the descriptions of the participant, and suspending preconceptions about the characteristics of the experience. The interviewer also helps participants report just their experiences and not their extrasampling general statements about their experiences, such as their self-theories or explanations about experiences.

What is the aim of DES, and what kind of knowledge do its users seek? Above everything else, DES strives for accuracy of accounts of individual experiences as they are lived in the moment. An analogy is that of taking a camera "snapshot" describes their sampling technique. Thus, they seek accurate accounts of brief moments (a few seconds) of phenomenal experience. Hurlburt and Heavey (2001) use data from DES to characterize the different ways that people experience in everyday life. It seems to be an excellent means of characterizing individual differences in the ways people experience. For example, DES research has found that some people have predominantly visual images with little or no verbal content whereas others have frequent inner speech with less visual imagery. DES also has been used to characterize personality disorders, such as borderline personality and Asperger's syndrome, a type of autism. Another interesting and perhaps unexpected outcome of this method is its revelation of the flaws in other types of psychological self-reporting. For example, Hurlburt and

Heavey (2001) beeped individuals who replied "yes" to the following item on a widely used depression inventory: "I am sad all of the time" (Hurlburt and Heavy, 2001). They found that people who endorsed that item were sad fewer than half their sampled moments. Hurlburt and Heavey concluded that it is wrong to believe that endorsement of this item should be construed as an accurate account of these individuals' direct experiences.

1.2.4 The Experiential Approach and Method[1]

We proposed an experiential paradigm designed to integrate human experiential science with the natural sciences in the 1970s and 1980s, long before the recent resurgence of interest in consciousness and consciousness studies (Barrell and Barrell, 1975; Barrell et al., 1985; Price and Barrell, 1980; Price and Barrell, 1984; Price et al., 1985). This paradigm retains much of the intent and principles of phenomenology. Thus, participants are trained to notice brief episodes of direct experience (several seconds) and to report on these experiences directly in the present tense without interpreting, explaining, or representing them in the form of stories, metaphors, or poetical reporting. The experiences pertain to specific topics such as types of emotions or situational problems. Examples have included anger, anxiety, jealousy, and performance anxiety. Once experiential descriptions are collected from a group of investigator–participants, the descriptions are subjected to qualitative analysis to determine the common factors within a particular type of experience. In some studies, the descriptions can also be subjected to quantitative analysis. For example, common dimensions of human experience, such as desire intensity, expectation, and emotional feeling states, can be characterized in both phenomenological qualitative terms and in quantitative terms (e.g., using psychophysical methodology). This approach and method provides discovery of common factors within specific types of experiences such as anger, anxiety, and pain as well as characterization of the interrelationships among the common factors within these types of experiences.

The paradigm consists of several stages that include (1) noticing the content of specific experiences (observing); (2) describing these experiences from a first-person perspective (reporting); (3) understanding these experiences through discovering common factors and their interrelationships (i.e., anxiety, pain, etc.); and (4) applying quantitative methods to test generality and functional relationships between common factors. Of these four stages of research, the first three are unique in that the investigators are often included as participants of their own research study (i.e., coinvestigators). Questions, not hypotheses, guide the first three stages.

For example, our study of performance anxiety was guided by the questions "What is it like to experience performance anxiety?" and "What are its common factors?" (Barrell et al., 1985). The aim of the first three stages is to discover the common factors within a given type of experience and their interrelationships. This aim is similar to that of phenomenology, which is to find the structural invariances in a given type of experience. The last stage utilizes accepted psychometric methods, derived mainly from psychophysics, to test hypotheses in human participants who are not informed about the study's hypotheses. Thus, the last stage is no different in principle from conventional psychological research. The psychometric methods and experimental designs would be similar in principle to those already used in psychological studies, especially those which employ psychophysical scaling methods. Unlike the first three stages, participants of last stage would *not* be the investigators. Thus, the last stage of an experiential paradigm would involve a third-person epistemology but one that is complementary to the first-person exploration of stages 1–3 described above. However, it is the combination of these stages that produces a more complete knowledge about experiential phenomena. It is a paradigm that could be directly applied to the study of consciousness in general and to highly specific kinds of experiences in particular.

An aim of the experiential method of Barrell and Price (Barrell and Barrell, 1975; Price and Barrell, 1980) is to generate qualitative descriptions of given kinds of experience, descriptions that express phenomena as they reveal themselves to the experiencing person. Thus, they retain the spirit and intent of phenomenology. They are to be agreed upon and well understood by all those capable of having the experiences in question. Each final phenomenological-experiential account of a kind of experience (e.g., performance anxiety) is to contain precise explicit statements about what is essential for a kind of experience, omitting particulars. These methods also may include a strategy of determining the necessary and sufficient factors for the type of experience in question. Finally, they allow investigators to discover the functional relationships of common factors of given kinds of experience. Functional relationships pertain to how one factor affects another and/or how multiple factors interact. Several examples are provided in topics of this book (e.g., emotions, choice, pain, placebo, background states of consciousness). Factors within experience can be scaled using psychophysical and other psychometric methods and the scaling of these factors can provide tests of *functional* hypotheses about the interactions between the various factors. The qualitative and quantitative aspects of this paradigm are presented in detail in the following four chapters.

1.2.5 What Do These Paradigms Have in Common, and How Are They Different?

All four paradigms are designed to seek clarity and accuracy in accounts of direct experience and attempt to remove or control for preconceptions and biases. They all attempt as much as possible to separate direct observation from interpretations and theory. Unlike scientific paradigms in other sciences, these paradigms don't necessarily begin with hypotheses or theories per se because their central aim is often that of describing or "capturing" the nature of human experience and specific types of experience. Often the studies are guided by a question such as "What is it like to experience anger at someone?" or "What is it like to experience jealousy?" However, the four paradigms differ somewhat in their reasons for describing experience. Phenomenological methods, including the experiential method, emphasize understanding the essential meanings within experience whereas this is not necessarily emphasized in classic introspectionism or in the DES method. The DES method differs somewhat from the other three paradigms in its emphasis on the fine details within experience and acute accuracy even for fine details.

Consistent with the paradigms described so far, Hurlburt and Heavey are concerned with the accuracy and veracity of reports of direct experience. The difference was, of course, while phenomenology focused on the underlying meanings of the immediate experience, they focused on the accuracy of the one-to-one correspondence of description to immediate experience. The phenomenological method is concerned with discovering what subjects generally share about the experience. There is an attempt to get to the "essence" of the experience, the general shared experience. In contrast, for Hurlburt and his colleagues, the important question is this: Can subjects accurately report their immediate experiences? It may be the case that an understanding of the general shared experience requires a positive answer to Hurlburt and colleagues' question.

The beeped experiences in the DES method are actually narratives described by the interviewer. They are stated in past tense, yet they seem to capture the general features of the experience as well as some details. The reported experiences of the experiential method are written descriptions of participants or coinvestigators and are written in present tense in order to foster a reexperiencing of the lived experience. In contrast to the DES method, emphasis is placed on the meanings of experience, with less attention to fine detail. Unlike the other methods, the experiential method attempt to arrive at "causes" (necessary and sufficient factors for a type of experience).

A similarity between all four paradigms just described is that they require training on the part of the participants. This is also true for psychophysics, as we point out in chapter 2. Although the DES and the experiential method have used both trained coinvestigators and untrained participants, the experiential method has placed greater emphasis on including coinvestigators in the studies. There are important methodological and epistemological reasons for doing so, as we discuss later. Coinvestigators undergo more extensive training in order to learn how to accurately and directly observe their experiences (thoughts, emotions, etc.). This training enables the ability to generate precise testable hypotheses about direct experience. These similarities and differences aside, Hurlburt has provided us with a very useful tool for noticing the content of our experience. The DES method of Hurlburt enables us to strengthen our capacity to observe because it is relatively unobtrusive and its accuracy is facilitated by immediate retrospective reporting. These characteristics also hold for most psychophysical studies as well (see chapter 2). With this improved ability to observe, participants can immediately reexperience "just previous" moments in order to provide data that may be eventually used to understand the meanings of the experience under study.

1.3 Neuroscience and Human Experience

Philosophers, some psychologists, and, most recently, neuroscientists have taken an interest in one or more of the paradigms just outlined (Aydede, 2005). For example, some neuroscientists have become very interested in the sense of agency, related to the experience of the source of one's own actions—as either originating from one's own intentions or from an outer cause (see chapter 10). This distinction is accompanied by different patterns of brain activity. Other neuroscientists have become interested in the neural causes and correlates of specific emotional feelings and in the multiple dimensions of pain experience (see chapters 5–8). These types of experiments require introspective measures along with some degree of phenomenology and, consequently, a general interest in experiential paradigms. Nevertheless, the neuroscience of human experience is not a concept that is commonly used by neuroscientists. The scientific programs of neuroscience meetings have sections described as "behavioral," and there are sections of neuroscience journals that use that same adjective, but the term "experiential neuroscience" has yet to appear in general public discourse. Perhaps the closest term is "cognitive neuroscience." However, only a small minority of research reports in cognitive neuroscience are explicitly about human phenomenal experience. This may in large part be the result of the influence of behaviorism in twentieth-century psychology, and most neuroscience studies that address psychological questions still do so within the context of behaviorist and functionalist frameworks. The main task of these attempts is to explain certain behavioral or cognitive functions from an external (third-person) viewpoint. A functionalist's view is that there is nothing in the vicinity of consciousness that needs explaining over and above explaining various functions, such as how cognitively related brain networks enable an organism's interactions with the environment and behavioral performance of some kind. The emphasis is on relationships between neural or computational mechanisms and behavior, even when the mechanisms are transparently associated with conscious phenomena (Chalmers, 1996; 2003; 2004). A functionalist approach deals with "easy" problems of consciousness, as just described, according to Chalmers (1996; 2003). In contrast, he asserts that the "hard" problem of consciousness is to explain the performance of functions and its accompanying neural activity in relationship to phenomenal experience. There is something that it is like to experience red, anxiety, beauty, and a painful toe, and it is these *experiences* that are in need of explanation, including their relationships to neural mechanisms. The problem is hard because it is difficult to understand how neural and material structures necessitate experiences. As Chalmers (2003, 2004) puts it, "Why don't these experiences just go on in the dark?"

A second reason for the hard problem is that there don't seem to be many strategic models for directly investigating phenomenal experience. We have given a preliminary account of several approaches above and will elaborate upon them in later chapters. Beyond experiential methods, we also need a strategy for integrating results of experiential science with the rest of the sciences. This overall strategy will be elaborated in remaining chapters. But first some questions have to be addressed.

1.3.1 Can Accounts of "Phenomenal Experience" Be Eliminated from the Neuroscience of Consciousness?

Some investigators and philosophers do not consider that there is a need to pursue the challenge of integrating neuroscientific data with human phenomenological reports. They claim that terms related to human meaning, indeed all mental terms, can eventually be eliminated from scientific explanation if science will one day discover consciousness to be nothing more than states of the brain. The philosopher Patricia Churchland seeks to eliminate phenomenal "consciousness" from science, claiming that our common-sense theories (folk psychologies) will be replaced by more advanced explanations and more exact neurophysiological theories. She claims that psychological *theories* will eventually be replaced by neurophysiological *theories* and that this replacement will help confirm that consciousness is nothing more than a state of the brain.

Certain psychological phenomena are defined by meanings, both intrapersonal and interpersonal. Meanings determine how situations are constituted in experience, as we have seen from examples described earlier. In the case of avoiders and confronters described above, the mode of attending and coping could only be understood when the meanings of the stressor and the stressful situation were understood. How would a neurophysiological theory and analysis eliminate the need to understand the meanings behind the two diametrically opposed orientations toward an external stressor that is the same for all study participants? Even if two distinct patterns of brain activity perfectly correlated with the "avoider" and "confronter" orientations, how could the explanation be completely devoid of any reference to how the participants construed the stress situation and devoid of any reference to the personal meanings that were developed? Other psychological phenomena are defined not only by meanings but also by psychosocial interactions. While these phenomena have corresponding neural activities in the brain, the original psychological terms are partly social and relational. As a result, these original phenomena and theories about them cannot be simply reduced to states of the brain. Many human experiences contain interactions between meanings, thoughts, and feelings, and yet these experiences are not exactly the same thing as corresponding states of the brain (see Velmans, 2009, for detailed argument). This would be the case even if they have exactly the same information structure. For example, suppose that the qualities and magnitudes of a given experience that contained a meaning and/or thought were very closely associated with corresponding magnitudes of neural activity within different places in the brain. Although they may have the same information structure, the appearances of neural activity and those of qualia are simply quite different. There is nothing in the brain that looks like a thought or a happy feeling. And there is nothing in a happy feeling that looks like neural activity.

Churchland links her claim about theory reduction with the claim that such a reduction may show that consciousness is nothing more than a brain state. Velmans points out that even if it were possible to replace existing psychological theories of consciousness with neurophysiological theories, it would not reduce conscious *phenomena* to being nothing beyond states of the brain (Velmans, 2009). He responds to this type of reductionist argument with a rather extensive series of explanations as to why such an approach would not work. His discussions will be succinctly summarized here. His first point is that when lower-level theories (e.g., neurophysiological) are used to explain higher-level phenomena (e.g., learning, memory, consciousness), the lower-level theories do not *replace* the phenomena. As he states, "In short, theory reduction is not equivalent to phenomenon reduction" (Velmans, 2009).

He then points out similar fallacies in other reductionist arguments. Reductionists and materialists often maintain that discovering the neural causes and correlates of consciousness would establish that consciousness itself to be a brain state (Place, 1956; Crick, 1994). The fallacy is fairly obvious. If consciousness is nothing more than brain states, it must be ontologically identical to (the very same thing as) brain states. However, causation and correlation do not establish ontological identity. Instead, the demonstration that neural activity causes phenomenal experience (e.g., pain) would suggest that the two phenomena are *not* ontologically identical. Ontological identity between A and B is shown when they are identical to each other, as demonstrated by the fact that *all* their properties are identical to each other. In this respect, their relationships are symmetrical. An example is that the "morning star" and the "evening star" were both eventually discovered to be the same planet Venus. In contrast, when causation occurs between A and B, they have different properties and the relationship between them is not symmetrical. An example, taken from Velmans (2009), is that when a rock is thrown into a pond it causes ripples. Although the thrown rock causes the ripples, ripples do not cause the rock, and the rock and the ripples have different properties. Height and weight are correlated with each other, but they clearly do not have identical properties. Several examples will be given in later chapters that show that neural activity both correlates with and causes different types of phenomenal experience, such as pain and reduction in pain. If that is the case, it is hard to support the claim that pain is exactly the same thing as neural activity.

Thus, there are two main points that refute reductionists' arguments: (1) Causes and correlations do not establish ontological identity, and (2) causes and correlations between two phenomena occur when they are *not* ontologically identical in every other instance in nature that we know about. If neural activity and mental activity are *not* ontologically identical, this lack of identity carries an interesting implication: The mind includes more than just the brain. The mind can be defined as *the agency of conscious experience*. From a third-person (external) perspective, it may include the brain, the spinal cord, the autonomic nervous system, the rest of the body, and the world itself. All of these components also perform or help perform body functions that occur without consciousness, such as sleeping and reflexive motor responses. This account is compatible with the view that interactions between these entities are critically necessary for consciousness and they take place between all of the entities just listed. If it were possible to take any one of them away without compromising the physical or physiological status of the remaining entities (e.g., the philosophers' thought experiment of a brain in a vat), we think consciousness would either become extremely compromised or disappear altogether. This is most obvious for the brain itself, as when consciousness is lost during sleep or anesthesia. Although the role of the world itself may be initially less evident, sensory deprivation experiments that incompletely eliminate input from the outside world reveal how consciousness can become extremely distorted and impoverished without worldly input (Mason and Brady, 2009, and references contained therein).

Another reductionist argument, discussed by Velmans (2009), is based on analogies with other reductions in science. Crick (1994) makes the point that reductionism is successful and that reductive approaches have shown that *hypothetical entities* such as genes were nothing but DNA molecules. He uses examples such as this as an analogy for qualia. He claims that when neural *correlates* of qualia are described and when we understand the nature of the correlates, we will come to understand corresponding forms of consciousness. Velmans points out the fallacy of this analogy as follows:

But it would be absurd to regard conscious experiences as "hypothetical entities" waiting for their neural substrates to be discovered to make them real. Conscious experiences are first-person *phenomena*. To those who have them, they provide the very fabric of subjective reality. One does not have to wait for the advance of neuroscience to know that one has been stung by a bee! (Velmans, 2009, p. 46)

Some philosophers claim that consciousness is more than a state of the brain but give no causal status to consciousness. Thus, they agree that there are neural causes and correlates of conscious experience. However, they claim that causal relationships only originate from neural activities and that conscious experiences cause nothing (epiphenomenalism). In their view, although phenomenal experience clearly exists, it is merely an epiphenomenon. But what empirical evidence can be used to support or refute this claim? Neuroscientists can demonstrate neural causes and correlates of phenomenal experience, yet no amount of neuroscience can rule out the possibility that there are causal interactions between qualia. The only evidence for or against causal interactions between qualia must come from first-person sources. For those who don't find credibility in first-person reports, they would probably fail to understand how the case can be made at all since their third-person observations would be restricted to neural or behavioral interactions. In this book, we claim that it is possible to verify or disconfirm causal relationships between qualia. We think a lot is at stake on this issue. For example, the claim that human beings have volition is contingent on the claim that qualia have causal efficacy. We have much to say about this issue in the final chapter (chapter 11).

1.3.2 Could Neuroscience and Experiential Science Mutually Facilitate Each Other?

Recent advances in neuroscience technology, particularly brain imaging, has fostered questions about human experience, such as those that are about the nature of human thought. It is as if neuroscientists cannot resist reflecting on the experiential implications of their unintended results. In our view, there has been no greater example of this than the discovery of the brain's "default" activity during associative thinking, a condition that is approximately described by the term "mind-wandering" (Bar et al., 2007). Associative thinking has been described as a conscious background state wherein subjects make unconstrained associations that are unrelated to the immediate external environment. Images and thoughts are linked together quickly in associative thinking (e.g., brain scanner—dark—end of daylight savings—got to set clock tomorrow—can't be late for work). In many control or baseline conditions of brain imaging experiments, participants are typically told to "rest quietly." Perhaps the assumption is that very little goes on in the mind or brain when given this instruction. Instead, however, a network of cortical areas show strong activations when participants are supposed to rest. This network typically does not include brain areas related to early stages of sensory processing, such as the primary visual, auditory, and somatosensory cortices, but rather a network of regions along the midline (medial region) of the brain: ventromedial prefrontal, anterior cingulate, and posterior cingulate cortices, as well as areas in the medial parietal and temporal cortices (see figure 1.1). This network of regions becomes activated during "rest" and during tasks that require associative thinking. This same network becomes deactivated during specific tasks requiring directed or focused attention. Although associative thinking is the "default" mode in the rest/baseline condition, it also can

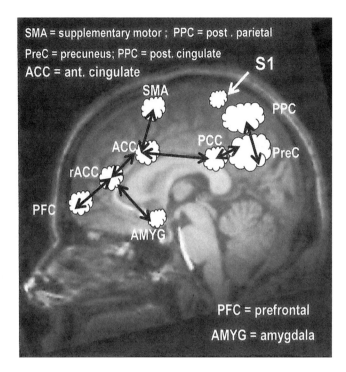

Figure 1.1
Midsagittal schematic (i.e., at midline of human brain between the two cerebral hemispheres). Brain regions interconnected by arrows are those involved in associative thinking: posterior parietal cortex (PPC), precuneus (PreC), posterior cingulate cortex (PCC), anterior cingulate cortex (ACC), insula, supplementary motor area (SMA), rostral anterior cingulate cortex (rACC), prefrontal cortex (PFC), and amygdala (AMYG).

be induced in specific tasks. As such, it can be made to be the independent variable of an experiment. When this is done, neural activity in this network of brain regions covaries with the degree of associative thinking (Bar et al., 2007). This example illustrates how questions about the nature of human thought can arise from initial observations of brain activity during imaging experiments. Thus, just as experiential science can foster testable hypotheses about brain mechanisms, so modern neuroscience can foster explorations about the nature of the human mind.

1.3.3   The Two Sides of the Human Experience Issue
Several interrelated points have been made thus far. We began by pointing out that human experience as both a topic and a method remains mostly

a blind spot in human knowledge, particularly in the sciences. We then addressed the necessity of understanding human experience in general and meanings in particular as essential for more complete explanations of scientific phenomena, such as human behavior and psychophysiological responses. Then four experiential paradigms were briefly described that we consider promising methods in developing a science of human experience. This attempt is in contrast to the rather strenuous attempts on the part of some philosophers, psychologists, and neuroscientists to eliminate, reduce, or ignore human experience altogether. The maintenance of the blind spot of human phenomenal experience has not been a passive endeavor.

To put the two sides of the "human experience" issue into stark perspective, consider the following thought experiment, which relies upon an extrapolation from existing methods. Suppose brain imaging technology improves to the point that it can map most of the relevant patterns of neural activity that take place during a given type of experience, such as pain, joy, or anxiety, for example. These patterns would include not only brain areas that become activated and deactivated but also the functional connections between them. Suppose still further that physiological recording improves to the point that it can also map all relevant activations and interactions that take place within and between the autonomic system, somatomotor system, and endocrine system, or, for that matter, the rest of the body. Then, with vastly improved technology, all the relevant neural and physiological activations for pain and the feeling of satisfaction are displayed on two very large screens, to be viewed "objectively" by scientists who are disposed to leaving human experience out of the experiment altogether. Thus, except for being told that the patterns on the left and right screens came from the person with pain (right screen) and another person with satisfaction (left screen), they would have no information about the experiences of the individuals who were in pain or felt satisfied. Would the investigators have a moment of deep insight where they would say, "Yes, of course, *this* is pain! And of course, *that* is the feeling of satisfaction"? Only when the observers had access to the experiential maps of the factors within pain or satisfaction could they hope to attain a more complete understanding of how neural and body computations map onto the experiential structures of these types of experiences. Of course, the most optimal way the investigators would have access to the experiential maps would be to actually *be* the participants who had these different experiences. The accounts of other participants, as used in more traditional types of experiments, would be used to confirm or disconfirm the direct observations of the investigators and would be complementary to them.

Experiential maps of these types of experiences might be provided with improved paradigms for analysis of human experience, paradigms such as the experiential method, psychophysical scaling methods, and the DES method described earlier. Correlations might then be established in imaging studies that provide insight as to how a fine-grained experiential account of an experience, such as a type of pain, maps onto a fine grained neurophysiological account of this type of experience. Of course, separate neuroscience studies that use methods other than neuroimaging, such as studies of effects of neural activation of specific brain sites and effects of damage to specific brain areas, would continue to add further knowledge about the causal relationships between neural processing and experiential factors. All of these approaches already exist to a major extent. Examples will be given in remaining chapters. Suppose still further that scientists become successful at carrying out these types of experiments. Would finding most or all of the neural causes and correlates of a type of experience (e.g., pain) provide a reductive explanation wherein the subjective account could then be eliminated? Could science then demonstrate that various types of qualia are nothing more than states of the brain? Our answer at this point is that a reductive explanation would be obtained, yet it would be an epistemological and not an ontological one. Thus, experiences would be more completely explained by neuroscience, yet "experiences" certainly could not be considered identical to brain states. Finally, we should remember that even the brain and brain states are concepts and are within conscious experience.

1.3.4   A Reflexive Model (Velmans, 2009)

According to Max Velman's reflexive model for understanding consciousness, the answers to these questions are an emphatic no! According to his reflexive model, the experiential and neural accounts reflect a circulation between sets of first-person and third-person observations. The first set reflects the experiential content of the phenomenon of study and the variables that constitute the phenomenon. For example, a type of pain is comprised of sensations with certain unique qualities, a sense of intrusion or threat, and a negative emotional feeling of a particular nature such as distress, annoyance, or anxiety. Observations about these aspects of pain necessarily are from a first-person perspective. The second set reflects the neurophysiological observations of brain activity, activity that could be demonstrated to correlate with and even cause these aspects of pain experience. A satisfactory explanation of how aspects of pain arise from neural mechanisms within the brain must utilize both sets of observations. The third-person account is not privileged over the first-person account and vice versa. Neither account is observer-free—each account requires the perspective of someone. Velmans takes this reflexive model a step further by proposing that the *same observer* could provide both first-person and third-person accounts. If so, the perspectives of the experiential reporter and the observer of brain activity could be switched, thereby providing a powerful epistemic access to relationships between neural and experiential activity.

1.3.5 Experiments Suggesting the Feasibility of an Empirical Version of the Reflexive Model

Brain imaging experiments already exist that are beginning to suggest the feasibility of the experimental methods and approach just outlined. Of course, these experiments are not as technically elaborate as the hypothetical experiments described above, yet they clearly point to the beginning stages of such a paradigm. A brain imaging study published by deCharms and collaborators at Stanford University has shown that it is possible for human participants to make two types of observations nearly simultaneously during brain imaging experiments: direct observations of their own pain experience and observations of their own pain-related brain activity (deCharms et al., 2005). However, the purpose of the experiment wasn't just to entertain the participants by letting them simultaneously watch their brains and experiences but to determine whether they could be taught to change their brain activity through feedback from real-time functional magnetic resonance imaging (rtfMRI). rtfMRI is an imaging method that indirectly measures neural activity by measuring changes in blood levels of oxygen in the microcirculation. Participants were trained to control the level of neural activation in their rostral anterior cingulate cortex (see rACC in figure 1.1), a region thought to be involved in pain experience, particularly its unpleasantness dimension (Rainville et al., 1997). When participants deliberately induced increases or decreases in rACC fMRI activation by using observed brain activation as feedback, there was a corresponding change in the intensity of pain caused by an applied noxious heat stimulus. Thus, both neural activity in rACC and pain reduced simultaneously or increased simultaneously depending on whether the task was that of decreasing or increasing pain. Importantly, there were several control conditions in the experiment. These effects on pain did not occur with similar training but without rtMRI feedback nor did they occur when a different part of the brain was used to provide the feedback. The effects also didn't occur when someone else's brain activity was used to provide the feedback, perhaps suggesting that you can't cheat on this test by using someone else's brain.

This experiment is extremely intriguing because it suggests the almost direct observation of an association between brain activity and a specific type of experience by *the same observer*. Yet it is also a simple experiment that just scratches the surface of understanding. Multiple brain areas are activated during even the most simple forms of laboratory pain (see chapters 7 and 8), and the interactions between pain-related brain regions are complex and can even change direction over time (Craggs et al., 2007). Given this experimental approach, one could envision experiments of this type wherein pain-related brain areas other than the rACC are used or wherein more than one region is used simultaneously or wherein the *interrelationship* between one brain area and another (e.g., somatosensory cortex → rACC) is used for the feedback. This strategy could gradually approximate the kind of ideal paradigm we have described for relating maps of experiential and neural patterns of activity. This should include the relevant phenomenology, perhaps using some of the paradigms briefly described earlier (i.e., psychophysics, phenomenology, DES, and the experiential method).

Notice that what has been eliminated from this suggested strategy is not human experience but the *perceived necessity of eliminating human experience* from science. Human experience is the phenomenon in need of an explanation and is an explanandum in its own right (Varela, 1996). Understanding experience may help immensely to understand the brain and vice versa. Since understanding experience is ultimately helpful in understanding ourselves and each other, it is difficult to understand the resistance of those who seek to eliminate the study of human experience or those who seek to ontologically reduce human experience to brain states. The philosopher John Searle suggests that it is as if "terror of the subjective" was a common condition among philosophers and scientists (Searle, 1996). Perhaps this terror could be mitigated somewhat by a clear method for investigation and understanding.

1.4 Beyond the Need for Expanding Science

Beyond our need to integrate phenomenal experience with the rest of the information in science, human beings everywhere have a deep desire to understand the inner experience of others. As David Bakan (1967) has pointed out, "Lawyers are concerned with the mental states of judges and juries.... Military commanders are particularly concerned with the mental states of those against whom they are warring.... Everybody has an interest in the mental states of motor vehicle operators." Developing a science of human experience and integrating that science with the natural sciences is a step in the direction of an alternative approach to resolving some major conflicts in the world.

Of course, a crucial step in understanding others is to understand ourselves, and that step is an end in itself. It is one of the aims of the experiential method. Although a science of human experience would make a novel and significant contribution to the world's knowledge, its principal aim would be that of improving the human condition. Knowledge for knowledge's sake is fine, but there appears no end in sight for the abundance of knowledge on earth. The development of the Internet has taught us that. What is drastically needed is a form of knowledge that is based on self-understanding and could be integrated with human values.

1.5   A Strategy for Developing a Science of Meanings (and Consciousness)

The remaining chapters discuss the methods, results, and interpretations of studies that reflect beginning stages of attempts to integrate a science of human experience with the natural sciences. A science of human experience would largely be about human meanings and also would constitute a science of consciousness. In chapter 2, we provide an explanation of psychophysics, with the purpose of showing that it includes a rudimentary form of introspection that is critical for developing a science of human meanings and consciousness. Chapter 3 extends this explanation in showing how psychophysical methods can be used to study human meanings and their interrelationships. Chapter 4 then elaborates on the qualitative aspects of human experience as a foundation for developing hypotheses to be used in experiments that have quantitative methods. Chapters 5 and 6 discuss how qualitative and quantitative methods can be integrated. Chapters 7 and 8 then provide examples of how this approach and method can be applied to the phenomenon of pain. The next two chapters do the same for the topics of placebo responses (chapter 9) and background states of consciousness (chapter 10). The final chapter discusses how this integration of experiential and natural science can be applied to human problems and to the understanding of consciousness, including volitional consciousness.

2 Lessons Learned from Psychophysics

What is psychophysics? Nearly everyone has experienced sensory phenomena that are reliable and interesting. When we turn on a three-way light bulb that has three stages—50, 100, and 150 watts, we readily notice that the difference between complete darkness and the brightness of 50 watts is large and that the remaining two differences in brightness become progressively less noticeable. This is so despite the equal intervals between the three stimulus levels. Apparently, our sensation of brightness is not a linear function of stimulus intensity but is approximately equal to the square root of the stimulus strength (perceived brightness = intensity of visual stimulus$^{1/2}$; see figure 2.1, right curve). This square root function applies to brightness, yet other sensory functions are very different (Marks, 1974; Stevens, 1975). For example, not surprisingly, our perception of length is a linear function of actual measured length (see figure 2.1, left curve). Our perception of pain, on the other hand, is approximately equal to the cube of the stimulus strength (perceived pain = stimulus intensity^3; see figure 2.1, middle curve). The total area of stimulation is also critical.

In testing a heated bath, we may notice that immersing a hand in the water feels slightly warm but that immersing most of the body feels much warmer and often much more pleasant, despite the approximately equal temperature throughout the bath. This experience illustrates the property of spatial summation. These relationships between the properties of physical stimuli and magnitudes of sensation and feeling can be studied precisely and are the subject matter of the science of psychophysics. Psychophysics is one of the oldest domains of research in psychology, the life sciences, and medicine. Its elegance is in its simplicity.

Despite the long history of this discipline, there are new lessons to be learned from psychophysics that go far beyond its immediate subject matter. These lessons are the reason for this chapter. We propose that psychophysics contains one of the key strategies for developing a science of

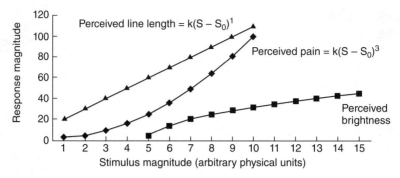

Figure 2.1

Three representative power functions with exponents of 1.0, 3, and 1/2 for perceived line length, pain, and brightness, respectively. Note that the function for length is linear, that for heat pain bends upward to the left, and that for brightness bends toward the right. In this figure and remaining ones of this chapter, the stimulus–response functions are highly simplified in order to teach psychophysical concepts to nonpsychophysicists. The original figures on which these curves are based can found in the references of this chapter (Marks, 1974; Stevens, 1975; Price et al., 1994). The terms S and S_0 refer to stimulus intensity and stimulus intensity at or near threshold, respectively. For purposes of illustration, the curves are arbitrarily separated in this schematic. The term k is a constant that applies to each physical continuum.

phenomenal experience. We think psychophysics is pivotal for integrating human experiential science with the natural sciences, such as neuroscience and other biological sciences. The central aim of this chapter is to explain our reasons for this proposal.

Recognizing that this might appear to be a tall order, here is an advance summary of the basic reasoning behind these proposals and the critical points of the chapter.

First, we provide a succinct description of psychophysics, including how experiments are generally conducted and how their results support the power law. The power law reflects a fundamental principle of sensory experience. We then delve deeply into the question of what observers are actually doing when they make psychophysical responses, especially direct estimations of magnitudes of sensations. A critical point is that we think that psychophysical responses reflect a simple and direct form of introspection and that it is more accurate to think of these responses as reflecting phenomenal experience than "emitted behavior." A second related point is that when *both* investigators and noninvestigators become psychophysical observers, knowledge of psychophysical relationships is derived from two complementary methods of verification and thereby achieves a higher level of certainty and veracity. We then raise the question of whether psychophysical approaches and methods can be extended to discover *other* psychological relationships and end with an account of experiments that demonstrate the feasibility of such an approach. This latter account provides a bridge to most of the remaining chapters that explain how psychological relationships can be characterized within natural contexts, that is, during actual lived experiences. Some chapters show how experiential dimensions can be related to neural activity and brain mechanisms.

2.1 Definition and Scope of Psychophysics

Psychophysics is an area of psychology that explores relationships between properties of physical stimuli and corresponding evoked experiences or behavioral responses. These relationships can be explored directly in humans; they can also be studied indirectly in nonhuman animals by using behavioral performance as a dependent variable. Psychophysical studies include those which measure the ability to detect stimuli and the ability to detect differences in stimulus intensity (e.g., How loud should an alarm be set to ensure that the occupants of a building are able to detect it?) and those which measure the relationships between stimulus intensity and the magnitude of experienced sensation or feeling (e.g., How loud do different alarm signals sound?) (Marks, 1974). To make our points stated in the beginning of this chapter, emphasis will be placed on the latter type of study.

The history of psychophysics contains two eras, the "old psychophysics" and the "new psychophysics." The viewpoint of the old psychophysics was that it was difficult, meaningless, or unimportant to measure sensory experience directly by having people rate magnitudes of their sensations (Fechner, 1860, and reviewed in Gescheider, 1997; Marks, 1974; Stevens, 1975). Instead, they usually adjusted stimuli in response to changes in their perception. This gave the appearance of measuring properties of the stimulus, an appearance that no doubt fostered scientific credibility. For example, measurement of the decline in experienced brightness over time was made by having observers adjust a comparison light to match the brightness of a long duration test light. This form of measurement dominated the study of the senses up until about the middle of the twentieth century and is still used in many studies of the senses. Fundamental to the new psychophysics is the viewpoint that human beings can directly provide quantitatively and qualitatively meaningful accounts of their sensory experiences, at least under certain conditions. The primary developers of methods for quantifying sensory magnitudes were S. S. Stevens (1975) and L. W. Marks (1974), and these efforts date back to the 1930s. Great strides have been made in methods for direct scaling of various types of sensory phenomena over the past seventy-five years.

2.2   Direct Scaling

Psychophysical direct scaling is the determination of the relationships between the physical intensities of stimuli such as tones, lights, and temperatures and their corresponding experienced intensities. Examples of different sensory modalities include loudness, brightness, cold, warmth, and pain (Snodgrass, 1975; Marks, 1974; Stevens, 1975). Sensations that differ in quantity, such as brightness or pain, can be directly scaled by having observers provide a quantitative representation of their experienced magnitude. There are several ways that such a representation can be made. The one probably most familiar is a simple 0-to-10 numerical rating scale. For example, it is now a common practice in many hospitals for patients to rate postoperative pain on such a scale with verbal anchors, such as "no pain" at 0 and "most intense pain possible" at 10 (Price et al., 1994).

In general, psychophysical studies use direct scaling methods that have better measurement properties than 0-to-10 numerical rating scales because they use scales or methods that measure true proportions or ratios of magnitude. For example, observers can provide representations of magnitudes of sensations in one sensory modality, such as perceived pain, by using another modality such as line length. This method is known as cross-modality matching. In one such an experiment, different intensity temperature stimuli were applied to the forearm and observers produced lines whose lengths represented their experienced magnitudes of pain. Since perceived line length is known to be a precise linear function of measured line length (see figure 2.1, left curve), line production in response to pain produced a highly reliable stimulus response function for groups of individuals (see figure 2.1, middle curve; Price et al., 1983). Another method of direct scaling is that of using a visual analog scale (VAS). A VAS is like a numerical rating scale, except that it has no numbers on its axis. Instead, participants make a mark on a vertical or horizontal line that extends over a continuum with verbal anchors, such as "no pain" at the far left and "most intense pain imaginable" at the far right (Price et al., 1983; 1994). Similar to line production, a VAS utilizes the principle of using length to represent magnitude (a form of cross-modality matching), and at least for some sensory modalities, line production and VAS scaling yields equivalent results (Price et al., 1983). Yet the VAS is easier to use than line production because of verbal anchors on the scales. With just a little practice, people use VAS in a highly reliable manner to rate stimuli. Tests show high reliability and repeatability of ratings on these scales (Price et al., 1983; 1994). Moreover, electronic or mechanical versions of VAS have been made to facilitate their use (Price et al., 1994, 2008b). The VAS has been used to scale not only sensory modalities, such as brightness, loudness, and pain, but also dimensions of personal meaning, such as perceived value of money, expectation, desirability, and intensity of positive and negative emotional feelings (Price and Barrell, 1984; Price et al., 1985, 2001).

The procedures for direct scaling and generation of a psychophysical stimulus–response function for a given sense modality can be briefly summarized. Observers are asked to use a given response continuum to represent their experienced intensity of a given stimulus. This response continuum may be another sensory continuum such as intensity of sound or it can be line lengths or numbers. They then match subsequent stimuli along this response continuum accordingly. For example, an observer initially produces a line whose length matches the experienced intensity of a light stimulus. A second light stimulus of a lower or higher intensity is then presented. The observer is asked to remember his or her response to the first stimulus and to produce a line to the new stimulus that represents the perceived change in light intensity. Subsequent stimuli are presented until an entire stimulus–response function is developed. Considerable practice and numbers of stimuli are sometimes needed to produce precise stimulus–response functions. In our view, an easier and more efficient way to conduct this type of experiment is through the use of a VAS. If extreme superlatives are used to anchor the scale (e.g., the brightest light imaginable, the most intense pain imaginable), participants find it easy to make the scaling response and the results are very consistent with line production. For example, both line production and VAS ratings result in the same power function for contact heat-induced pain (Price et al., 1983).

2.3   The Psychophysical Power Law

When stimulus–response relationships are determined using direct scaling methods, they have consistently been shown to follow a power function. The power law implies a very simple and parsimonious concept that equal ratios of *stimulus intensity* result in equal ratios of *subjective intensity*. To the nonpsychophysicist, this statement means that proportions of perceived stimulus intensities remain stable. For example, the perceived relations between the lighter or darker parts of a photograph are the same under bright or dim illumination. The power law can be expressed by the following simple equation:

$$\Psi = k(S - S_0)^X,$$

where Ψ = perceived magnitude, k is a constant, S_0 is stimulus magnitude at threshold for a sense modality tested (e.g., warmth threshold), and X is an exponent for a given sense modality under a standard set of conditions.

A power function whose exponent is 1.0 (i.e., $\Psi = k(S - S_0)^{1.0}$) predicts that two stimuli whose ratio of *measured intensities* is 2:1 will result in two *experienced intensities* whose ratio is 2:1. The simplest example is perceived length, which is a precisely linear function of measured length (see figure 2.1, left curve). This relationship is maintained regardless of whether one uses measured intensities of 2:1, 4:2, or 8:4 to construct the 2:1 ratio and regardless of whether length is measured in inches or millimeters. Using this same stimulus ratio (2:1) in the case of a power function whose exponent is 2 (i.e., $\Psi = k[S - S_0]^{2.0}$) results in a ratio of perceived magnitudes that is 4:1, similar to the simple algebraic equation of $y = x^2$ (see figure 2.2). In the case of a power function with an exponent of 0.5 ($\Psi = k[S - S_0]^{.5}$), a stimulus ratio of 2:1 will result in a response ratio of 1.4 (see figure 2.1, right curve for brightness). Figure 2.2 schematically illustrates how the principle of "equal stimulus ratios produce equal response ratios" applies to a power function with an exponent of 2. Different sense modalities have characteristic power function exponents (see figure 2.1 and table 2.1). Power functions with exponents below 1 bend downward to the right (e.g., brightness), functions with exponents of 1 are linear, and functions with exponents greater than 1 bend upward (see figure 2.1). For example, heat-induced pain has an exponent of about 3, which means that it bends upward toward the left (see figure 2.1, middle curve), and perceived warmth has an exponent ranging from 0.5 to about 1.6 depending on the total area of stimulation (Marks, 1974; Stevens and Marks, 1971).

Regardless of which way a power function bends, there is a stable experience of proportionality of magnitude throughout the stimulus–response function. For example, perceived brightness of a brief-duration light stimulus is always approximately proportionate to the square root of the

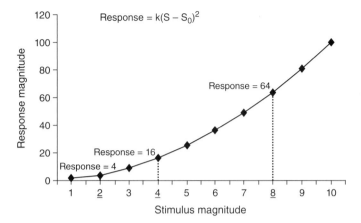

Figure 2.2
Illustration of the principle that equal stimulus ratios result in equal response ratios for a power function whose exponent is 2. Note that a stimulus ratio of 2:1 will yield a response ratio of 4:1 regardless of whether 4:2 or 8:4 is used to make up the 2:1 stimulus ratio.

magnitude of the light, regardless of whether the stimulus intensity is very weak or strong.

The determination of a given power function and its exponent sometimes entails a combination of magnitude matching and magnitude production. Magnitude matching consists of matching numerical values to stimuli of different intensities whereas magnitude production is adjusting magnitudes of different stimuli to match different numerical values. The power function exponent is often slightly different between the two methods, and some psychophysicists consider the average of the two methods to be a more accurate estimate of the true power function exponent than that provided by only a single method (Stevens, 1975; Gescheider, 1997).

Table 2.1 lists the power function exponents of several sensory modalities, including brightness, warmth, heat-induced pain, cold pain, sourness, sweetness, loudness, and perceived line length. This list is only a limited sample of all sensory modalities for which power function exponents have been determined; it merely provides representative examples. However, most of the power functions listed in table 2.1 have been verified in multiple experiments that have used different methods of direct scaling.

Table 2.1
Power function exponents for different sensory modalities

Sensory Modality	Power Function Exponent
1. Brightness of a brief flash of light	0.5–0.6
2. Contact heat pain	2.2–3.5
3. Warmth	0.5 to 1.6 depending on stimulus area
4. Perceived line length	1.0
5. Sound	0.55
6. Indentation of the skin	0.5–0.7 with a small probe
7. Cold pain	1.0–1.1
8. Sweetness	1.2
9. Sourness	0.77

2.4 Individual Differences in the Power Function

The power function exponents listed in table 2.1 require an important caveat. For some modalities, there are considerable individual differences in the derived exponent. For example, pain induced by contact heating of the skin has an average exponent of 3.5, yet the derived exponent differs considerably across individuals (Nielsen et al., 2005). The function, like that displayed for pain in figure 2.1, bends upward in the vast majority of people, yet it varies considerably among people. Some individuals have exponents as low as 2 while others are over 8 (Nielsen et al., 2005, 2007, 2009). These differences in stimulus–response power function exponents are related to the fact that people vary enormously in pain sensitivity, a variation that is not commonly recognized by health-care professions. Other modalities, such as perceived visual intensity, have less individual variability (Stevens, 1975; Gescheider, 1997).

2.5 The Relationship of the Power Law to Ratio Scale Measurement

Reliable power functions are related to the validation of a specific type of scale as having ratio scale properties. A ratio scale provides accurate measurement of ratios or proportions of magnitude, unlike ordinal scales that only measure the rank order of magnitude. A ratio scale also has a true zero point, unlike interval scales such as the Fahrenheit scale of temperature (e.g., the freezing point of water is 32° F). A ratio scale level of measurement is most useful to science. Thus, physical quantities such as distance, mass, and velocity are measured using ratio scales. Since power

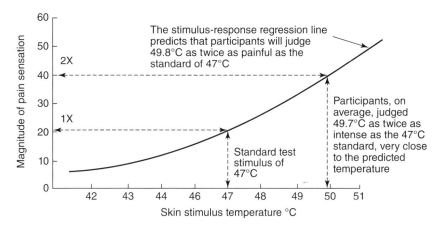

Figure 2.3
The power function of experienced pain evoked by contact heat stimuli. Visual analog scale (VAS) ratings of 45°–51° C predict that participants will find that on average 49.8° C is twice as intense as 47° C. The predicted temperature matched the actual observed temperature.

functions related to the senses reflect reliable relationships between ratios of *stimulus* intensity and ratios of *experienced* intensity, then the demonstration of a power function is one line of evidence that a given measurement scale is a ratio scale. However, power function exponents can sometimes vary as a function of physical contextual factors such as the range of stimulus intensities used and as a function of biases in observers' judgments. Thus, multiple tests are necessary to demonstrate that a given psychological scale is a ratio scale and does not foster systematic biases.

An example is the demonstration that the VAS is a ratio scale of pain. As shown in figure 2.3, VAS ratings of five-second 45°–51° C contact temperatures to the forearms of 23 participants resulted in a power function that bent upward to the left. Subsequently, the same 23 participants directly chose a temperature that was experienced as twice as painfully intense as a 47° C standard (see figure 2.3). After the standard was presented, the stimulus intensity was gradually increased until participants pressed a button acknowledging that the pain was now twice as intense as the 47° C standard. This task reflects a direct judgment of a ratio of two pains. This task was different than their previous VAS ratings of 46°–51° C stimuli because it involved simple and direct judgments of ratios of perceived intensity. VAS ratings of these temperature stimuli and separate judgments of ratios should be in quantitative agreement if the VAS is a ratio scale.

According to the stimulus–response curve in figure 2.3, participants should have selected 49.8° C as twice as intense as the 47° C standard. The mean temperature actually chosen was 49.7° C, a value very close to that predicted. This test was replicated using several other standard temperatures within the range of 45°–51° C (Price et al., 1983; 1994). The reliable power function, in combination with the quantitative agreement between VAS ratings and separate judgments of intensity ratios, helps confirm that this VAS is a ratio scale. Furthermore, these results would not likely have been obtained if the VAS had no true zero point because a true zero point on a scale is necessary for accurate estimates of ratios or proportions of magnitude. The demonstration of a true zero point was further confirmed by showing that VAS ratings at or near pain threshold were not significantly different from zero. Finally, the power function generated by VAS ratings was found to be nearly identical to those generated by other methods, such as cross-modality matching and verbal descriptor scaling (Price et al., 1983; 1984; Duncan et al., 1989). The latter type of scaling uses words that convey relative magnitude, such as mild, moderate, slightly intense, intense, very intense, and most intense imaginable. These words can be quantified when observers numerically rate the intensities implied by these various descriptors. Results from verbal descriptor scaling can then be quantitatively compared to those obtained using VAS. The consistency in the derived power function across several different scaling methods further validates the VAS method as having ratio scale properties and helps to establish the power function itself.

As one might discern from examples given above, psychophysics contains several strategies and uses converging and independent lines of evidence, similar to methods used in other branches of science. The power function of a given sense is often determined by multiple experiments that use different methods. Similar to scientific methods in general, psychophysics contains a system of checks and balances that can be used to detect biases and accuracy across different experimental approaches. Thus, different methods of rating of heat-induced pain result in the same average stimulus–response function across groups of participants. A validated method allows participants to represent experienced pain intensity in response to a range of stimulus intensities extending from 45° C to 51° C applied to their forearms. Different methods of scaling have been compared throughout the era of the new psychophysics and have been used to validate power functions for multiple sense modalities as well as for other dimensions of human experience, such as perceived criminality and desire for a goal.

2.6   Adding Variables to Psychophysical Experiments: Spatial and Temporal Summation

Experienced sensation intensity is a function of not only stimulus intensity but also other variables such as the size and sometimes the duration of the stimulus. An example of spatial summation of warmth was given at the beginning of the chapter.

Warmth and pain experiments have provided excellent examples of spatial summation, as shown in figure 2.4 for warmth and figure 2.5 for pain. Experienced warmth probably provides the best example of combining the variables of stimulus size and intensity in psychophysics. Spatial summation of warmth takes place generously over large areas of the body surface, and as stimulus area increases, the overall perceived intensity of warmth increases (Kenshalo et al., 1967; Marks, 1974; Hardy, Wolff, and Goodell, 1940; Marks, 1974; Stevens and Marks, 1971). However, the slope of the stimulus–response function obtained when relating stimulus temperature to perceived warmth decreases in magnitude with increasing stimulus area, as shown schematically in figure 2.4. Furthermore, the perceived warmth intensity functions converge at a common point (44° C)

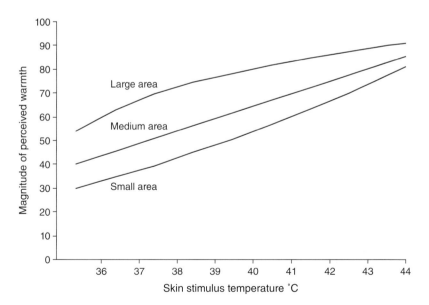

Figure 2.4
Spatial summation functions for warmth, using small, medium, and large stimulus areas.

near pain threshold (Marks, 1974). Spatial summation is a large factor near warmth threshold and becomes less of a factor as warmth approaches pain threshold. Another way of describing these functions is that the power function exponent of warmth decreases systematically as the stimulus area increases. This means that an increase in temperature of a small area of skin will cause a large change in warmth sensation (as would be expected for a power function with an exponent close to 1.6) whereas a change in warmth for a very large area will be less detectible (e.g., power function exponent of 0.5). You can test this relationship the next time you are getting ready to take a bath or get in the hot tub. Immersing your index finger in the bath may feel slightly warm, and immersing your whole hand will feel noticeably much warmer. However, the change in warmth as you immerse your whole leg versus half your leg in warm water (e.g., 39° C) would be less noticeable. These experiences are predicted by the family of curves shown in figure 2.4.

Considerable spatial summation also occurs for both the intensity and unpleasantness dimensions of heat-induced pain (Douglass et al., 1992; Greene and Hardy, 1958; Hardy, Wolff, and Goodell, 1940; Price, Larson, and McHaffie, 1989; Price et al.,1992). This spatial summation is illustrated in simplified schematic form in figure 2.5. Notice that although spatial

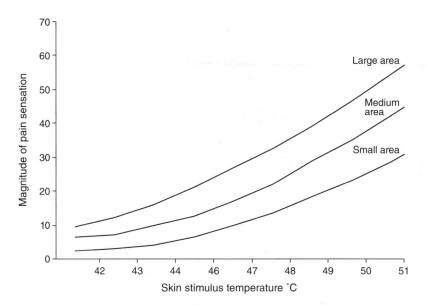

Figure 2.5
Spatial summation functions for pain.

summation occurs throughout a wide range of temperatures, it is far larger at temperatures that are suprathreshold for pain (47°–51° C) than at those near pain threshold (42°–46° C). This pattern is the reverse of that of perceived warmth. In contrast to spatial summation of warmth, which *decreases* with increasing stimulus temperature, spatial summation of heat-induced pain *increases* with increasing stimulus temperature (cf. figures 2.4 and 2.5). Notice too that the psychophysical curves for warmth tend to bend downward whereas those for pain bend upward. The spatial summation properties of warmth and pain may be related to their biological functions. Perceived warmth (and for that matter the sense of coolness) may be integrated over large body areas, and this integration serves the function of thermal regulation. Pleasant warm experiences and unpleasant cold experiences initiate desires (and behaviors) to seek warmer environments, at least up to a certain temperature. Thus, it may be adaptive to immerse oneself in a pleasant and small warm environment (e.g., a hot tub) in the larger cooler context of a backyard in the winter. The result might prevent hypothermia and could be enjoyable. Immersing large body areas in hot tubs serves both thermal regulation and human hedonics. The motivating force of pain serves quite a different function altogether. For pain, the motivating force is escape or avoidance. The separate contributions from stimulus area and stimulus intensity have adaptive significance because they reflect a mechanism that is sensitive to the total amount of biological threat to the integrity of body tissues. All other factors being equal, a strong *sensation* of pain (imagine a 7 on a 10-point pain sensation scale) in a large area is likely to be more *unpleasant* or *distressing* than the same level of pain sensation in a very small area. And it is biologically more dangerous.

Temporal variables also can be added to psychophysical experiments. For example, a long-duration light stimulus may appear less bright over time as a result of adaptation, and repeating a brief tactile stimulus may cause a gradual decline in perceived intensity over time as a result of habituation (Stevens, 1975; Marks, 1974; Gescheider, 1997). On the other hand, very brief (two-second) repeated stimulation of some types of pain-related receptors (connected to unmyelinated C-axons) results in temporal summation as shown by the observation that each successive heat pulse to the skin results in a progressively more intense burning sensation (Price et al., 1992). In this case, repeating the same type of brief heat pulse at two- to three-second intervals results in progressively more intense sensations of delayed burning pain despite no increases whatsoever in actual stimulus intensity and even in the peripheral receptor responses. The physical properties of all of the brief heat pulses can be made to be nearly exactly the same! This phenomenon, which depends on special central nervous system mechanisms, has interesting neurophysiological, psychological, and philosophical implications that are discussed in chapter 8.

2.7 Adding Different Types of Stimuli to Experiments: Multisensory Integration

Finally, stimuli from different senses can be combined as well as presented in isolation. Psychophysical studies of combined sensations are very important because we often use multiple senses to perceive and evaluate objects. This is probably the rule rather than the exception. Remember the last time you ate your favorite kind of food. The experience was likely to be an integration of taste, smell, texture, and visual appearance. In fact, there are fundamental principles of multisensory integration (Stein and Meredith, 1993). Thus, when multiple senses are used in perception, sensations from different modalities (e.g., visual and auditory) can inhibit or enhance each other depending on several factors such as their locations in space.

As an example, a brief, broadband auditory stimulus was found to significantly enhance the perceived brightness of a brief light stimulus (Stein et al., 1996), but only when the sound and the light stimuli originated from the same physical location in space. The effect was most pronounced at the lowest visual intensities near threshold and became progressively less at higher light stimulus intensities. Yet, despite the significant influence of the auditory cue, a power function that maintains the proportionality among perceived visual intensities was retained. The enhancement of visual intensity by an auditory stimulus is likely to serve the function of enhancing the ability to detect objects in the environment, such as a small chirping bird in a tree. Imagine walking by a tree with a small bird perching on one of its limbs. You may be looking vaguely in the direction of the tree but don't orient to anything in the tree, despite the fact that the bird is within your visual field. Then the bird chirps. The physical locations from which both the auditory and visual stimuli originate are exactly the same; they both come from the same bird. Another technical way of putting this is to say that they are in topographic register. You are then more likely to abruptly orient to and notice the chirping bird. Psychophysical experiments carried out on cats and humans elegantly demonstrate how auditory and visual stimuli mutually enhance the disposition to orient to objects in the environment and detect their location (Stein and Meredith, 1993). Of equal interest is the observation that inhibition rather than enhancement occurs when visual and auditory stimuli originate from different locations in space. Thus, a chirp from a bird in a tree in back of you makes it less likely that you will orient to the bird in the tree in front of you. When the chirp comes from behind you and the silent bird is in front of you, you are less likely to perceive either bird. Since they are not in topographic register, the auditory and visual stimuli mutually inhibit one another. Well-established central neural mechanisms support these facilitatory and inhibitory interactions (Stein and Meredith, 1993).

2.8   Remaining Skepticism about Psychophysics

The progress made in psychophysics is one of the cornerstones of psychology, and psychophysics is probably the least controversial subdiscipline of this science. For example, there are no longer major controversies regarding whether the senses follow power functions versus logarithmic functions, and there are even few controversies regarding the numerical values of power function exponents. As early as 1965, Ekman and Sjoberg (1965) summed up the progress of psychophysics as follows:

After a hundred years of almost general acceptance and practically no experimentation, Fechner's logarithmic law was replaced by the power law. The amount of experimental work performed in the 1950's on this problem by Stevens and other research workers was enormous. The power law was verified again and again, in literally hundreds of experiments. As an experimental fact, the power law is established beyond any reasonable doubt, possibly more firmly established than anything else in psychology.

This is not to say that psychophysics has not had it share of detractors and skeptics. As pointed out earlier, the view of the old psychophysics was that you cannot measure sensation directly. There are those who still maintain this view and there are even those who seem to imply that psychophysics is not a science at all. A good example is the argument presented by Rakover that suggests that psychophysical theory does not fulfill the requirements of the theory of measurement accepted by science (Rakover, 2002). He bases this claim on an assertion that psychological concepts do not have fundamental measurement units. He asks us to consider the variable of length as an example of fulfilling the procedure of fundamental measurement:

We cannot only know if object a is longer than object b but also how many units of length a is longer than b. If for instance a is <---------->, b is <-----> and the measurement unit is <->, then a is longer by five length units than b and a is twice the length of b.

This procedure sustains several important mathematical properties such as transitivity and additivity. (Rakover, 2002,)

He claims that this measurement procedure cannot be applied to psychology. He uses taste as an example:

We have a heap of 60 corn kernels. I add (or remove) 30 kernels. Without doubt I have significantly altered the heap's weight and volume. But have I altered the taste of the corn by the addition or removal of kernels? Obviously not. The addition or removal of the kernels does not alter the "corny" taste. There is no measurement unit for taste whereby we may increase or decrease the taste of the corn, as we did in the physical case. (Rakover, 2002)

There are serious (and not so serious) flaws in this argument. In the first place, sensory experience has both qualitative and quantitative dimensions. Why would anyone expect to alter the qualitative taste of corn by changing the number of corn kernels? Five, ten, and 50 cooked corn kernels would all taste like corn. His example is one of misplaced emphasis on quality, not quantity, of experience. Moreover, it is hardly a method that psychophysicists use to alter taste! Normally the intensity of taste is altered by changing the concentration of a diluted substance such as sugar or citric acid, as will be discussed later. Concentration of a substance can be precisely measured in physical units (e.g., moles/liter). For most people, the magnitude of sweetness increases monotonically as a function of the concentration of sugar molecules, as anyone can easily demonstrate for himself or herself. Adding one-half a teaspoon, a whole teaspoon, or two teaspoons of sugar to tea or coffee results in progressively sweeter taste experiences. Beyond this simple, common-sense fact, what is left to be established is the precision of this relationship. Does it follow a reliable power function (or some other type of function), and how precisely can such as function be measured? The central flaw in Rakover's argument is that he fails to explain why application of the procedure of fundamental measurement is impossible *in principle* for all psychological variables. Using Einstein as an example, he claims that if Einstein's IQ was 150, it would make no sense to propose that his IQ equals the IQs of three individuals with extremely low IQs (150 = 50 + 50 + 50). Similar to his corn example, this is not the way that psychologists think about analyzing differences in intelligence. But why extrapolate from this kind of example to all psychological variables available? We have provided a reasonable case that power functions and ratio scales can be developed for several sense modalities as well as other dimensions of human experience. If these scales are ratio scales, they must have interval scale properties as well. This means that both ratios of magnitude and differences can be meaningfully measured, albeit not with the same precision as measurement of length or other physical phenomena. In addition to the development of ratio scales, units of psychophysical magnitude have been developed for several sense modalities (Marks, 1974; Stevens, 1975). For example, one psychophysical unit of magnitude is termed the just-noticeable difference, and for some sense modalities these units have been precisely quantified (Marks, 1974; Stevens, 1975). Even pain has been measured in distinct scale interval units, termed dols (Hardy et al., 1955).

Another reason for the remaining skepticism surrounding psychophysics may be a holdover from the domination of psychology by behaviorism during the twentieth century. Given the firmly ingrained suspiciousness surrounding the measurement of subjective phenomena among some researchers and philosophers, it is indeed ironic that the most quantitative, precise, and reliable results within psychology come from psychophysics, the measurement of subjective experiences in response to physical stimuli.

2.9   Psychophysics and Neuroscience

Psychophysics is not just a branch of psychology. It has also become an integral part of neuroscience, especially within the last few decades. Even during the earliest part of the "new psychophysics" era, investigators were correlating the responses of neurons with psychophysical functions. For example, a classic study by Borg et al. (1967) reported that the neural responses within the chorda tympani nerve (the taste nerve) were directly proportional to the perceived magnitude of taste. Because of the accessibility of the taste nerve to physiological recording in human participants, neural activity and perceived magnitude of taste could be recorded nearly simultaneously. When sour taste was generated by graded concentrations of citric acid, the stimulus–response functions for *both* experienced magnitudes of sourness and responses of neurons within the taste nerve were power functions with the same exponent of 0.77. On the other hand, when the same type of experiment was done for sucrose (sweetness), the power function exponent for *both* neural activity and perceived magnitude was 1.2. The confirmation of the power function for sweetness, including a degree of external validation from neural recordings, helps to refute Rakover's claim that the principle of fundamental measurement does not apply to psychological variables, such as experienced sweetness and perhaps "corniness."

The correspondence between power functions for neurons that supply peripheral receptors and those of perceived magnitude has been demonstrated for several sense modalities, including mechanical pressure to the skin, brightness, loudness, and different types of pain, to name just a few examples (Gescheider, 1997; Marks, 1974; Price, 1999; Stevens, 1975). In most cases, the power functions are nonlinear (exponents greater than or less than 1). Since, in general, the neural recordings were made for neurons that supply sensory receptors, these results suggest that peripheral receptor function may comprise most, if not all, of the basis for nonlinearity between stimulus intensity and experienced sensation magnitude.

This possibility suggests that all or most of the nonlinear transformation about sensory intensity might occur at the earliest stage of sensory reception (i.e., the sensory receptor), with linear transmission of signals thereafter. Mountcastle and his colleagues (Mountcastle, Talbot, and Werner, 1962; Mountcastle, Talbot, and Kornhuber, 1966) have explicitly maintained such a position with regard to somatic sensations (Mountcastle Talbot, and Kornhuber 1966). The parallels between experiences of sensation intensity and magnitudes of neural responses extend confidence that psychophysical experiments truly examine human experiences of sensory phenomena and at the same time begin to uncover some of the fundamental mechanisms of the senses. For example, the principle that equal stimulus ratios result in equal response ratios (i.e., the power law) must also be a fundamental physiological principle because it has been demonstrated for neurons that directly supply sensory receptors as well as for neurons within pathways of the central nervous system, including the somatosensory cortex. Usually, the power functions of the neurons are very similar to the corresponding psychophysical power function for a given sense modality.

Of course, the foregoing account is somewhat of an oversimplification because some nonlinear transformations have been found within the central nervous system, particularly for some types of pain (see chapters 7–8). With the advent of the ability to record from single neurons of central nervous system pathways, neuroscientists have studied the basis of sensory encoding of several senses. Although it is beyond the scope of this chapter, suffice it to say that combining psychophysics with various types of neurophysiological recordings has proven to be a very successful approach in elucidating sensory mechanisms as well as mechanisms of other functions related to emotions (see chapters 4–5), pain (see chapters 7–8), and attention.

Another example of the cooperative relationship between psychophysics and neuroscience are studies of multisensory integration, a phenomenon described above. Thus, neural mechanisms underpinning both the enhancement and inhibition that takes place when different senses are simultaneously activated have been worked out to a major extent. These interactions are now known to occur in the superior colliculus, an area of the midbrain that is involved in behavioral orientation toward stimuli in the external environment (Stein and Meredith, 1993). They also take place at cerebral cortical levels (Stein and Meredith, 1993). Similar to the psychophysical interactions between sound and light stimuli, mutually facilitatory and inhibitory interactions take place in neurons of the deep layers of the superior colliculus. Thus, when presented alone, a brief light stimulus may evoke a small number of impulses in a given superior colliculus neuron as would a brief sound stimulus. However, when the sound and light stimuli are combined and presented simultaneously, the evoked impulse discharge is typically much greater than the sum of the responses to individual sound and light stimuli presented alone. In other words, when presented together, there is a synergistic interaction between effects of visual and auditory stimuli. However, this synergistic interaction only occurs when the stimuli originate approximately from the same physical location. When they originate from different locations in space, the responses to visual and auditory stimuli are mutually inhibited. In these respects, the neural interactions parallel the behavioral observations described earlier (i.e., orienting to combinations of visual and auditory stimuli). In combination with other neurophysiological and anatomical information, we can begin to understand basic neural mechanisms that underlie multisensory experience. Understanding these mechanisms could not occur without psychophysical experiments.

The explosive growth of brain imaging in the last twenty years has fostered explorations of relationships between human experiential dimensions and neural activity within several functionally distinct regions of the brain. Questions that were impenetrable decades ago are now beginning to be addressed and even answered to some extent. In fact, these questions are topics to be covered in later chapters of this book. To take just one example for the moment, the experience of being absorbed in something varies along a continuum ranging from "not at all absorbed" to "completely absorbed." This dimension is one of many that contribute to background states of consciousness. It can be scaled using methods similar to those used to scale experienced brightness or loudness of sound. Experiments described in chapter 10 show how the degree of experienced absorption covaries with activity within areas of the brain known to be involved in the regulation of consciousness. The measurement of experiential dimensions in human brain imaging experiments, along with good experimental designs, addresses exciting questions and in some cases provides exciting answers. Both the questions and the answers are psychologically and biologically significant. Some experiments are also psychologically significant because they provide an opportunity to analyze psychological variables that are related to each other rather than to just stimuli, as we discuss later.

Finally, psychophysical measurement and sensory testing is becoming increasingly utilized in medical research, especially for subjective phenomena such as pain. Characterization of mechanisms of diseases which are difficult to diagnose, such as fibromyalgia, irritable bowel syndrome, and complex regional pain syndrome, have been made in studies that utilize psychophysical methods of sensory testing (Price, 1999; Price et al., 2009).

2.10   Does Psychophysics Depend on Introspection?

Presumably, the types of dependent variables that we have described for psychophysics are within direct human experience and are not just utterances of participants who want to please the investigator during the experiment. But is this really the case? What are participants actually doing when they represent their experience of the brightness of a light or the painfulness of a heat stimulus? We need to examine these questions with care if we maintain that the methods of psychophysics are crucial for developing a science of human experience and if we want to integrate this science with the rest of the natural sciences.

One simple answer to these questions is that participants of psychophysical experiments are noticing the contents of their experience and representing this content by verbal or numerical ratings or by using another sensory continuum such as line length or VAS rating. Another way of making this claim is to say that participants are relying on a simplified form of introspection. Unfortunately, the term "introspection" has vastly different meanings to different people and contains negative connotations for many psychologists. This is especially the case for those who maintain that an entire school of "Introspectionism" was discredited during the early part of the twentieth century, as was discussed in chapter 1. Another problem with the term "introspection" is that it has so many misguided definitions. For example, here are some common definitions derived from an Internet search:

"Looking into one's mind, to find what one thinks and feels." (*Oxford Dictionary of Philosophy*, 2008) "Introspection is the self-observation and reporting of conscious inner thoughts, desires, and feelings." "It can also be called contemplation of one's self, and is contrasted with extrospection, human self-reflection." (Wikipedia on Answers.com:Introspection 2011)

In our view, although some of these definitions capture part of the sense in which we use the term, we think they all have serious flaws. In all cases, there is no distinction between simply *noticing* or observing what is in experience versus reflecting, interpreting, analyzing, or ruminating on the contents of experience. Our specific use of the term "introspection" refers to just noticing what is present in moment-to-moment experience without reflecting on or interpreting the meaning of the content, as we pointed out in chapter 1. It is like taking a snapshot. A comparison to neuroanatomy illustrates this point. A neuroanatomist we knew taught his students how to "see" when they looked at neurons under the microscope. He recommended that when you examine Golgi stains of neurons of the gray matter of the brain, you need to relax your gaze and open yourself up to simply noticing what is there in front of you. You learn to simply see the different neurons with all of their anatomical diversity, axonal projections, and interconnections. He recommended saving the theorizing and reflecting for later. When you are making attempts to "see," theory and reflection just get in your way. With practice, you begin to see more of what is there. It is well established that psychophysical observers can be trained to detect very low intensity stimuli and notice extremely small differences in intensity. Visual threshold, for example, is almost as low as it could possibly be, because human observers can learn to detect just a few photons (Gregory, 1966; Bruce et al., 1996). As another example, psychophysical observers can detect the difference between temperatures of 47.0° C and 47.2° C applied to their skin (Bushnell et al., 1984; Price et al., 2008b). If humans can learn to witness more and more of their sensory experience, we must wonder how well they can learn to observe subtle changes in experience in general. What is the just-noticeable difference in a desire, for example? You may notice a gradual increase in desire to be seen by your physician as you sit in the waiting room. How many levels of desire occur in such a situation?

We think it is also possible to introspect experiential dimensions that have personal meaning, such as emotional feeling and desire, so that the issues of detection and ability to observe apply to these dimensions as well. This issue will be raised again in subsequent chapters. For the present, we think the main challenge of introspection is learning to notice the content of immediate experience and the ability to represent or report on this content. Of course, participants of psychophysical experiments may bring their explicit or implicit beliefs and theories to the laboratory, and there are psychological experiments that are about how these factors influence sensory perception. Examples of this type of influence will be presented in chapters that are about placebo effects (chapter 9) and effects of hypnosis (chapter 10).

Thus, when participants of psychophysical experiments are noticing aspects of their sensory experience, what counts is their representation of just those aspects of sensory experience that they are engaged in witnessing. Their utterances related to other experiences (e.g., thoughts about how long the experiment is going to last) may be informative about the degree to which they are paying attention to the task at hand, but what counts is their sensory experiences. The main bulk of psychophysics is not concerned with the relation of stimulus parameters and *any* response on the part of the observers. Most often and crucially, it is concerned with the relation between the stimuli and *sensations*—conscious sensations. Thus, someone's representations of the magnitude of sensations inevitably reflect a simple form of introspection. In later chapters, we discuss introspections that have more varied and complex content, including meanings and emotional feelings. Nevertheless, we think the principles are similar to those applicable to psychophysics.

We have made a rather large point of this issue because the history of psychology in general and psychophysics in particular contains abundant attempts to eliminate the appearance of subjective content from its subject matter. These attempts appear quite odd when the subject matter is some form of human experience. Even one of the major proponents of the "new psychophysics," S. S. Stevens, attempted to operationalize psychophysics in a way that avoided reference to what observers actually experience.

He argued for example that

[u]nder this view, the meaning of sensations rest in a set of operations involving an observer, a set of stimuli and a repertoire of responses. Sensations are reactions of organisms to energetic configurations in the environment. The study of sensations becomes a science when we undertake to probe their causes, categorize their occurrences, and quantify their magnitudes. (Stevens, 1966, p. 218)

According to Stevens, this set of operations makes psychological science like a physical science. For example,

[w]e know the temperature of a body only through that body's behavior which we note by studying the effects the body produces on other systems. It is much the

same with sensation; the magnitude of an observer's sensation may be discovered by a systematic study of what the observer does in a controlled experiment in which he operates on other systems.... He may, for instance adjust the *loudness* in his ears to match the *apparent intensity of various amplitudes of vibration* applied to his fingertips and thereby tell us the relative rates of growth of loudness and the sense of vibration. (ibid., p. 225—our italics)

When observers are required to adjust the growth of loudness to match the apparent intensity of vibration, this matching allows responses to heard loudness and felt intensity of vibrations to be expressed in terms of the settings of two dials which control the intensities of both auditory and tactile stimuli. This operational approach gives the task an *appearance* of externalizing subjective estimates of magnitude and expressing them on two scales. The appearance is one that belongs to the investigator, not the participant of the study. Imagine what performing this task would be like. You are having varying magnitudes of sensations of vibrations. You notice that they get stronger, then weaker, then stronger, and so on. As you notice these changes, you adjust a dial that causes stronger and weaker loudness of sound. You then "match" changes in sensations of loudness to changes in sensations of vibration. It is clear that there would be a lot of sensations going on in this situation. The person conducting the test is also having a lot of sensory experience, just a different kind, that of watching and recording dial numbers for both loudness and vibration intensity.

Max Velmans points out the pitfalls of Stevens's attempt to eliminate subjective experience from the psychophysical task. As he states,

... the difficulties of *removing* conscious experiences from psychophysics or of *redefining* them in this operational way should be clear from Stevens' inability to describe what subjects are required to do in a way that avoids reference to what they experience. In the auditory/tactile matching task S is required to match the intensity of *what he hears* to the intensity of *what he feels*, a procedure which can hardly be said to have removed his experience from the experiment.

... Stevens['] contention that the "meaning of sensation rests in a set of operations involving an observer, a set of stimuli and a repertoire of responses" (i.e., a set of operations that avoids reference to what a subject experiences) seems more an attempt to assimilate the study of sensations to a behaviorist preconception of psychological science, than an attempt to describe what subjects in perception experiments actually do. (Velmans, 2009)

Perhaps, then, it is more realistic to conceptualize estimates of sensation magnitude as accounts of phenomenal experience than emitted behaviors. However, we must keep in mind that so far we have only discussed relatively simple forms of human experience that are generated in highly structured settings. The case will be made later that more complex experiences can be observed in ordinary everyday environments and that these experiences are amenable to scientific analysis in a manner similar to that employed in psychophysics. We also want to distinguish these simplified forms of introspection from other types of observation and self-report, such as those generated by those psychological questionnaires that request information about what individuals believe to be true in general about their experiences or their personality.

2.11   Why Is It Important That Both Investigators and Noninvestigators Participate in the Same Psychophysical Experiments?

There are aspects of the account we have given so far that are enormously troubling to some people. How can there be a serious science of subjective experience when science relies on objective data that are publicly verifiable? To illustrate this dilemma, we can compare a simple physical experiment with that of a psychophysical experiment. The physical example comes from elementary chemistry. Suppose you are told that adding salt to water will lower its freezing point. You take several cups of water and dissolve various amounts of salt in the different cups and put them in the freezer. You then find a thermometer and measure the temperature at which the various cups of water freeze and verify that dissolving salt in water lowers the freezing point. You can even plot a function of the relationship between the amount of dissolved salt and the degree to which the freezing point is lowered. You can show the results to anyone who is interested and/or have someone else replicate the experiment. When others conduct this experiment themselves in their own kitchen, they can phone you to determine whether their results are the same as or different from yours. These procedures describe the essence of public verifiability. Public verifiability does not require that everyone be present in the same laboratory (or kitchen) when the results occur, and in fact this rarely ever happens in science. In just about all branches of science, public verifiability depends on following accurately described experimental procedures, attempting to replicate or disconfirm a hypothesis by repeating the same experiment in different laboratories, and reporting replications and disconfirmations publicly. These reports include actual public presentations or articles in peer-reviewed scientific journals.

Can the principle of public verifiability be demonstrated in experiments that are about human experience? Suppose you are presented with the stimulus–response curve for contact heat-induced pain shown in figure 2.5

and told that this is how human beings experience the growth of pain sensation as stimulus temperature increases. Is this stimulus–response relationship publicly verifiable? If you happen to be a psychophysicist, even one who has never tested heat pain on anyone, you can verify this function by applying these temperatures to the forearms of participants and having them rate pain sensation intensity on scales. You can use different types of scales, and you can have observers match temperatures to different magnitudes along the scale, as we discussed above for magnitude matching. In short, in doing the experiment yourself, you can replicate the stimulus–response curve in many different ways or, for that matter, disconfirm it. Moreover, this same experiment can be replicated or disconfirmed in other laboratories that follow the same procedures or follow different methods of scaling. In this respect, a psychophysical experiment is as publicly verifiable as the elementary chemistry experiment.

For some people, however, there is a nagging difference between the chemistry experiment and the one on heat pain. In measuring the temperature of water as it freezes, you can directly observe a physical result. In the case of heat-induced pain, no matter how many times you have other people rate heat pain and generate stimulus–response curves, there is something missing in your knowledge of the relationship between temperature and pain. After all, you only have access to what other people are reporting, not the sensations themselves.

One way around this dilemma is to apply the temperature stimuli to your own forearm, randomize the various stimulus intensities, and rate the stimuli yourself. This experiment can even be done on a blind basis, particularly if the various stimulus intensities and their order of presentation are computer programmed. In other words, you can participate in your own experiment in addition to collecting ratings of other participants. In so doing, there are two types of observations in this psychophysical study, not just one. One type is the usual observations of the individual ratings of the participants and the development of stimulus–response curves, statistical analysis, and so on. This type of observation is "third person" as discussed before. The other type of observation is your direct experience of the various intensity stimuli, the "first-person" observation. If the results from both first- and third-person observations are in agreement, then the knowledge claim that contact-induced heat pain is a positively accelerating (curve bending upward toward left in figures 2.4 and 2.5) function of stimulus temperature is now supported by other individuals' representations of their direct experience as well as your own direct experience. You, as the self-directed investigator, can make other observations as well. For example, when we applied these temperatures to our own forearms, we readily noticed that the difference in pain between 45° C and 47° C was distinctly less than the difference in pain between 47° C and 49° C even though both intervals were 2° C. Based on the nature of the curves shown in figure 2.5, these differences are clearly expected.

It is important to point out that the first-person observations really reflect the perspective of the persons receiving the stimuli and the third-person observations reflect the perspective of persons collecting and observing the ratings, regardless of whether the persons are participants or investigators. Importantly, either group can make first- or third-person observations, that is, these perspectives can be switched. When the participants of experiments are directly noticing the magnitudes of sensations, they are making observations that from their perspective are first-person observations. It is the same perspective that an investigator has when he or she applies the stimuli to his or her own forearm. There is nothing we see that would violate any scientific or epistemological principle if investigators and psychophysical observers switched roles. In so doing, the knowledge claims of psychophysics would be based on a more rigorous methodological approach and yield results with greater certainty and veracity. Since the combination of first- and third-person observations is complementary, the conclusions of psychophysical studies could be strengthened by this approach. In all other respects, too, psychophysical results can be publicly verifiable in the same sense as that intended for biological and physical sciences. Studies of human sensory experiences are certainly not unique in their potential for merging first- and third-person observations. As we discuss in later chapters, we propose this same approach for several types of psychological and neuroscience experiments.

No doubt there are researchers who would question our proposal that scientists should use themselves as subjects (e.g., Gallagher and Overgaard, 2005). Gallagher and Overgaard remind us that investigators have certain hypotheses and have results that they hope to find and thus are more likely to be biased as participants of their own study. We have heard this concern many times and understand its rationale. However, we think that this problem may actually be greater when investigators *don't* use themselves as participants. In the first place, explicit evaluations of biases of either investigators *or* participants are by no means routinely made in psychology studies, except in those psychology experiments that are about biases and expectations. Investigators become susceptible to bias the moment they form their hypotheses or design their experiments, and there are multiple ways they can transfer their biases to their participants. Biases have numerous origins, including being influenced by the past or existing literature, imagining how something works, and having a vested interest in supporting one's past results. Far from being a problem for our position, involving the investigators themselves as observers has the potential of eliminating or minimizing the impact of such biases within the formal framework of our proposal. The participation of investigators as psychophysical observers offers a means whereby bias can be recognized and dealt with more effectively. If the subject matter is that of a particular type of experience, such as a type of pain or an emotion, then wouldn't it be better for the investigators to encounter these phenomena in their own direct experience as the basis for formulating hypotheses and designing experiments as opposed to *only* relying on published accounts of others or their imagination? The former approach reflects being objective about the subjective whereas the latter approach reflects being subjective about the subjective. Not surprisingly, many psychophysical studies rely on both participants' and investigators' psychophysical responses (Stevens, 1975; Marks, 1974). Both sets of data are usually in agreement. Correlations between psychophysical and neural activity also have the potential of further validating psychophysical relationships as well, as discussed in this and remaining chapters.

2.12   Some Conclusions about Psychophysics as a Paradigm for Studies of Sensory Experience and Experience in General

Psychophysics is a simplified and highly structured paradigm in which conditions are arranged to explore relationships between stimuli and sensory experiences. Similar to some other sciences, the outer conditions of psychophysics are simple and in many respects similar to those of physical experiments. Devices that deliver well-measured and controlled stimuli are used in a quiet setting wherein participants are comfortable and free to use some method by which to signal their detection of stimuli (e.g., pushing a button) or represent their experienced magnitude of sensation or feeling (e.g., cross-modality matching or rating on a VAS).

Psychophysical experiments are about direct human experience in an important respect, yet they are designed to confirm or disconfirm specific hypotheses already stated in advance. One limitation of this approach is that their hypotheses are almost always based on presuppositions and often the presuppositions originate from results of previous studies. Their purpose is confirmatory, not exploratory. Highly simplified and structured psychophysical experiments raise the question as to whether they have applicability to phenomena as they occur in ordinary lived situations, a concern that is raised by phenomenologists and by psychologists who seek ecological validity. Highly simplified physical and social contexts are not unique to psychology. Newtonian physical principles that confirmed the laws of motion and force were discovered using highly simplified and structured physical objects—yet Newtonian physical principles are used in constructing complex structures such as jet airplanes and cyclotrons. Thus, the highly simplified and constrained contexts of psychophysical experiments may provide important knowledge about relationships between physical properties of stimuli and human experiences, and this knowledge has to be extended in scientific studies that determine whether these same relationships apply within wider and more naturalistic contexts. Psychophysical contexts are not artificial, just highly structured and simplified. As we discuss in the next chapter, it may be possible to use methods similar to those of psychophysics in experiments that are about relationships between psychological variables. This approach contrasts with conventional psychophysics in which controlled physical stimuli constitute the independent variables.

3 Psychophysical Methods and Human Meanings

Human sensations are dimensions of phenomenal experience and can be studied using psychophysical methods. Can these same methods be applied to studies of meanings and relationships between meanings? In this chapter we initially explore this question by discussing past attempts to extend the field of psychophysics to studies of human meaning. We then ask the reader to carry out two experiential explorations and consider the results of these explorations in relation to actual studies that are about dimensions of meaning. In particular, we use the example of the possible interrelationship between human desire, expectation, and emotional feeling intensity.

3.1 Can the Methods of Psychophysics Be Used to Investigate Experiences Based on Meanings?

The sensory stimuli of many psychophysical experiments contain very little association with personal meaning. For example, the stimuli may simply consist of sounds that participants are asked to rate. One might even construe their meaning as "sounds which I'm paid to rate." They are neither pleasant nor unpleasant, and they don't evoke interest beyond attempts to be consistent and accurate. On the other hand, some stimuli seem to be associated with relatively simple forms of intrinsic meaning, such as the pleasantness of warmth or the unpleasantness of intense heat. In psychophysics, these feelings are considered hedonic functions. Still further, there are some types of "stimuli" that are heavily invested with meaning, even personal meaning. Examples include the perceived criminality of stated offenses, the status of occupations, and the perceived value of different amounts of money.

3.1.1 Feeling Good about Money

It may be surprising and even amusing that money provided the basis of the first psychophysical conjecture. In 1728, conjectures were far more common than experiments, and a 24-year-old mathematician named Gabriel Cramer suggested that the subjective value of money grows less rapidly than stated numerical amounts of money, whether measured in pennies or dollars. *Cramer (1728) conjectured that the psychological value of money grew only as the square root of the number of pennies.* Put another way, he proposed that the perceived value of money was a power function with an exponent of one-half, similar to brightness (see figure 2.1). This function predicts that you would feel good if you received a dollar, but you would have to receive about $4 to feel twice as good. The square root of four divided by one is two. Similarly, it would take about $40 to make you feel twice as good as receiving $10 (the square root of forty divided by ten is also two). Remember that the power law states that equal stimulus ratios produce equal response ratios (e.g., the stimulus ratio needed to double the pleasure of receiving amounts of money is 4:1). We only know about Cramer's conjecture because another mathematician, Daniel Bernoulli, mentioned Cramer's idea in a footnote in his own paper in 1738 (Bernoulli, 1954/1738). Bernoulli himself conjectured that the perceived value of money was a logarithmic function of actual money presented.

Given the lack of actual experimentation, it is easy to see why these two alternatives were not resolved until the twentieth century. Both a logarithmic function and a power function with an exponent of one-half look very similar when graphed on paper. Both functions bend downward to the right, similar to the bottom curve shown in figure 2.1 for brightness. Fechner's law (Fechner, 1860), which asserts that the experience of sensory magnitude is a logarithmic function, may well have been influenced by Bernoulli's conjecture. When experiments finally addressed this issue, it was determined that the perceived value of money followed a power function whose exponent ranged from about 0.4 to 0.5 (Galanter, 1962). The function was derived by asking participants to state how much money it would take to make them feel twice as happy as receiving a stated amount of money (e.g., $10, $20, etc.). Using visual analog scale (VAS) ratings of imagined desirability and pleasantness in response to hypothetical gifts of money, we also derived a power function whose exponent was 0.4 (Price and Barrell, 1984). This function was in quantitative agreement with a second method, that of making separate and direct judgments of how much money it would take to double the positive feeling of receiving various amounts of money (similar to the power function and ratio scale test for pain discussed in chapter 2!). The similarity in power function exponents across the two methods helps to validate the scales used for desire and emotional feeling ratings. Thus, power functions apply to perceived magnitudes of human experiences that are based on values and personal meanings. It is astonishing that they are similar in this respect to those derived from studies of the senses. Perhaps there is a commonality of psychological and neural mechanisms that encode experienced magnitude, regardless of whether it involves sensory perception or experienced feeling.

3.1.2 Feeling Bad about Crime

The procedures used to scale perceived brightness and loudness have found immediate translation into scaling other variables such as the perceived seriousness of crimes, the perceived status of occupations, and even the perceived degree of national power (Shinn, 1969). Ratio scales of these perceived dimensions of experience can be erected even though the "stimuli" are verbal descriptions of specific meanings which have no known inherent numerical scale of their own. For each description, a subject can perceive the meaning and magnitude of the experienced dimension, such as perceived seriousness of a crime. For example, ratio scales of the perceived seriousness of criminal offenses have been constructed by presenting subjects with brief descriptions of actions, each more or less illegal (Ekman, 1962). These ratio scales of perceived criminality have been shown to be reliable and generalizable across different occupational and national groups (Ekman, 1962; Stevens, 1975). The perceived severity of a criminal offense evidently depends on perceived meanings rather than exact particulars of the situation. Thus, if an offender breaks and enters a building, one can reliably estimate the seriousness of this act independent of the color of the building or the city in which the building is located. Indeed, precise ratio scales of criminal acts have been derived using descriptions of crimes in which the descriptions of victims and the exact nature of objects used in the crime were omitted (i.e., the word weapon was used as opposed to gun or knife).

If one can reliably estimate perceived magnitudes of experienced variables based on *descriptions* of acts or situations, then in principle one ought to be able to do this when *viewing* situations or possibly during *participating* in situations. Magnitudes of experiential variables may be estimated in much the same way as one would estimate the magnitudes of certain conceptual dimensions such as "severity of crime" or "national power." For example, we could construct a ratio scale of anxiety. To do this, we might ask a subject to use an anxiety VAS to represent the amount of anxiety he or she is experiencing. In fact, validated VASs of anxiety are commonly used in psychology experiments. The scales are anchored on the left by "no anxiety at all" and on the right by "the most intense anxiety imaginable." Several situations could be constructed in which the subject experiences anxiety and makes VAS ratings. Likewise, it also would be possible to scale such dimensions as the "degree of unfairness," "expectation," and "strength of desire" using a similar procedure. In fact, experiments have shown that it is possible to reliably measure such variables as the "desire to avoid pain," "expectation," and the magnitude of "negative feeling" in several different contexts (Price and Barrell, 1984; Price et al., 1984; 1985; 2001; Vase et al., 2003). Moreover, these experiments have provided evidence for interrelationships between these variables, a topic of chapters 5 and 6.

The construction of ratio scales for dimensions of experience that pertain to meanings allows us to perform arithmetic functions on the data. An interesting example is the demonstration of additivity for the ratio scale of perceived criminality (Ekman, 1962; Stevens, 1975). The extraction of the additive components of the complex delinquent acts was achieved through the process of analyzing the results of magnitude estimations. For example, the perceived criminality of stealing $5 was found to be equal to that of trespassing in a locked building. It was found that trespassing in a locked building *and* stealing $5 was perceived as twice as criminal as each crime performed independently (Ekman, 1962). Even more complex functions can be tested with ratio scaling. If both simple and complex functions can be validated with ratio scaling methods, it should be possible to validate a hypothesis in which two or more experiential variables are expressed as having a definite relationship to one another. For example, the perceived probability of a negative outcome and magnitude of the consequences should it occur could both be rated on ratio scales. If so, then relationships between perceived probability and imagined negativity of the outcome could be understood. This approach could be very useful in risk assessment.

3.2   Can Psychophysical Methods Be Used to Discover Reliable Interrelationships within Experience?

3.2.1   Two Experiential Explorations Which Are Important to Carry Out
Consider the following questions:

1. Are there reliable causal relationships between desires, expectations, and emotional feelings?

2. Do you think they are significant?
3. Can they be known with any certainty?
4. Do you think they can be studied scientifically?

We would like the reader to consider these questions before and after engaging in two simple explorations about imagined emotional feelings in response to hypothetical desires and expectation levels. In doing these exercises, it is important to use imagined emotional feelings as the guide as opposed to trying to "solve" the task theoretically. In responding to the different expectation levels, take each level of expectation as a new experience, not letting your previous response to expectation level blend in with the new imagined one. For example, each exercise starts with imagining that you do not expect to achieve the desired goal. When you move on to a higher level of expectation, imagine that it is a totally new experience that is not related to how you imagined feeling during the preceding expectation level. Also, imagine that the magnitude of your desire is about the same across all levels of expectation.

In the first exercise, imagine that you are in a situation wherein you could receive a large prize (e.g., $10,000) or award—something that you would really want and enjoy. Now look at figure 3.1. The vertical scale shows faces for a range of feelings. The scale extends from "worst feeling

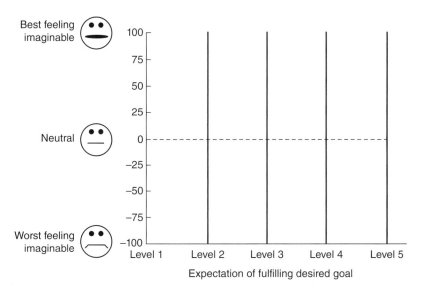

Figure 3.1
Reader exercise in rating hypothetical feeling intensities in two hypothetical scenarios.

imaginable" (bottom of scale) ... to neutral (middle of vertical scale) ... to "best feeling imaginable" (top of scale). Place a pencil mark on each vertical line, including the left vertical axis. Each mark represents how good or bad (happy/unhappy) you imagine feeling for each expectation level.

Level 1: I expect that I will not get this prize/award (mark left vertical axis)
Level 2: I expect that there is a small chance that I will get this prize/award
Level 3: I expect that there is a 50/50 chance that I will get this prize/award
Level 4: I expect there is a large chance that I will get this prize/award
Level 5: I am certain that I will get this prize/award

Now connect the five marks and look at the curve. Is it linear or curvilinear? You might consider doing this exercise two or three times to get a kind of average.

The second exploration is similar and can be compared to the first one. Imagine that you are in a situation wherein *you really want to avoid losing something or someone of value*, such as the life of someone close to you. (It could even be yourself.) Using the same figure 3.1, place a pencil mark on each vertical line for each of the following levels of expectation:

Level 1: I will lose (mark left vertical axis)
Level 2: There is a large chance that I will lose
Level 3: There is a 50/50 chance that I will lose
Level 4: There is a small chance that I will lose
Level 5: I am certain that I will not lose

Now connect the five marks and look at the curve. Again, doing the exercise two or more times to get a kind of average might be helpful. Is it linear or curvilinear? Is it similar or different than the one obtained in the exercise on receiving a prize?

We have found that when individuals use their imagined happy/unhappy feelings to rate imagined emotional feeling intensity in response to stated probabilities of receiving different amounts of money, the results were similar to those presented in the upper curves of figure 3.2. Don't be concerned if the curves you just produced are not exactly like those of figure 3.2, which is based on averages of several participants who each gave several ratings at each data point.

The purpose of the preceding exercises is not to formally replicate the curves of figure 3.2 but to give the reader a general experiential sense of the relationships between desire, expectation, and emotional feeling magnitude. The curves in figure 3.2 are derived in experiments wherein participants imagined different probabilities of avoiding several days of rain (an avoidance goal) or imagined different probabilities of receiving differ-

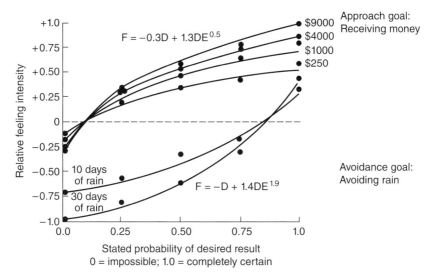

Figure 3.2
Positive and negative emotional feeling intensity as a function of expectation and desire in the hypothetical case of receiving money and enduring different durations of rain.

ent amounts of money (an approach goal; Price and Barrell, 1984). For the curve related to wanting to acquire a pleasant or happy consequence, the curve is likely to bend slightly downward to the right and feelings are positive over most of the range of expectation. In contrast, for the goal of wanting to avoid a negative consequence, the curve you derived is likely to bend upward to the left and feeling is negative over most of the range of expectation. If you used imagined feelings in these exercises, it is likely that the resulting curves look something like the ones in figure 3.2.

3.3   Results of Experiments Using Hypothetical Scenarios

Remember the questions that were posed at the beginning of the previous section (e.g., Can we discover experiential laws or relationships?). Does performing these explorations change perspective on these questions? Of course, these "experiential explorations" are not actual scientific experiments, yet they suggest that such functions are possible. A more formal experiment that addresses these questions utilized an experimental approach taken by Galanter (1962) to scale simple hypothetical experiences similar to the ones just presented (Price and Barrell, 1984). The experiment required participants to respond to their imagined intensities of desire and expectation in two hypothetical situations, (1) anticipating the possibility of receiving different amounts of money ($250 to $9,000) with different stated probabilities and (2) anticipating the possibility of different durations of continuous rain combined with different stated probabilities of rain occurring,[1] Imagined emotional feeling intensity increased as a function of stated probabilities of receiving money and as a function of amount of stated money. This should not be a surprise to anyone. People can get excited when they imagine the possibility of receiving money, and both the amount of money and likelihood of receipt influence this imagined excitement. No doubt, similar factors contribute to the vicarious excitement of watching game shows on television. What is interesting are the subtleties of these relationships and how they interrelate with Galanter's (1962) work on perceived value of money. Anyone can verify or disconfirm them quite easily, for example, by doing the experiment using index cards that combine money values with stated probability values. As an approximation, one can imagine magnitudes of emotional feeling in response to combinations presented in figure 3.2.

We found that when participants imagined actually receiving different amounts of money, both their rated emotional feeling intensity and the desirability of having a given amount of money were power functions with an exponent of 0.4, identical to the one obtained by Galanter in 1962 and similar to the 0.5 exponent conjectured by Cramer in 1728 (quoted in Stevens, 1975). This function is similar to the one shown for perceived brightness (see figure 2.1). Thus, emotional feeling intensity and desirability were either strongly and linearly related to each other or experienced as the same variable when participants imagined actually receiving different amounts of money.

Surprisingly, emotional feeling intensity (imagined excitement) but *not* desirability grew as a power function of stated probability when the latter varied from 0 to 100%. In contrast to imagined emotional feeling, desirability remained the same, on average, throughout the range of stated probabilities but increased as a function of stated amount of money. Feeling intensity, on the other hand, was a power function of stated probability with an exponent of 0.5. This exponent was the same for all stated amounts of money. Thus, figure 3.2 presents a family of curves that all bend downward toward the right, similar to some sensory psychophysical functions such as warmth. An equation was derived that accommodated all four upper curves in figure 3.2: $F = -0.3D + 1.3D \times E^{1/2}$, where F is emotional feeling intensity, D is desire, and E is stated probability. For the *approach* goal of receiving money, F depends on a multiplicative interaction between D and E because the curves intersect between 0 and 1.0 and in fact cross over between 0 and 0.25. Hence the term $D \times E^{1/2}$ reflects this interaction. We note that in this highly structured and simplified experimental context, we assume that stated probability is very close to subjective probability. We would not make that assumption in actual lived situations, as we point out in chapter 5.

Imagining receiving money may be exciting, but what about imagined unpleasant events such as pain or bad weather? In a second variant of this same experiment, we asked participants to scale imagined emotional feeling intensity and desire in response to two continuous durations of rain, ten days and thirty days, with different stated probabilities of rain occurring. When participants imagined actually having to endure different durations of rain, both feeling intensity and desire were nearly linear functions of stated durations of rain, similar to that of perceived line length. Feeling intensity grew less negative when participants imagined greater probabilities of avoiding the unpleasant rains (see figure 3.2, bottom curves). Positive emotional feeling only occurred when the probability of avoiding rain was certain (i.e., 100% or 1.0 on the x-axis). This may be related to the imagined relief of avoiding rain entirely. In the case of the *avoidance* goal associated with rain, the relationship of stated probability to feeling intensity is a power function with an exponent close to 2, consistent with the fact that the family of curves all bend upward toward the left (see figure 3.2, bottom curves). Similar to the *approach* goal of receiving money, desire, *on average*, was only a function of stated duration of rain (i.e., magnitude of the prospective outcome) and not a function of stated probability. An equation was derived that accommodated the two bottom curves in figure 3.2: $F = -D + 1.4D \times E^{1.9}$, where F is emotional feeling intensity, D is desire, and E is stated probability. For the *avoidance* goal of wanting it to not rain, F is a function of a multiplicative interaction between D and E because the curves intersect between 0 and 1.0 and in fact cross over between 0.75 and 1.0. Hence the term $D \times E^{1.9}$ reflects this interaction.

There are several aspects of these curves that are noteworthy. They resemble the families of curves found in sensory psychophysics, particularly those that contain multiple variables (e.g., spatial summation of warmth and pain in chapter 2). Despite having multiple variables, single equations parsimoniously account for each family of curves, and the two derived equations are similar in form but have different exponents. In the case of imagining actually receiving the projected outcome, desire and feeling have similar magnitudes both in the case of money and rain.

Finally, the curves for *approach* goal (receiving money) and *avoidance* goal (rain) functions appear symmetrical to each other (figure 3.2 and perhaps figure 3.1). This symmetry reminds us that when basic principles are found in nature, they sometimes have aesthetic qualities.

The functions suggest the possibility of reliable interrelationships between variables of experience, which admittedly are not measured as precisely as variables of Newtonian physics. No doubt, there is more variability and measurement error in former than in the latter. The multiplicative interactions between D and E are consistent with value-expectancy models in decision theory (Shah and Higgins, 1997), yet the former make the distinction between approach and avoidance goals, which have very different power function exponents (0.5 vs. 2 or 1.9). Although they are power functions, they differ in several ways from psychophysical laws. First, like psychosensory laws, *both* the independent and dependent variables could be psychological if we substituted subjective probability for stated probability in figure 3.2 (Stevens, 1975). A good example of a psychosensory law is the relationship between perceived volume (V), density (D), and loudness (L) of sound wherein $L = V \times D$ (Stevens, 1975). However, unlike psychosensory laws, the emotion-related variables need not be strictly associated with stimulus variables, as explained in chapter 5.

3.4   Can Similar Functions Be Discovered in Lived Situations?

Although the equations for approach and avoidance goals have symmetry and simplicity, they are all based on highly structured and simplified *imagined* conditions. The explorations carried out by the reader (see figure 3.1) may help decide whether they apply even to imagined situations. The remaining question is whether they have any relationship whatsoever to actual experiences of wanting to acquire pleasant or avoid unpleasant outcomes in actual lived situations. To the extent that participants become involved in *imagining* these hypothetical situations, we think they bear some relationship to actual experienced events because we can imagine hypothetical excitement, anxiety, and disappointment as well as vicariously experience emotions of others. Imagination is a part of everyday human emotions. Nevertheless, demonstration of these interrelationships between desire, probability, and happy/unhappy feelings in actual lived situations would inspire much greater confidence that these relationships reflect true psychological principles. It would also help if these relationships were verified from both first- and third-person perspectives, as we have outlined above for psychophysical experiments. Otherwise, the families of curves shown in figure 3.2 may be mathematically interesting but could be construed as empty abstractions by people who don't verify the functions in their own experience. What if these curves account for some human emotional feelings of everyday life and provide positive answers to the questions posed at the beginning of this section: Can they be meaningfully and reliably verified in scientific studies?

If they could be replicated in actual lived situations, such as waiting for the train to pass so that you can get to work on time or waiting to hear the results of your latest experiment or physical examination, then these functions would acquire a degree of ecological validity, as termed by psychologists. Thus, if directly experienced probabilities were substituted for stated probabilities and if the objects of desire were about real outcomes sought by study participants, then these functions would take on a higher level of importance and meaning. They also could represent understanding of the nature of thoughts and feelings. We have introduced sets of formulas that suggest the possibility of delineating functions that account for some types of emotional feeling. If dynamics of human feeling could be made numerically explicit, this result would in no way detract from the very human experience in which it is rooted.

As Michael Polanyi (1969) wrote,

Imagine a set of mathematical formulas that would answer questions that we might ask about such matters of experience. The object of such experience must be other than the mathematical formulas which are to explain it, and hence these formulas are meaningless unless they bear on non-mathematical experiences.

Designing experiments wherein these interrelationships between desire, expectation, and emotional feeling intensities are verified in the ordinary contexts of life is a tall order. Such experiments would require an acute level of self-observation, and we would have to collect both qualitative and quantitative data that were complementary and interpretable. We would need an experiential method and sets of procedures/methods to conduct such ambitious experiments. Beginning in the 1980s and continuing to the present, we developed an experiential paradigm for the purpose of testing interrelationships between dimensions of human experience. The qualitative aspects of this paradigm constitute the topic of the next chapter (chapter 4). In chapter 5 we discuss how qualitative and quantitative methods can be integrated to provide both an experiential and quantitative understanding of some types of emotions.

4 Describing, Characterizing, and Understanding Phenomenal Experience

4.1 The Possibility of Experiential Science

4.1.1 The Conditions for Observation

In this chapter, we explain methods that could provide a scientific foundation for describing, characterizing, and understanding the qualitative nature of human phenomenal experience, starting with a close examination of the "outer" and "inner" conditions that would make such a science feasible. We maintained that considerable efforts were needed to arrive at and test hypotheses that pertained to experiences associated with such phenomena as emotions, motivation, and choice (chapters 2 and 3). In this chapter we undertake a close examination of how experiential studies can be designed, observations about experience obtained, and results understood. In chapter 5 we discuss how these qualitative methods can be combined with quantitative methods to answer some significant questions about the structures of specific types of human experiences, such as emotional feelings and the experience of choice.

Some of these steps are not unique to a science of experience, but to some extent are embedded in all of the sciences. Astronomy serves as an example. Modern astronomy requires telescopes and other technologies with which to observe and characterize planets, stars, galaxies, black holes, and related phenomena, yet the external conditions for observation have to be optimal. Telescopes have to be used at high altitudes or in space; advanced technology has to be used to capture and analyze images. Even our physical position in the universe is critical. Our planet is situated between the center and perimeter of our galaxy and between adjacent arms of two spirals. Had our planet been closer to the center or to the perimeter of our galaxy or embedded within a spiral, the physical conditions would not allow telescopes to peer into the vast reaches of the universe. Even if life were possible within the middle of a galaxy's spiral, light would simply be too dense there for observations of distant regions of the universe. The external conditions that allow life and perhaps consciousness to exist are the same ones that allow astronomical science to take place.

So also there are several conditions that need to exist for a science of human consciousness, including optimum "outer" and "inner" conditions. They require tools for observation and external situations that optimize inquiry into distinct phenomena such as thinking, imaging, and emotional feelings. However, instead of relying mainly on advanced technology, an experiential science has at least three requirements: (1) a trained ability to directly witness what is directly present in experience, (2) a temporary suspension of our presuppositions and usual interpretative mode of inquiry, and (3) a utilization of the same inferential and deductive methods of the other sciences once the observations are made and the data are collected. An experiential science also requires that we either provide external conditions that increase the likelihood that certain phenomena such as emotions will occur or otherwise use "free-ranging" sampling methods that "capture" ordinary experiences as they occur in the moment. As discussed already, there has been and continues to be enormous controversy about the extent to which these types of enterprises are feasible. The ensuing discussion begins with examples of "failed attempts" in order to help specify the conditions that are required for an experiential science. These examples are then followed by discussions of different levels of experiential science, starting with reflections on psychophysics, the topics of chapters 2 and 3, then continuing with the experiential sampling method of Hurlburt and colleagues (Heavey and Hurlburt, 2008; Hurlburt, 1997; Hurlburt and Akhter, 2006; 2008; Hurlburt and Schwitzgebel, 2007) and ending with the experiential method (Price and Barrell, 1980; Price and Aydede, 2005; Price, Riley, and Barrell, 2001). Instead of addressing the question of whether *any* science of consciousness is possible, we attempt to simply characterize the practices of each method and to compare and contrast them. We recognize that not everyone will agree about the level of experiential inquiry that is possible and that controversy about this issue will no doubt continue for a while.

4.1.2 "Failed Attempts" at Self-Report?

There is a vast literature that claims enormous fallibility in people's ability to accurately report their experiences. For example, under many, if not most, conditions, eyewitness testimony is inaccurate, filled with distortions, and easily influenced by suggestions and subtle physical and social cues (see pp. 234–291 and references in Hurlburt and Schwitzgebel, 2007).

Moreover, people are often very inaccurate about the accuracy of other people's eyewitness testimony (Hurlburt and Schwitzgebel, 2007). Another similar phenomenon is that people often miss seeing changes in their environment that might appear obvious to someone else who already knows about the changes. This phenomenon is referred to as "change blindness" (Levin et al., 1997). An example is from a movie clip which shows two actors in a busy restaurant talking to each other. The scene continuously includes the plates on their table. As the camera focuses on actor A the plates are red, but when the focus switches from actor A to B, the plates suddenly turn white. Despite what one might consider an obvious change, only about 10% of the participants watching the scene report seeing it. However, people are not blind just to change but also to the very fact that such a phenomenon as "change blindness" even exists (Levin et al., 2000). If asked whether they would actually notice an abrupt change such as the example just given, approximately 85% of people claim that they would certainly notice abrupt changes.

Some psychologists and philosophers such as Schwitzgebel (see chapter 10 in Hurlburt and Schwitzgebel, 2007) often use phenomena such as these as the basis for their skepticism about the possibility of developing an experiential science that relies on people's ability to directly and accurately report their experiences. Added to this conundrum is the reluctance for people to suspend or bracket their presuppositions (as recommended by the phenomenologists) about the nature or content of their experiences. For example, the philosopher Bernard Baars claims that "human beings talk to themselves every moment of the waking day" (Baars, 2003, p. 106). This claim is nothing more than a presupposition, one that may be based more on armchair reflection than on any effort to empirically determine what people's direct experiences are like. We shall see later that actual empirical evidence indicates that Baar's generalization is incorrect.

However, this skepticism put forth by philosophers and psychologists itself raises some interesting questions. To what *extent* are the people giving eyewitness testimony or the people with "change blindness" misreporting their *experiences*? Consider the example above of change blindness. If someone doesn't see the color change, then the color change may simply not have been in their experience or the color change *was* briefly in their experience but not long enough to install a working memory of it. In any case, when they are reporting on what they were just experiencing, their experience may or may not include changes in the color of the table plates (e.g., red to white). The possibility that they might miss something doesn't necessarily invalidate their overall experience or even their ability to self-report, especially if what they are asked to report is their phenomenal experience. What might have been most essential in the example of the scene of the "two actors in a busy restaurant" are the meanings contained within their interchange. We may all "leave out" or "fill in" when we report an experience. These facets of reporting may be considered "errors" in relation to a hypothetical objective account, such as the filmed portrayal of persons and objects in a scene. However, is it an error from the standpoint of being an accurate account of someone's experience? Most critically, is it an error from the perspective of the essential *meanings* that are within someone's experience? The color of the plates in the example of change blindness may not significantly impede recognition of the meanings portrayed in a scene or other types of phenomenal experience. Whether these "errors" invalidate self-report depends on the reasons why someone is self-reporting. For example, if the study is about essential meanings that underpin a type of emotion or background state of consciousness, then the accuracy of *how* one is experiencing is more critical than the exact environmental particulars in a situation, as we discuss later.

As pointed out by Hurlburt, the use of eyewitness testimony literature and other studies that discredit observation about experience also do not address the possibility that people can be trained and instructed to provide accurate reports about their experience (Hurlburt and Schwitzgebel, 2007). We have already seen this development in the case of psychophysics. What about reporting of experiences in more common and natural settings? Whereas eyewitness observations do not involve preparation or practice and commonly involve only single opportunities for observation, the methods to be described involve training, support, clarification, and multiple chances to make observations. Let us turn to the question about what levels of observation and analysis are possible in different methods that utilize self-report of experience.

4.1.3 What Is Needed in Experiential Science?

There are several approaches and methods in psychology that claim to engage in qualitative research on human experience. One of the specific methods includes the thought-listing method. Using this method, participants are asked to list the thoughts or ideas relevant to a message as they process the message, that occur later as they consider their current attitude toward the message, or that occur later while judging their preferences (Cacioppo et al., 1997). Other methods include questionnaires that probe recent experience. Much social and human science research deals with verbal reports or responses to questionnaires that are about generalizations about experience (e.g., I feel sad—none, some, most, or all of the time). Verbal responses contribute huge amounts of both qualitative and quantitative data for human psychology. They can be taped, transcribed, codified, and analyzed for certain frequencies of responses, such as beliefs, attitudes, and so on. However, many of these methods begin with presuppositions. Thus, a thought-listing method presupposes that people are having thoughts in their recent experience. Instead, they can just as well have other kinds of phenomenal experience, such as "inner seeing," images, and feelings, as we shall explain. Likewise, when participants endorse items on questionnaires about themselves, they are often asked to make generalizations, often sweeping ones, about themselves as persons or about their experience in general. What if someone really doesn't know the answer? For example, it is entirely conceivable that some individuals really don't know whether they feel sad none, some, most, or all of the time or the prevalence of their own happiness. It is clear to us that we need methods that directly capture human experience as it is lived in the moment. We now compare three experiential paradigms, dealing with questions about what conditions and procedures are necessary and what level of observation is possible in conducting experiential science.

4.2 A Comparison of Three Experiential Paradigms—Psychophysics, the Descriptive Experiential Sampling (DES) Method, and the Experiential–Phenomenological Method

4.2.1 Psychophysics

As discussed in chapter 2, psychophysics is a simplified and highly structured paradigm in which conditions are arranged to explore relationships between stimuli and sensory experiences. Psychophysics offers an important reminder of the critical roles of "inner" and "outer" conditions in studies of human experience. How are such conditions arranged in psychophysics? The outer conditions of psychophysics are simple and in many respects similar to those of physical experiments. Devices that deliver well-measured and controlled stimuli are used in a quiet setting wherein participants are comfortable and free to use some method by which to signal their detection of stimuli (e.g., pushing a button) or represent their experienced magnitude of sensation or feeling (e.g., cross-modality matching or rating on a visual analog scale). Yet "inner" conditions also are critical and have to be carefully arranged. Thus, participants are usually instructed beforehand to attend to some aspect of their experience when the stimuli occur, such as experienced sensation intensity, spatial extent of sensation, or the magnitude of pleasantness/unpleasantness they experience. Of course, arrangements can be made to observe and assess other aspects of their experience while performing the psychophysical task. For example, the experiment can be about how pain is affected by aspects of one's conscious state, such as during an experiment that is about hypnotic analgesia. Participants can rate their experienced degree of absorption, their degree of attention, their attitudes toward their context, or any number of factors. As in the large majority of psychology experiments, the hypotheses are proposed before the experiment is conducted and participants are simply asked to describe, rate, or use some other method to represent the contents of their experience. Both stimulus characteristics, such as intensity, and aspects of conscious experience, such as absorption, may constitute some of the independent variables of such an experiment.

Experiments such as these are about direct human experience in an important respect, yet they are designed to confirm or disconfirm specific hypotheses already stated in advance. One limitation of this approach is that their hypotheses are almost always based on presuppositions, and often the presuppositions originate from results of previous studies. Their purpose is confirmatory, not exploratory. Another limitation is that experiments involving psychophysical methods arrange highly simplified and, some might say, artificial physical and social contexts. They raise the question as to whether they have applicability to phenomena as they occur in ordinary lived situations, a concern noted by phenomenologists and by psychologists who seek ecological validity. This concern was raised in the previous chapter.

The purpose of reiterating psychophysics as a paradigm for the study of human experience is that it is already a widely acceptable method that is an integral part of psychology, neuroscience, and medicine. It contains a system of checks and balances and multiple methods for confirming and disconfirming hypotheses that is similar in principle to all of the natural sciences. And it offers a critical bridge to understanding neural mechanisms that help explain sensory processing, thinking, and emotions. Thus, it can be used to interface experiential science with brain science.

4.2.2 Simply Discovering What Human Experience Is Like: The Descriptive Experience Sampling Method

Paradigms that use stimuli to explore human experience do not provide much information as to how people have experiences under the ordinary conditions of everyday life. Psychology and particularly studies of consciousness are in drastic need of an approach and method for exploring experience as it is lived. This need has long been recognized (Giorgi, 1970). One promising method for exploring phenomenal experience, the DES method, already has been described in chapter 1. It uses a random beeper in the participants' natural environment to signal them to notice their experience that was ongoing just prior to the beep. Participants then take notes about that experience, and after several such beeped experiences they meet with the investigator to clarify and describe the experiences. The iterative nature of this method allows the participant's observational and reporting skills to improve over the course of the sampling days. The purpose of the interview with the investigator is to provide a simple answer to one question posed for each beeped experience "What were you experiencing at the moment of the beep?" A complete and detailed answer is sought for that question, while avoiding interpretations, explanations, and confabulations on the part of the participant.

The outer and inner conditions of the DES method are remarkable and drastically different than those of psychophysics just described and almost all of psychology in general. The main purpose of this method, unlike psychophysics, is exploratory, not confirmatory. For the most part, both the outer and inner conditions of this method are just ordinary consciousness as encountered in everyday life. There are no "stimuli" that are delivered, and participants are not instructed to prepare for anything or to be in some special state of attention or awareness. In fact, the randomness of the programmed beeps prevents such preparation. People are simply beeped, and then they attend to and take notes on what was in their experience at the moment of the beep. The purpose of this method is simply to capture the content of experience as it is lived, without presuppositions, analyses, confabulation, or even some kind of indirect representation of experienced magnitudes (e.g., ratings or categories). The outer conditions also include using the electronic beeper, the willingness and ability to take brief notes for each beep, and the conditions of the interview. As we described in chapter 1, the interviewer has to be skillful in using this method.

The Nature of the Data

What, then, is the nature of the data and knowledge derived from this method? The reports of direct experience are derived from the notes taken immediately after noticing the beep, and the interview then clarifies the notes. A report based on these notes and the interview is then written by the interviewer. Let us examine an example of such a report in detail. We have chosen a representative experiential account of Melanie (not her real name), the study participant of Hurlburt and Schwitzgebel's 2007 book.

Melanie was considering the appointments she had later in the morning, particularly the time pressure of getting to her second appointment, which was across town from the first. She had a mental image of sitting in her car and being stopped at a red stop light at a generic intersection. She could see the stoplight and the road stretched out in front of her and her hands on the steering wheel. Melanie was also cognitively aware that she was anxious, but the feeling of anxiety was not in her awareness at the moment of the beep. (Hurlburt and Schwitzgebel, 2007, p. 308)

This account contains images and meanings, ones that point to a goal of getting to an appointment on time (a meaning) and an implicit uncertainty about this goal (also a meaning). The latter is accompanied by an image of being stopped at an intersection and a road stretched out in front of her (see figure 4.1). She notes that during this experience she was not actually stopped at an intersection and there was no actual road. It was just an imaginary scene. The account seems to contain at least the cognitive part of an emotion that is described simply as an awareness of being anxious. However, the *feeling* of anxiety is said not to be in the brief

Figure 4.1
Our imagination of Melanie's imagined scene.

moment just prior to the beep. Her experience is further clarified in an interview with both Hurlburt and Schwitzebel (2007, pp. 173–177).

In the interview, it becomes clear that the brief moment just before the beep was embedded in a sequence of thoughts, images, and then feelings that she noticed. First, there were thoughts about what she was going to do this morning and the fact that she had this appointment. Then she became quite focused on this fact. The beep occurred as she was becoming focused. After the beep, she noticed becoming "a little bit more tense, after I thought about it, than before." The sequence ends with a general feeling of anxiety about wanting to be somewhere on time. However, strictly speaking, this report would not count as a report of anxiety because she did not report the feeling of anxiety as occurring just before the beep. This account provides a very small piece of information about an experience that may have preceded anxiety. It suggests but certainly does not prove that the cognitive content or *meaning* of experience in this sample may have something to do with a future necessity combined with a vague uncertainty.

To use the metaphor of the camera, the shutter duration of this "snapshot" is very brief, appearing to capture a quick image and immediate associated meanings, despite the fact that they are embedded in a temporal sequence. However, in clarifying the entire sequence of thoughts, images, and feeling in proximity to the beep, it becomes evident that a concern with being on time emerges out of general thoughts about the day. This concern is manifested as both thought and an image, followed by *feeling* anxious (after the beep). The DES method takes very brief "snapshots" that contain moments of actual lived experience as it ordinarily occurs. Usually the data are just these brief moments. In the example from Melanie just given, it is clear that these moments can be part of an extended sequence of experience.

Knowledge Derived from DES Studies

If several people are studied using DES, what kind of knowledge does this method generate? What does it tell us about the ordinary consciousness of human beings? For example, are we more different than alike in our moment-by-moment experience? Studies using DES have yielded some very interesting answers to these questions, some of which are very surprising.

One study by Heavey and Hurlburt (2008) characterized frequently occurring phenomena of direct experience within and across people. They discovered that the five most frequent types of experience included feelings, sensory awareness, inner seeing, inner speech, and unsymbolized thinking. These five categories were distinct and included the following:

1. *Feeling* is contained within emotions such as sadness, happiness, humor, anxiety, joy, fear, nervousness, embarrassment, anger, and so on. An example is in the interview of Melanie above where she reports feeling anxious *after* the beep. It would not be counted as a feeling in the report itself because it happened well after the beep (seconds?). If the beep had occurred later than it did, it may well have captured the anxious feeling itself.

2. *Sensory awareness* is attending to a particular sensory aspect of one's environment, and the sensory experience is a primary theme or focus of experience. An example is my attending to the computer screen during a pause in writing. I focus on the cursor blinking and the whiteness of the page. No thought, just watching the cursor and screen.

3. *Inner seeing* is seeing something in imagination that is not actually present. A really good example is Melanie's image of seeing the intersection and the road stretched out before her while sitting in her car (see figure 4.1). All of this is in her imagination.

4. *Inner speech* is speaking words in your own voice but with no external (real) sound. An example occurred just now when I heard myself think "I've got to think of an example of inner speech. Should I use one of my own or just one of Hurlburt's?" I wasn't talking out loud or making any sound, yet the words were mostly clear to me. My thoughts were expressed in approximately these words.

5. *Unsymbolized thinking* is thinking a particular definite thought *without* the awareness of words, images, or any other symbols used to make up that thought. As an example, my wife and I were in a restaurant and I was watching a waiter carry a tray on which there were many tall filled glasses. As the waiter approached a nearby table, I was hoping that the glasses wouldn't fall over. (A beeper that I purchased from Russell Hurlburt beeped!) However, this hoping did not involve any inner speech or any symbols. If translated into words, an appropriate sentence would be "I hope the glasses don't fall over." However, there were no words and no concepts of "glasses" or "tray" or "fall over." This category is of great interest and relevance to the DES method because both psychologists and philosophers have denied that this type of thinking exists and because its presence comes as a surprise to those who notice it for the first few times. Its denial by others appears not to be based on any experiential test that anyone has done on themselves or others.

To what extent are these types of phenomenal experience present in "normal" people? Heavey and Hurlburt (2008) randomly sampled moments of experience of 30 participants who each provided 10 samples. The participants were college students who were stratified according to psychological symptoms. Thus, participants each responded to a questionnaire that was about their general level of psychological distress (Derogatis, 1987; revised in 1994) and 3 participants were selected from each of 10 score levels on the questionnaire, making a total of 30. Part of the basis for the study was to determine if the five types of sampled experiences related to general level of psychological distress that were present in the lives of the participants. One of the main findings of this study was that each of the five categories listed above occurred in approximately one quarter of sampled moments. Thus, the results suggest that all five categories listed above are quite common in human experience, even unsymbolized thinking. Other categories were discovered, but they each accounted for a very small percentage of the total number of samples.

A second and perhaps unexpected finding is that the frequency of these five types of experience varied considerably across individuals. For example, 5 participants had no inner speech in any of their 10 samples, whereas one participant experienced inner speech in 75% of his samples. The majority of participants (22 of 30) exhibited a dominant form of experience, with one of the 5 types of phenomena occurring in 50% or more of their sampled experiences. Inner seeing was the most common dominant form of experience, followed by feelings, and then inner speech.

This study is important for several reasons. It overturns the conclusions of other studies and philosophers' assertions that claim that we are constantly experiencing feelings or that we are constantly experiencing inner speech. It does so through a method that avoids presuppositions and simply samples experience randomly and as it is lived in the moment. This study also reveals unsymbolized thinking, a common phenomenon of experience that is not widely recognized in the scientific literature on consciousness. There were no strong or statistically significant associations between the frequencies of occurrence of the five types of experience, thereby demonstrating that these types of experiencing are, for the most part, independent of each other. Finally, an unexpected finding was that higher frequencies of inner speech were associated with lower levels of psychological distress (Heavey and Hurlburt, 2008).

Other studies by Hurlburt and colleagues reveal interesting experiential characteristics of people with different medical and psychological conditions, so that the DES method appears to extend to group as well as individual differences. One DES study of three adults with Asperger's syndrome, a form of autism in individuals who still have high functioning, showed that their thoughts were primarily or solely in the form of images, commonly visual ones (Hurlburt, Happe, and Frith, 1994). By contrast, normal adults show the variability in types of experience described above (Heavey and Hurlburt, 2008). In another DES study, seven undiagnosed participants who shared a high rate of speech were compared to seven normal-speech-rate individuals (Hurlburt, Koch, and Heavey, 2002). The authors found that high-speech-rate individuals had fewer instances of simple inner speech, more instances of complex inner experiences, fewer feeling experiences, and more "just doing" experiences. This study demonstrates the capacity to link characteristics of phenomenal experience to a clear type of behavioral characteristic. This type of result may have much wider implications. If behavioral traits are linked to types of experience, then characterizing, understanding, and perhaps even treating conditions such as autism, depression, and various types of psychoses may be facilitated. This approach would contrast with one that utilizes a behavioral approach or cognitive–behavioral approach. When several samples of direct experience are taken from different groups of human participants, the DES method differentiates several conditions. Schizophrenics really do experience themselves and the world differently than other people, as do depressed or anxious people (Hurlburt and Schwitzgebel, 2007).

How Is the DES Method Validated? Does It Provide Accurate Accounts of Direct Experience?

From the perspective of much of psychology and neuroscience, a means of establishing the validity of the DES method is not immediately obvious because samples of momentary experience are not necessarily closely linked to anything in the environment—there is no external event that can be used to validate what was experienced. As we discussed in chapter 1, even the same situation or external event can give rise to radically different meanings; human experience is often dependent on meanings. Furthermore, we may be lost in our imagination or in our inner speech at the moment of the beep, and the environment has a highly variable influence on what we are experiencing. The notes are closer to the experience, but they are at least one step removed from what was actually experienced. What is the nature of these notes? A critical question also can be raised about the interview. Although its purpose is to clarify each sample of experience, does the report of the experience depend so much on the interviewer that it makes the experiential report untrustworthy?

These questions have been answered to some extent by Hurlburt and his colleagues. In one study, Hurlburt and Heavey (2002) obtained six random samples each from 10 participants, and two interviewers independently interviewed them and rated samples on the presence or absence of the five types of inner experience described earlier. The interobserver reliabilities were very high (.90–.98, using Spearman–Brown adjustment), comparable to highly reliable questionnaires. Another kind of reliability of DES occurs within individuals. Participants who have a predominant form of experience, such as inner speech, have been found to be reliable in having that form of experience (Hurlburt and Heavey, 2008). Someone who has a predominant pattern of inner speech doesn't suddenly become a person who is a predominant "feeling" person or someone with predominantly unsymbolized thinking.

Reliabilities such as these may be necessary for validity and accuracy, but they are not sufficient. To be valid and accurate, it would seem necessary that the participants agree with the written reports of the interviewer. Upon reading the report, the participants may or may not find that it corresponds to what they experienced. Thus, we think that the participant should provide some independent means of verifying the content of the sampled experience and thereby share the task of validation. However, Hurlburt and Akhter (2006) argue against this approach. They make a diametrically opposing claim that "it is *hazardous* to check validity against your own experience" because, as they state, "Presuppositions *always* exquisitely match your own experiences" (p. 206). This claim seems to put the DES method in a curious bind. Participants can't check whether the report of the interviewer matches their experiences, thereby excluding a means of further validating this method. If the participant should claim that the report does *not* correspond to his or her experience, then one should at least question the accuracy of the interviewer's report. If the participant makes this negative claim, how can we tell whether it is based on an interviewer's inaccuracy or on the participant's presupposition? If we really knew that presuppositions *always* match experience, then such potential criticisms by participants could be ignored but at the cost of an opportunity for checking the accuracy of the report. Thus, it appears that there is a missing piece in the DES method, an independent means of verifying the contents of sampled experiences.

This limitation aside, the nature of the interview itself and the training of the interviewers help ensure correspondence between the report of experience and that which the participant claims is her or his experience. Interviewers are trained to determine what was actually present in the sampled moments, without leading the participant[1] or supplying the participant with presuppositions or interpretations. Moreover, they discourage the participants themselves from supplying them as well. The high reliability between interviews lends some confidence that the DES experiential method reduces distortion by these factors. In fact, participants are often surprised by their sampled experiences for the very reason that they do not correspond to their presuppositions. For example, Heavey and Hurlburt (2008) note that when people begin participation in DES, they have more inner speech samples and few, if any, samples of unsymbolized thinking. As they become more practiced, some participants supply many more samples of unsymbolized thinking and are very surprised at the phenomenon.

Thus, both the practice of the participant and the interview technique are critical for the accuracy and validity of the DES method. The role of the participant in the interview is to provide a description of the experience that is as accurate and faithful to the experience as possible. This requires that the participant neither hide nor add to the content, but just simply report what was present in the experience. The role of the interviewer is to help the participant accomplish this aim, and this role requires several skills and guidelines. The interviewer tries to grasp the subject's experience, as experienced by the participant. This requires listening carefully, not intruding upon or leading the descriptions of the participant, and suspending preconceptions about the characteristics of the experience. The interviewer also helps participants report just their experiences and not their extrasampling general statements about their experiences, such as their self-theories or explanations about experiences.

4.2.3   Discovering and Confirming Hypotheses about Human Experience: The Experiential Method

The DES method is exploratory and addresses the questions of what ordinary experience is like for people in general and for people that have certain ongoing psychological conditions (e.g., autism, depression, schizophrenia). It simply seeks to explore the nature of experience during ordinary situations and doesn't begin with hypotheses or theories, unlike the vast majority of studies in psychology. However, some investigators are interested in specific phenomena or questions about phenomena, such as the nature of specific types of emotional feelings, pain, pleasure, or background states of consciousness. A method that randomly samples moments of experience could not efficiently address such questions unless it was interfaced with methods that arrange conditions in which specific phenomena (e.g., anxiety, excitement, etc.) are likely to occur. Perhaps an ideal method would be one that addresses specific questions about experience yet is both exploratory and confirmatory. It would have two stages of verification. The purpose of the first stage would be to generate hypotheses and would be mainly exploratory while the second stage would explicitly test hypotheses generated in the first stage. We developed an experiential method, starting in the 1980s, that contained both of these stages (Barrell et al., 1985; Price and Barrell, 1980; 1984; Price, Barrell, and Barrell, 1985, Price, Riley, and Barrell, 2001; Price and Aydede, 2005). The cornerstone of this method is awareness of experience as it has just taken place in the moment. This general idea is not at all new and is an integral component of ancient teachings, spiritual traditions, and even some forms of psychotherapy (e.g., Gestalt therapy; Perls, 1969). It can be a remarkable process for attaining self-knowledge and self-transformation (Givot, 1998). To study specific topics of interest, such as emotions and states of consciousness, certain outer and inner conditions have to be arranged. Although this method was briefly described in chapter 1, the following discussion will elaborate on the purpose of this paradigm, the nature of the procedures that are used, the form of the results, and how the data are interpreted and understood.

The Outer and Inner Conditions of the Experiential Method

The conditions for the experiential method are in some ways similar to those of the DES method, but have a number of critical differences. Unlike the DES method, the experiential method begins with a study group posing a general question to their experiences such as anger, feeling understood, or jealousy (Barrell and Barrell, 1975; Price and Barrell, 1980; Barrell et al., 1985; Barrell and Richards, 1982; VanKaam, 1959). The question is general, clearly understandable, and specifically directed to *how* one experiences a given phenomenon rather than only the target of experience or the stimulus conditions in which the phenomenon manifests itself. Thus, if the question is about anger at someone, we focus on the experience of being angry rather than only on the person at whom we are angry (i.e., the target). The assumption here, taken from phenomenological analysis (Husserl, 1952; Merleau-Ponty, 1962; VanKaam, 1959), is that the process of experiencing rather than the specific targets of experience leads us to an understanding of the essential factors within the phenomenon. For example, the specific person(s) at whom we are angry and the specific physical contexts may vary considerably from one situation to another. However, noticing *how* we experience someone (e.g., as unfair) is more likely to reveal the content of experience that is common across situations and across individuals (Barrell and Jourard, 1976; VanKaam, 1959). Most important, the study group members are to pose the question to their own experiencing of the phenomenon. The assumption here is that an understanding of the reality of an experiential phenomenon is most accurate if it is about one's *own* experience (Bakan, 1967; Barrell and Barrell, 1975; Brandt, 1970; Sardello, 1971).

Similar to DES, the experiential method samples experiences of ordinary life by taking "snapshots" of lived experience. However, these snapshots use a somewhat longer "shutter duration," to return to the analogy of the camera. In studying emotional feelings, for example, samples of experience had to be long enough to capture both the meanings of an emotion and the qualities of the feelings associated with them whenever they were also present. Thus, accounts of such experiences are necessarily longer than those of the DES method, lasting several seconds and usually not much longer. These accounts are obtained by having coinvestigators (also known as coparticipants) notice and then write brief descriptions of these moments.[2] The descriptions follow certain guidelines, many of which are similar to those employed by Hurlburt and his colleagues (Hurlburt and Akhter, 2006; Hurlburt and Schwitzgebel, 2007). The guidelines are as follows:

1. Briefly describe the setting in which your experience takes place. Where were you? What were you doing?
2. Attempt to get back into and reexperience a short interval of time when you had the experience of X (e.g., anger or anxiety).
3. Make the interval between the actual experience and your description as short as is feasible, preferably right after the experience. Do not write descriptions hours after the actual experience.
4. Make the descriptions brief, a few sentences or a short paragraph.
5. Just describe what was in your experience, without interpreting, judging, or adding anything to make the description poetical, amusing, or clever.
6. Write the descriptions in first-person, present tense since even an immediately past experience is to be reexperienced.

Learning to Notice
We found out that designing your own courses in the Psychology Department at West Georgia University provided very interesting opportunities and challenges for conducting these kinds of studies in the context of upper division and graduate courses on research. Initially, we focused on

simple psychophysical experiments in which students rated various physical stimuli and dimensions of experience based on meaning. S. S. Stevens used a similar approach in teaching classes at Yale University. In addition to practicing scaling, our students practiced noticing what was taking place in their experience and then describing qualitative aspects of their experience. This sometimes took the form of completing a sentence starting with "Now I am aware of..." The completed sentences sometimes referred to thought , (e.g., Why are we doing this?"), sensory images (e.g., changes in sunlight coming from a window), or feelings (e.g., Hope I don't embarrass myself. Feel anxious). Another exercise also was helpful in developing some skill in self-observation. They were to practice *just noticing* what had just taken place in their experience and then writing one or just a few sentences down in first-person present tense. They were instructed to just report what was there without judging, interpreting, telling a story, or being poetical ... *unless* one or more of these processes were in their direct experiences. This admonition is similar to that used in Hurlburt's DES method where participants are told to just tell the truth, the whole truth, and nothing but the truth. If judging happened to occur directly in their experience, they were told to notice it but to not judge the judging. Importantly, they were not to *actively* search for the answer to the question "Now I am aware of..." They just had to be aware of what was directly in their present experience. It is largely a matter of being parallel to experience,[3] regardless of whether we are experiencing from the viewpoint of our imagination/cognition ("outer viewpoint") or from an embodied viewpoint ("inner viewpoint").[4] Noticing should occur in a present-oriented context, that is, either in the present or in reexperiencing situations that had just occurred. Since people find it difficult to notice at exactly the same moment one is experiencing a phenomenon, this form of observation often consists of an immediate retrospective account of what has just occurred in experience.

The Act of Observing in the Experiential Method

Similar to the DES method, the experiential method describes and characterizes phenomenal experience as it is lived in the moment. It is a form of self-observation that is very different from armchair reflections, filling out detailed psychological questionnaires, engaging in phenomenology, or the usual manner of providing self-reports during psychological experiments. What we mean by self-observation is taking an immediate impression of what is taking place in a moment of consciousness, like taking a snapshot of what is happening (Givot, 1998). The content can include sensations, perceptions, feelings, beliefs, moods, movements, thoughts, and images. This type of self-observation already exists to a limited extent in science in rudimentary forms, as was discussed in chapter 2. In this and later chapters, we demonstrate that these attempts can be taken a step or two further with some interesting consequences. For example, self-observation for the experiential method requires awareness rather than absorbed reflection ... unless one is studying absorbed reflection. However, even if someone is observing absorbed reflection, he or she would have to wake up momentarily to notice it. Awareness includes simply noticing whatever is present in experience[5] (see also note 3). This is not active effort but rather an intention to notice.

Unlike DES, the experiential method addresses questions that pertain to specific topics, such as the nature of human emotions and states of consciousness. However, consistent with the principles of phenomenology, the questions are open-ended and exploratory. For example, we have asked "What is like to feel anger toward someone?" or "What is like to feel anxious about an outcome?" The results of these explorations are descriptions of experience that contain common factors or meanings.

The Nature of the Data

The first part of this descriptive task in reexperiencing is that of briefly (in one or two sentences) describing the situation wherein the experience takes place in order to set the context of the experience and to foster an optimum mindset for reexperiencing. For example, if someone was reexperiencing anxiety about an outcome, he or she would initially describe the physical and/or social situation in which the experience has just taken place. The rest of the description records simply what the individual is noticing in his or her experience—thoughts, images, feelings, and so on. This part of the description is also relatively brief, consisting of no more than a single paragraph. Let us take a simple example of anxiety about a specific outcome, one that was obtained from an investigator–participant:

I was in the examination room waiting for the doctor to show up and tell me about the results of my biopsy for cancer. I could hear some doctors talking to each other outside the door but I couldn't make out their words. The following was my experience:

They sound serious. I think he's going to tell me that I have cancer but I'm not sure. I feel a "knot" in my stomach. What is he going to say? I imagine him telling me the bad news.

I have a visual scene of him being in the room telling me I have cancer. I feel anxious as I imagine this.[6]

Notice that the description of the setting and context (examination room, hearing doctors outside) is separated out from the thoughts and images that are more integral to the experience. Uncertainty is clearly evident in this description ("…but I'm not sure"; "What is he going to say?"). Notice also what is not stated but is nevertheless strongly implicit in this overall description. Clearly, this person doesn't want to be diagnosed with cancer ("bad news"). There is a bodily feeling that relates to some or all of this ("…a 'knot' in my stomach"), but it is not entirely clear where this feeling occurs during the experience. Was it there only in the beginning, the end, or throughout the experience? Despite this ambiguity, this description conveys meanings of a potential undesirable outcome and uncertainty, coupled with a bodily feeling.

It is interesting to compare this account of anxiety with the DES report of Melanie's anxiety given earlier. Similar to the example just given, Melanie's report begins with a description of her situation, what she was *doing* at the time of the experience: "Melanie was considering the appointments she had later in the morning.…" However, the duration of her sampled experience appears to be shorter than that of the example of meeting with the doctor. It contains an image (stoplight and the road stretched out in front of her) and noticing *that* she had been anxious but no bodily feeling of anxiety. Could it be that the meanings that support an emotional feeling don't necessarily coincide exactly with the bodily feeling itself? The exact timing of cognitive content and associated bodily feelings has a long history of uncertainty in the psychology of emotions. This uncertainty also is evident in both DES and the experiential method. Nevertheless, in contrast to the DES method, the experiential method allows the capacity to capture most or all of an entire episode of an emotion, so that most or all of the elements that constitute the emotion can be identified and characterized in a single episode. It also provides a means of allowing the experiencing person to provide the report, instead of taking notes, as in the DES method. Of course, the report itself has to be discussed and described in group meetings with other coinvestigators, similar in principle to the interview of the DES method.

To further clarify the nature of an experiential report, we can distinguish it from those reports which would not be considered experiential (Barrell and Barrell, 1975; Price and Barrell, 1980). These alternative report styles would include *interpretative, poetical,* and *historical* accounts. For example, an interpretative report of anger might be, "I have physiological activity which continues to increase. Anger happens when someone has embarrassed me. I think it is a coping device to keep from being manipulated."

What is specified in this report are concepts (i.e., physiological activity), causes (i.e., embarrassment), and inferences (i.e., coping devices) that are not immediately given in experience. Thus, only after a reflection disconnected from immediate experience do we classify a feeling, name the cause of our anger, or infer its basis.

Poetical or historical self-reporting also doesn't reflect what is directly given in experience. A poetical account of anger might consist of statements such as, "It is like a volcano which suddenly erupts." In this case, imagination interferes with noticing and experiential reporting. One's feelings are viewed metaphorically as objects in the world. The report is from an outside viewpoint without an indication of awareness for this viewpoint. Similarly, an historical account of experience necessitates that one view oneself in the past instead of in the present. For example, "When I was angry, I started to scream and yell." In this way, experiences of the past are placed at a distance from one's present context, a situation which tends to separate the observer from direct contact with experiences.

In contrast, the experiential report refers to immediate experience and is written in the first person, present tense, since even previous data are to come from a reexperiencing of those situations. Initially we may find ourselves engaging in a "free-associative" type of self-reporting. Such a type of reporting may consist of thoughts that might automatically occur during anger. "He can't do this to me. I don't deserve this. I want to get even but I can't." These expressions appear to pertain to a particular situation and person. With continued practice of describing experiences, the descriptions more often directly referred to felt meanings, such as "being wronged," "victimized," or "treated unfairly." In the studies that we conducted, each group member contributed several descriptions of experience that were in the first person, present tense, and either written or transcribed from tape. As we have mentioned, each description was preceded by a sentence or two that described the situation in which the experience occurred in order to frame the context of the experience and to reexperience the episode of interest. The following is a representative example of an experiential description of a few seconds of anger:

I was waiting for the plumber to show up. He was late and the following experience occurred.

Where in the hell is he? What happened to reliability? Can't depend on anyone. He could have at least called and said he would be late. My whole damn day has been thrown out of whack!!

There are some questions about such descriptions that we can ask at this point. Descriptions were written as if these were actual sentences that participants thought. Do participants think in sentences? We have already seen that inner speech does constitute about a quarter of randomly sampled experiences. Partially worded experience (i.e., fragments of sentences) also has been shown to occur in experience (Heavey and Hurlburt, 2008). However, unsymbolized thinking occurs in about a quarter of sampled experiences, and this type of experiencing can be translated into words. Recall the example given earlier of "hoping that the glasses won't fall over" without the explicit words or symbols. Nevertheless, the sentence provides a fairly accurate account of the meanings and images that were embedded in the experience. Thus, one can think of these descriptions as a translation of meanings and feelings into words. Is it critical that sentences in this description follow the exact order in which they originally occurred in the actual experience? Or in other words, would the meanings of this experience be critically altered if the sentences were completely rearranged? We think not because the same meanings and factors would remain, factors such as "a sense of unfairness" or "being wronged" and an implicit or explicit desire for an absence of this wrongful act. Clearly, in the case of waiting for the plumber to show up there was someone who was unreliable, undependable, and inconsiderate, all culminating in an undesirable effect on one's day. Nor does it matter whether the words used in this description are *exactly* the ones that occurred during the thoughts of this experience. Suppose instead the sentence "My day has been ruined" had been used? The alternative sentence would still capture the same meaning. The words point to meanings in the experiential method, and the same meanings can be stated in multiple ways. A meaning can be described by multiple words, and a single word can have multiple meanings. To understand human experience, the goal is an analysis of meanings and not just the exact words. Descriptions that were vague, excessively long (more than a full paragraph), and complex were discouraged because they interfered with the aim of identifying the simple factors within a given type of experience, mainly because the boundaries of one experience would start to overlap those of another. Although experiences can sometimes be vague, excessively long, and complex, we deliberately chose relatively simple experiences that were easier to characterize.

Another critical issue is to what extent descriptions are reconstructions of the original lived experience. It is unlikely that the descriptions lead to an exact replica of the original lived experience. In reexperiencing an episode, participants may engage in a kind of abstract remembering that doesn't necessarily involve putting oneself back in the original situation. Or they may imaginatively put themselves back in the previous situation and think/feel the experience anew. In using the experiential method, we have emphasized the latter alternative as much as possible. Like other methodologies (e.g., psychophysics), it is largely a matter of training. There is no way to absolutely eliminate the possibility that some participants "recreate" or even fabricate their accounts. If such distortions were systematic, however, it would seem unlikely that all coinvestigators would arrive at the same common factors that characterize a type of experience. The use of multiple descriptions from each coinvestigator, guidelines for participation (given above in section 4.2.3), and methods that establish the presence or absence of group consensus mitigates much of the concerns about "creating" experiences that did not take place in the first place.

A closely related question is about the extent to which participants embellish or distort their reported experiences when they write them. Participants in these studies dealt with this problem in their own reporting partly because they were coinvestigators who expressed a sincere interest in understanding types of experiences. Part of our ongoing analysis was to monitor the descriptions for these potential problems, and participants were responsible for checking the accuracy of their own reported experience and questioning each other's descriptions. Group meetings were held in a context wherein participants reflected on and discussed the descriptions, with careful attention to accuracy. This entire process is the counterpart to the interview phase of the DES method. Descriptions that didn't follow the guidelines of this method were eliminated from the collected data. Such descriptions were noticed sometimes by the author of the description and sometimes by others. Importantly, each description was read and discussed by the group, and the authors of each description sometimes redescribed their experience using different words.

Discovering the Common Factors

Once group members produced several descriptions that pertained to the topic of interest (e.g., anger, anxiety), members would each begin to identify the common meanings or factors within all of their descriptions of a given kind of experience (e.g., anger), and they would do this prior to group meetings (Price and Barrell, 1980). They began this process by analyzing the descriptions in such a way as to determine what is present in all situations in which this phenomenon occurs. The aim of this approach is similar to that of phenomenology (Merleau-Ponty, 1962; VanKaam, 1959). At this point, it is important to reflect in such a way that no preconceptions are brought in for the purpose of interpretation. The assumption is that the answers to our question can be seen *directly within the data*. We are to reflect upon the data, continuing to ask, "What is present in all situations in which anger toward someone occurs?" "Which of these common factors are necessary or sufficient for this type of experience?" The lists of common meanings/factors were submitted for group discussion and analysis at regular meetings. In arriving at consensus about the common factors, one would find expressions that replaced those that were concrete or overlapped in meaning (Barrell and Jourard, 1976; VanKaam, 1959). Thus, the statement "He can't do this to me" and "I don't deserve this" might be reduced to a single expression that more precisely describes the feeling and applies to all situations in which one is angry at someone. This process is similar to phenomenological reduction (VanKaam, 1959). In this example, a reduced expression could be "I think and feel that what has been done to me by this person is unfair." Unfairness is a very broad category of meaning. Its synonyms include "injustice," "wrongness," and "grievance, among others. The slightly different connotations of these words suggest the likelihood of somewhat different forms of anger. Nevertheless, they all convey a meaning that some agent (e.g., person, God, the Devil, country, animal, universe) has done something wrong (or has threatened to do something wrong) and this wrong act is something that we take personally. Everything is a potential target for anger.

Discovering Relationships

Once the common factors were agreed upon, the factors were subjected to an analysis in which the study group reflected upon two kinds of relationships within the phenomenon. The first is the discovery of *definitional hypotheses*, statements about the necessary and sufficient experiential factors for the occurrence of a given phenomenon. The second is the discovery of *functional hypotheses*, statements about the relationships between these experiential factors, including quantitative relationships between one factor and another. These relationships must apply to the several situations that one has experienced in order to answer the question.

To continue our analysis of anger as an example, we can formulate the following definitional hypothesis: Two factors that are each necessary and, taken together, sufficient for the experience of anger at someone are (a) a perceived act of unfairness that is experienced, either directly or imagined, as already having been committed by someone and (b) a desire for this specific act of unfairness to be absent. We also could formulate a hypothesis about a functional relationship between the perceived extent of unfairness and the magnitude of anger: Given that one has a desire for fairness, anger increases as the perceived extent of unfairness increases. A similar functional hypothesis can be formulated for desire. The factors of perceived unfairness and desire for the absence of unfairness clearly vary in magnitude. It is certainly plausible that anger increases as a function of both factors, so that anger itself can vary from a mild annoyance to a seething rage. As we pointed out in chapters 2 and 3, it is possible to develop and validate scales of these experiential dimensions so that these hypotheses can be tested with methods traditionally used in psychophysical studies. Furthermore, they can be tested in participants who were not involved in arriving at the hypotheses themselves.

A definitional hypothesis is facilitated by performing an analysis in which we determine whether each experiential factor is necessary or sufficient for a given phenomenon (Barrell and Jourard, 1976). To do this, we would attempt to place ourselves in or reexperience situations in which the phenomenon is present and the factor is absent and vice versa. For example, one could ask whether it is possible to feel anger at someone without a sense of unfairness. Is this factor necessary for anger? If we simply felt that some outcome ran contrary to our desires and expectations, could we feel anger? The answer, according to our experiences and those of our group members, is that we might feel frustration or disappointment, but we would not *necessarily* feel anger. Only when we sense that the outcome is unfair do we feel anger. This sense of unfairness would include feeling that one is the victim or at least identifying with the victim. However, we could even feel hurt, cheated, mistreated, or injured and not be angry because it would be possible to experience these meanings without sensing unfairness. For example, we could feel that we somehow deserved the outcome. Therefore, a sense of unfairness is necessary but not sufficient for anger. Conversely, we could ask whether we could sense unfairness and not feel angry, that is, is this factor *sufficient* for anger? Certainly it would be possible to impartially judge an act as unfair and not feel personally involved. Anger must include additional factors. When we are angry, we desire the unfairness to be absent or to not have taken place. This desire is necessary for the experience of anger.

Finally, one could raise the question "Is it necessary for the act to be perceived as being completed?" Suppose someone were to only threaten us with the possibility of an unfair act. First, we could perceive the threat itself as an unfair act and become angry. Second, if we imagine the completed occurrence of the act, we also can become angry. Finally, if we only focus on the uncertainty of the undesirable occurrence and ignore the unfairness, we could become anxious. Therefore, an unfair act imagined or perceived as complete is necessary for the experience of anger. Although this could be construed as a third factor, the imagined or perceived completeness of the act is included in the factor of perceived unfairness (factor a).

It was also discovered that in addition to the factors of unfairness and desire for its absence, anger could be combined with other emotions. Thus, the desire could be manifested as wanting to eliminate the source of unfairness during frustration. Desire also could be manifested during disappointment, sadness, or even feeling depressed when the unfairness was perceived as irrevocable and there was no experience of the possibility of setting things right. Anger could even be experienced in combination with excitement or satisfaction when one experienced themselves or others as eliminating the source of unfairness, as in the case of revenge. The factors were to be agreed upon by all members of the study group and supported by the large majority of descriptions obtained from group members (Barrell and Barrell, 1975; Price and Barrell, 1980; Van Kaam, 1959).

Experiential Equivalence and Difference

Experiential equivalence refers to the idea that different words can be used to signify the same experiential meaning. To test this possibility, an individual determined whether his or her experience could be accurately stated in alternative ways (i.e., in the words of other group members) without altering the essential conclusions about a type of experience. Such alternative expressions were considered experientially equivalent and listed as a single common factor. For example, as discussed earlier, one could use words like "wronged" and "injustice" instead of "unfairness." However, these alternative words referred to the same factor within experience. "Unfairness" seems to be the best choice because it had the same general meaning as the other words and seems to have the broadest application to experiences of anger.

Experiential Validity

Group consensus was based on experiential *verification*—actual past experiences were examined and reexperienced and used to argue for the inclusion, removal, or retention of a common factor. This process made public verifiability possible because it allowed other persons to examine and test for the presence or absence of a specific common factor within their own experience. Therefore, as one's own experiences are being used, direct testing of the consensus can be accomplished within each group member's experiential system. This direct experience of the relationship of words to meanings becomes a most accurate test of validity. What we mean by validity is that a self-report (e.g., anxiety) optimally accounts for what that person has, in fact, experienced. The only direct way to test this match is to have the person question whether the relationship applies to his or her own experiences.

An approach that is similar to the one described by us was developed by VanKaam (1959). This approach was applied to the experience of "really feeling understood by someone." He devised a method of controlled analysis of human experience that consists of describing experiences and reducing their descriptions to their essential factors. The descriptive phase involved a process in which he asked a group of students to relive and describe their experiences of a given phenomenon in a manner similar to the one we have described. These descriptions were then subjected to a sequence of operations, the aim of which was to identify the common factors of the experience in question. The final identification of these common factors was based on the requirements that each factor must be (a) expressed explicitly in some descriptions, (b) expressed explicitly or implicitly in the large majority of descriptions, and (c) compatible with descriptions in which the factor in question is not expressed or this factor must be shown not to be an expression of the experience under study.

An aim of both the experiential method and an earlier method of Van Kaam (1959) is to generate qualitative descriptions of given kinds of experience, descriptions that express phenomena as they reveal themselves to the experiencing subject. They are to be agreed upon and well understood by all those capable of having the experiences in question. Each final description is to contain precise explicit statements about what is essential for the experience, omitting particulars. However, important differences exist between the approach we have described and that of Van Kaam. For one, the experiential method enlists coinvestigators to form these descriptions. Another difference is that it more exactly specifies the mode of attending and questioning. A third difference is that it includes a strategy of determining the necessary and sufficient factors for the experience in question. Finally, it allows the investigators to discover the functional relationships of common factors of given kinds of experience. Thus, this can generate both *definitional and functional* hypotheses as described earlier. It is important to emphasize that unlike other sciences and psychology in particular, the experiential method doesn't *begin* with theories or hypotheses. Rather it begins with general questions posed to experience and *arrives* at definitional and functional hypotheses through self-directed experiences (Barrell and Barrell, 1975; Price and Barrell 1980; Price et al., 2007). Both types of hypotheses can then be tested in studies that use quantitative methods in conventional psychological studies. Some of the remaining chapters describe how a phenomenon is initially characterized by the experiential method and then tested in subsequent studies that use psychophysical methods and, in some cases, brain imaging (e.g., hypnotic state in chapter 10).

Who Is the Researcher? A Second-Person Component to Experiential Paradigms

Regardless of whether the list of common factors is decided by coinvestigators or investigators who do not participate in their own experiments, the participant and the investigator must train their sensibility to each other so that interpretations of experiences ultimately and accurately follow the observations (i.e., the direct experiences). The participant must train his or her skills in noticing and reporting experiences, and the investigator must train his or her ability to provide an undistorted report of what the participant is experiencing. As Kordes (2009) notes, "This confirms the need (and ethical urge) for a dialogical approach…" Both participants and investigators are researchers in an important sense because observation of experience is not "from the outside" but one of participatory coresearch. Kordes asks, "Is it possible to research the experience of another being unless that person has an honest and deeply existential interest in observing his/her experience?" We think this interest must occur in both investigators and participants.

Is This Method More Efficient Than Simply Reflecting on Experience?

After carrying out studies using the experiential method, the identification of the common factors and their interrelationships may sometimes seem obvious in retrospect and perhaps even trivial. It may seem particularly obvious once you see the list of common factors. One might think, "Of course anger at someone entails a sense of unfairness and a desire for the unfairness to be absent!" But oddly enough, when we invite people to identify the common meanings of anger, most of them have a hard time articulating them. They say things like "When I feel anger toward someone, I feel hot inside" or "Anger always occurs when I feel defensive or when I'm really upset with someone." For those we have asked, including colleagues at work and friends, they find it difficult to determine whether each factor is necessary or sufficient for anger. Thus, the results of the experiential method sometimes appear obvious in retrospect, and that is good because it brings confidence in the results. Of course, there is always the possibility that we are inaccurate about our characterization of emotions such as anger or anxiety. At this point, you can ask yourself whether the proposed common factors for anxiety or anger apply to your own experience and whether the factors are implicit or explicit in experience. Use your actual experience as the means of making this determination.

Of course, we use "anger toward someone" and "anxiety about an outcome" as examples because they are relatively simple and common forms of emotional experience. One can simply watch or read news reports to see and feel anger and sometimes feel anxiety. A more rigorous test of this method might use a more complex experience such as performance anxiety, a specific form of anxiety. The following discussion of this topic illustrates how this complex experience can be characterized using the experiential method.

4.3   An Experiential Study of Performance Anxiety

4.3.1   The Question, Group, and Examples of Descriptions
Our approach to understanding this phenomenon was to discover the ways in which people experience performance anxiety and, in particular, the ways in which specific meanings instantiate this experience. Similar to the examples of anger and anxiety given above, we used the experiential method to discover *how* people think, feel, and experience meanings in situations of performance anxiety. This differs from some approaches to performance anxiety that conceive of it as a response to stimulus conditions outside of the person. This approach may turn out to have functional benefits. If people can learn how they constitute their own performance anxiety, they may discover how to reduce it and return to a more optimal level of functioning.

A study group composed of six coinvestigators (three males, three females) explored the following question: *What is it like to experience performance anxiety?* (Barrell et al., 1985). The research consisted of two phases. During the first phase, each group member used the experiential method to provide six first-person present tense descriptions of experiences of performance anxiety. These were easily generated in most cases since all group members had performances that they had to give and all members regularly experienced some degree of performance anxiety. Participants sometimes wrote descriptions before giving a performance of some kind (e.g., a lecture) and sometimes wrote them shortly after giving a performance. Performance anxiety could occur even well before the actual performance since it could be based on imagined performance. During the second phase, group meetings were scheduled in order to reach a group consensus regarding the common factors of performance anxiety and to establish which ones were necessary and/or sufficient for this kind of experience. The use of a small number of participants made it possible to conduct an in-depth analysis that requires a full understanding of any exception to specific results of the study. All variance in results between participants had to be accounted for, and any one contradiction was capable of negating the overall conclusions. In contrast, the use of an excessively large number of participants allows the investigators to ignore small variations in behavior or experience and leave them unaccountable. We think the former approach gives us more confidence in generalizing the results. It does not preclude a second phase of research, one that involves testing the hypotheses in large groups of participants through the use of well-validated scaling methods.

The following three descriptions are representative of experiences of performance anxiety. This set represents the same experience (performance anxiety) as it occurred across different types of situations. This was done intentionally to increase the generality of the results of this study. Contrary to more traditional research approaches that attempt to control experimental situations and make them as similar as possible, we have attempted to use situations that vary widely. Each situation does have in common that it was an actual lived situation that occurred for one of the study group members. Each description was introduced by describing the situation in which the experience occurred, and the experience was then described in first-person present tense. Descriptions were meant to serve as snapshots of experience, showing as clearly as possible what occurred in experiencing a given situation. Each of the following descriptions was written by a different group member, and each description was preceded by a description of the situation in which the experience occurred (in italics).

Situation 1
I was getting ready for graduation ceremonies. While looking in the mirror at myself, I was hurrying but having trouble trying to get the cap and gown to look right.

Fumbling around. How should this cap and gown be worn? Suppose it is wrong. People will laugh and I will feel like a fool. Dr. X standing out in front of all those people. No one will ever forget it. I will have to leave the area and run away and start a new life.

Situation 2

I was at a meeting with the individuals that I work for. I respect all of these people. They are older, experienced, and expert at what they do.

I feel withdrawn. I feel afraid to say something. My body feels tight and stiff; kind of paralyzed. My thoughts seem slow and I notice that I am quiet. I am concerned about what these people are thinking of me. I feel that I am not contributing and I feel an urgency to say something. I want to participate. They seem very powerful. I wonder if they approve of my work and if I am valuable to them. I am afraid that I will do or say something that seems unintelligent.

Situation 3

I entered the classroom to give a lecture and the following experience occurred.

I am looking around the room. I am seeing faces and eyes all looking at me. I hope I look Ok. I am looking down at my legs. Do I look fat? I hope I look ok—makeup, hair? Well, am I going to get any response? I wish they wouldn't just sit there looking at me. Why won't these people respond to me?

4.3.2   Discovering Common Factors and Their Necessary and Sufficient Relationships

Members examined and questioned their own descriptions after collecting six or more of them with the aim of discovering the common factors throughout the variety of their own experiences of performance anxiety. These common factors may be found to be explicit or implicit in the descriptions. Examples of the most useful questions asked were as follows: "Does this factor occur in all my experiences of performance anxiety?" "Could I experience performance anxiety without it?" "Is this factor necessary for performance anxiety?" "Are these factors sufficient for the experience of performance anxiety to occur?"

The second phase of discovering common factors consisted of reaching a group consensus regarding the common factors of performance anxiety (Barrell et al., 1985). Each group member contributed his or her list of independently discovered factors to a cumulative list. Group meetings were held in which the common factors were subjected to an analysis involving tests for experiential equivalence and difference, experiential proof, and the testing of necessary and sufficient relationships.

Once a list of common factors was agreed upon, each factor was evaluated as to whether it was necessary for the experience of performance anxiety. There is always the possibility that a consensus can be prevented by an exception to the rule. An attempt was made to find an exception in which performance anxiety could occur without the proposed common factor. If so, the factor was eliminated from the list. The result was a list of necessary common factors that contribute to the structure of performance anxiety, irrespective of the specific situation or person doing the experiencing. That the same general experiential structure applied across widely diverse situations and different persons demonstrates that the factors generalize across all instances of performance anxiety.

Next, each individual independently set out to discover whether this group of common factors could lead to an alternative experience. In other words, are these common factors sufficient to result in performance anxiety, or might they also lead to another experience? Do we need an additional factor or factors, or do we have enough? If it was discovered that these factors were not sufficient, each individual was to reexplore the experience repeating the previous process. If no such alternative was discovered, the list of factors was considered both necessary and sufficient. Finally, the repeated occurrence of these specific factors resulting in the same experience was the measure of reliability.

4.3.3   Common Factors of Performance Anxiety

The following factors represent a consensus found to be common across all the experiences of performance anxiety observed by group members. Taken together, they constitute a structure of performance anxiety. Each factor is a necessary condition for the occurrence of performance anxiety, and all factors taken together are sufficient for the occurrence of the experience. Each factor can be briefly described as follows:

1. Believe that there is an audience made up of important people who can judge you (this can be just one person).
2. Consider the possibility that you could fail in front of them.
3. Have a strong need to do well to avoid failure.
4. Feel unsure of yourself (uncertainty) as to whether or not you will do well.
5. Focus on yourself.

The factors can be explained in more detail as follows:

1. *Presence of important people judging you*   In each description, the other persons are experienced as potential judges or witnesses of performance. This factor is explicit or implicit in all of the situations. There is an image of an audience of several people in all of the descriptions. Included in performance is speaking and/or social interaction (descriptions 2 and 3) or just the appropriate appearance (descriptions 1 and 3). The significance of others was most explicitly stated in description 2, "They seem very power-

Figure 4.2
A view of the "audience" from the perspective of someone with performance anxiety.

ful. I wonder if they approve of my work." This form of judgment relates to the perceived power of the others to in some way influence this person's future. (See figure 4.2 for a view of the "audience" from the perspective of someone with performance anxiety.)

2. *Possibility of visible failure*   At the onset of this experience, an individual considers failure and what it might mean. The individual may consider his or her catastrophic expectations at this point in time. This consideration is reflected in the words "like a fool" (description 1) or "unintelligent" (description 2). These consequences carry the implication of being rejected by others. The idea of permanence also arises here. If individuals believe their weakness will become obvious to others, it is possible that they will not easily forget it. Their negative evaluation may long outlast the immediate situation of performance. Worse yet, this memory may last a long time in the performer. In conducting this experiential study, it became clear to us that performance anxiety may be sustained in long-term memory, and specific negative episodes of performance anxiety can be reexperienced.

3. *Felt need to avoid failure*   Behind performance anxiety can be individuals' belief that they may not be as good as others think and the possibility that they might discover the truth. Another possibility is that someone can believe that they may be as bad as others think and that they might verify this through seeing the performance. People have a need to be regarded positively, which might include being liked, being thought of as special, or being respected. In performance anxiety, there exists a felt need to avoid losing this positive regard and thus a need to avoid failure in some aspect of performance, such as needing to be prepared, needing to look right (descriptions 1 and 3), and needing to make intelligent contributions (description 2).

4. *Feeling unsure of yourself (uncertainty of outcome)*   Uncertainty of the outcome is revealed implicitly or explicitly in the three situations. It is manifested as questioning either the outcome (descriptions 2 and 3) or the appropriateness of one's appearance (descriptions 1 and 3). It is exemplified by expressions such as "I wonder if they approve of my work?" (description 2). Uncertainty about the outcome of performance may stem from uncertainty about skill or knowledge of how to do the task.

5. *Focus on self*   The focus of one's experience is on his or her own appearance and behavior in relation to the other person(s), and this is evident in all three descriptions. Often in the experience, one is aware of existing in his or her own subjective space, that is, an "enclosed space" that distances the performer from the others. At this moment, the others exist minimally, if at all. During the experience, questions arise such as "How am I doing?" "Will I be able to do well?" Performers notice their own performance or imagined performance and take an outside and often judgmental view of this as if they were another person. For example, in description 1, "I will feel like a fool, Dr. X, standing in front of all those people." The imagined possibilities of appearance are indicated in description 3 by the words "Do I look fat? I hope I look ok." In this description, this person experienced a lack of involvement with the others and a distance between herself and the others, a distance created by the monitoring process. This monitoring process was largely about her appearance.

The following questions may arise: Why these common factors? Are others also possible? Furthermore, there may be doubt as to whether the factors proposed here get to the essence of performance anxiety. Although more profound levels of understanding may be reached through common factors such as fear of isolation, configurations of such factors would fail to differentiate performance anxiety from other types of experiences. One major purpose of the performance anxiety study was to identify the experiential structure that uniquely defines performance anxiety, rather than undertaking a more global assessment of how this type of anxiety relates to other emotions.

4.3.4   Possible Applications

Identification and clarification of these common factors may reveal possible alternative solutions to the problems of performance anxiety. If each factor is *necessary* and if all five factors taken together are *sufficient* for performance anxiety, removal of any one factor is a possible means of eliminating performance anxiety. Factors can be removed in some of the following ways. Take, for example, the experience of seeing yourself from an outer viewpoint. In this viewpoint, you view yourself as if you are being "looked at" through the eyes of others. If you start looking through your own eyes at the task at hand instead of imagining being looked at by others (inner viewpoint; see note 4), then common factors related to *concern about the presence of potential judges*, *possibility of visible failure*, and *self-focus* can diminish or even be eliminated. Clearly, we contribute to this experience by imagining the response of significant others and by catastrophizing. Effective strategies of reducing performance anxiety may include identifying, characterizing, and understanding the common factors of the phenomenon.

4.3.5   The Epistemology of the Experiential–Phenomenological Method

An important question that can be addressed to any experiential paradigm is what kind of important knowledge does it generate that is different from that produced by other approaches in philosophy and psychology? Similar to other approaches, an experiential approach is concerned with knowledge that is reliable, generalizable, valid, publically verifiable, and objective. Most critically, this knowledge simply should be the truth about the nature of the investigated phenomena. The following discussion will focus upon the ways in which these features uniquely apply to knowledge obtained from the experiential method and upon the ways in which this knowledge differs from that obtained by other approaches.

This paradigm yields small number of common factors, such as desire/need, expectation, and feeling. The latter include extent of felt arousal and valence—how happy/unhappy, pleasurable/unpleasurable one feels. The emotional feeling is felt as within the body to some extent, more for other people than others. The feelings are qualitatively different for jealousy, anxiety about an outcome, frustration, sadness, excitement, and satisfaction (see chapter 5).

Coinvestigators using experiential methods would be interested in propositions concerning the nature of specific types of experiences. Such an interest has historical roots in the tradition of Fechner, Ebbinghaus, Wundt, and Titchener, whose concern was to find laws that characterize the "generalized, normal, human, adult mind" (Boring, 1957; Titchener, 1908; 1924). A group of coinvestigators would be in a unique relationship to their topic of interest since each coinvestigator would be both a participant and a coinvestigator in the study.

When a coinvestigator questions and explores his or her experiences of a given phenomenon, that questioning and exploration is an integral part of the verification process itself. The hypotheses which are derived from such an approach can be verified as qualitatively accurate facts about one's own experience. The steps used to arrive at experiential hypotheses contain tests of *intrasubjective* reliability, generalizability, and validity. To be reliable and generalizable, an experiential hypothesis must apply to experiences of someone at different times and across different situations. For example, someone who is disposed to have performance anxiety would likely experience the same five factors listed above before or during performances in many different contexts. Thus, in the example of performance anxiety, each factor is necessary and, taken together, all five factors are sufficient for this type of experience. Since each factor also has different magnitudes, functional hypotheses can be tested when scales are validated for each factor. For example, one hypothesis about performance anxiety is that it increases as a function of the experienced need to avoid failure. Of course, the remaining factors would have to be statistically controlled in experiments that test this functional hypothesis. The testing of functional hypotheses requires the use of scaling procedures. Examples of such tests are given in the remaining chapters.

To be *experientially* valid, however, an experiential hypothesis must express to the person that which it claims to express. Thus, the hypothesis is made up of words and has validity only if what the words represent in experience is verified. This relationship between words and experience can be directly perceived using a method in which the subject matter is one's own experience. However, this direct relationship of words to experience has to be intersubjectively verified as well. Members of the study group had to share this task, with a sincere interest in the phenomenon of study and with the absence of verbal coercion by anyone in the group. Finally, one may notice that reliability, generalizability, and validity of experiential hypotheses are greatly facilitated by the fact that the exact objects of experience or the details of the physical or social conditions are not part of the hypotheses themselves.

To the extent that experiential hypotheses can be subjected to experimental methods that utilize reports of participants, they can be tested in the usual sense for reliability, generalizability, and validity by using traditional psychometric methods. It may well be that hypotheses which are generated from this qualitative method apply to many persons across different contexts. On the other hand, there may be cultural and demographic variables that significantly influence how some phenomena are experienced. One also must keep in mind that the written reports of experience are intended to capture direct experience but do not always do so. From the perspective of the coinvestigator, certainty about the truth of a hypothesis would be optimized by repeatedly reencountering and confirming the same type of experience and then subjecting the derived hypothesis to controlled experiments on other persons. These two aspects of the experiential method are epistemologically complementary.

Hypotheses generated from an experiential approach require intersubjective agreement. They must be seen to apply to one's own experience of a given type and to apply to experiences of other group members. And they must be distinguished from presuppositions and preconceived theories. The "objectivity" of this approach relies on the capacity to reach intersubjective consensus. As pointed out by Velmans (2009), this consensus is actually required for all sciences. There is no single observer-free perspective (i.e., external viewpoint) that stands apart from the intersubjective consensus of investigators. Thus, there is intersubjective consensus among physicists on the mathematical formula for gravity and less consensus on the role of observation in quantum mechanical phenomena.

Intersubjective agreement is more objective than that of other approaches. Neither reviewing the literature nor "thinking about" experience will necessarily bring one into direct contact with the phenomena of experience. Direct contact with experience would minimize the role of preconception or imagination in arriving at experiential hypotheses. Sardello (1971) refers to direct contact as objective since "it requires of its participants an attitude of respectful openness to the entirety of their subjective existence and allows through direct experiential involvement the reality of the phenomenon to be revealed the way it is." The experiential approach contains a mode of observation and analysis consistent with this principle. There is no guarantee that investigators attempting to use the experiential method will be dispassionate, truthful, and uninfluenced by bias or preconception. A study group with a sincere existential interest in the nature of a type of experience, in combination with the methods and procedures of this paradigm, at least provides a means of minimizing such factors.

4.4   Conclusions: Identifying the Common Factors and Forming Hypotheses

Experiential methods such as the DES and the experiential–phenomeno-logical method have common objectives of accurately describing and characterizing brief episodes of human experience. The DES method is idiographic and simply describes experiences as they are sampled on a random basis. The experiential–phenomenological method addresses specific topics and questions about experience, such as the nature of emotions or states of consciousness. The latter method requires a wish to understand the qualitative structures of human experience and a specific type of self-observation consisting of awareness and the capacity to notice what is present in experience while suspending active effortful attention, presuppositions, beliefs, and at least initially, interpretations. Similar to other sciences, however, it also requires the capacity to determine the common factors for different types of experience (e.g., anger, anxiety). Analyses can then be carried out to determine which of the factors (or combination of factors) is necessary or sufficient for an experiential phenomenon (definitional hypotheses). When scales are developed for each of the factors, experiments can be conducted to determine how the magnitudes of the factors interact and influence the magnitude of the phenomenon of interest (functional hypotheses). The extent to which different components of experiential methods can be integrated remains an open question. The following chapter will explore the ways in which qualitative and quantitative methods can be interfaced.

5 Merging the Qualitative with the Quantitative: The Roles of Desire and Expectation in Emotions

We maintained that psychophysics has implications that extend well beyond its immediate subject matter (see chapter 2). First, evidence was provided that the power law applies not only to sensory phenomena but to other dimensions of human experience, including those associated with personal meaning (see chapter 3). Second, we maintained that the precise quantitative relationships in psychophysics are verified by using a rudimentary form of introspection, which is a method that some people thought had disappeared from science. We then suggested that when *both* investigators and noninvestigators engage in psychophysical observation, knowledge of psychophysical relationships is obtained in two complementary ways, directly experiencing sensory phenomena and the usual method of observing/analyzing responses of study participants. This combination of approaches thereby achieves a higher level of certainty and veracity. We then raised the questions of whether psychophysical methods could be extended to discover psychological relationships between two or more psychological variables (i.e., "psychological laws") and whether they could be verified within ordinary lived contexts. To do so, however, would require training and some ability to notice one's experience, including both its qualitative and quantitative character. Chapter 4 presented paradigms for analysis of qualitative contents of lived experiences, such as common emotions (e.g., performance anxiety). In this chapter, we show how qualitative methods can be merged with quantitative methods to further explain the nature of some human emotions.

It is noteworthy that when qualitative factors of certain specific types of emotions are identified using an experiential method, they are often found to consist of just a few associated factors within experience—an approach or avoidance goal, a desire or need to fulfill that goal (D), an expectation within a range extending from impossibility to certainty (E), and an associated feeling (F) (Price and Barrell, 1984; Price, Barrell, and

Barrell, 1985; Price, Riley, and Barrell, 2001). Examples were given in the preceding chapter. Performance anxiety always seemed to contain a perceived judge or judges of performance, a need to avoid an inadequate performance, and an uncertainty of fulfilling this need. Anger was about an experience of injustice or unfairness coupled with a desire or need to set things right. Thus, although specific types of emotions relate to different overall meanings and situations, they often contain common dimensions of experience (D, E, F) as well as goals toward which these factors are directed. We have found that these factors are implicitly or explicitly expressed in first-person descriptions of both simple and complex emotional experiences (e.g., performance anxiety, jealousy). This commonality becomes even more evident when qualitative and quantitative analyses are combined. They not only underpin some emotions but also seem to be integral components of choices and motivation (see chapter 6). These same emotional factors underlie dimensions of pain and suffering (see chapter 7) as well as some types of placebo effects (see chapter 9). We suggest that these explanations of some emotions are supported by recent results of neuroscience and later propose how a neurobiology of these phenomena could be guided by experiential science (see chapter 6).

5.1   Emotion Experiments Combining Qualitative and Quantitative Methods

5.1.1   A Brief Personal History
When we first attempted to merge qualitative with quantitative methods (1979–1980), we proposed that the valence or positive/negative intensity of an emotional feeling (F) is the product of desire (D) and expectation (E). This is expressed by the simple formula $F = D \times E$. This proposal was similar to previous value $\times$ expectancy models and Siminov's "information theory" of emotions that proposed multiplicative relationships (Siminov, 1970; Shah and Higgins, 1997). However, our choice of the terms "desire" and "expectation" was based on their closer proximity to actual direct experience than "information" or even "value." Thus, one can highly value an object but not have a concrete need or desire for it in the actual experience of feeling or wanting. In this initial study, participants provided data for actual lived situations wherein they wanted something to happen or not happen. Using visual analog scales (VASs), they rated D, E, and F for single episodes of relatively simple emotional experiences (e.g., impatience while standing in line). They wrote a first-person present tense description of each episode, using the qualitative methods described in the previous chapter.

The aim of this simple experiment was to qualitatively and quantitatively characterize relationships between D, E, and F. We had no thoughts about the distinction between approach and avoidance goals because we were unaware of Kurt Lewin's (1943) approach–avoidance typology that had been around for decades. When we plotted the data assuming linear relationships, the results were not impressive. Although linear curves could be fit to relationships between D, E, and F and, as hypothesized, F was predicted by D × E, the variability surrounding each mean rating (standard deviation) was very large. Then we closely examined the experiential descriptions and noticed that participants' goals were either about approaching something, avoiding some unpleasant outcome, or much less commonly a mixture of the two types of goal. We wondered what would happen if we grouped the questionnaires into two categories involving approach and avoidance goals.

The results resembled the curves of figure 5.1 and were replicated in subsequent studies that hypothesized different curves for approach and avoidance goals (Price and Barrell, 1984, Price, Barrell, and Barrell., 1985; Price et al., 2001). In comparison to linear equations derived in our initial unpublished study, the variability surrounding the mean ratings was much

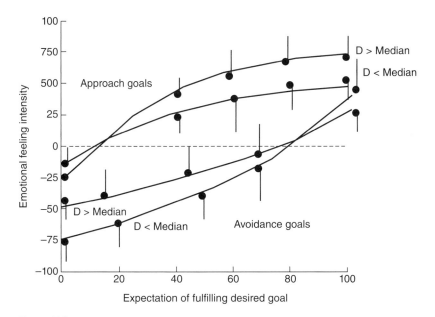

Figure 5.1
Emotional feeling curves. D, desire. (Based on data from Price and Barrell, 1984.)

smaller. Similar results were found for hypothetical scenarios (see figure 3.2) and actual lived situations. We think this historical account is an example of a benefit of using an experiential approach in forming psychological hypotheses.

5.1.2 Terminology of Goals, Desires, and Expectations

It was critical that participants understood the nature of the dimensions that they were asked to rate. Even simple terms can be challenged by ambiguities inherent in language. Thus, we provide here an account of the variables of D, E, and F as well as the distinction between approach and avoidance goals. These factors are directed toward an enormous range and variety of human experience, yet there are common features of each factor.

Goal

A goal is a result or process that someone wants to happen now or in the future or to have taken place in the past. It can occur in the form of spoken works, inner speech, nonsymbolized thinking, or images. It can be the grandest and most significant outcome imaginable, such as immortality, or simply having a higher ambient temperature in the house. It is always something that one wants to acquire or avoid, and goals vary tremendously in significance. In examining the qualitative descriptions, we found that approach and avoidance goals could usually be easily distinguished. Approach goals were focused on attraction—pleasurable stimulation, pleasurable meaning, inner peace, and the like. In general, people felt good about approach goals and about anticipating them. For example, one can imagine feeling the joyful meaning of a creative accomplishment just before it is finished or the excitement of winning a game in the last minute. On the other hand, avoidance goals were found to be associated with fear, distaste, disgust, and other negative states. Examples of avoidance goals included wanting to prevent or escape experiences of physical discomfort, failure, loneliness, helplessness, rejection, pain, boredom, and even death. It is important to emphasize that the distinction between approach and avoidance goals is in phenomenal experience and not in the situation from the perspective of an outside observer. For example, the young man asking for a date, illustrated in figure 5.2, could have multiple and even diametrically opposed types of images and associated feelings as he is asking "the question." His approach-goal image might be seen as the romantic outcome of the left image and his avoidance goal as the catastrophic outcome of the right image.

Figure 5.2
Alternating between approach and avoidance images.

Despite their occasional complexity and subtlety in actual human experience, concepts of approach and avoidance have a long history in psychology (Lewin's, 1943, approach–avoidance typology), and approach–avoidance behaviors occur for virtually all animal species, even single-cell organisms such as paramecia (Stein and Meredith, 1993). We also found that a goal can be that of obtaining a result (winning a game) or engaging in a pleasant process (listening to pleasant music). Result goals can be directed toward the immediate future, long-term future, or past. In contrast, process goals are more oriented toward the present or short-term future.

Desire

Desire is *wanting* and is always related to a goal—there is always the object of a desire. To want is to want something. However, although any desire always aims toward an object, it is also separate from it. For example, if we are thirsty and reach for a glass of water, it is clear that our desire (urge) "belongs to us" and the water is "out there" in the world. We most often want what we don't have. Desire can be directed toward an enormous number of goals, such as those related to achievement, control, knowledge, aesthetics, or love, to name just a few examples. It is even possible to want to want or to want to not want. Thus, desire can be its own object, as when someone experiences an empty life without anything to desire and wishes it were otherwise. The absence of desire also can be the object of desire when someone feels trapped or caught up in desire.

Is there a quantitative dimension in the experience of desire? Certainly almost everyone has had the experience of disappointment related to a previous desire and expectation of success. Upon reflection, we can see how an experience of desire can influence subsequent experiences. For example, the higher our desire for a successful outcome, the greater our later disappointment should we not achieve it. Thus, whereas a goal has specific qualitative content, as shown by examples given earlier, desire is the degree of wanting the goal. There is always a magnitude for each desire, and it can range from the smallest desire imaginable to the most intense desire you can imagine having.

Expectation

The word "expectation" has multiple meanings in common language. It can refer to the events that we expect to happen, as when we say "I expect *that* it will rain tomorrow," or more directly to the likelihood of events, as when we say "I think it is *very likely* to rain tomorrow." For the purposes of the studies to be discussed later, it is about our *experienced likelihood* of our desired outcomes which include either processes or results. Similar to desire, expectation has a wide range of magnitude, extending from the experience of impossibility to that of complete certainty. Sometimes expectation is termed subjective probability by psychologists and is distinguished from objective probability. We used the term "expectation" only in the former sense because it is the expectation from our experienced point of view that counts in our emotions, decisions, motivations, and performances. We can be told multiple times that it is likely we will succeed in our mission, but it only counts and affects our motivation if it is "likely" from our experienced perspective. In discussions of the emotion models that will be described, expectation refers to the *experienced likelihood of fulfilling our desired goal*, regardless of whether the goal is approach or avoidance.[1]

Feeling Good and Feeling Bad

Feeling good and bad also has multiple meanings in common language. The term "feelings" can be used to describe experiences of the physical state of the body, as when we say "I am feeling really good today, really rested and relaxed." We also use the word "feeling" to describe emotional feelings such as happiness, sadness, and anxiety. Our term "feeling" is about how emotionally good or bad we feel in relationship to our goals, desires, and expectations. Barrett (2004, 2007) refer to feeling good and feeling bad as "pleasure" and "displeasure," and we think they mean the same thing.[2]

5.1.3 Combining Qualitative and Quantitative Data during Interpretations

Strong conclusions cannot be made from a single experiment or even two experiments. We felt the need to replicate the results shown in figure 5.1 and extend them by determining whether these quantitative results could be related to qualitatively distinct types of emotions such as anxiety or excitement. Thus, in a second study we determined whether the combination of quantitative and qualitative results could be used to characterize types of emotional feelings, such as feeling *depressed, frustrated, anxious, excited, satisfied,* and *relieved* (Price et al., 1985). This second study was designed and conducted in a manner identical to the first, except that participants chose experiences that related to the six emotional feelings just listed. These six feelings were chosen because they were the ones most commonly expressed in participants' experiential descriptions. As in our previous studies, each description was read by a research assistant who had no knowledge of the hypotheses. The results of this second study are summarized in figure 5.3, which illustrates quantitative relationships of dimensions of emotional feelings and at the same time characterizes distinct types of emotions.

Some examples of experiential descriptions obtained in this study help to identify specific types of emotional feelings:

I was just watching a basketball game and had the following experience:

Only a few seconds left on the clock. Game is tied at 65…. our team is at the free throw line. Feel heart racing. The guy on the free throw line is one of the best shooters on the team. I watch the ball go through the basket. Now we will almost certainly win! I'm excited.

Goal   to have our team win.
Desire intensity   91/100 on VAS
Expectation (impossible to complete certainty of obtaining goal)   95/100 on VAS
Feeling intensity (+100 = best feeling imaginable)   +87/100 on +VAS
Type of goal   approach
Type of emotional feeling   excitement

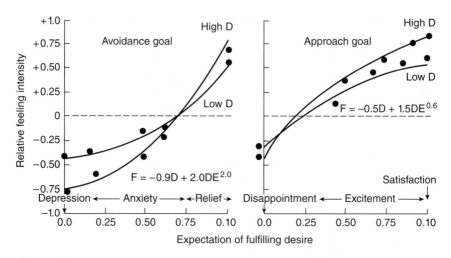

Figure 5.3
Avoidance and approach goal functions in relationship to types of emotional feelings. The range of expectations over which each type of emotion was experienced is shown by the lines with arrows. Expectation values were transformed to a 0–1.0 scale for computation purposes. The actual scales were 0–100. F, feeling; D, desire; E, expectation. (Adapted from data of Price, Barrell, and Barrell, 1985.)

Here is an example of an account of an experience that pertained to an avoidance goal:

I have been driving around Columbia looking for a trailer hitch; Today is Sunday and almost every store is closed in South Carolina.

I am sitting in my car talking to my brother. I'm telling him I can't believe this. I feel like I am wasting my time. I realize that every place I go to is closed. I feel tension in body.

Goal   I want to avoid continuing to waste all this time.
Desire intensity   89/100 on VAS
Expectation (impossible [0] to complete certainty [100] of obtaining goal)   18/100 on VAS
Feeling intensity (neutral to worst feeling imaginable, –100)   –73/100 on –VAS
Type of goal   avoidance
Type of emotional feeling   frustration

This experiment clearly differed from psychophysical experiments in which investigators have precise quantitative control over stimulus parameters. As investigators, we had no control over "stimuli" whatsoever, and we weren't even certain about what stimuli were present. We didn't know what objects in the environment caused our participants to feel excited, frustrated, or disappointed. This was not relevant because the experiment was not about physical stimuli. Our reasoning was that as long as the independent and dependent variables could be specified, understood by participants, and rated on well-validated scales, then the relationships between the variables could be characterized in approximately the same way as in psychophysical experiments. Thus, desires, expectations, and feelings could be about free throw shots or trailer hitches—it didn't matter. This approach differs radically from experiments wherein the investigators attempt to achieve maximum levels of external stimulus control.

As with the first study, the magnitude of positive and negative feeling intensity (+F or –F) was shown to be a multiplicative function of *both* D and E. Thus, the curves for high and low D intersect between zero and 100% (complete certainty of fulfilling goal), in the case of both approach and avoidance goals. The influence of E also differed according to whether the goal was approach or avoidance, bending downward to the right in approach goals and upward to the left in the case of avoidance goals. Equations derived for these functions were $F = -0.5D + 1.5D \times E^{0.6}$ and $F = -0.9D + 2D \times E^{2.0}$ for approach and avoidance goals, respectively.

As can be discerned from figure 5.3, emotional feelings are negative over most of the range of expectation in the case of *avoidance* goals and positive over most of the range of expectation in the case of *approach* goals. These results supported our proposal that relationships between dimensions of at least some types of human emotions could be discovered in ordinary experiences of daily life. They followed power functions of expectation and had exponents close to 0.5 for approach goals and 2.0 for avoidance goals. The six emotions were most easily distinguished quantitatively on the basis of level of expectation and qualitatively on the basis of types of goal—approach or avoidance. Each type of emotional feeling can be characterized by a range of expectation over which it is most likely to occur. The arrows in figure 5.3 show the range of expectation over which 95% of each emotion was distributed. For example, 95% of experiences labeled as anxiety were between 20 and 78 on the expectancy axis, suggesting that anxiety is characterized by a broad range of uncertain expectation. Frustration occupied a more narrow range of lower expectations in comparison to anxiety. Depression occupied a narrow range close to 0 (impossible). Positive emotions, not surprisingly, were closer to certainty of obtaining the desired outcome. These emotions may be most usefully characterized if one simultaneously considers the quantitative data, the meaning of the emotional feeling (including whether it is approach or avoidance), and the associated body sensations. Each emotion can be characterized in terms of these factors and illustrated by representative examples.

Satisfaction (Happiness and Relief)

The emotions of satisfaction included happiness and relief. These positive emotional feelings related to the experience that one's goal had been fulfilled or was almost certain to be fulfilled in the future. The goal of satisfaction was that of obtaining something of positive value (71%), an approach goal, whereas that of relief was avoiding negative consequences (29%). The body feelings of these forms of satisfaction were described in terms of a diffuse or whole-body feeling, such as relaxation, warmth, or calmness in the case of approach goals and relaxation in the case of avoidance goals. The following is a participant's account of a few moments of satisfaction:

I had cooked for hours and everything was on the table and ready to eat.

Everything looks great. It was worth it. It is perfect. I have a glowing feeling. I feel pleased with myself. I did it.

This description contains implicit yet strong references to a *desired* outcome (e.g., It was worth it), *expectation* (I did it), and an associated *feeling* (I have a glowing feeling. I feel pleased with myself).

Excitement

Excitement was most often described as a positive feeling and as an approach goal (91% of 88 accounts) and was associated with high levels of certainty of goal fulfillment (see figure 5.2). If the body feeling tone was in the description, it was usually described in terms of movement or an urge to move, often distributed in the limbs. There appeared to be a readiness for action or an already-acting-toward the anticipated goal. The following is a representative account of a single experience of excitement:

As a friend explained an investment to me, I became more and more interested.

I feel myself moving quickly, almost wiggling as I talk to him. I want to make this investment quickly before I miss out. I think there is little risk and a good chance to make a lot of money. I notice myself talking rapidly and trying to show him that I want to make this investment.

An explicit reference is made to a *desire* (I want to make this investment...) and *expectation* (I think there is little risk and a good chance...), and a positive feeling of excitement.

The feeling of excitement is implicit in the description of the urge to move ("...talking rapidly and trying to show him that I want to make this investment.").

Anxiety

Anxiety was associated with *avoidance* goals (59 of 65 accounts) and expectation levels within the middle of the expectation range (see figure 5.3). It was based on an uncertain expectation of suffering negative consequences in the future. When described, the body feeling was that of inner tension often concentrated in the stomach area or chest. Sometimes it was sometimes described as a feeling of an increased heart rate. Thus, the feeling was often "visceral" as compared to an outer muscular tension. In this respect, it differed from frustration (see below). The following is a participant's description of anxiety:

I was about to call a friend to tell her that I would not come to her party. As I dialed the number the following experience occurred:

I don't really have a good excuse. I try to think of one. I am thinking "What can I say? Will she believe me if I say I don't feel good? Hurry, think of something." I feel my heart beating faster as the phone rings.

The goal of this experience is clearly implicit, yet it is one of the participant's wanting *not* to experience the consequences of the friend's disbelief. Reading this, we have no exact idea what those consequences might be. The participant may not have had a clear idea about this either. Yet it is evident that he wishes to not suffer these consequences, whatever they may be. The uncertainty in this account is evident in the question that the participant poses: "Will she believe me if I say I don't feel good?" The body feeling is an indication of anxiety within the context of the rest of the description. We must note that, for the purposes of simplicity and clarity, all accounts of anxiety were ordinary experiences of anxiety directed toward an outcome, regardless of whether there was a single explicit negative event or an outcome with vague or extended consequences, as in the example just given. Thus, this person may not have experienced imagining several distinct consequences of not being believed but nevertheless wanted to avoid them. In other descriptions, anxiety was pointed more explicitly toward a negative outcome ("I hope he doesn't miss this field goal. Otherwise, we're going to lose this game!").

Frustration

Frustration was associated with avoidance goals (78 of 80 accounts) and low expectations (see figure 5.3). It was described as a negative emotional feeling based on the experience of having one's goal interrupted or blocked. Regardless of whether it was preceded by an experience of an approach or an avoidance goal, the implicit or explicit goal in accounts of frustration was that of removing an obstacle or obstacles or moving through resistance. The negative consequences in frustration included the presence of the obstacle (i.e., being blocked) and the consequences of being blocked. Hence, frustration involved an avoidance goal (98% of accounts) that was directed toward the immediate future or present. The goal of frustration often included a temporal element of wanting to remove the obstacle *now*. The body feeling tone was usually described as somatic tension (71 of 80 accounts). When parts of the body were included in the description, it often included the upper body—the head, neck, arms or shoulders. The following is a single account of frustration:

I was trying to get to work on time and I had to stop for a train that was going by.

I can't believe this. I need to get to work on time. How long will this take? I look down the tracks to see how long the train is. It seems to have no end. Box cars passing. I grip the steering wheel and feel shoulders tense up.

The goal in this description refers to a sense of being blocked in relation to a need to be on time. The level of expectation for this goal is implied by the question "How long will this take?" in conjunction with the statement "It seems to have no end." The latter is not likely to be related to a literal belief about the length of the train, and this is not critical for understanding the experience.

Feeling Depressed (i.e., Sadness, Grief, Melancholy, Disappointment)

Feeling depressed was described as a negative emotional feeling based on the experienced absence of goal fulfillment and/or the experienced unlikelihood of future goal fulfillment. It was related in some instances (26% of 81 accounts) to feeling that one has lost something of value (e.g., a loved one) or has acquired negative consequences (e.g., spending time in jail). Consequently, the level of expectation for goal fulfillment was found to be very low, approaching impossibility (see figure 5.3). The expectation related to an improbable future goal and/or to an experience of already having lost something. The body feeling was described in terms of weakness, numbness, heaviness, or not wanting to move. Similar to satisfaction, feeling sadness, grief, and disappointment were most often described as a whole-body experience. The following is a single account of feeling unhappy and depressed:

Michael and I just split up and I had this experience:

I feel very weak. Nothing really matters to me anymore. I feel so empty inside, like something is missing. "What do I have to look forward to now?" I start to cry.

The implicit desire is for a relationship (and/or meaning?) and the low expectation is implicit in the question "What do I have to look forward to now? The feeling is clearly suggested by the words "weak," "empty inside." However, there is an apparent ambiguity in this account because if we take the statement "Nothing really matters to me anymore" at its literal face value, it implies an absence of desire. The statement "I feel so empty inside, like something is missing," on the other hand, implies the felt loss of something of deep significance. Was desire absent or still very high? The quantitative results help to resolve this issue. Her D rating was 88, and her E rating was zero. Apparently, her "grief" was based on a meaning of impossibility coupled with a desire for a relationship with someone. Sadness, grief, and inconsolable melancholy may be similarly constituted in this way. Another type of depressed feeling may be present when people appear to give up the immediate desire for a goal and the intention to act on this desire. Although desire can be given up, the significance or value of the goal can remain, as in the case of resignation. They may appear as numb or empty, and when asked, they might report that their lives have become devoid of meaning. Or they might alternate between these two types of feeling. In the example just given, it is evident (by the desire rating and the emotional expression of crying) that resignation hasn't happened yet. The account of this particular experience illustrates how the combination of qualitative and quantitative analysis helps to clarify the emotion in a specific circumstance.

Each of these five types of emotional feelings was characterized by a combination of qualitative and quantitative methods. The quantitative methods serve to demonstrate that desires, expectations, and associated emotional feelings are present, implicitly or explicitly, in all five types of feelings, and each emotion can be characterized by an expectation range over which it is most likely to occur. However, these ranges overlap, so that the qualitative analysis further specifies the nature of the emotion in terms of meaning of the emotional feeling. The bodily feeling of the emotion also reflects its meaning. Thus, the feeling of frustration was characterized by a desire to move past an obstacle or through resistance, reflected in the person's thinking and in body feelings of tension. On the other hand, anxiety was characterized by a more passive stance wherein one either "waited out" the uncertain catastrophe or attempted to decide on the right course of action. The body tension in anxiety was directed inward and perceived as a more "visceral" sensation, as if to prepare for and absorb the shock of negative consequences. Both the thinking and the body preparation of excitement reflected a movement toward or an urge to move toward expected pleasure whereas that of satisfaction was a whole-body feeling of being absorbed in the pleasure itself. Similarly, the whole-body feeling of weakness or heaviness in sadness reflected the felt absence of goal fulfillment and the felt hopelessness of acting in the future.

In addition to characterizing these common emotions, the model of emotions presented in figure 5.3 serves to explain how D, E, and type of goal (approach or avoidance) interact to produce changes in emotional experience. The focus on negative consequences during an avoidance goal has the effect that, unless one is close to certainty of avoiding these nega-tive consequences, one will feel negative emotionally and often anxious, frustrated, disappointed, or even depressed (see figure 5.3). This aspect of emotional experience is captured by the positively accelerating curves in figure 5.3, wherein it can be seen that feelings are negative throughout most of the range of expectation. Imagine waiting in the doctor's office to hear the results of a test for a deadly disease. Your goal is likely to be that of wanting the test results to be negative (i.e., no sign of disease). It is plausible that your desire would be high under these circumstances. What level of expectation would be required for you to feel good? This hypotheti-cal situation is similar to the emotion exercise presented in chapter 2. The best one can feel during a goal of avoiding negative consequences is relief. On the other hand, the focus on positive and/or pleasurable consequences with nothing or little to lose has the effect of maintaining emotional feel-ings at positive levels over most of the range of expectation (top curves, figure 5.3). Quantitative changes in desire and expectation can lead to qualitative changes in the type of emotion experienced. For example, as expectation of avoiding negative consequences lowers, a shift is likely to occur in one's experience of their relationship to the goal and one's inten-tions to act or not act. As expectation lowers, the focus on uncertain nega-tive consequences during anxiety may be replaced by a focus on obstacles to preventing catastrophe and, hence, frustration or despair. Likewise, the latter may be replaced by the felt hopelessness of grief, deep sadness, or depression as expectation lowers toward impossibility. A shift in goal ori-entation also can change the emotion experienced as well as the quantita-tive influence of expectation. For example, in receiving a medical treatment for a persistent pain, one could focus on the consequences of a more healthy condition of reduced pain and a moment later on avoiding the devastating consequences of a chronic pain condition. Even when expectations of these two possibilities remain uncertain, the shift from an approach goal (greater health) to an avoidance goal (avoiding devastating consequences) could produce a shift from a positive feeling to a negative feeling of anxiety (upper curve at expectation of 50% to lower curve at expectation of 50%).

These results and experiential considerations help to resolve an ongoing question in studies of emotions: Are emotions better characterized as having natural types, such as happiness, sadness, and anger, or as having dimensions such as expectations (or beliefs), desires (or needs), arousal, and valence? (Barrett and Wager, 2006). These experiential studies show that both natural types and experiential dimensions can be used to explain both components of emotions. They are not mutually exclusive. It is important to emphasize that we have focused on the experiential phenomenology of emotional feelings. Emotions also often have overt behavioral expressions and physiological patterns of activity. A reasonable explanation of emotions should relate dimensions of experience to behavioral expression and to patterns of physiological activation.

5.1.4 How Does Arousal Relate to Types of Good and Bad Feelings?

Arousal is the degree to which one feels "awake," "energized," or "ready to respond." There are alternate definitions of arousal, and they seem to refer to one or more of these terms. Similar to other experienced dimensions that constitute emotional feelings, very little research has been conducted on the direct *experience* of arousal, despite the fact that it is a common variable in emotion research. There may be qualitatively different forms of arousal (e.g., somatic vs. visceral). Nevertheless, participants of emotion studies commonly rate arousal on scales, and these ratings are often used to characterize different emotional states and/or relate emotions to physiological responses (Barrett, 2004; Barrett, 2007; Lane et al., 1997). How does arousal interrelate with the dimensions of emotions and types of emotions that have been discussed so far? Lisa Barrett summarizes results of different experimental methods, including those which sample lived emotional feelings using a random beeper, that map emotional experience onto two dimensions, valence (how good or bad the feeling is) and arousal (Barrett, 2004). Strikingly, the different methods show that different types of emotions can be characterized by their relative positions on the two dimensions. "Disappointment," "unhappiness," or feeling "blue," on average, were experienced as very negative yet had somewhat low levels of arousal. "Nervous," "afraid," and "fearful," on the other hand, were also quite negative yet were rated as more arousing. A similar dynamic seemed to apply to positive emotions. Feeling "pleased," "glad," or "satisfied" was associated with low levels of arousal in comparison to the higher arousal ratings for feeling "excited," "lively," and "elated."

These general results support both qualitative and quantitative characterization of emotions discussed earlier (see figure 5.3). Emotional feelings that pertain to the absence or near absence of goal fulfillment (e.g., sadness, depression, disappointment) do not immediately entail an experienced readiness to respond (i.e., high arousal). Similarly, emotional feelings that pertain to fulfillment of a goal, such as satisfaction, are not accompanied by high arousal either. In contrast, an urge or preparation to respond is clearly present in experiential descriptions of excitement and frustration. Emotional feelings that suggest anxiety (e.g., nervous, scared) also had higher levels of arousal in comparison to sadness (Barrett, 2004). The arousal may be felt "somatically" or "viscerally," depending on whether it is actively directed toward making the right choice (somatic) or passively preparing for possible negative consequences (visceral; Barrell and Price, 1977). Arousal is no doubt higher when emotional feelings have higher desire or significance, yet arousal level is more closely linked to specific types of emotions than are desire and expectation. Desire and expectation seem to be the most direct mediators of positive/negative feeling intensity.

5.2   Toward an Experiential and Quantitative Characterization of Emotions

5.2.1   A Concept and Definition of Emotions

Emotions require both cognitive appraisal and physiological activation in an interdependent manner. Cognitive appraisals, in turn, are often comprised of two general dimensions—(1) significance or desire and (2) expectation or level of perceived fulfillment. As Arnold (1970) has pointed out, emotionally related significance or desire is often in relationship to "something good for me" or "bad for me," that is, as something to be approached or avoided. Profiles of bodily states during emotions reflect these factors. For example, the feeling of unlikely fulfillment of a desire may be accompanied by felt body tension if one focuses on the intention to remove the obstacle to fulfillment. Similarly, feelings of weakness or heaviness accompany the meaning of hopelessness of acting on one's desires during episodes of feeling sad or depressed. The *extent* of physiological activation will generally increase with significance or desire. The *pattern* of physiological response is influenced by the nature of one's intentions, attitudes, and expectations of fulfillment. For example, an intense emotional feeling of frustration may arise when a chronic pain patient experiences a low expectation of being able to carry out an important physical task. The felt sense of this frustration is one of bodily tension accompanied by an urge to remove the source of the interruption (Price, Barrell, and Barrell, 1985). The patterns of physiological arousal, including both autonomic and somatomotor activation, help to provide the felt sense of the emotion (Damasio, 1994; 1999; Price, 1999). The felt sense of an emotional feeling comes from the body. However, the physiological patterns of response and consequent body feelings are representations of the meanings and intentions of the felt emotions. Thus, an emotional feeling is *the felt sense of a cognitive appraisal that occurs in relation to something of personal significance (often in relation to desire and expectation)*. Similar to some classical theories of emotion, modern explanations of emotion mechanisms recognize the interaction between meanings and physiological activation patterns yet provide a more precise explanation of these interactions.

5.2.2 The Role of Patterns of Physiological Reactions in Emotions and Emotional Feelings

Anyone who is curious about the critical roles of peripheral patterns of physiological reactions and central nervous system activity in emotions should begin with *Descartes' Error* (1994) and *The Feeling of What Happens* (1999) by Antonio Damasio. Although the following account by no means provides a definitive explanation of this issue, we present a succinct summary of it here in order to show how it could be integrated with the emotion model that we have put forth in this chapter. According to Damasio, the felt sense of an emotion is provided by input to the brain from an enormous number of diverse peripheral sources, including those of visceral, musculoskeletal, hormonal, and neurochemical origins. These diverse peripheral sources, in turn, are regulated and affected by the brain itself, so that emotions reflect a dynamic interplay between brain and body. Damasio's account of emotional feelings extends classical theories of emotions, particularly the James–Lange theory, by a much more precise explanation of the interrelationships between cognition and profiles of physiological responses. According to his view, an emotional feeling requires that neural signals from viscera, muscles, joints, and neurotransmitter nuclei, all of which are activated during the process of an emotion, reach certain subcortical nuclei and the cerebral cortex. Endocrine and other chemical signals are said to be additional inputs to the central nervous system via the bloodstream and other routes. Thus, the felt changes in the body produced by these means accompany specific images, thoughts, or meanings. Thus, there are representations of emotions in the body as well as in the brains of people who feel these emotions. In subsequent work, Damasio relates body and brain representations of emotions to two kinds of consciousness (Damasio, 1999). The first kind of consciousness is termed "core consciousness." It can be conceptualized as the moment-by-moment awareness of the state of the body and self and the perceptual aspects of what is taking place in the present. The other kind of consciousness is "extended consciousness," and it is largely autobiographical. It is based on extended awareness of the past and the future, and it links present perceptions to memories and reflections. It is sustained by "core consciousness." Different emotional feeling states reflect these two kinds of consciousness. They provide the felt sense of meanings, particularly as they relate to what is desired and expected by the organism.

Damasio's (1994; 1999) explanations take into account classical theories of emotions and extend them by a more precise explanation of the interrelationships between cognition and profiles of psychophysiological responses. Thus, the felt changes in the body produced by these responses accompany specific thoughts or meanings. For Damasio, "the essence of feeling an emotion is the experience of such changes in juxtaposition to the mental images that initiated the cycle." But exactly what are these mental images and what are their relationships to the profiles of physiological responses? Of course, Damasio has a lot to say about these relationships. Instead of repeating them here, we simply suggest that first-person models of emotion could be integrated with an explanation of the kind that he provides. It is often the case that the mental images that "initiate the cycle" combine appraisals of one's immediate situation with what one wants or wants to avoid. During emotional feelings, we may commonly move away from or toward something in our experience. An experiential perspective and method might greatly facilitate the kind of explanation that Damasio is proposing.

Let's take the present moment as an example. What do you want to happen next—more understanding of human emotions, cessation from boredom, or something else? With this "want" comes a certain associated feeling. If you have a mild to strong desire to understand and feel nearly certain that you do, you may feel mild to strong excitement or satisfaction, depending on your exact circumstances and meanings. If you are trying to understand and feel confused and blocked, this may be felt as frustration. All of these alternative experiences have a corresponding *felt sense* that is generated from muscles, viscera, circulating hormones, and neurochemical agents (Gendlin, 1962; 1978; Damasio, 1994; 1999). The pattern of somatic and visceral input provides a representation that is associated with the goal and intention of our experience coupled with desire and expectation. Recall from earlier discussion of emotion studies (see figure 5.3) that there was an urge to move in excitement, a felt tension of removing an obstacle or pushing through resistance in frustration and so on. Thus, we are contending that Damasio's "images that initiate the cycle" often pertain to what we immediately perceive, want, and expect to happen or not happen. The meaning of an emotional feeling is expressed by a pattern of responses within the body. These responses also generate a profile of neural responses in distributed networks of the brainstem and cerebral cortex, a profile that underpins the felt sense of emotions.

The input to the brain during emotional expression also can feed back upon the experienced meaning and feeling of the emotion, as shown by the work of Ekman (1993). He showed (as did Charles Darwin) that specific types of expressed emotions have facial patterns of action—angry, sad, happy, and fearful faces look a certain way and are different from each other. When people simulate these emotional expressions by contracting the relevant muscles in their face, they can experience the corresponding emotional feelings to a certain extent (Ekman, 1993). Thus, looking angry may evoke a small feeling of anger; looking happy may evoke mild happiness.

Thus, contrary to the long-held view that patterns of physiological responses are too undifferentiated to account for the wealth of emotional feelings, considerable evidence exists for exquisitely precise physiological profiles for different emotions, profiles that contribute to the feelings of the emotions. The work of Ekman just described suggests that feedback from specific facial muscle groups contributes to different emotional feelings. Similarly, considerable evidence supports the contribution of feedback from different visceral organs to emotional feelings. An example is a study by Harrison and colleagues at the Sussex Medical School in the United Kingdom (Harrison et al., 2010). They combined brain imaging (fMRI) and multi-organ physiological recording to distinguish two distinct forms of disgust which have different meanings. One form, which they termed "core disgust," was evoked by having participants watch videos of actors smelling, eating, and mock vomiting visually repulsive food. The participants rated their experienced magnitudes of disgust and other feelings such as nausea. The other form of disgust was termed "body boundary violation" and was evoked by videos of surgical operations from surgical training archives. As before, participants rated dimensions of their experiences of this form of disgust. The experience of core disgust was closely associated with increased rates of gastric responses in the stomach and increased activity in the *right* anterior insular cortex. In contrast, the disgust of body boundary violation was strongly associated with decreases in parasympathetic activity, increased heart rate activity, and increased activity in the *left* anterior insular cortex. Strikingly, the peripheral physiological changes closely predicted the changes in activity within the insular cortex and differentiated between the two forms of disgust that held separate meanings. The authors conclude that "organ-specific physiological responses differentiate emotional feeling states and support the hypothesis that central representations of organism homeostasis constitute a critical aspect of the neural basis of feelings" (Harrison et al., 2010). We agree. However, although this study is elegant, it greatly emphasizes third-person observations. The first-person data consist of ratings of simple dimensions of experience. If studies of emotional feelings included qualitative and quantitative experiential methods in combination with methods used by Harrison and colleagues, the understanding of human emotions might advance to a much higher level altogether. For example, both the peripheral and central physiological profiles of response may be representations of meanings that could be more completely discerned through experiential analysis. This approach could work not only for disgust but for several types of simple and complex emotions. Both peripheral and central profiles are likely to entail distributed networks of structures—discrete "centers" for each type of emotional feeling do not appear to exist.

Because the emotion model in figure 5.3 was derived from actual lived experiences, it was not feasible to directly measure patterns of relevant physiological activity. Collecting relevant physiological data in these types of studies would be possible though challenging. Consider the potentially enormous amount of physiological data that would be needed, including multiple measures of muscular and visceral activity. Such types of studies would be ambitious but, if successful, might support a synthesis between Damasio's explanation of emotional feelings and the experiential dimensions that underpin emotional feelings. For example, as a start it would be important to measure EMG activity of several muscle groups in the shoulders, arms, and facial regions during studies of frustration. This approach is similar to the one used in the study of "avoiders" and "confronters" described in chapter 1. Without an experiential approach and method, the external variables (threat of electric shock to one of several body areas) that induced a stress response might have led to marginally increased heart rates and marginally increased trapezius EMG responses in the overall population of that study. Since these responses would be combined across avoiders and confronters, they may or may not have been statistically significant. Only when the meanings and the manner of experiential coping were identified (i.e., avoiders vs. confronters) could one see robust profiles of psychophysiological responses, profiles that easily relate to two diametrically opposed experiential orientations.[3]

Some Important Caveats and Implications

It is important to emphasize that in order to conduct the emotion experiments described earlier, participants had to utilize situations in which there was only one goal and one type of goal and in which there were relatively stable levels of expectation and desire that persisted long enough to provide stable qualitative and quantitative data. Thus, chosen situations consisted of those in which people were waiting for results to occur or in which there were experiences of satisfaction, disappointment, or relief that persisted for at least several seconds. Inevitably, these accounts were certainly not representative of all human emotions. We recognize that some human emotions rely on experienced significance and complex meanings and may contain little or no desire or expectation. However, personal significance is required for emotional feelings, and desire is a subclass of significance. We also recognize that mixed emotions and rapid emotional changes commonly occur and may even be more common than those present in our experiments. For example, someone may be initially experiencing frustration. Upon a moment's reflection, the individual might sense the source of this frustration to be unfair. His or her frustration would then be combined with anger. Multiple simultaneous meanings like this often fuel complex and mixed emotions. This may well be one of the reasons why understanding of human emotions has been so difficult in psychology. Thus, some emotional experiences may contain elements of both approach and avoidance goals, and we often rapidly shift from avoidance to approach goals and vice versa. For example, anyone who has watched a sporting event with a strong vested interest in the outcome can probably remember strong rapid shifts in feelings, such as from excitement to disappointment and from anxiety to relief. These rapid shifts also occur in athletes themselves with distinct consequences in their behavior and performance (Barrell and Ryback, 2008).

Emotions have the potential to be modulated by changes in perspective and awareness and by new information. Thus, emotional feelings are often a continuously evolving stream, much like consciousness itself, as has been pointed out by Lisa Barrett and her colleagues (Barrett, 2007; Barrett and Wager, 2006). Thus, excitement can turn into anxiety, and vice versa; frustration can turn into sadness. Excitement can turn into satisfaction. Sometimes when we are engaged in emotional feelings, we can step back and notice them rather than be absorbed in them. Impartial witnessing of emotional feelings can take place without having to change them. However, in working with people with emotional and motivational problems, including professional and college athletes (Barrell and Ryback, 2008), we have noticed that continued observation as to how emotional feelings originate in experience leads to the insight that emotions are not just phenomena that are triggered by stimuli in the environment (e.g., other people). Emotions are created within ourselves through meanings and consequent desires, expectations, and emotional feelings. The method we developed for noticing and understanding emotions is an end in itself because once someone understands how negative emotions arise in experience, then that simple understanding is sometimes enough to help mitigate problems with their occurrence.

5.3   Working Directly with the Emotion Model

Does people's knowledge of these relationships within emotional feelings make any difference to them? Some participants in our studies and athletes have found that it is easier to notice how feelings of excitement, satisfaction, anxiety, frustration, anger, and sadness arise in experience and it is easier to see how these feelings lead to behavioral consequences (Barrell and Ryback, 2008). We can notice that understanding dimensions of emotional experience can help to understand the emotional experience as a whole. For example, we can work backward in the emotion model, starting with what the emotion feels like. Suppose you are asking someone for something highly significant, such as a large promotion. As you begin to ask the question, your hands feel cold and clammy. You feel your heart racing, and you feel this awful inner tension in your stomach. You experience your breathing as fast and uneven. You can barely move; you feel frozen. Does this sound like excitement or anxiety? To us, it sounds like anxiety. Thus, the goal and images in this experience are not likely to pertain to a happy acceptance of this request but rather to the avoidance of rejection. The body feeling of an emotion can teach us about our goal and whether it is an approach or avoidance goal. Understanding this experience could be even further refined by asking yourself about levels of desire and expectation. If the desire is high and the expectation uncertain (e.g., 50–50), feeling an unpleasant anxiety means that the goal is avoiding something.

On the other hand, suppose you feel excited as you ask "the question." You still feel your heart racing, but now you feel an urge to move, and you have joyful images of acceptance in your experience. Your assessment of your goal, desire, and expectation would probably reveal an approach goal, a strong desire, and high expectations of fulfillment. Unfortunately, life is sometimes a little more complicated than these two hypothetical scenarios. It is possible to shift moment by moment from an approach to an avoidance goal, and expectation levels can vary over time, even seconds. It is possible to feel an alternation between anxiety and excitement, and the body sensations could reflect a mixture of these two emotions. Alternation between excitement and anxiety is a common occurrence, and it no doubt influences decisions and motivation. This alternation is consistent with ambivalent experiences of everyday life. These are some of the reasons so much discussion has been presented so far on the emotion model. The experience of body "feelings" associated with specific emotions can act as a barometer for what we desire and expect. This idea is partly inspired by Eugene Gendlin's work (Gendlin, 1962; 1978).

Another use of the emotion model is to reveal that which we deny in our experience. For example, we may rate our expectations on the basis of some "objective criterion" or something that we conceptualized intellectually rather than our true experienced expectation, and we may deny or overplay the strengths of our desires. Noticing the body feelings of emotions, particularly the strength of those feelings, however, may lead to a more accurate account of our goals, desires, and expectations. The felt sense of an emotion can provide information that helps us to understand implicit goals, intentions, desires and expectations. Again, it is a case of working backward in the emotion model.

Goals, desires, expectations, and consequent emotional feelings are often open-ended, with some goals leading naturally to subsequent ones. For example, frustration may lead to a sense of unfairness and anger. Alternatively, frustration may lead to anxiety if someone changes their focus from the interruption to the dire consequences of interruption. Sometimes there is a natural progression of factors/meanings that lead to an existential bottom line. One of the descriptions of performance anxiety (see chapter

4) showed a progression of catastrophes, leading to a bottom line: "Dr. X standing out in front of all those people. No one will ever forget it. I will have to leave the area and run away and start a new life." The if–then technique of Gestalt therapy can be used to discover extended meanings and bottom line catastrophes (Perls, 1969; Perls, Hefferline, and Goodman, 1951). Suppose that you are anxious and have a strong need to avoid failure. The questioning could go something like the following:

If you fail, then what do you imagine will happen?
"If I fail, then my best friends will look down on me."

And if your best friends look down on you, then what will happen?
"I will feel rejected."

And if you feel rejected, then...
"I will be all alone."

The existential bottom line of avoiding failure for this person would be that of avoiding isolation and loneliness. Other variations could include the following: "If I fail, then I will be stuck at my current job. And if that happens, I will feel helpless." Alternatively, "If I fail, I will feel stupid. I would have to live with my stupid self. If I have to do that, I will feel that my life is meaningless, empty, and nothing."

Existential bottom lines are sometimes difficult to pinpoint because they are hard to see in an objective light. Unfolding the goal is the key. The experiential method, combined with some psychotherapeutic techniques, such as Gestalt therapy, could be used to clearly characterize both the immediate and deeper meanings of common fears and other emotions. Coparticipants or coinvestigators could learn to become aware of the origins of these deeper meanings. They could learn how they create these meanings in their experience and the extent to which people generate them in similar ways. Thus, meaninglessness, helplessness, and loneliness are not just objective states of situations but are largely generated by meanings that we impose on them.

5.4   Are Desires and Expectations Constituents or Causes of Emotional Feelings?

There are two ways to envision the relationships between desires, expectations, and emotional feelings. The first is to see them as constituents of emotions, much like the weight of an object is made up of height, circumference, and density of mass. On this account, desires and expectations are simply dimensions that constitute emotions. The analogy with weight suggests, however, that this case cannot be easily made. None of the physical dimensions that constitute weight can exist without the other. In contrast, if either desire or expectation can exist without the other, then some types of emotional feelings may be caused by desire and expectation rather than being constituted by them. An expectation can be emotionally neutral and may be necessary but not sufficient for some types of emotional feelings. It is harder to imagine a desire without a feeling. That causal relationships can occur between desire, expectation, and emotional feelings is suggested by the graphs of figures 5.1 and 5.3. However, these graphs were constructed by taking cross-sectional "snapshots" of single episodes. The independent variables were not systematically varied by the experimenter as they are in some experiments. On the other hand, they were systematically varied in experiments utilizing hypothetical scenarios, and the derived functions from these experiments were similar to those of lived situations. This similarity provides support for causal relationships between D, E, and F. However, ratings of these variables pertained to the same approximate moment in time. Causal relationships between these dimensions may occur quickly, perhaps more quickly than the development of physiological patterns of reaction that are part of different emotions. According to classical and modern theories of emotion, the "feelings" of the emotions depend, at least in part, on these physiological responses (James, 1890; Schacter and Singer, 1962; Damasio, 1994; 1999; Barrett, 2007). Effects of D and E on F may be moderated or mediated by these physiological responses.

Demonstration of causality is sometimes considered to depend on the capacity to exercise direct control of the independent variables (e.g., the stimuli). If variables such as D, E, and F can be reliably scaled and measured, then relationships between them can be established in the same way as in other scientific experiments in which causal interactions are demonstrated without direct control of the independent variables. For example, experimental control is not absolutely required to demonstrate causation in the physical sciences. Astronomical observations allow nature itself to provide variation in the independent variables, and astronomers, in effect, take "snapshots" of objects in moments in time. They do so in order to record magnitudes of the independent variables (the mass and velocity of objects) and the dependent variables (e.g., their positions in relation to each other). The same approach can be taken on experiential dimensions that are causes of emotional feeling intensity. By taking snapshots of moments of experience (lasting a few seconds), relationships between desire intensity, expectation level, and positive or negative feeling intensity can be constructed using the same principles of observation and data analysis that are used in all sciences.

However, the precision of the functional relationships that serve some emotions may be less than those of laws demonstrated in the physical sciences. More measurement error undoubtedly exists in the case of emotions. In this respect, relationships between emotion dimensions may be similar to psychophysical relationships. On the other hand, improvements in attention, awareness, and scaling methods may reveal greater precision of these relationships. The question of precision is also integrally related to the issue of individual differences and hence cultural and demographic influences. As pointed out in chapter 2, large individual differences exist for some psychophysical functions, such as heat-induced pain, yet all participants responses could be fit to a positively accelerating power function with an exponent greater than 2.0. The power function exponents for the avoidance and approach goal curves were close to 2.0 and 0.5, respectively (see figures 5.1 and 5.3), but these exponents were derived from group mean responses. Do these same exponents apply to all individuals, or do they vary considerably across individuals in the same way that heat pain curves show individual variation (see figures 2.1–2.2 and figures 3.1–3.2)? If so, then this potential variability suggests that people vary in dispositions to have low or high emotional feelings by virtue of dispositions to have low or high desires and/or expectations (e.g., general degree of optimism or pessimism).

5.5 Conclusions

We have explained how qualitative and quantitative observations can be integrated to arrive at a model that helps explain some common human emotions. The model was derived by using two stages of the experiential–phenomenological method. The initial observations were used to establish both definitional and functional hypotheses, and the hypotheses were then tested in participants using scaling methods similar to those used in psychophysics. The results yielded qualitative and quantitative characterization of common emotional feelings. We think this approach contrasts radically with traditional studies of emotions that attempt to explain them from an external viewpoint (i.e., in terms of behavior) or on the basis of physiology alone. Even most studies that rely on self-report avoid actual lived experiences and tend to focus on hypothetical scenarios, pictures that are presented, or "words." A comprehensive theory of human emotions will require integration of experiential science with the rest of the sciences, particularly neuroscience and physiology of somatic and visceral regulation. The next chapter will explore how the emotion model can be integrated into a model of choice and how both models are supported by neuroscience research.

6 Choosing

More than any other time in history, mankind faces a crossroads. One path leads to despair and utter hopelessness. The other, to total extinction. Let us pray we have the wisdom to choose correctly.

—Woody Allen

The question of "how the experience of choosing relates to actual choices" has not been satisfactorily answered in the scientific literature on decision making, despite the centrality of decision theory in psychology and economics. Despite the long history of decision theories, the first-person experiential phenomenology of choosing has not been integrated with the economics, psychology, and neuroscience of decision making (Kordes, 2009). This problem is magnified by the ubiquitous nature of choosing. The experience and consequent act of choosing occurs throughout everyday life and determines the course of our lives. Rational and irrational choices cause both individuals and nations to succeed or fail. The histories of individuals and countries can be largely explained by the choices that were made. Given the importance of this topic, how can a science of human experience advance understanding of human choice?

Using an experiential perspective and examples of experiential studies of choice, this chapter explores the nature of interrelationships between emotions and choice in order to provide a preliminary answer to this question. Both the psychology and neuroscience of emotions have shown emotions to be interrelated with several phenomena, including decision making. Even some types of responses to placebo are based on emotions (chapter 9). We begin by very briefly tracing the history of the psychology and economics of decision theories, pointing out that models of decision have gradually incorporated factors that relate to human emotions. We then discuss how explanations of emotions presented in chapter 5 could be used to help explain the phenomenon of choosing. This approach, which is grounded in experiential phenomenology, is in stark contrast to over a century of decision theories that tend to avoid first-person data. We then discuss how a neuroscience of emotions and choice could be enhanced by experiential science.

6.1 Classic and Modern Theories That Predict Choice

6.1.1 Early Models

Early models of choice emphasized "objective" probabilities and people's values of objects as two major factors that determined which option would be selected in a given situation (see Mellers, 2000, for review). For most of the twentieth century, decision theories emphasized human preferences and stated probabilities, leaving out consideration of anticipated pleasures or displeasures (Von Neumann and Morgenstern, 1947). This type of model was replaced by one that substituted human *beliefs* for stated probabilities, later conceptualized as subjective probabilities (Savage, 1954; Edwards, 1992). At this point, subjective factors that approximated our definition of "expectation" (chapter 5) appeared in studies of human decisions. Subjective expected utility theory became the dominant approach to choice theory.

A next step, however, was to determine whether subjective expected utility theory could describe and predict actual choices. Economists and psychologists soon found that choice behavior often deviated from rationality (Kahneman and Tversky, 1979; Tversky and Kahneman, 1981). Thus, people were found to idiosyncratically arrive at their expectations, and it was demonstrated that people often used information in nonrational ways. A common and simple example is that of predicting outcomes of coin flips. One person might predict the likelihood that the next coin flip would yield tails after seeing five instances of heads (e.g., "six in a row is just too unlikely!") while another person might predict heads (e.g., "the best predictor of the future is the past!"). Both predictions run counter to probability theory because each coin flip has a 50% probability of turning up heads or tails and is independent of the past history of results. Regardless of whether people use information in a rational or irrational manner, subjective probability, not objectively stated probability, was found to be a much better predictor of choice. Deviations from subjective utility theory also were found to occur as a result of anticipated disappointment associated with choosing the wrong option. For example, when choosing between gains with high stated probabilities, people were found to be risk averse. Thus, most people preferred gaining $3,000 for certain over an 80% chance of receiving $4,000. Apparently, a goal of assuring oneself of a gain is an added factor in the decision process. On the other hand, when faced with no chance of avoiding a $3,000 loss and a 20% chance of avoiding a $4,000 loss, people usually prefer the more uncertain option. Thus, when choosing between losses with stated low probabilities of avoiding any of them, people tend to choose the more risky option. In the example just given, at least there is hope in the 20% chance to avoid losing $4,000 rather than the catastrophe of the certain loss of $3,000. Choices were also found to be influenced by whether options were framed as approach or avoidance goals (Tversky and Kahneman, 1981) and they applied to situations about gaining or losing money and to choosing between alternative medical treatments. Percentages of choice about one treatment over the other reversed when medical treatment goals were framed as "saving lives" versus "avoiding deaths" (Tversky and Kahneman, 1981).

That people have risk-averse preferences in choosing among gains and risk-seeking preferences in choosing among losses has been termed the "reflection effect" and is an integral concept of prospect theory (Kahneman and Tversky, 1979; Tversky and Kahneman,1981). When people evaluate potential outcomes, they imagine or anticipate feelings that will occur with the best and worst outcomes as well-anticipated regrets had the other option been the better choice (Mellers, 2000).

Because these accounts are largely speculative and indirectly supported by empirical data, different theorists use different terms to describe emotional factors that influence choice. Thus, emotional terms such as "hope," "fear," "beliefs," and "feelings of uncertainty" are used, without a common agreement as to how they actually apply to the experience and act of choosing.

6.1.2 Decision Affect Theory

In an advance over preceding decision theories, Barbara Mellers (2000) provides a formulation of decision making based on an explicit comparison of anticipated emotional feelings provided by two or more options. Her theory is called "decision affect theory." Each option contains "*utility*" (the perceived value of an object), *belief* (expectation?) that the option will result in the desired outcome, and anticipated *regret* should the option not chosen turn out to be the better choice. Anticipated regret has been shown to have a salient influence in experiments using gambling tasks (Coricelli, Dolan, and Sirigu, 2007). Decision affect theory includes all three factors, and each option is described mathematically by a formula that includes multiplicative interaction between factors. The formula for choice then is the quantitative weight of a set of factors for one option over the weight of a second similar set of factors for the remaining option(s). Put another way, the option that produces the highest overall positive score, presumably in the form of positive feelings, is the one that is more likely to be chosen.

Concepts of "utility," "belief," and "anticipated regret" have a heuristic purpose in explaining choice theories, but they do not directly address whether they actually occur in someone's experience of choosing. If different types of emotional feelings moderate or even mediate choices, then choosing may be associated with anxiety, excitement, or satisfaction or with anticipations of these feelings. If so, they might ultimately modify or even replace the constructs used in decision theories. In chapter 5 we raised the question as to whether emotions are better conceptualized as natural types such as sadness, disappointment, and excitement or as dimensions of experience such as desire and expectation. We presented an account of how dimensions of experience and types of emotions can be integrated within a single framework. The same type of integration may well apply to choices and motivation. Thus, when we choose, we may be guided by anticipated excitement or anticipated anxiety associated with the various options. However, it might be equally appropriate to propose that we are guided by multiple goals, desires, and expectations. Both alternatives are testable and may be applicable. An experiential method and perspective would facilitate understanding of how we arrive at decisions.

6.2   Challenges to a First-Person Science of Choosing

Kordes (2009) points out that the most studies of the process of choosing fail to clearly specify whether decision making is a behavioral category (third-person perspective) or an experiential one (first-person perspective). Similar to mainstream psychology in general, researchers tend to view the process of choosing as something "out there" separate from the experience of doing the choosing. As Kordes states, "Decision making (like most experiential phenomena) is reified—it is dealt with in a way similar to the one taken in the case of physical phenomena (for example gravity, which is 'out there' whether I notice it or not)." Clearly this approach is inappropriate because at least some *experiences* of choosing (i.e., careful deliberate choosing) appear to have a strong bearing on what is chosen. Although the experiential literature on decision making is sparse, we focus the remainder of this chapter on construction of a first-person science of decision making and its integration with third-person science (e.g., neuroscience, social psychology).

Before we undertake this challenge, it is important to acknowledge that different experiences of choosing may vary enormously according to how much one is aware of choosing and according to how much the choosing is experienced as deliberate or automatic. In other words, they vary according to the extent to which someone experiences making a choice. For example, studies carried out on firemen who had to make a "decision" about whether to attempt to rescue someone or leave the building performed only one of these acts (but not the other) without experiencing a choice (Klein, 2002). The same behavioral choice can be experienced quite differently. When ordering a dessert in a restaurant, we may sometimes immediately choose without much thought and other times carefully weigh different options. On the other hand, when a higher court judge is deciding to vote on repealing an existing law, this decision may require an enormous amount of deliberation, consideration, and mental effort. Our discussion focuses on those experiences which feel most like choosing from an individual perspective. This approach is taken in order to provide a framework for scientific investigation. After all, we have to start somewhere.

6.3   Experiential Studies of Choosing

6.3.1   Qualitative Studies of Hurlburt

Two types of experiential studies have been conducted on choosing. One type of study utilized the descriptive experiential sampling (DES) method (Hurlburt and Heavy, 2006). Recall that DES uses a random beeper in the participant's natural environments to signal participants to notice their experience that was ongoing just prior to the beep. They then take notes for each of several sampled experiences and meet with the investigator for interviews to clarify and describe the experiences. The purpose of the interview with the investigator is to provide a simple answer to one question posed for each beeped experience: "What were you experiencing at the moment of the beep?" According to Kordes (2009), this method combines first-, second-, and third-person observations because it is dialogical. As he points out, "…it would be most accurate to say that both participants of the dialogue and investigators are researchers. What we are dealing with is thus not a case of observation 'from the outside,' but rather one of participatory co-research."

In one study, Hurlburt and Heavy (2006) randomly sampled moments in the manner described in chapter 4. As before, they determined several categories of experiencing, for example, "sensations," "inner speech," "inner seeing," and so on, and again found the category of "unsymbolized thinking": "...the experience of thinking some particular, definite thought without the awareness of that thought's being represented in words, images, or any other symbols." A striking finding of their study was that about 80% of reports that were categorized as unsymbolized thinking occurred during episodes in which participants reported "weighing" different options. In situations not involving options, the same participants experienced their thoughts in other ways as well, such as inner speech. Results of the study suggest that the experience of choosing commonly relies on "unsymbolized thinking" but does not provide definitive evidence that choosing requires this form of thinking. It raises a general question as to what types of thinking, feeling, or imaging are necessary or sufficient for experiencing choice. Listening to people choose out loud in restaurants and elsewhere suggests that choosing can sometimes have a somewhat verbal representation.

6.3.2   A Qualitative–Quantitative Study of Choosing

The qualitative–quantitative model presented in chapter 5 proposed that magnitudes of some types of positive and negative emotional feeling, termed "valence" by many emotion researchers, is codetermined by type of goal, magnitudes of desire, and expectation level. The functions that characterize this model were established for hypothetical scenarios and for lived situations that varied enormously in physical and social contexts. The same approach and methods were used to study experiences of choosing (Price, Riley, and Barrell, 2001). First, a preliminary study used hypothetical choices involving stated probabilities of receiving money or enduring rain, similar to scenarios described in chapter 2. The main experiment, however, involved choosing during widely different contexts.

The rationale for the study was relatively simple: The choice between two positive outcomes with different expectations may be largely determined by how good (or bad) we feel about each of the two options. It seems reasonable to propose that we would choose the option that we feel is most likely to make us feel the best. In choosing between two negative outcomes, we would choose the option that we feel is most likely to make us feel the least bad.

Some Hypothetical Situations

The hypothetical examples of figure 6.1 help frame this simple idea in quantitative terms. A 100% chance of receiving $1,000 would, *on average*

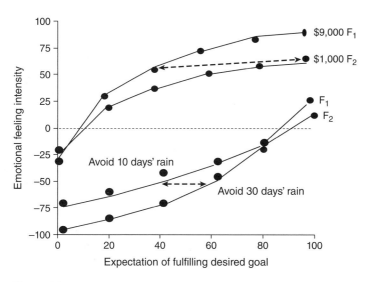

Figure 6.1

Approach and avoidance goals for hypothetical scenarios involving money and enduring rain. Dashed horizontal lines connect points on the two upper curves that would be of equal feeling intensity (i.e., a 100% chance of receiving $1,000 would be just as attractive as a 40% chance of receiving $9,000). Similarly, a 50% chance of avoiding thirty days of rain would be as unpleasant as a 15% chance of avoiding ten days of rain. Curves are based on approach equation $F = -0.3D + 1.3DE^{1/2}$ (money) and avoidance equation $F = -D + 1.4DE^2$ (days of rain).

for a population of individuals, be equivalent in positive feeling intensity to a 40% chance of receiving $9,000 ($F_1 = F_2$). This equivalency is shown by the upper dashed horizontal line in figure 6.1. Based on the idea that choice is determined by a comparison of anticipated feelings associated with each option, the tendency to choose the $9,000 option ($F_1$) would increase if its experienced probability were to increase above 40%. It would also increase if the perceived probability of receiving $1,000 ($F_2$) were to decrease below 100%. We can propose that the tendency to choose the higher value but lower probability $9,000 option is a function of $F_1 - F_2$, where F_1 and F_2 are hypothetical feeling intensities provided by options with the highest (e.g., $9,000) and lowest (i.e., $1,000) possible gains, respectively. These feeling states, F_1 and F_2, can either be directly rated or calculated according to the emotion functions derived in earlier studies.

Consider the options represented in figure 6.1. Is the choice between a 40% chance of receiving $9,000 ($F_1$) and certainty of receiving $1,000 ($F_2$) somewhat difficult? Which option feels better when presented alone?

Which one feels better when you have to choose between them? This F_1 – F_2 model predicts that the choice would be difficult when $F_1 – F_2$ is close to zero, and we observed this to be the case in a group of 40 people.[1] A slightly better model was more predictive when an additional risk or "regret" factor was added.[2] Similarly, when the same participants were asked to choose between different possibilities of enduring different durations of rain, a similar model of $F_1 – F_2$ was predictive of choice (see notes 1 and 2).

Emotional Feelings and Choice in Lived Experiences

Although experiments on hypothetical events have high control over the "stimuli" and provide prospective data about choices, they are not about real choices that people have in everyday situations. Gambling experiments in experimental psychology have the same limitation. Using a qualitative–quantitative method similar to that used in emotion studies (see chapter 5), we tested whether emotional feelings could help explain decisions (Price, Riley, and Barrell, 2001). Two questions guided this study. First, do the same functions shown in figure 6.1 apply to emotional feelings during choosing? Second, do these functions and feelings predict one's strength of choice (SC) for one option over the other? Participants rated desire (D), expectation (E), and feeling intensity (+F or –F) for each option and their strength of choice (SC) for the option that was chosen. Similar to emotion studies, both first-person qualitative descriptions and quantitative data were obtained during actual decisions.

The following ratings and descriptions for one participant serve as an example:

I was standing in front of the ticket office when the following experience occurred:

This is probably going to be one of the best games of the season. Image of being in the stadium watching the game. Really short on money right now. Need to save. Maybe I'll have more money next week. But this is going to be a really good game.

Alternative A   Buy ticket to game and enjoy it (Approach Goal).
Alternative B   Not buy ticket and avoid spending money (Avoidance Goal).
Desire associated with A = 80 (0–100)
Expectation of enjoying A if A is chosen = 48 (0–100)
Feeling about A = +39 (0–100)
Desire associated with B = 49 (0–100)
Expectation of saving money if B is chosen = 100
Feeling about B = +20
Strength of Choice (SC) = 75 (where B = 0 and A = 100). A was chosen.

Note that the positive feeling about A was approximately twice as that of B and the strength of choice highly favors A. A was chosen, and he went to the game.

Since participants rated D, E, and F associated with each option, these ratings could be subjected to the same type of analysis used to generate curves for the emotion model presented in chapter 5 and illustrated in figure 6.1. When this was done, the relationships between D, E, and F were very similar to those derived previously. They followed the same equations as shown in figure 6.1: $F = -0.3D + 1.3DE^{1/2}$ (approach); $F = -0.9D + 1.4DE^2$ (avoidance). These results suggest that actual or anticipated emotions that are about choosing follow the same functions as some emotions in general.

We then determined the extent to which ratings of D, E, and F predicted the strengths of choices that were made, or, in other words, the degree of preference of one option over the other. A simple model of $D \times E$ modestly predicted strength of choice ($r = .55$). However, the $F_1 - F_2$ model (see figure 6.1) was a significantly better predictor ($r = .72$) as were direct ratings of the feelings about the options ($r = .84$).

The experiential descriptions clarified what the desires, expectations, and feelings were about, as exemplified in the description given above about whether to buy a ticket to a sporting event. The descriptions pertained to lived situations and to the moments of choosing. As in the case of emotions based on D and E, the decisions could be about anything. There were no stimuli to be measured, and no experimenter was present when each choice was made.

Nevertheless, a concern that could be raised about this study is that it relied on reconstructions of each choice experience and therefore on retrospectively obtained data. When participants reconstruct their experience, is it possible that they adjust their ratings of D, E, F, and SC to account for the actual choice that was made? The results of this single study cannot rule out this possibility. Participants might want to appear consistent in their responses. They may have a need to "explain" their responses, and they may even have their own theory of choice. If that is the case, it is remarkable that the functions that predict choice follow the power functions for approach and avoidance emotions (see figure 5.1). How would participants know how to make this happen? And does everyone have the same theory of choice? The results of the preliminary experiment involving hypothetical options were consistent with the main study on lived choice experiences. The latter is more ecologically valid, yet it relies on retrospective data and has potential for bias. The study using hypothetical scenarios is prospective, yet it has little ecological validity. The general similarity in results across both experiments supports the idea that deliberate choices are based on weighing emotional feelings (or anticipated feelings) that, in turn, are based on desire and expectation.

6.3.3 Are the Factors within Choosing Immediately Transparent?

We are not claiming that people are fully conscious of their desires, expectations, and feeling states during choosing, nor are they necessarily verbally representing these dimensions in "inner speech." As discussed earlier, Hurlburt's research shows that decision between options is commonly accompanied by unsymbolized thinking (no words, symbols etc.). Yet in reconstructing their experiences, including ratings of D, E, and F, participants were able to translate their experience into both a verbal and quantitative account. Their experiences of desire and expectation were more commonly stated in indirect terms, such as "I hope this is going to be a fun event" or "Is it likely to snow heavily if we go to the mountains this weekend? I don't want to go if that happens." Yet if Hurlburt's results are correct, these thoughts may not have been experienced in words or symbols that denote desire, expectation, and feeling. Nevertheless, D, E, and F (or anticipated feelings) may be critically associated with options even if they are implicit in experience.

Choices are often made impulsively and quickly. We probably make many trivial decisions each day on the basis of impulse, and occasionally we have to make very important choices rapidly. Decisions about marrying or divorcing someone, on the other hand, would likely contain much more deliberation, especially if they were difficult decisions. This type of choice would more explicitly include D, E, and F. Thus, when people consider important options during volitional choosing, they are likely having emotional feelings about these options, however subtle they may be. Other investigators have arrived at similar conclusions using very different types of data (Damasio, 1994; 1999; Mellers, 2000).

6.3.4 Predicting Choices

For the sake of simplicity and our reasons to show how an experiential account of emotions and choices can be integrated, we have restricted our discussion to choices between two simple alternatives. We have not discussed how experienced outcomes are influenced by factors of surprise and novelty or the lack of such factors. Overall, our explanation is similar to Meller's expected pleasure theory that asserts that people select the option that maximizes their expected pleasure and minimizes their expected pain. Meller's theory adds elements of surprise and anticipated regret. For example, it describes the facts that surprising smaller wins can be more pleasurable than expected large ones, that a loss can feel like a win if an even larger loss was expected, and that a regrettable action can feel worse than a regrettable inaction if perceived control increases an expectation of the act. The predictability of emotional feelings is critical for predictability of choices in both explanations.

Finally, we should not leave the impression that the task of predicting decisions is always as simple as the studies and examples we have described. Decision analyses contain huge complexity and have multiple paradoxes, particularly when options contain multiple outcomes and have multiple goals, desires, and expectations (Birnbaum, 2008). It is possible, however, that even complex decisions could eventually be addressed by experiential methods. Thus, the overall feeling for each option may be an integration of all the goals, desires, expectations, and feelings contained within it. A choice might be made on the basis of comparing overall feelings provided by two or more options. These overall feelings would pertain to anticipated gains, losses, and regrets that are linked to goals within each option. Clearly much more experiential research is needed. The extent to which one is conscious of these factors during a choice also is a matter for considerable exploration.

6.4 Neurobiology of Emotions and Choice

A commonality of psychological functions that predict feeling intensity, choice responses, and perhaps motivation suggests the existence of interrelated psychological dimensions. These dimensions are directly experienced during at least some conditions and can be the variables of an experiential science. Of course, the psychological dimensions and their interactions relate to corresponding neural mechanisms. The neuroscience of emotions and choice is in an early stage, yet some interesting questions have emerged. Are there neural mechanisms that could account for the emotion and choice models described earlier? Do approach and avoidance goals have different neural circuitries? Finally, are there brain regions and connections that compare feeling states or anticipated feelings associated with options?

6.4.1 Brain Areas Involved in Human Emotions and Choice
If anything has been learned in the last few decades about the neural representations of human emotions, it is that they include widely distributed networks of several brain structures as opposed to discrete centers for each

type of primary and secondary emotion (Murphy, Nimmo-Smith, and Lawrence, 2003). These areas include both cortical and subcortical regions, including critical midbrain regions such as the periaqueductal gray (Panskepp, 2006). Based on neurology, brain imaging, and other neuroscience disciplines, it has been amply demonstrated that emotions require processing in multiple brain structures that serve all forms of sensory processing, somatomotor and autonomic system output, memory, and cognition. They require processing in multiple cerebral cortical, limbic, and even lower brainstem structures. Yet there are brain structures that seem most proximate to the feelings and motor output associated with emotions. Reward areas that are affected by dopamine release, such as nucleus accumbens and ventral striatum (figure 6.2), are involved in good and bad feelings of emotions as are the amygdala and lower brainstem areas (e.g., periaqueductal gray, figure 6.2; Panskepp, 2006). Other areas are about expectations and anticipation and related information processing. A few of these cerebral cortical areas are shown in figure 6.2. Thus, different parts of the anterior cingulate cortex (ACC) are involved in attention, cognition, and/ or emotional feeling (dorsal ACC; dACC; rostral ACC; rACC) and different

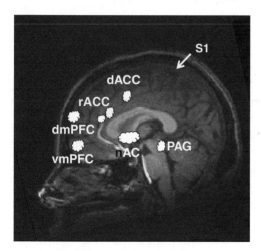

Figure 6.2
Some brain regions involved in emotion and choice. Shown is a midsaggital view of the brain (between cerebral hemispheres) with white areas designating the following regions: dorsal anterior cingulate cortex (dACC), rostral anterior cingulate cortex (rACC), ventromedial prefrontal cortex (vmPFC), dorsomedial prefrontal cortex (dmPFC), nucleus accumbens (nAC), ventral striatum, and periaqueductal gray (PAG).

parts of the medial prefrontal cortex are involved in decisions and expectations. Not shown in figure 6.2 are emotion-related areas that are displaced from the midline, such as the insular cortex, amygdala, orbitofrontal cortex, and dorsolateral prefrontal cortex. Neurological, psychophysiological, and brain imaging studies have illuminated how these different brain structures further explain emotions and the relationships between emotions and choosing (Rushworth and Behrens, 2008). However, studies of the neural basis of emotions do not characterize them experientially.

6.4.2 Neurological and Psychophysiological Studies

Interrelationships between emotions and choice have been proposed on the basis of several studies that are very different than those of psychological studies. The first is work by Bechara and colleagues showing that psychophysiological responses indicative of emotional states precede choice responses and that both rational choices and their associated physiological responses are deficient in patients with ventromedial prefrontal cortical (figure 6.2) or amygdala damage (Bechara et al., 1997; Bechara et al., 1999; Damasio, 1994; 1996). These brain structures are involved in both cognition and emotion. Their research provides complementary support for the idea that emotional processes underpin choices, including rational choices. In particular, they have formulated the "somatic marker" hypothesis to help explain the interdependence between choice and emotional processes. This hypothesis proposes that as an outcome associated with a specific option is considered, a somatic state is produced that consists of both somatomotor and autonomic components and this somatic state "marks" an imagined outcome. According to Damasio (1994), this "somatic marker" can function as an automated alarm signal that can lead to immediate rejection of a course of action and allow choice among fewer alternative options. Somatic markers are suggested as increasing the accuracy and efficiency of the decision process, and their absence reduces them. Somatic markers may act covertly in the otherwise deliberate evaluation of option–outcome scenarios.

Experimental support for this mechanism comes from studies that show that the learning of risky choices in a gambling task is accompanied by increased anticipatory skin conductance responses (SCRs) while participants pondered risky choices (Bechara et al., 1997). These increased SCRs began to develop even prior to the explicit realization of which choices were risky. Patients with ventromedial prefrontal cortical damage continued to choose disadvantageously even after learning these risky choices in a gambling task and, unlike normal participants, never developed anticipatory SCRs. In a similar subsequent study, both patients with bilateral amygdala damage and patients with ventromedial prefrontal damage were impaired on the gambling task and failed to develop anticipatory SCRs (Bechara et al., 1999). However, patients with only ventromedial cortical damage were able to generate SCRs when they actually received a reward or punishment (play money), whereas patients with *both* amygdala and ventromedial cortical damage did not generate SCRs either in response to anticipation or to actual outcomes. The more severe psychophysiological and emotional deficits of the latter patients were consistent with their inability to make critical life decisions that serve to maintain personal success and even safety in everyday life. The overall lesson of these studies, in light of consideration of experiential studies of choices and emotions, is that brain structures that are critically involved in emotions are also necessary for choice.

The idea that choices are based on emotional processing and that emotional feeling supports rational decisions potentially overturns a viewpoint held for centuries—namely, that rational decisions and emotions serve very different functions that are often at odds with one another. Instead, Damasio (1994; 1999) proposes that emotional limbic circuitry and even lower brainstem regions act in concert with prefrontal cerebral regions when choices and feelings are directed toward even the most rational issues. Areas of the brain involved in cognitive functions co-opt limbic and brainstem circuitry when choices are made. And these choices are dependent on feelings directed toward alternative options. The feelings associated with each option may reflect the first-person counterpart of the "the somatic marker." Although they used very different methods and addressed somewhat different questions, the overall explanation put forth by Damasio's group lends general support to explanations given earlier, including affect decision theory.

6.4.3 Are Different Brain Circuitries Involved in Approach, Avoidance, and Weighing Options?

The psychological models of emotion and choice described earlier propose that we somehow "weigh" feeling states associated with each option. The option that produces a sum of feelings that is felt as the most positive or least negative is the one that is chosen. The dynamics of these processes indirectly suggest the possibility that there are partially different brain circuitries for different aspects of emotions and the overall process of choosing. Thus, there may be partially different brain circuitries for approach as compared to avoidance goals. In addition, the brain regions that process the feeling states may not be entirely the same ones that "weigh" the feelings provided by the options. The regions would have to at least partially overlap because brain regions that compare the options would require access to information provided in the feeling states. For similar reasons, brain areas that compare options may partially overlap with or connect to ones that relate to behavior or plans for behavior (i.e., motivation). Brain mechanisms involved in emotions, motivation, and choice are complex, and we attempt to simplify the discussion of the possibilities just raised. We think there is at least good preliminary evidence for partially separate brain regions and connections for approach as compared to avoidance goals and evidence for different brain areas involved in the different stages of choice responses.

6.4.4 Brain Areas and Mechanisms That Serve Feelings about Options and Weighing of Options

Research conducted in the 1990s began to suggest somewhat separate motivational and emotional neural subsystems for approach and avoidance goals. Both Lane et al. (1997) and George et al. (1995) found somewhat different cortical regions of activation for appetitive (approach) and aversive (avoidance) emotional states, showing that aversive and appetitive emotional states are not simply represented by different levels of activity within the same brain structures. This overall view has since received support from many brain imaging studies, but the story is a little complicated. For example, in an analysis of 106 brain imaging studies of human emotions, Murphy and colleagues found partial support for asymmetry in representing approach as compared to avoidance emotions (Murphy et al., 2003). Whereas approach emotions were represented more in the left cerebral hemisphere, avoidance emotions were represented symmetrically in both hemispheres. More recently, several studies have more specifically characterized how different brain structures may be related to different dimensions of emotions that process choices and to different stages of choice responses themselves. Brain imaging studies of expectations, reward and punishment evaluation, and experienced values during decision making provide further support for the idea that emotional feelings related to approach and avoidance account for choice responses. A study by Hans Breiter and colleagues (2001) was one of the first to use brain imaging (fMRI) to track brain areas involved in both expecting and receiving monetary rewards and losses while participants engaged in a game of chance. They were exposed to different types of "spinners," each of which had different types of outcomes: (1) a "Bad" spinner with losses (e.g., –$6.00,

–$1.50), (2) a "Mixed" spinner with wins and losses (-$1.50 or +2.50), and (3) a "Good" spinner that had gains of $0, $2.50, and $10.00. Participants knew which type of spinner was being used on any given trial and rated how good or bad they felt about each spinner. Their brains were functionally scanned while each spinner rotated as well as when the actual outcome was presented. Several brain regions known to be involved in emotions were activated during the phase wherein spinners were spinning and participants were expecting but not certain of exact outcomes. A set of brain regions activated during this expectation phase included the extended nucleus of the amygdala, the orbitofrontal cortex, nucleus accumbens (nACC in figure 6.2), and hypothalamus. These regions are part of a widely distributed network of brain areas that are involved in emotions, including good feelings that accompany gains of some kind. Thus, the orbitofrontal cortex is associated with perceived value or desirability of outcomes as is the amygdala to some extent. Nucleus accumbens is well-known for its role in the feeling of reward and is activated by euphoria-producing drugs. Most of the same regions that were activated during the spinning phase of the trial, wherein expectations were generated, also were activated during the outcomes when participants learned how much they had won or lost. There was little evidence of a strict anatomical segregation of anticipated versus experienced outcomes. Areas that were activated when participants expected to feel good were generally the same ones that were activated when they actually won. To some extent, this similarity also occurs for other types of expected and actual outcomes, such as pain, for example (see chapter 7).

What is remarkable is that this same network of brain regions (e.g., amygdala, orbitofrontal cortex, nucleus accumbens) is involved in "feelings" about all kinds of outcomes—for example, those related to tactile stimuli, gustatory stimuli, money, and euphoria-producing drugs. Common brain circuitry for the enormous diversity of potential outcomes is consistent with a model of emotions that pertains to a common set of variables (i.e., D, E, and F) that are not immediately contingent on particular environmental conditions or "stimuli" that evoke them. Desire can be *about* anything we want, as can expectation and feelings (see chapter 5). Put another way, the interrelationships between desire, expectation, feelings, and choice follow a common set of functions for widely diverse physical and social contexts. Of course, factors within such contexts have moderating influences, yet the proximal causes are within experience.

A pivotal study by Karina Blair and her colleagues (Blair et al., 2006) investigated the brain imaging correlates of two critical aspects of decision making: (1) *decision form*, which is the distinction between choosing between two objects to gain the greater reward (approach–approach decision) or choosing between two objects to avoid the greater of two punishments (avoidance–avoidance decision), and (2) *the difficulty of choice*. Such difficulty depends on how close or far apart the objects are in reward value or punishment value. While in the fMRI scanner, participants were presented with pictures, and each picture had two common objects in it, such as a duck, a shoe, or a house. Each object had either an associated reward value (e.g., +300, +500, +700, or +900 points) or a punishment value (e.g., –900, –700, –500, –300, or –100 points). They were familiarized with reward and punishment values of each object before the scanning session. Then, on each trial during the brain scanning session, a pair of objects was displayed and participants had to choose the object with the greatest reward value in approach–approach choices and had to choose the object with the least punishment value in avoidance–avoidance choices. There were also trials that involved approach–avoidance decisions. The authors measured reaction times to the choice responses and error rates, measured as the number of times participants "incorrectly" chose the object with the least reward value or the most punishment value. All participants were told that the overall object of the choosing session was to win as many points as possible. They could only win points on approach–approach trials; the only question was how much. In avoidance–avoidance trials they could only lose points. Their memory for the exact number of winning and losing points associated with each object was no doubt imperfect so that they had a somewhat uncertain expectation of winning or losing when viewing the various objects. We can assume they had varying degrees of desire to win on approach–approach trials and to avoid losing on avoidance–avoidance trials.

Activity in brain regions was then correlated with decision form—approach or avoidance goal decisions as well as decision difficulty. Overall, their results conformed to two general proposals made earlier. The first is that brain regional activity within the right ventromedial prefrontal cortex (see vmPFC in figure 6.2), right amygdala, and temporal lobes was associated with approach–approach decisions while other brain regions, such as the right dACC (see dACC in figure 6.2) and bilateral insula, seemed more involved in avoidance–avoidance decisions. Other studies show that approach responses are strongly associated with activity in the ventromedial prefrontal cortex whereas avoidance responses, presumably produced by punishment, are strongly associated with activity in the more lateral orbitofrontal cortex (O'Doherty et al., 2001; Anderson et al., 2003). Thus, neural representations of emotional functions related to approach goals are at least partially separate from those related to avoidance goals.

The second proposal is that areas of the brain that are related to weighing the reward or punishment value of the two competing options are partially different than those that are related to expected reward or punishment and emotional feelings associated with these expectations. Thus, a second major finding of the study by Blair et al. (2006) was that activation in dACC (see dACC in figure 6.2) increased as a function of difficulty of the decision, the second aspect of decision making. The dACC is most heavily involved during avoidance goals and in the "weighing" of the different options, regardless of whether they are approach or avoidance. With regard to weighing the options, activity in dACC increased when the *differences* between two reward values or between two punishment values decreased. These decreases presumably made the decisions difficult. Some areas within the ACC have long been known to be heavily involved in attention. The effort of attention in making close decisions is likely to be proportional to the level of neural activity in these regions.

A study by Abigail Marsh and the same colleagues in the study just discussed (Blair et al., 2006) examined the functional roles of the dorsal ACC (dACC; figure 6.2) rostral ACC (rACC), and medial prefrontal cortex (figure 6.2) in two aspects of decision making: (1) the number of available decision options and (2) the level of expected reward (Marsh et al., 2007). Their participants were trained to recognize the reward value associated with each of several visual options and then were presented with groups of two, three, or four of these options. This variability in number of presented options was used to systematically increase the complexity of the choice task. Then they were asked to select the option associated with the highest reward. Given the nature of the rewards, obtaining them could be construed as an approach goal because most outcomes were rewarding to varying extents. Participants were given points, and none of the options were punishing. Neural activation in dACC and dorsomedial PFC was associated strongly with the total number of decision options (i.e., 1, 2, 3, or 4 options) but only weakly with increases in the level of expected reward. This finding is similar to results of Blair discussed above and other studies that show that dACC is involved in conflict resolutions and in the difficulty of decision making (see Rushworth and Behrens, 2008, for review).

On the other hand, Marsh and colleagues found that activation in rACC/mPFC and amygdala was associated with magnitude of the expected reward but not increases in the number of decision options (i.e., complexity of the choice task). One way to think of these results in simple terms is that the areas of the brain associated with weighing the different options (dACC and dmPFC) are somewhat different from those that are associated with generation of emotional feelings associated with each option (rACC/mPFC, figure 6.2). Of course, these two functions are likely to be intimately interrelated. Areas of the brain that are most proximately associated with generating the motor output related to the decision (e.g., reaching for the chosen duck, exclaiming "Hey, I choose the duck!") are most closely linked to brain areas, such as the supplementary motor cortex, that are associated with the actual motor outcome of a decision (Rogers et al., 2004). For example, the dACC and the supplementary motor area are known to be anatomically and functionally interconnected. Thus, interactions between experiential factors that underlie the process of choosing and subsequent choice-related behavior may well be represented by interactions within corresponding brain areas that link cognitive/emotional aspects of choices to motor acts or plans for motor acts.

In combining the results of Blair et al. (2006) and Marsh et al. (2007), we see that dACC and vmPFC have complementary yet dissociable roles in decision making. Both were shown to be related to decision form, approach or avoidance, but differentially. The dACC showed greater responses when both choices were avoidance whereas the vmPFC showed greater responses when both choices were approach goals. In addition, the neural responses in dACC, but not the vmPFC, related to the closeness of the desirability of the choices on display. All of these results suggest that brain processes related to emotional feelings are critical in determining choice responses and that some brain areas are preferentially involved in weighing the anticipated good or bad feelings associated with projected outcomes.

6.5 An Alternative Approach in the Neurobiology of Emotions, Choice, and Motivation

6.5.1 Integrating First- and Third-Person Understanding of Emotions and Choice

There is a general compatibility between experiential studies of emotions and choice and those studies that have used neuroimaging in humans to study emotions and choice responses. Both types of studies propose a close relationship between emotional processing and choice responses, and the studies by Blair et al. (2006) and Marsh et al. (2007) propose at least partially separate brain circuitry for avoidance as compared to approach goals.

A number of brain imaging studies propose that areas of the brain that are related to comparing options are at least partially separate from brain areas that generate the emotional states. These separate functions and stages of processing have the potential to be integrated with emotion and choice models discussed earlier. However, the latter explanations are framed in experiential terms whereas the brain imaging studies have mostly used a behavioral approach. For example, the latter measure error rates and reaction times to the decision response. We contend that a much more efficient and powerful approach might use participants' direct scaling of the factors that comprise emotional feelings and preferences of options (i.e., strength of choice ratings). Using these factors in analyses of brain activity, it should be possible to discover the neural correlates of functions shown in figure 6.1. Thus, direct scaling of expected outcomes, desirability of expected rewards, undesirability of expected punishments, and emotional feeling states could be used to directly correlate magnitudes of dimensions of direct experience with that of activity in networks of brain structures. Ideally, the moment-by-moment functional connections between these structures also could be related to moment-by-moment experiential results. Activity in some brain structures in figure 6.2 might have the same functional curves that are displayed in figure 6.1. In other words, the functional interactions between brain areas might mirror those which occur between dimensions of experience (e.g., D, E, F, and strength of choice). This approach could be very helpful in determining whether the experiential and neural activity maps have similar information structures. And none of the analyses would result in an ontological reduction of experiential phenomena to neural phenomena. Both would always remain in the explanation. The neural activity maps could be representations of experiential maps. The feasibility of this potential approach is supported by several brain imaging studies that already utilize direct scaling of multiple dimensions of human experience. For example, Rainville et al. (1997) found that activity in ACC area 24b was closely associated with participants' direct ratings of emotional feeling intensity but not sensory intensity associated with experimental pain.

6.5.2   Can an Experiential Approach and Method Also Help Explain Motivation?

Desire is necessary but not sufficient for motivation, which is the strength of one's intention to carry out some effort or action. We can have several desires that we never intend to act on. Can a motivational model be based on desires and expectations in a manner similar to the way a model of choosing can be related to human emotions? Such a possibility seems compatible with the idea that motivation involves a choice between acting or not acting on a given desire or choosing between alternative actions involving different desires. Based on work at the University of Florida as well as numerous consultations for several college and professional athletes, one of us (JJB) has proposed a model for motivation (Barrell and Ryback, 2008).

Motivation can be framed as *the strength of desire to make an effort to fulfill a goal* and not simply desire. Moreover, several factors that may represent the essential causes or common elements related to motivation are the following:

1. Identification of the goal—In short, what do you want? This can be an approach or avoidance goal, something that is enjoyable or fearful. Another aspect of the goal is that it can be a process or result goal (see chapter 5).
2. Strength of desire for the goal, that is, importance of the goal.
3. Level of expectation that one knows *how* to fulfill the goal.
4. Level of expectation that one *can* fulfill the goal.
5. Level of expectation that one *will* fulfill the goal.

The final two factors are desires and expectations that can undermine motivation:

6. Strength of desire to avoid the effort necessary to fulfill the goal. (How much do you want to avoid what it takes to fulfill the goal?)
7. Level of expectation that the goal will be fulfilled without effort. (How sure do you feel that the goal will simply happen and be fulfilled in time, come as a gift etc.?)

We propose that optimal motivation occurs when factors 1–5 are enhanced while factors 6 and 7 are reduced. This model, which is based on several dimensions of D and E, is testable. It has been shown to predict behavior and enhance performance (Barrell and Ryback, 2008).

6.6 Integrating Experiential and Neural Models of Emotions, Choice, and Motivation

This chapter began with discussions of how variables related to emotions have become integrated into theories of decision making. A strategy for utilizing experiential methods to better understand relationships between emotional feelings and choosing was then outlined. Although considerably more work has to be done, experiential first-person studies of emotions, choice, and motivation have the potential to be integrated with the rest of the psychological and neuroscience literature. Most critically, experiential science could help characterize the choices that people make in widely different circumstances (not just gambling experiments). Finally, there is a potential neurobiology of emotions and choices that could rely on first-person models. At a deeper level, this approach could provide a more direct access to the neurobiology of the actual human experiencing of these phenomena. We think that this approach may yield explanations that would be better understood and appreciated by people interested in scientific accounts of these phenomena, including nonscientists. For example, remember the emotion explorations suggested in chapter 3 (hypothetical feelings in response to receiving a large award or loss) and the questions about how one would experience choices presented in figure 6.1 of this chapter. The types of experiential studies that we have described also have to be combined with physiological measures, including those provided by brain imaging. For that matter, brain imaging studies on a wide range of psychological topics need experiential methods and much more ecologically valid designs. It is time to move beyond reaction times and error rates and remove the blind spot pertaining to direct human experience. Experientially recognizable explanations are critically needed in research on emotions, choice, and motivation.

Jaak Panskepp sees this challenge as one of the most important in the field of affective neuroscience:

I believe one of the biggest challenges in emotion research is for us to open up discourse about the nature of affective-motivational experience, not just in humans but all mammals. I think most people in the world outside of the scientific-philo-sophical formal approaches to the study and discussion of emotions believe that the *experience* of affect, the valenced feeling aspect of emotions, is the defining characteristic and hence the most important dimension of emotional life. Yet it remains the least studied and the least discussed property of emotionality, with considerably more effort devoted to the autonomic arousal, behaviourally expressive features, and more recently the abundant cognitive correlates. (Panskepp, 2008, p. 89)

Analysis of emotional feelings may be a key to understanding complex and ubiquitous phenomena such as pain (see chapters 7 and 8) and the placebo effect (chapter 9). Analysis of emotions and states of consciousness also may offer a novel approach to the study of volition (chapter 11).

7   Human Pain and Suffering

Pain is but the breaking of the shell that encloses the understanding.
—Khalil Gibran

Human concern with the phenomenon of pain is at least as old as human civilization itself because relief of pain is as integral to survival as any of our biological functions. Medical relief of pain comes at an enormous cost to countries that can afford it and is almost unavailable in the poorest of countries. The problems presented by the existence of pain are largely conceptualized as mechanistic puzzles to be solved by neuroscientists, psychologists, and clinicians. However, as David Morris (1994) has pointed out, the problem of pain extends well beyond its immediate mechanisms because pain is shaped by individual human minds and by specific human cultures. Pain also is a topic that seems to fascinate philosophers, and they often use pain as a model with which to reflect on the nature of the human mind and consciousness. A major challenge that is common to all disciplines that attempt to understand pain is how to observe and characterize the *experience* of pain. There is no way to circumvent this challenge if pain is an experience. We begin this chapter with the history of attempts to define pain and then describe its phenomenology. Then we show how an experiential perspective is helpful at arriving at a definition of pain that is most useful to science and health-care professions. The definition that we propose relates to hypotheses that are about what experiential factors are contained in pain. We then discuss studies that test functional interrelationships between these factors, followed by a discussion of neuroscience research that explores their neural correlates and causes. Like other chapters, this chapter exemplifies how an experiential perspective can initially be used to study the nature of a conscious phenomenon such as pain and then be used as a strategy in studies of pain mechanisms.

7.1   Attempts to Define Pain in the Twentieth Century

Despite its enormous importance in medicine and biology, it is astonishing to discover that physical pain has been defined so poorly throughout the twentieth century, and pain definitions have serious problems even now. This poses huge problems in science and medicine because if pain is left as a vague and open-ended concept, then how can we conduct meaningful scientific research on pain or provide adequate medical treatments? We propose that an experiential approach can provide precision and clarity to the definition of pain with consequent improvements in scientific and conceptual understanding of this phenomenon and in diagnosis and management of pain. We begin with past difficulties in defining pain and show that the lack of an experiential approach to this phenomenon lies at the heart of the problem. We think it is possible to provide semantic precision and clarity to the definition of pain. An improved definition of pain could lead to research that clarifies the dimensions of pain and their interactions. An improved understanding of pain phenomenology should also lead to an improved neurobiology of pain. This chapter on physical pain and pain-related suffering serves as yet another model for how an experiential method can be interfaced with the natural sciences. It can also be interfaced with health-care practice.

7.2   Definitions of Pain Prior to the International Association for the Study of Pain

Two individuals in the twentieth century proposed noteworthy definitions of pain. Sternbach (1968) proposed the first one, which defined pain as an abstract concept that refers to *"(1) a personal, private sensation of hurt, (2) a harmful stimulus which signals current or impending tissue damage, and (3) a pattern of responses which operate to protect the organism from harm"* (italics ours) . According to Melzack and Wall (1983), this definition is wrong on all three counts. First, if pain is a "hurt," how does one define a "hurt"? One could just as well define "hurt" as a pain, so this part of the definition is circular. Second, both clinicians who treat pain and researchers who study pain know that pain can occur in the absence of tissue injury or long after the injury has healed. It is also the case that injury can occur without pain. Any definition of pain that rigidly links tissue injury to pain meets with numerous exceptions. Finally, while it is often the case that pain is accompanied by protective or avoidance behaviors, such behaviors are neither necessary nor sufficient for pain. Pain-related behavior can be suppressed during the presence of pain. Furthermore, the same pain-like behaviors can be expressed during the absence of pain because they can occur during other threatening events that do not necessarily entail physical pain. It seems unlikely that this definition would help to advance knowledge of pain mechanisms.

The second definition proposed by Mountcastle (1974) was that *"pain is that sensory experience evoked by stimuli that injure or threaten to destroy tissue, defined introspectively by every man as that which hurts"* (italics ours). This definition is flawed for reasons similar to the ones applicable to Sternbach's definition. Mountcastle's definition even more closely links stimuli to the experience than does Sternbach. The main problems with both definitions are that they conflate physical and experiential phenomena, such as the stimulus or tissue injury with the response, and they are circular with respect to the experiential factors (e.g., pain = "hurt").

7.3 The International Association for the Study of Pain's Definition

According to the official definition of the International Association for the Study of Pain's (IASP's) taxonomy committee, pain is *"an unpleasant sensory and emotional experience associated with actual or potential tissue damage, or described in terms of such damage"* (italics ours). (Mersky and Bogduk 1994, p. 210). This definition is unique in that it was the first to explicitly recognize that the phenomenon of pain is an *experience*, yet one that comprises both sensory and affective dimensions (as also proposed by Melzack and Casey, 1968). Although we have supported this IASP definition in the past (Price, 1988), we presently think that it is confusing and that it does not represent a clear case of an experiential definition. The definition postulates an association between an experience of sensation, unpleasantness, and actual or potential tissue damage, but it is not at all clear from whose point of view such an association exists. Is it based on the judgment of an outside observer or on the experience of the person in pain? Although this was not likely the intention of its authors, the definition could be construed to imply that if an observer (e.g., health-care professional) cannot determine an association between the reported experience and actual or potential tissue damage, then the experience is *not* that of pain. This problem relates to our present knowledge that an association between unpleasant sensation and tissue injury or even the potential for tissue injury is neither necessary nor sufficient for the experience of pain. It may not even be a common factor in pain experience from the perspective of those in pain. Does someone with a stomachache associate the sensation with tissue damage or even the potential for tissue damage? Does someone who has tactile allodynia (pain from normally nonpainful types of stimuli such as brushing) for several years really associate the burning sensations with actual or potential tissue damage? And although many patients with neuropathic pain do describe their pains in "terms" of tissue damage, others do not. Does an "ache" automatically entail an experienced association with tissue damage?

Melzack and Wall (1983) also criticized the IASP definition, even though they considered it the best one yet formulated. Like us, they found the merits of this definition to be its explicit recognition of the loose association between tissue injury and pain and its inclusion of the emotional dimension of pain experience with its sensory dimension. Nevertheless, they state their main concern as follows:

The problem it encounters lies in the word "unpleasant." Pain, to be sure, is unpleasant; but it is much more. The unpleasant—or "negative-affective"—dimension of pain is really comprised of multiple dimensions. It is the kind of "unpleasantness" that makes people scream, fight, undergo crippling, disfiguring operations, or commit suicide. What is missing in the word "unpleasant" is the misery, anguish, desperation, and urgency that are part of some pain experiences. The qualities of "unpleasantness" are complex and comprise multiple dimensions that have yet to be determined. (p. 45)

Instead of providing their own definition of pain, however, Melzack and Wall make a very strange claim, which is that pain research has not yet advanced to the stage at which an accurate definition of pain can be formulated. They state, "At present, we must be content with guidelines *toward* a definition rather than a definition itself. *Too much remains to be learned about pain mechanisms before we can define pain with precision*" (p. 46, italics ours). If someone claims that the analysis of pain mechanisms (e.g., neuroscience, molecular biology) is required to determine a definition of a type of experience, it is hard to see how the scientific inquiry about pain could have even started! And this is not the state of affairs in other sciences. Even in the physical sciences, the basic concepts of "energy" and "matter" are still being continually redefined, yet no one can deny the incredible advances of modern-day physics and chemistry.

We think that Melzack and Wall were wrong about what is required to formulate a definition. Definition is normally a semantic affair—a word is often a pointer to a phenomenon or some aspects of it. If we can at least agree that pain is a kind of experience, then what we really need to do is make observations of this experience to identify common factors and interrelationships among these factors. In the case of pain, these factors are likely to be types of sensations, meanings, and feelings. Thus, the strategy discussed in previous chapters can be applied to understanding pain. The experiential approach and method may be ideally suited for such a project. This approach should then allow us to define a word whose meanings we already intuitively know but which are now stated in a more precise and explicit way. Beyond this approach, no additional empirical science is needed to produce a definition. Knowing the pain-related neural pathways, neurotransmitters, and integrative centers of the brain need not be required to provide a definition of pain. Semantic precision and clarity are essential for the definition of pain because pain researchers and professional health-care givers should find it very useful to have precise and clear guidelines about where and when to apply the term "pain" to study participants or patients.

7.4   Using First-Person Experiential Studies to Guide a Definition of Pain

The definitions of pain just discussed do not seem to use an explicit phenomenological method or, for that matter, even an experiential perspective. A major aim of the experiential method described in chapter 4 is to arrive at definitional hypotheses that consist of the necessary and sufficient factors that constitute a given type of experience and statements about which factors are necessary or sufficient for it to be present. These factors can then be used to construct a definition for an experience such as pain, anger, or excitement. For example, we have seen that this method provides definitions of specific types of emotional feelings, such as performance anxiety (chapter 4). Surprisingly, there is historical precedent for such an approach in the case of pain. Studies conducted between 1920 and 1977 used different variants of a coinvestigator/ participant model to discover the factors that constitute different types of physical pain. These studies illuminate the feasibility of determining a consensus about what constitutes pain and providing its definition. These factors are likely to include unique sensory qualities combined with other aspects of experience, such as emotional feelings, that are present during pain. Identification of unique sensory qualities and feelings may help clarify what make an experience a pain and not some other sensory experience such as an itch or a tickle.

7.4.1   Studies by Head (1920)
The neurologist Henry Head studied different types of pain, using himself as the only subject. He must have been intensely curious because he

studied various types of pain before and after cutting one of his own peripheral nerves (Head, 1920). During the slow course of nerve regeneration, unmyelinated axons (C-fibers) reestablished their connections to skin areas that had been rendered totally numb by cutting the nerve. These reestablished connections occurred before myelinated axons (A-fibers) restored their connections. He could then study the pains evoked in skin areas that were temporarily supplied *only* by C-fibers. Of course these areas were still numb, yet when repeated needle pricks or strong heat stimuli were applied to them, he observed a slow-onset burning sensation that grew in intensity with repeated pinpricks. This sensation also outlasted the series of applied stimuli. He found this form of sensation somewhat poorly localized and accompanied by special feelings of unpleasantness, or what he called "feeling tone." He found that the unpleasantness of the burning sensation experience was associated with temporal summation (each successive pinprick felt worse), spatial spread, and an increase in arousal. It was later learned that the "arousal" was the result of sympathetic activation from impulses in C-fibers. Head termed this form of experience "protopathic sensibility".

When axons from myelinated axons regenerated, application of a pinprick evoked an initial sharp sensation followed by a protopathic sensation as just described. We now know that the initial sharp sensation is the result of impulse conduction in finely myelinated axons connected peripherally to specific types of "nociceptors," termed A-delta nociceptive afferent neurons. Head found that the initial pinprick sensation was unpleasant but for reasons that were different than that of protopathic pain. It felt sharp and penetrating, probably much like the sensation of receiving a strongly delivered needle injection. Such an experience is undoubtedly unpleasant, especially if one is taken by surprise. Unlike protopathic sensibility, the pinprick sensation was well localized and did not long outlast the stimulus. Head categorized experiences such as this "epicritic sensibility."

7.4.2 Studies by Landau and Bishop

Similar to Head, Landau and Bishop (1953) used themselves as coinvestigator/subjects to determine the sensory and affective qualities that are unique to pains evoked by stimulation of skin receptors connected to thinly myelinated (A-delta) and unmyelinated (C-fibers) axons. Brief simultaneous stimulation of both types of nociceptors leads to "first" and "second" pain when the stimulus is applied to an extremity, and the two pains are related to faster and slower impulse conduction in A and C axons, respectively (Lewis and Pochin, 1938). Using standard stimuli, they attempted as much as possible to simply notice the qualities and intensities of first and second pain prior to reflecting on their causes or making interpretations. Both Landau and Bishop observed that first pain was sharp or stinging, well localized, and brief whereas second pain had qualities of dullness, aching, throbbing, or burning. Second pain also outlasted the stimulus that evoked it, and the location of the pain was diffuse, often radiating into areas well beyond the location of the stimulus. These results replicated and extended those of Head (1920). With the advent of modern neuroscience, neural mechanisms were discovered that help explain these sensory features of first and second pain. The qualities of unpleasantness also were different for the two types of pain. Whereas the unpleasantness of first pain was related to its intrusive sharpness and intensity, that of second pain was related to its sense of vagueness, poor localizability, dull and diffuse nature, and long duration. Both Landau and Bishop independently verified these characteristics of the two types of pain.

7.4.3   Studies of First and Second Pain

Results of Head (1920), Landau and Bishop (1953), and Lewis and Pochin (1938) have since been replicated and extended by studies of first and second pain using both qualitative and modern psychophysical methods (Price, 1972; Price et al., 1977; Staud et al., 2001; 2008). Both participants of these studies and sometimes the investigators themselves consistently found that the unpleasantness of first pain was strongly associated with a meaning of immediate intrusion and, in some cases, threat. Simply stating the likelihood of an electric shock to the skin was also experienced as threatening, as has been demonstrated in numerous psychology experiments. As in earlier studies, the experienced intrusiveness of second pain was associated with its spreading, dull, aching, burning, or summating qualities. Thus, meanings of threat or intrusion were manifested differently yet common for these highly controlled types of experimental pain. The feelings of unpleasantness or disturbance were the most common, yet negative feelings such as "annoyance," and "anxiety/fear" sometimes accompanied the meanings of threat and intrusion. The long-lasting and summating qualities of second pain have been shown to have neural causes and correlates as attested by experiments that study responses of single spinal cord neurons (Mendell and Wall, 1965; Price et al., 1978) and by recent brain imaging experiments (Staud et al., 2007, 2008).

7.4.4   A Proposal for an Improved Definition

There seem to be common factors within the experiences of very different types of pain, as exemplified by studies of first and second pain and by studies of pain patients. Based on common factors, we propose an improved definition of pain. It addresses concerns with past definitions and yet closely resembles the widely accepted IASP definition. We think that it mitigates the problems inherent in the latter:

Pain is a somatic or visceral experience that is comprised of (1) unique sensory qualities that are like those which occur during tissue damaging stimulation, (2) a closely related meaning of intrusion and/or threat, and (3) a related feeling of unpleasantness and/or other possible negative emotion(s).[1]

Unlike all preceding definitions, it is explicitly derived through an experiential perspective and method, similar to the approach used to characterize other types of human experiences. It is based on factors within particular experiences of pain, including those of investigators and participants unfamiliar with hypotheses. It also can be verified or disconfirmed by noticing your own phenomenology of pains, preferably in proximity to when they actually occur. Such an approach might be preferred over conceptual debate alone.

7.4.5   Are These Same Factors Present in All Types of Pain?

The studies just discussed help confirm that there are unique sensory qualities, meanings, and unpleasant feelings for different types of pain. Their results are useful in building a definition of pain, yet they raise the question as to whether the same experiential factors exist within all pains. Clearly there is an enormous diversity in pain experiences. Gustafson (2005) has claimed that a consistent definition of pain is not possible because of this extreme diversity. We think he gives up too early on a definition because some categories of phenomena are extremely diverse. An example from zoology helps to explain our reasons. If one considers the types of birds on earth, one can easily appreciate the enormous diversity in size, appearance, and detailed physical structure of various types of birds. Hummingbirds, peacocks, and ostriches all look very different from each other, and the latter can't even fly. Yet they are all birds. A bird is defined in a precise way in zoology despite this diversity. Likewise, pains have similar dimensions despite their different qualities, duration, intensities, and other features. For example, the word "pain" is often applied to the sharp sensation and unpleasantness following a brief pinprick as well as to a low-grade, dull backache. Nevertheless, if different types of experience have unique sensory qualities commonly used when people say they have pain *and* they contain unpleasantness or disturbance, then the word "pain" can apply to diverse types of experience.

Our question of whether the same factors could be applied to very different forms of pain was partly addressed through interviews with chronic pain patients. During the early 1980s we were given the task of developing a pain questionnaire for the Medical College of Virginia's (MCV's) Pain Center. Part of this task was that of interviewing chronic pain patients on a regular basis from 1980 to 1982. Each patient was asked the following question: "What is your pain like at this moment?" Often the patients would start to explain their pain and/or talk about past painful events instead of talking about the nature of their pain as it was taking place in the moments of the interview. With repeated questioning and focusing on the experience itself, patients would usually say things like "It hurts!," "It's burning," "It feels like someone stuck a hot poker in my back!," "I'm miserable." Further precise qualitative characterization was derived by giving them the McGill pain questionnaire that provided several alternative words to describe sensory qualities of their pain. The Medical College of Virginia pain questionnaire was also developed and based on visual analog rating scales of pain sensation intensity, pain unpleasantness, cognitive meanings, and pain-related extended emotions (see note 1; see also Harkins et al., 1989; Price et al., 1983; Wade et al., 1992; 1996; 2011). It was used to characterize and quantify different dimensions of pain. Administration of both the McGill and MCV pain questionnaires to large groups of pain patients helped establish that vastly different chronic pains all had (1) unique "pain-like" sensory qualities, (2) meanings of intrusion and/or threat, and (3) related feelings of unpleasantness and/or other negative emotions (Price et al., 1987; Harkins et al., 1989; Melzack and Torgerson, 1971). These observations extended those made in earlier studies of the twentieth century and support our proposed definition.

Despite enormous diversity in disease conditions and types of pain, the three factors just listed were found to be present in multiple types of clinical pain, including different categories of musculoskeletal pain, neuropathic pain, cancer pain, and labor pain (Harkins et al., 1989; Price, 1988; 1999; 2000; Price et al., 1987). Results from large samples of different kinds of pain patients at both MCV and the University of Florida have since been used to characterize the common factors in pain and their functional interrelationships (Harkins, Price, and Braith, 1989; Price, 1999; Riley et al., 2000; 2002; Wade et al., 1992; 1996; 2011).

Although the definition we have provided is similar to the IASP definition, we think there are critical differences and additions. First, an *association* with tissue damage is replaced with the observation that the sensations are *like* those which occur during tissue damage or during stimulation that would result in tissue damage if it were maintained over time. Thus, if someone reports their sensory experience as burning, aching, pricking, or stinging, these unique sensory qualities are *like* those known to occur when nociceptive stimuli (stimuli that cause tissue damage) are applied to tissue. This is a statement of similarity rather than association, and these sensory qualities can occur without any tissue damage whatsoever and without an association with tissue damage in anyone's experience. However, such an association certainly can and often does occur.

The sense of intrusion and/or threat stems partly from the observation that the sensory qualities themselves dispose a sense of intrusion or assault upon the body. The features of second pain serve as a prime example. With repeated stimulation, second pain temporally summates, spreads spatially, and becomes arousing. Most critically, the sensory qualities (burning, aching, and dull) are like those which occur during tissue damage. Thus, the sense of intrusiveness and threat is fostered by sensory qualities in various ways. Pain can be experienced as *constrictive* pressure, as implied by words such as "pinching," "pressing," "cramping," or "crushing." It can also be experienced as *punctuate pressure,* as described by words such as "pricking," " boring," or "stabbing" or as *intense thermal sensation*, verbalized as "burning," "scalding," or "searing" (Melzack and Torgerson, 1971). Sometimes patients used metaphorical words, describing their pain *as if* their skin was being stabbed or burned. The intrusive and threatening qualities relate to the meaning that something is happening to or within the body in such as way as to evoke harm. However, we need to carefully point out that this experience of intrusion/threat isn't necessarily that of *physical* harm. Although it can and often does relate to physical harm, it can also be just a sense of being "taken over" or overwhelmed by the sensation and by the attention it commands. For example, some pain patients with nerve-injury pain (i.e., some forms of neuropathic pain) know that the burning sensations in their skin are *not* related to physical harm or impending physical harm. Yet they still have pain. They know that burning sensations do not come from anything hot being placed on their skin because their burning sensations are evoked by touch and sometimes even when nothing is contacting their skin. In addition, years of burning sensations and being told that the cause is from abnormally functioning nerves support their lack of experienced association of "burning" with damaged skin. Their sense of intrusion or threat is about the threat to their state of being and the intrusion into their consciousness. Pain always involves a meaning of *threat or intrusion of the self* that is directed toward one's body, well-being, sense of psychological stability, or all of these aspects.

If the sensory qualities themselves dispose one to a sense of intrusion/ threat, one might question whether pain-like sensory qualities and the sense of intrusion/threat are separate factors. We think they are separate for two reasons. First, the sense of intrusion or threat can be based on more than just the sensory qualities of pain. Pain occurs within a psychosocial and physical context and is influenced by several factors within experience. For example, a backache is likely to be experienced as less intrusive and threatening when someone is sitting in their living room as compared to when they are trying to work. Parallel influences from contextual and psychosocial factors abound in pain experience (see figure 7.1). Thus, although pain-like sensory qualities may dispose one to a sense of intrusion, this meaning can be strongly combined with the experienced context of the pain. The second reason is that sensory qualities integral to pain

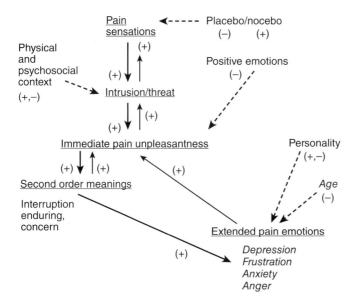

Figure 7.1
A schematic used to illustrate interactions between the basic dimensions of pain, meanings of pain, and extrinsic factors (dashed arrows) that moderate the intensities of these dimensions of experience. Inhibitory and facilitatory influences are represented by + and −, respectively.

can occur without any sense of intrusion or threat whatsoever under at least some circumstances. For example, some people like to eat hot, spicy foods. The food often contains capsaicin, a chemical known to stimulate oral nociceptors (receptors that respond to tissue damaging stimuli) in the mouth. A low concentration of capsaicin does not actually cause tissue damage. It just chemically stimulates oral nociceptors. This agent produces a burning sensation that is combined with other flavors in the food. The burning sensation is experienced as intrusive or threatening by some people and not by others, presumably corresponding to approximately the same people who find this experience painful and not painful, respectively. This means that the sensory qualities that normally occur during pain are necessary but not sufficient for pain and that there is often more to pain-related intrusion/threat than sensory qualities. However, one could argue that when burning sensations reach a high enough level, even people who like hot spicy foods would find the burning sensations intrusive or threatening and therefore painful. Perhaps this is the reason why some American Thai restaurants provide alternatives of mild, medium, American hot, and Thai hot on their menus.

Finally, the meaning of intrusion/threat is closely related to the feeling of unpleasantness or disturbance, sometimes accompanied by some other negative emotion. The inclusion of this alternative, "and other possible negative emotion(s)," helps to mitigate the concerns of Melzack and Wall, who criticized the IASP definition for not including negative feelings that are often integral to pain (despair, anxiety, annoyance, etc.). Our revised definition, with its phrase "unpleasantness and other possible negative emotion(s)," accommodates the observation that in addition to the simple feelings of unpleasantness or disturbance, pain can include both immediate and extended emotional feelings, such as depression, anxiety, or anger. Is pain-related unpleasantness the very same thing as intrusion/threat? The meaning of intrusion/threat reflects a primitive meaning of pain that is partly built into the immediate sensory experience. The feeling of unpleasantness or disturbance reflects the felt sense of that meaning (Gendlin, 1962; Price, 1999), and both the meaning of threat and its accompanying feeling can be enhanced or diminished by physical and psychosocial context (see figure 7.1).

The immediate unpleasantness or disturbance of pain is often accompanied by a present desire to reduce or terminate it and a level of expectation that it can or will be reduced, as is evident in several studies of both experimental and clinical pain (Chung et al., 2007; Price, 1999; Vase et al., 2003; 2005; Price et al., 1987; Rainville, Bao, and Chetrien, 2005). If this is the case, then an emotional feeling is present, as specified by the emotion model discussed in chapter 5. The next time you have an acute pain episode, notice whether it contains an implicit or explicit desire and/or an expectation, factors that are essential for some types of emotional feelings, such as anxiety or frustration. Thus, given that most of the chronic pain patients who presented at the MCV pain center had high desires for pain reduction as well as uncertain to unlikely expectations of having significant pain reduction, one would expect them to have pain-related emotional feelings of depression, anxiety, and frustration, consistent with the emotion model discussed in previous chapters. These emotional feelings relate to desires and expectations of terminating or reducing them, the fundamental factors within at least some human emotions (see chapters 3–6). The meaning of intrusion/threat, desire for its termination, expectations, and consequent emotional feelings would be closely related but separate variables. Pain-related emotional feelings are often the bottom line of pain, especially if pain persists over time. We propose that unique sensory qualities, a sense of intrusion/threat, and pain-related unpleasantness/disturbance are each necessary and, taken together, sufficient for pain, as reflected in our definition. This proposal extends a long-held consensus that pain is multidimensional, containing sensory, cognitive-evaluative, and affective dimensions (Melzack and Casey, 1968), yet it casts these dimensions in more experientially recognizable terms.

7.4.6   Do People Implicitly Use This Definition When They Use the Word "Pain"?

The definition we have provided is inclusive of three factors, yet not everyone uses the word "pain" to reflect all three of them—not everyone implicitly defines pain in the same way. We have noticed that some people use only the first factor to denote pain, as when they say "My leg is painful and aches, but it doesn't bother me." Others use the word "pain" to denote all three factors. For the purposes of experimental research and clinical treatment of pain, we think the three-factor definition is more experientially accurate and much more useful. Both pain researchers and people whose pain is being investigated need to have a common understanding and definition of pain, and all dimensions of pain, including its affective dimension, need to be studied. Similarly, the inclusive definition is by far more useful in treating pain patients because the emotional dimensions of their pain constitute a major proportion of their problems with pain.

Using the quantitative stage of the experiential method, we have found that several psychological factors cause people to rate sensory and affective dimensions very differently under at least some circumstances. Thus, the functional relationships between these dimensions have been tested in several studies to be discussed.

7.5   Characteristics of Pain-Related Emotions

7.5.1   Immediate Pain Unpleasantness

The stage of immediate unpleasantness of pain is about the meaning of pain as it relates to what is taking place in the present and is sustained by what Damasio refers to as "core consciousness" (Damasio, 1994; 1999). Core consciousness can be thought of as the moment-by-moment awareness of the state of the body and self and the perceptual aspects of what it taking place in the present. The link between immediate pain unpleasantness and core consciousness is evident when one directly experiences the distress, intrusion, and threat that occur in the present (see figure 7.1). Both unique pain-like sensations and meanings related to one's present context can make separate contributions to immediate pain unpleasantness, as shown by studies to be described.

7.5.2   Multisensory Contributions to Immediate Pain Unpleasantness

Certainly, the sensory qualities associated with pain dispose us to experience them as unpleasant under most circumstances. Thus, similar to nausea, intense thirst, or intense hunger, nociceptive sensations are usually closely linked to the immediate unpleasantness of pain. However, the immediate unpleasantness of pain sometimes includes additional sensory components that are part of a more integrated experience. Consider the following hypothetical example of being suddenly stung by an insect such as a bee. This unpleasant experience is accompanied by abrupt visual, auditory, and somatosensory attention to the bee. The stinging nociceptive sensation is only part of what is threatening. Seeing and hearing the bee at the same time only make the experience more threatening and fearful. This is actually an example of multisensory integration, as described in chapter 2. The stinging sensation, the arousal, and the feelings of one's own autonomic and somatomotor responses all culminate in an experience of sudden intense threat, intrusion, and fear. Memory of past consequences of bee stings can also add to this experience. One can easily appreciate that a bee sting would be even more emotionally disturbing if one remembered one's previous allergic reaction to a sting.

This example serves to illustrate that emotional feelings that are a part of pain experience are derived from meanings and that these meanings are based not only on the physical sensations of pain but on the contexts in which they occur. Part of the context is the integration of different sense modalities, as in the case of the bee sting. Other contextual factors, including psychosocial interactions, can lead to the association of pain sensations with present or near future consequences as a result of one's immediate situation. In either case, the affective dimension of pain is integrally related to the cognitive-evaluative dimension of pain and is not separate from it. Cognitive-evaluation is *an integral component* of the affective-motivational dimension of pain.

7.5.3 How Do Pain Sensation and Immediate Pain Unpleasantness Interact?

Given our three-factor definition of pain, *functional* hypotheses pertaining to how these pain-related factors interact can be tested in studies that use psychophysical scaling methods and participants unfamiliar with the study hypotheses. Testing functional hypotheses is an integral part of the experiential method (as discussed in chapters 2–6) and psychology in general. Numerous studies support the view that the sensory and immediate affective dimensions of pain are separate and unique, even though they are often closely associated (Price, 1999; 2000). Two related experiments clearly illustrate this view and help establish the direction of causation between the two dimensions (Rainville et al., 1999). Both experiments were part of a hypnosis study in which pain was induced in subjects by immersing their left hands in a moderately painful water bath heated to 47° C (about 5 on a 10-point scale). In the first experiment, hypnotic suggestions were alternately given to enhance or decrease pain unpleasantness *without* changing pain sensation intensity. In the second, the hypnotic suggestions were targeted specifically toward enhancing or decreasing pain sensation intensity and nothing whatsoever was stated about pain unpleasantness.

Pain unpleasantness, but not pain sensation intensity ratings, were changed in the directions suggested in the first experiment, a result that was not too surprising (see figure 7.2, top graph). However, *both* pain sensation intensity and pain unpleasantness ratings changed in parallel in the second experiment despite the fact that the suggestions did not mention pain unpleasantness at all (see figure 7.2, bottom graph). Pain unpleasantness decreased and increased passively as a consequence of alternations between reduced and increased pain sensation intensity. This study helps to establish that pain sensation is more of an immediate cause of pain unpleasantness than is the latter a cause of pain sensation. Thus, there is

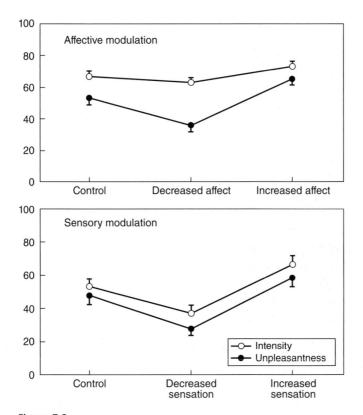

Figure 7.2
Mean pain intensity (open circles) and pain unpleasantness (closed circles) ratings in two hypnosis–pain experiments. The top graph shows selective effects of suggestions targeted toward pain unpleasantness. A large decrease in pain unpleasantness occurred with no significant changes in pain sensation intensity. The bottom graph shows parallel changes in both pain sensation and pain unpleasantness dimensions despite the fact that hypnotic suggestions were given only for changing the intensity of pain sensations. (Adapted from Rainville and Price, 2003.)

a sequential or serial relationship between the sensation of pain and its associated unpleasantness, as shown in figure 7.1. Other psychophysical experiments and studies of pain patients also support a serial relationship between pain sensation intensity and pain unpleasantness (Price, 1999; 2000; Price, Harkins, and Baker, 1987). At the same time, the first experiment showing selective effects on unpleasantness also suggests parallel influences on pain unpleasantness (see figure 7.2, top graph). If pain unpleasantness can be selectively altered, pain sensation cannot be the exclusive cause of pain-related unpleasantness. In clinical contexts, parallel influences appear quite frequently because patients' emotional responses are often not just about the pain but also about the physical and social implications of having the pain. These parallel influences, which shape the meaning of the pain, are represented in the schematic of figure 7.1. These kinds of influences can be illustrated by a study in which different types of pain patients were studied, patients with cancer pain and women who were in labor. This study hypothesized that the ratio of unpleasantness ratings to pain sensation intensity ratings would be higher in cancer patients, whose pain is likely to be associated with a serious threat to health or life, in comparison to labor pain patients, whose pain is very intense but likely to be less threatening (Price, Harkins, and Baker, 1987). A corollary hypothesis was that women in labor who focus mainly on the birth of their child would have lower ratings of pain unpleasantness than women who focus mainly on pain or on avoiding pain.

Labor pain patients and cancer pain patients used visual analog scales (VASs) to rate their levels of pain sensation intensity and degree of unpleasantness that occurred at different times during their clinical condition. Cancer pain patients were distinguished by the fact that their VAS unpleasantness ratings were higher than their VAS sensory ratings whereas the reverse was true for labor pain patients, as shown in figure 7.3. Furthermore, significant differences in pain VAS-unpleasantness ratings were observed among labor pain patients as a function of whether the patient focused primarily on pain or avoiding pain (avoidance goal) as compared to focusing on having the baby (approach goal). Patients who focused primarily on having the baby rated their experienced magnitude of pain unpleasantness as approximately one-half that of patients that focused primarily on pain or avoiding pain. This difference occurred for each stage of labor. In contrast, no significant differences in mean VAS pain sensation intensity ratings occurred between these two groups of patients at any stage of labor. For example, average pain sensation intensity ratings were nearly identical across transition and pushing stages (see figure 7.3).

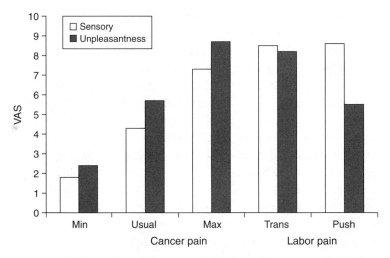

Figure 7.3
Average sensory (white bars) and unpleasantness (Unpleas; gray bars) ratings for
cancer pain patients (Min = lowest pain, Usual pain, and Max = maximum pain)
during the preceding week. Unpleasantness ratings were significantly higher than
sensory ratings at usual and maximum intensity ($p < .01$). Unpleasantness ratings
of labor pain patients were significantly lower than sensory ratings during the transition (Trans; $p < .05$) and pushing (Push; $p < .001$) stages of labor. VAS, visual analog
scale. (Adapted from data from Price, Harkins, and Baker, 1987; Price 1999.)

The combination of all these results indicates that someone's goals (e.g.,
having the baby/avoiding pain), desires, and expectations about outcomes
can strongly influence unpleasant feelings associated with different clinical
pain conditions. The influence of these factors is most apparent when
divergent psychological orientations exist *within* a clinical pain condition.
Thus, the unpleasantness of cancer pain was enhanced by meanings that
extended beyond that provided by the sensory qualities, including thoughts
and images about the tumor location and the future implications of having
this pain and source of pain. In contrast, labor pain often has an immediate implication that a baby is being born. The positive emotional consequences of this implication may offset, to some degree, the unpleasantness
of labor pain. This interpretation is further supported by the much greater
degree of labor pain unpleasantness among women who mainly focused
on avoiding pain (an avoidance goal) as compared to those who focused
on the birth of the baby (an approach goal). As noted above, unpleasantness ratings of the latter were approximately half that of the former. Part
of what constitutes pain unpleasantness is the *immediate implication* of the

pain condition. Results obtained in studies of experimental and clinical pain demonstrate that cognitive-evaluative factors can selectively and sometimes powerfully modify the immediate unpleasantness of pain.

7.5.4 Extended Suffering: Pain-Related Emotions Based on Reflection/ Rumination

Both empirical studies of experiential factors of pain and consideration of the experience of pain itself indicate that there can be two stages of pain-related feelings distinguished by the time frame over which cognitive appraisals are directed (Price, 2000; Wade et al., 1996). These stages and their interrelationships are illustrated schematically in figure 7.1. The first, discussed already, is the *immediate unpleasant or disturbing feelings* that are often closely linked with the intensity of the painful sensation and its accompanying arousal. The next stage is more cognitively mediated and is based on more elaborate reflection related to that which one remembers or imagines. These involve meanings directed toward the longer term implications of having pain. These meanings are related to perception of how pain has or will interfere with different aspects of one's life, reflection on how difficult it is or has been to endure the pain over time, and concern for the future consequences of having pain (see figure 7.1). Persistent pain can be experienced as a serious threat to one's freedom, the significance of one's life, and ultimately one's self-esteem (Bakan, 1967; 1968; Buytendyck, 1961). Whereas the *immediate unpleasantness and disturbance* is based on the present, pain-related extended emotions are based on the past and consideration of the future. Thus, just as one may be immediately fearful, distressed, or annoyed about presently experiencing the intrusive sensations of pain, one can also feel anxious or depressed about the long-term implications. Pain is often experienced as an immediate threat not only to one's body, comfort, or activity but also to one's well-being and life in general. It is, then, the meanings of how pain influences one's life activities and future that fuel much of the stage of pain-related extended emotions, a stage that may be thought of as suffering. This extended stage of pain-related emotions is related to Damasio's concept of "extended consciousness" (Damasio, 1994; 1999). It is largely autobiographical and is concerned with memories and reflections that sustain the identity of the individual, one that includes a sense of one's history and self. It is not a necessary part of pain because pain can occur without secondary appraisals, as in the case of some brief laboratory pains. The distinction between immediate and extended emotion also applies to other situations that do not involve physical pain. Extended meanings of

The museum of existential despair

Figure 7.4

loneliness, emptiness, helplessness, and meaninglessness can be experienced in association with any chronic debilitating condition, including chronic pain (see figure 7.4).

7.5.5 Other Versions of Pain-Related Suffering

David Morris (1994) discusses the need to recognize pain-related meanings among pain patients and has elaborated on the ways that culture, attitudes, and setting affect these meanings. Pain patients bring entire constellations of meaning with them when seeking treatments for pain. He gives a compelling example of a conversation that he had with a chronic pain patient that illustrates extended pain-related emotions:

She told me that the high point of her life was playing the organ for her church choir. She lived for the twice-a-week practices and Sunday performances. Now, with pain immobilizing her elbow, she could no longer manage the keyboard. Her days held nothing that she looked forward to. The constant aching had robbed her of any hope. Life seemed empty of everything except pain. When I asked her if she had explained this to the staff of the clinic, she replied that they had not asked. Her medical history, as one might expect, read exactly like the history of an elbow. (Morris, 1994, p. 275)

Two points can be made about this narrative. The first is that different stages and dimensions of pain-related suffering and their interactions are illustrated, albeit implicitly, in this example. The statement "The constant aching had robbed her of any hope" illustrates how the qualities and intensity of pain sensation and immediate pain unpleasantness lead directly to a felt sense of interruption and implications for future interruption. Pain had robbed her of life's meaning. The second point is that the patient's medical history contains virtually nothing about this patient's lived meanings that undoubtedly contributed a lot to her suffering. Although the particulars are likely to differ radically across chronic pain patients, it is likely that they experience at least a partial commonality of meanings. If that is true, then it should be possible to assess their presence and perhaps even measure their magnitudes. A scientific analysis of meanings in studies of pain and suffering would be helpful in this regard.

Based on earlier work by Buytendyck (1961; Bakan, 1968) and later empirical work (Price, 1999; 2002), we propose that the stage of pain-related extended emotions is based on three meanings. The first is that the painful condition has and will continue to *interrupt* one's ability to live, such as one's ability to function or to live a meaningful life. The second is that the painful condition and its accompanying domination of consciousness are a *burden that one is enduring over a long time*. Finally, the condition of persistent pain may mean that *something permanently harmful might happen or has happened* (see figure 7.1).

The meaning of intrusion during immediate pain unpleasantness and the meanings of life interruption, enduring, and concern for the future in the stage of extended pain-related emotions are directed toward the painful sensations, the context in which they occur, and the implications of avoiding harm. Each of latter three meanings is easily related to desires and expectations about avoiding or reducing the interruption, burden, or future negative consequences. Numerous contextual factors that relate to information about the nature of the painful condition and about potential means of reducing it and its consequences converge to determine one's level of expectation that pain and its consequences will be reduced. As such, extended emotional feelings associated with pain may be determined by desires and expectations in the same way that some human emotions are determined by these two factors (Price et al., 1985). High desires accompanied by very low expectations can attend emotional feelings of frustra-tion or depression whereas uncertain expectations can attend emotional feelings of anxiety, as was discussed in chapter 5.

In addition to the three meanings just discussed, more complex emo-tions can evolve as well. Thus, anger can attend the sense of unfairness of chronic pain. Guilt or remorse can attend patients' experiences of impaired relationships that have resulted from chronic pain. Despair, helplessness, loneliness, and emptiness can attend the felt impoverishment of one's life and separation from significant others (see figure 7.4). Finally, even the loss of meaning can itself constitute a meaning, as shown by Morris's conversation with a chronic pain patient given above. Despite this com-plexity and diversity, the factors of goal, desire, and expectation codeter-mine the intensity and nature of many types of emotions that are integral to the experience of both acute and persistent pain. The following discus-sion provides empirical support for different types of extended pain-related emotions.

7.5.6   Testing the Stage of Pain-Related Suffering

This stage of pain processing has been studied by administering a VAS for each of five pain related negative emotions—depression, anxiety, frustra-tion, anger, and fear—and for three meanings that are likely to be main contributors to these emotions—interruption of life activities, difficulty of enduring, and concern for future consequences (Bush et al., 1993; Harkins et al., 1989; Wade et al., 1990; 1992; 1996; 2011). It was critical for the patients to understand that these emotions and meanings were in relation-ship to their chronic pain. Thus, a question about anxiety, for example, was framed in the following way: "In relationship to your pain, how anxious have you felt over the past week?" The combined ratings of these five emotions in combination with ratings of interruption, difficulty of enduring, and concern for future have been shown to represent a psycho-logical stage that is unique and separate from that of immediate pain unpleasantness. The evidence for this separately measurable stage consists of two types of studies: (1) those which test the relationships between the psychological stages of pain processing and (2) those which demonstrate selective effects of personality traits and demographic factors on the stage of pain-related emotions (i.e., suffering). The first uses a form of path analysis (i.e., structural equation modeling) to test the functional interac-tions between the stages of pain (Lackner, Jaccard, and Blanchard, 2005; Riley et al., 2000; 2002; Wade et al., 1996; 2011). The second type of study establishes the stage of pain-related emotions to be unique and separate from immediate pain unpleasantness because it demonstrates a selective effect of personality trait or psychosocial factor on this later stage (Harkins, Price, and Braith, 1989; Riley et al., 2000; 2002; Wade et al., 1992). The reasoning behind this approach is similar to that used to demonstrate that pain unpleasantness to be unique and separate from that of pain sensation intensity as when some types of hypnotic suggestions alter the unpleasantness of pain without changing the strength of the pain sensation (see figure 7.2).

Effects of Personality Traits

Similar to the selective effects of some types of contextual factors and hypnotic suggestions on pain unpleasantness, personality traits and some demographic characteristics such as age can selectively and powerfully influence pain-related suffering. Two separate studies have shown that personality traits exert their largest effects on extended pain-related emotions or suffering. One type of personality trait that disposes people to suffer during pain is neuroticism. Most of us know someone who can massage a small disappointment into a catastrophe and who usually seems to find the most maladaptive response to a personal problem. Both Eysenk and Eysenk (19675) and Costa and McCrae (1985) have established neuroticism to be a personality trait characterized by a strong disposition to engage in negative emotions and maladaptive behaviors. Neuroticism is also closely related to catastrophizing, a disposition to ruminate on the pain, exaggerate its threat, and perceive oneself as hopeless (Wade et al., 2011). Two studies of chronic pain patients explored the effect of neuroticism on pain sensation intensity, the immediate unpleasantness stage, and extended pain-related emotions (i.e., suffering). Both studies found that patients with high neuroticism did not rate the sensory intensity or the unpleasantness of their clinical pain differently than patients with low levels of neuroticism, yet both studies found that high neuroticism patients had much higher levels of pain-related extended emotions such as depression, anxiety, frustration, and anger (Harkins et al., 1989; Wade et al., 1992) as rated on scales of the MCV pain questionnaire. Selective effects of race and sex on extended pain-related emotions also have been found (Riley et al., 2000; Riley et al., 2002).

Effects of Age

Using a similar approach, the extent to which age influences the magnitude of the various stages of pain processing was examined in 1,712 chronic pain patients (Riley et al., 2000). Similar to personality traits, no overall

effects of age were evident for pain sensation ratings or immediate unpleasantness ratings of chronic pain. However, age had large (greater than 1.5
VAS units) and selective effects on the extended pain-related emotions and
illness behavior, with older adults (older than sixty-five years old) manifest-
ing lower mean ratings of negative emotional feelings as compared to
younger patients. Older pain patients had considerably lower ratings of
pain-related anxiety, frustration, and anger and significantly lower com-
posite ratings of the five pain-related emotional feelings. Why do older
people have selectively lower levels of suffering in proportion to the intensity and immediate unpleasantness of pain? We found that they had much
lower levels of concern for future consequences in relationship to their
pain and somewhat lower levels of experienced interruptions of their lives
(Riley et al., 2000). Lower extended affect in older patients may be related
to lower lifestyle disruption. For example, older pain patients would less
likely be dealing with concerns such as the interaction of pain with their
employment, their children's college tuition, or other midlife issues.

The selective impact of neuroticism and age on extended emotions of
chronic pain (suffering) further validates the sequential model of pain
processing and reinforces the uniqueness of this later stage of pain-related
emotions.

Can Extended Pain-Related Emotions Feed Back upon and Influence Earlier Stages?

The observation that neuroticism enhances (Harkins, Price, and Braith,
1989; Wade et al., 1992) and age reduces (Riley et al., 2000) pain-related
suffering without changing the sensory intensity or immediate unpleasantness of pain is similar in principle to the observation that pain sensation
intensity maintains and is more of a cause of pain-related unpleasantness
than vice versa. However, can changes in pain-related emotions result in
changes in pain unpleasantness or pain sensation? In other words, are
there recursive effects across these stages of pain? To test this possibility,
Rainville and his colleagues alternately enhanced and decreased pain-
related emotions such as depression, anxiety, anger, and sadness by using
hypnotic suggestions that targeted these emotions (Rainville et al., 2005).
Changes in these extended pain-related emotions were accompanied by
corresponding small changes in ratings of immediate pain unpleasantness
but not ratings of pain sensation. Thus, there appear to be some recursive
effects between pain-related suffering and immediate pain unpleasantness.
The recursive effects are smaller than the effects in the other direction,
as represented in the schematic of figure 7.1. Thus, selective changes in

suffering would have weaker effects on earlier stages of pain processing whereas changes in magnitudes of pain sensations would more potently affect all subsequent stages.

7.6 Overview of Neural Processing of Pain: Parallels to the Stage Model

The sequential model of sensory intensity–unpleasantness–suffering has since been replicated in several studies using large samples of pain patients (Lackner et al., 2005; Riley et al., 2000; 2002; Wade et al., 1996; 2011). This model provides a psychological framework that can be discussed in relation to ascending pathways and brain circuits, as well as to mechanisms by which pain can be modified. Ideally, the neuroscience of pain-related ascending pathways and brain circuitry should further explain psychological models of pain, such as the serial/parallel processing model of figure 7.1. This approach reflects integration of first- and third-person data.

The stages of pain processing described in preceding sections are related to our present understanding of the neuroscience of pain. Underlying neural substrates of sensory as well as primary and extended emotional dimensions of pain include multiple ascending spinal pathways to the brain and both serial and parallel processing in the brain, illustrated schematically in figure 7.5 (Price, 2000). This neural complexity is understandable given the experiential complexity of pain. The neural representation of the experience of pain is likely to be related to a distributed network of brain structures that participate in the different dimensions of pain, such as arousal, identification of unique sensory qualities and their intensity, response selection, emotional feelings, and finally emotional expression and motivation. This network of brain circuitry is itself controlled by inhibitory and facilitatory interactions within the brain, as well as descending inhibitory and facilitatory control within brain-to-spinal cord pathways (Basbaum and Fields, 1978; Fields and Price, 1997; Price, 2000; Rainville et al., 1997). Thus, different aspects of pain can be enhanced or reduced by interactions that take place at any one of several points in the schematic shown in figure 7.5. A major pathway for pain modulation, known since the 1970s, is that of a brainstem-to-spinal cord pathway that utilizes endogenous opioids. Both intracortical and brain-to-spinal cord mechanisms will be discussed in chapter 9 in association with the topic of placebo analgesia. Explanation of pain processing in terms of multiple ascending pathways and a distributed brain network has gradually emerged in the last 20 years and has replaced the classic textbook view of one or two ascending pathways and single discrete "pain centers" in the brain.

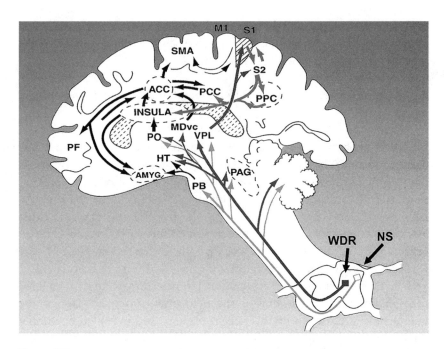

Figure 7.5
Schematic of ascending pathways, subcortical structures, and cerebral cortical structures involved in processing pain. PAG, periaqueductal gray of midbrain; PB, parabrachial nucleus of the dorsolateral pons; PO, ventromedial part of the posterior nuclear complex; MDvc, ventrocaudal part of the medial dorsal nucleus; VPL, ventroposterior lateral nucleus of the thalamus; ACC, anterior cingulate cortex, targeting various subcomponents (area 24 a, 24b, and dorsal ACC); PCC, posterior cingulate cortex; HT, hypothalamus; S-1 and S-2, first and second somatosensory cortical areas; PPC, posterior parietal complex; SMA, supplementary motor area; M1, motor cortex; AMYG, amygdala; PF, prefrontal cortex; WDR, wide response range; NS, nociceptive-specific neurons ascending to the brain from the spinal grey matter. (Adapted from Price, 1999, 2000.)

That multiple pathways and brain regions are required for pain is intimately related to the fact that pain is both a sensory phenomenon and an emotional state, and pain sensation may be a salient but not sole determinant of these emotions. Thus, consistent with modern views of the mechanisms of emotional feelings formulated by Damasio (1994; 1999), Arnold (1970), and Price et al. (1999; 2000), the emotional state that accompanies pain reflects a synthesis from several psychophysiological sources. These include brain activity related to pain sensation, arousal, and autonomic, neuroendocrine, and somatomotor responses, all in relationship to meanings of the pain and the context in which it occurs. The following discussions attempt to describe and explain these relationships.

7.6.1 Ascending Nervous System Pathways for Pain

The principal ascending pathways for pain originate in specialized receptors in body tissues, called nociceptors. These receptors are specialized to respond to stimuli to tissues that either cause damage or would cause damage if they were maintained for a sufficient length of time. Nociceptors are connected to primary afferent neuron axons that synapse onto neurons of the dorsal gray matter of the spinal cord shown at the bottom right in figure 7.5 (wide response range and nociceptive-specific neurons). There are different classes of primary nociceptive afferent neurons that supply different types of tissues, such as skin, muscle, joints, and viscera. Spinal cord neurons that receive primary nociceptive neuron input are at the origin of ascending pathways to the brain, and some of them have different roles in pain. The main somatosensory pathway is that of the spinothalamic tract that originates in the spinal cord and projects to a ventroposteriorlateral thalamic nucleus (VPL) and other thalamic nuclei (PO and MDvc in figure 7.5). VPL, in turn, projects to the somatosensory cortices (figure 7.5), whereas other thalamic nuclei project to limbic cortical areas and somatosensory cortices to a lesser extent. Both pathways to the somatosensory cortices and insular cortex (elongated dashed oval of figure 7.5) play roles in experiencing sensory qualities and intensity as well as feelings of unpleasantness or disturbance by reason of serial connections to brain areas involved in emotions. In addition to this major pathway, there are ascending spinal cord pathways that target areas of the medulla, midbrain (e.g., PB and PAG of figure 7.5), and hypothalamus (HT, figure 7.5). There also is a pathway that indirectly targets the amygdala by way of a synapse in the pons (PB of figure 7.5; Bernard and Besson, 1990). These various target structures are involved in pain because they participate in somatosensory processes, widespread cortical activation, and therefore arousal, body regulation (hypothalamus), and affective states that are initiated quickly. For example, the central nucleus of the amygdala has been strongly implicated in fear, emotional memory/behavior, and autonomic and somatomotor responses to threatening stimuli (Bernard and Besson, 1990). Various hypothalamic nuclei have also been implicated in some of these functions.

Based largely on their central targets, all of these pathways, including the somatosensory cortices, are very likely to participate in the emotional dimension of pain. The sensory dimension of pain is at least partly in series with and therefore is one of the causes of the emotional dimension. Both unique sensations and psychophysiological responses of arousal and autonomic activation contribute to the overall experience of pain, especially its immediate unpleasantness. Some (but by no means all) aspects of pain-related emotions may occur automatically as a result of direct input to cortical limbic areas such as the amygdala. Multisensory integration (discussed earlier and in chapter 2) and higher order cognitive functions that are associated with activity in frontal cortical areas contribute to extended pain-related emotions (i.e., suffering).

7.6.2 Brain Pathways and Regions Interrelating Sensory and Affective Dimensions of Pain

Once impulses in ascending spinal pathways reach different targets within the brain, both serial and parallel circuitry is activated (figure 7.5). The serial interconnections are established by the pathway to VPL and to somatosensory cortices that is anatomically interconnected with a ventrally directed corticolimbic pathway that integrates somatosensory input with other sensory modalities such as vision and audition and with learning and memory (Friedman et al., 1986). This pathway proceeds from primary and secondary somatosensory cortices to posterior parietal cortical areas and to the insular cortex and from the latter to the anterior cingulate cortex (ACC), an area involved in pain unpleasantness, attention, and motivation associated with pain (see figure 7.5). The ACC is, in turn, interconnected with subcortical limbic structures (e.g., amygdala, perirhinal cortex, and hippocampus), the prefrontal cortex, and the supplementary motor area. All of these structures are critical for pain-related emotions and for the different stages of pain-related emotions (Friedman et al., 1986; Price, 1999, 2000). The ACC is pivotal in this regard because it projects to limbic areas involved in primitive aspects of emotions, to areas involved in higher order meanings (prefrontal cortex), and finally to premotor areas involved in escape or avoidance (see figure 7.5). This serial network converges on the same limbic and subcortical structures that can also be directly accessed by other ascending spinal pathways. For example, as shown in figure 7.5, the amygdala receives input from both the ACC and an ascending spinal pathway. Dual pathways to the amygdala reflect parallel processing. This dual convergence may be related to a mechanism whereby multiple neural sources contribute to pain emotions. The contribution of the somatosensory areas to pain emotions occurs as a result of their influences on deeper limbic structures (insula, mid-ACC) and is consistent with the schematic of figure 7.1. The latter is based on experiential and neurological data and studies that use interviews and psychophysical methods. An example of the latter is the study illustrated in figure 7.2. Thus, pain unpleasantness was shown to be at least partly the result of pain sensation intensity. That the somatosensory cortices are involved in emotions, even complex ones, as well as somatic sensation is not surprising in view of a study by Adolphs et al. (2000). They showed that patients with damage to the somatosensory cortex are unable to recognize emotions that are expressed in photographs of people having different emotional expressions.

7.6.3 The Pivotal Role of the Anterior Cingulate Cortex in Pain Unpleasantness

As illustrated in figure 7.5, the ACC receives anatomical projections from several sources, including the insular cortex. ACC, in turn, is part of the brain's attentional and motivational network because it projects to prefrontal cortical areas involved in executive functions and to the supplementary motor area involved in response selection (Devinsky et al., 1995). Parts of the ACC are consistently activated during pain, and in fact the ACC is the most consistent brain region activated in brain imaging studies of pain (Casey and Bushnell, 2000). Brain imaging studies show that ACC is more directly involved in pain affect than in appreciating the sensory qualities of pain. Rainville and his colleagues (Rainville et al., 1997) conducted a neuroimaging study about the subjective qualities of pain sensation and pain unpleasantness. The design of this study was similar to that described earlier and used hypnotic manipulations to selectively enhance and then reduce pain unpleasantness *without* changing pain sensation intensity (e.g., similar to figure 7.2, top graph). As before, participants of this study rated pain sensation intensity and pain unpleasantness of moderately painful immersion of the left hand in a 47° C water bath. They found that suggestions for enhancement of unpleasantness increased magnitudes of both pain-unpleasantness ratings and neural activity in the ACC (area 24b) in comparison to the condition wherein suggestions for decreased unpleasantness were given (figure 7.6, top pair of images [plate 1]). Consistent with subjects' mean ratings of pain sensation intensity, neural activity in S-1 somatosensory cortex, were not statistically different across the two experimental conditions. These studies suggest that ACC may be more proximate to the production of pain unpleasantness than somatosensory cortical areas. However, the latter also contribute to pain-unpleasantness by virtue of their interconnections to insular cortex and hence ACC (see figure 7.5).

A second similarly designed study by Hofbauer et al. (2001) used hypnotic suggestions to modify the intensity of pain sensation. In this experiment, the suggestions were effective in producing parallel changes in ratings of pain sensation intensity and neural activity in S-1 somatosensory cortex, that is, increased and decreased activity in S-1 during higher and lower pain sensation intensity respectively (figure 7.6, bottom pair of images [plate 1]). It is important to recognize that the stimulus intensities were exactly the same across experimental conditions that produced different subjective magnitudes of unpleasantness or pain sensation. These experiments reflect a strategy designed to identify neural structures differentially involved in two separate dimensions of pain experience. It is necessarily simplistic because sensory and affective dimensions of pain cover broad and complex experiential territories.

7.6.4   The Role of the Insular Cortex in Dimensions of Pain

The insula is a large cortical area buried deep within left and right cerebral hemispheres and is surrounded by white matter. Hence the term insula means "island." Its role in pain is that of interfacing somatosensory input with brain circuitry involved in anticipation and feelings of threat and intrusion. It is thereby a link between pain-related sensations and emotional feelings (Koyama et al., 2005; Wiech et al., 2010). It is functionally divided into a posterior, mid-, and anterior regions. The posterior and midinsula appear directly related to both sensory and emotional dimensions. Electrical stimulation of sites within this region evokes pains experienced in specific body areas. The pains have "pain-like" sensory qualities (e.g., burning, stinging) and are unpleasant (Ostrowsky et al., 2002). The anterior insula, which is interconnected with the mid and posterior insula, is involved in both the direct experience and anticipation of pain and is highly influenced by contextual factors (Wiech et al., 2010). Brain imaging studies show that neural activity in the anterior and posterior insula increases not only as a function of stimulus intensity but also as a function

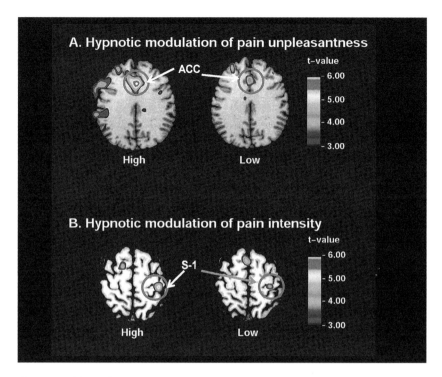

Figure 7.6 (plate 1)
The top pair of brain images shows results of a brain imaging study revealing selective modification of neural activity (measured by regional cerebral blood flow) in the anterior cingulate cortex (ACC) by hypnotic suggestions that targeted only pain unpleasantness (based on results from Rainville et al., 1997). Note the higher activity in the high pain unpleasantness condition (top left brain image, circled area) as compared to the low pain unpleasantness condition (top right brain image, circled area). In a second brain imaging experiment, activity within the S-1 somatosensory cortex was higher in the high pain sensation intensity condition (lower left image) as compared to the low pain sensation intensity condition (lower right image). (Based on results from Hofbauer et al., 2001.)

of *expected* pain (Koyama et al., 2005). Expected pain intensity influences not only how much neural activity occurs during anticipation of pain but also during the pain itself. Increased and decreased neural activity, in turn, predicts the intensity of pain. The anterior insula also critically influences whether or not someone labels his or her experience as pain, as shown by a study that combined psychophysics with brain imaging (Wiech et al., 2010). When laser stimuli were applied at intensities near pain threshold, instructions that induced a high degree of perceived threat resulted in a greater likelihood of labeling the experience as pain as compared to instructions that led to a low degree of perceived threat (Wiech et al., 2010). Anterior insula activity was significantly higher in the high-threat as compared to the low-threat condition. In addition, ACC activity and its functional connections with the anterior insula were enhanced in the high-threat condition. All of these results help clarify neural circuitry that serves the relationships between sensory qualities, meanings of intrusion/ threat, and unpleasant emotional feelings. They also provide neurophysiological support for our experiential definition of pain and show the extraordinary sensitivity of pain experience to contextual factors.

7.6.5   Insular–ACC–Prefrontal Cortical Connections and Their Relation to Extended Pain Emotions

Response priorities change over an extended period of time. Pain unpleasantness endured over time engages prefrontal cortical areas involved in reflection and rumination over the future implications of a persistent pain condition. Both the insula and ACC may serve this function by coordinating somatosensory features of pain with prefrontal cerebral mechanisms involved in attaching significance and long-term implications to pain, a function associated with pain-related emotions (Devinsky, Morrell, and Vogt, 1995; Price, 2000; Verne et al., 2003a). Thus, ACC may be a region that coordinates inputs from parietal areas involved in perception of bodily threat with frontal cortical areas involved in plans and response priorities for pain-related behavior. Both functions would help explain observations on patients with prefrontal lobotomy and patients with pain asymbolia as a result of insular cortical lesions. The former have deficits in spontaneous concern or rumination about their pain but can experience the immediate threat of pain once it is brought to their attention (Foltz and White, 1962; Hardy, Wolff, and Goodell, 1952). In contrast, asymbolia patients appear incapable of perceiving the threat of nociceptive stimuli under any circumstances (Berthier, Starkstein, and Leiquarda, 1988; Weinstein, Kahn, and Slate, 1955). The role of medial prefrontal cortical areas in secondary pain emotions is also supported by a brain imaging study of pain in irritable bowel syndrome (IBS) patients (Verne et al., 2003a). These patients' rated both their clinical as well as experimentally induced (heat pain) pain. In comparison to age- and sex-matched volunteers who did not have IBS, patients with IBS gave higher ratings of pain sensation intensity and pain unpleasantness and much higher ratings of extended pain-related emotions. These differences were, respectively, associated with higher levels of brain activity in the somatosensory cortex (associated with pain sensation intensity), ACC (associated with unpleasantness), and the medial prefrontal cortex (associated with extended pain emotions). For example, high medial prefrontal neural activity was found in the IBS patients who had high levels of pain-related anxiety, consistent with both the psychological model of figure 7.1 and the neural model of figure 7.5.

7.6.6 Decoupling Primary Pain Processing from "Suffering" in Zen Meditators

Some ancient Eastern texts help teach a form of Zen meditation that practices being present to current experience, somewhat like the approach taken in the experiential method. In addition, this form of meditation fosters a state of mind characterized by a shift away from rumination, reflection, interpretation, and other forms of cognitive evaluation (Bohdi, 2005). In comparison to nonmeditators, practitioners of Zen meditation had lower pain sensitivity and did not report typical increases in pain that occur just by attending to it in an ordinary way (Grant, Courtenmanche, and Rainville, 2011). However, when attending to it mindfully, without interpretation or judgment, they reported decreases in both the sensation intensity and unpleasantness of pain. A subsequent study showed neural correlates of some of the differences in pain processing between nonmeditators and meditators (Grant, Courtenmanche, and Rainville, 2011). Unlike control participants, who showed *increases* in prefrontal cortical activity during experimentally induced pain, meditators had *decreases* in the same prefrontal cortical areas. The functional coupling between prefrontal cortical areas and areas related to earlier stages of pain processing (insula and ACC) was also less in meditators. These differences further underscore the neural substrates that support the distinction between early (pain sensation intensity and unpleasantness) and extended stages of pain (i.e., suffering) and support a relatively unknown cognitive method of pain control. Another study of mindfulness meditation showed potent reductions in pain sensation intensity (57% reduction) and pain unpleasantness[2] (40%) evoked by noxious heat stimuli (Zeiden et al., 2011).

7.6.7 Relating Brain Activity to Multiple Dimensions of Pain

The strategies used in the brain imaging experiments described above not only clearly and essentially draw on the introspective reports of participants (e.g., psychophysical ratings) but also strongly suggest that adopting more refined experiential methods could only help here. In particular, an experiential perspective and method could help clarify, better describe, and expand the results of the specific experiments from which the results are obtained. For example, a more detailed account of experiences of Zen meditators could help clarify just how they instantiate pain reduction.

We can't just look to the environment for an adequate explanation. There is nothing about the stimulus in Rainville et al.'s (1997) and Hofbauer et al.'s (2001) brain imaging studies of hypnotic analgesia that allows one to predict changes in the emotional or sensory intensities of pain that were produced by the hypnotic suggestions. Sensory and emotional intensities of pain covary much more closely with impulse frequencies of neurons in the central nervous system than with the physical characteristics of stimuli. Given the high variability between the stimulus characteristics and the resulting subjective experiences, it is clear that the relationships between pain experience and neural activity can only be explored through careful analysis of *both* phenomenal experience and neural activity, including neural activity at different levels of the nervous system: receptors, spinal cord, brainstem, and cortical areas. It should by now be obvious that drawing on experiential methods is indispensable for such an exploration.

Parallels between experience and neural activity do not prove that the neural activity sufficient for a given subjective quality of pain exists within one specific brain region, such as the somatosensory cortical area in the case of pain intensity/sensory qualities or ACC area 24b in the case of pain unpleasantness. However, activity in these regions may be necessary for processing a dimension of pain under many circumstances. We can envision how knowledge of patterns of activity in these brain regions may eventually form at least part of a coherent explanation of how patterns of brain activity entail the existence of different types of pain.

7.7 Some Conclusions about Existential Meanings of Pain and a Strategy for the Future

Experiential studies show that sensations during pain are linked to a primitive meaning of intrusion and/or threat and are experienced as immediately unpleasant or disturbing. In some circumstances, such as enjoying spicy food, even this primitive meaning can be greatly attenuated to the point that the experience is not considered painful. However, if the experience of pain-like sensations and meanings of threat and/or intrusion have sufficient duration, the experience can lead to additional meanings of interruption, a concern for future consequences, and having to endure a burden over time. All of these meanings are focused on the pain itself. If individuals in chronic pain then shift their focus to their entire existence as a person, these meanings can in turn be linked to existential meanings: helplessness, loneliness, and being reduced to nothing by the pain (figure 7.4). For example, if pain patients feel that their life is interrupted, they can feel that they are getting nowhere and their life has become empty or nothing. Alternatively, they may feel that they are being cut off from significant relationships are therefore lonely, trapped, or helpless to deal with the interruptions. All of these meanings, including those which are immediate and those based on rumination and reflection, are associated with levels of desire and expectation, resulting in a range of emotions (depression, anxiety, frustration, despair, etc.). Some progress has been made in relating some of these experiential dimensions of pain to activity in neural pathways and regions of the brain.

Understanding pain and its mechanisms would be most optimally achieved by starting with observations of the experience of pain at the beginning rather than after the neuroscience. This view is compatible with Gallagher and Overgaard's (2005) idea that human neuroscience experiments, particularly those involving brain imaging, can be well served by "front-loaded phenomenology" wherein an experiential–phenomenological study precedes and informs the design and measures used in a neuroscience experiment. As we have seen, an optimum strategy is for the investigators to carefully notice what an experience of pain entails and then discover the common factors, or what phenomenologists call structural invariances. This strategy includes noticing one's own experience and others' reported experiences of pain. Definitional hypotheses and functional hypotheses, and for that matter, a working definition of pain, results from this method. Both definitional and functional hypotheses can then be tested in both laboratory and clinical settings, using direct scaling methods of psychophysics. Causal interactions between the dimensions of pain can then be examined from an experiential perspective. Thus, pain-related emotional feelings depend on both serial and parallel inputs, and there are two stages of pain-related emotion. Analysis of these two stages can potentially be integrated with neuroscience. This is more than an intellectual exercise. Understanding both psychological and neural mechanisms of pain are critical for treating pain and making pain much less of a health-care problem.

8 Second Pain: A Model for Explaining a Conscious Experience?

The previous chapter traced the history of studies wherein investigators used their own direct experiences to characterize the nature of "first" and "second" pain evoked by a single intense stimulus. The early studies were followed by a considerable number of psychophysical studies, including those conducted in combination with brain imaging (Staud et al., 2007, 2008). What makes "second pain" so interesting from the perspectives of both experiential science and neuroscience is that it has features that are very unique and somewhat unpredicted by the nature of physical stimuli or responses of peripheral receptors (connected to C axons). As discussed in chapter 7, a single intense stimulus often gives rise to impulse input from faster conducting A-delta axons followed by impulses from slow conducting C axons. The former and latter, respectively, evoke first and second pain. Second pain has burning, aching, or "dull" qualities, exhibits slow temporal summation with repeated stimuli (i.e., each "second pain" becomes stronger), and often outlasts a stimulus that evokes it. Similar to other forms of pain, it also spreads into body regions outside the area of the stimulus as the sensation becomes more intense. The combination of these characteristics makes second pain an experience that cannot be easily explained by the nature of the physical stimuli that give rise to it. It is better explained by studies of neurons, pathways, and interactions within the central nervous system. For these reasons, it is an interesting model for relating first-person experience to third-person neural mechanisms. Since features of second pain and its neural correlates have been studied for decades, this model may be one that serves as a useful example for explaining a conscious experience.

There are several historical reasons for choosing this model, which is the basis of this chapter. First, there is a long history of characterizing the experience of second pain, using both qualitative and quantitative observations (first-person data). Second, there is also a long history of characterizing the neural correlates and causes of second pain and its temporal summation (third-person data). As Chalmers (2004) has pointed out, a science of consciousness will articulate the systematic connections between first- and third-person data through refined analysis of their correlations and causes. The quality of explanation of second pain will depend on the quality of both first- and third-person observations, for which there is always room for improvement. Systematic principles which link first- and third-person data will also have to be discovered. A science of consciousness will not reduce first-person data to third-person data, as explained in chapter 1 and by Velmans (2009) and Chalmers (2004). Chalmers suggests that "we can expect systematic bridging principles to underlie and explain the covariation between third-person and first-person data. A theory of consciousness will ultimately include these principles." This chapter traces the evidence for the reasons why second pain and its temporal summation is experienced in a specific way. This explanation may support a general strategy that can be used to explain a type of conscious experience.

8.1 Mechanisms of Temporal Summation of Second Pain

Landau and Bishop's 1953 study of first and second pain (discussed in chapter 7) was followed up by several psychophysical and neuroscience studies starting in the 1970s and continuing to the present (Price, 1972; Price et al., 1977; Staud et al., 2001, 2004, 2005, 2007, 2008; Vierck et al., 1997). These studies used either a series of multiple electric shocks or, more commonly, a series of computer-driven heat pulses to the hand or foot to evoke first and second pain (see figure 8.1). Each stimulus in the series evoked first and second pain and had the same physical configuration throughout a train of shocks or heat pulses. In all of these studies, subjects' mean ratings of first pain did not increase in intensity throughout each series (Price et al., 1977, 1994). However, unlike the first pricking or sharp pain, the burning second pain progressively increased in mean intensity and duration throughout a series of shocks or heat pulses when the interstimulus interval was three seconds or less but not when it was longer. This temporal summation occurred in the absence of changes in the intensity and duration of the repeated shocks or heat pulses. Each stimulus had an identical duration and peak intensity (e.g., peak temperature was 51° C in the case of heat pulses). Temporal summation also was confirmed in our own direct experience. We found that second "burning" pain became stronger and more diffuse and unpleasant with repeated stimuli (Barrell

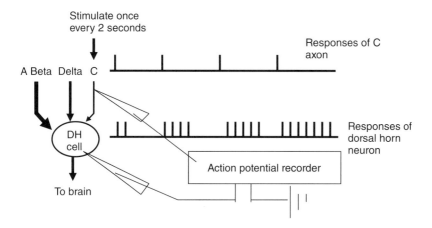

Figure 8.1
Schematic of how neurophysiology experiments have verified that slow temporal summation of C-fiber postsynaptic responses occur within the dorsal gray matter of the spinal cord dorsal horn. This schematic is based on a considerable number of similar experiments over the last forty-five years. Regardless of whether impulses are generated in C-fibers by electrical shocks or by heat pulses to the skin, temporal summation occurs in the second-order dorsal horn neurons and not in the stimulated peripheral receptors for pain. Temporal summation occurs in the second-order dorsal horn neurons (earliest level of central nervous system) and not in the stimulated peripheral receptors for pain. DH, dorsal horn.

and Price, 1975; Price, 1972). Moreover, second pain outlasted the series of stimuli that produced it, lingering several seconds beyond the last stimulus. If these results cannot be explained by progressive increases in stimulus intensity, what mechanisms can explain them?

Mechanisms underlying temporal summation of second pain must occur somewhere in the nervous system. But where? Based on numerous neurophysiology studies, it has long been known that when the same series of heat pulses or electrical shocks described above are applied to the skin, repetitive stimulation does not result in temporal summation of anything measured in the skin or even in the responses of peripheral receptors (Price, 1988; 1999; see figure 8.1). The results are quite different for the dorsal horn neurons of the spinal cord, on which both the axons of A and C nociceptive neurons make synaptic contact. Individual neurons in the spinal dorsal horn respond with a delayed response to stimulation of C-axons that are connected peripherally to nociceptors. This delayed response increases in magnitude with each successive stimulus to C-fibers,

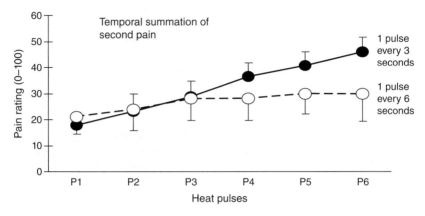

Figure 8.2
Temporal summation of second pain as a result of repeated heat pulses (P1 to P6) to the foot (Staud et al., 2007). A stimulus frequency of 0.33 and 0.17 Hz corresponds to a stimulus delivered once every three seconds and six seconds, respectively (see graph with filled circles and open circles, respectively). Note that temporal summation occurs with a 0.33 Hz but not 0.17 Hz stimulation frequency. This summation is similar to that of single dorsal horn neurons. (Adapted from Staud et al., 2007.)

as illustrated schematically in figure 8.1 (for original results, see Mendell and Wall, 1965; Price et al., 1977, 1978; Thompson and Woolf, 1990; Woolf and Thompson, 1991). Similar to the delayed responses of the dorsal horn neurons, second pain also increases progressively in magnitude but only if the interval between the stimuli are three seconds or less, as shown in figure 8.2. The combination of these studies, including those directed toward peripheral axons, dorsal horn neurons, and psychophysical responses of second pain, demonstrates that temporal summation of second pain can be partially explained by neural mechanisms within the dorsal horn of the spinal cord. What is fascinating about this demonstration is that the second pain experience correlates closely with responses that occur in the dorsal horn despite the absence of any progressive changes that take place in the stimulus, tissues, or receptors. These parallels between psychophysical responses and neural responses have been confirmed not only in the case of single neurons of the spinal cord but also in multiple areas of the brains of human participants who make pain ratings (Staud et al., 2007, 2008). Brain regions throughout the "pain matrix," including regions of the thalamus, somatosensory cortex, and regions of the brain that are more proximately related to the emotions of pain (e.g., anterior cingulate cortex; ACC), all display the phenomenon of temporal summation in response to repeated C-fiber stimulation. An example of the neural

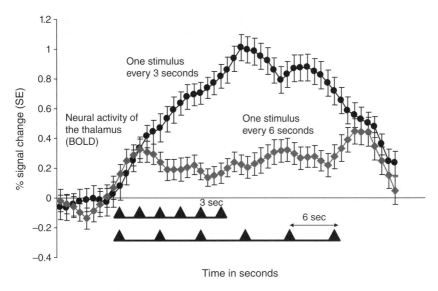

Figure 8.3

Temporal summation of neural activity (as measure by blood-oxygen-level depen-
dency; BOLD) within the posterior thalamus. Similar to the pain ratings of figure
8.2, temporal summation occurred with one stimulus every three seconds but not
with one stimulus every six seconds. The heat pulses were identical in form and
intensity across all series of heat pulses. (Adapted from Staud et al., 2007.)

responses associated with temporal summation of second pain is shown
in figure 8.3. These responses occurred within a pain-related area of the
thalamus (ventroposterior lateral nucleus) and were obtained from the
same participants who experienced temporal summation of second pain
(see pain ratings in figure 8.2). Similar to second pain, neural activity
increased linearly during the series of heat pulses, and it long outlasted the
series of pulses (figure 8.3). This area of the thalamus is part of a major
pathway that begins in the spinal cord and proceeds through the thalamus
to the somatosensory cortical area. This temporal pattern of thalamic
neural activity was very similar to that found in a widely distributed
network of brain regions that responded to repeated C-nociceptor stimulation (see figure 8.4). The brain regions shown in figure 8.4 are involved in
very diverse functions, yet these functions all relate to an integrated and
unified experience—a burning, diffuse, arousing, unpleasant pain that one
would like to terminate or avoid. Thus, brain areas that most proximately
represent sensory qualities (somatosensory cortices, insular cortex), emotional feelings (insular cortex, ACC), preparations to escape or withstand

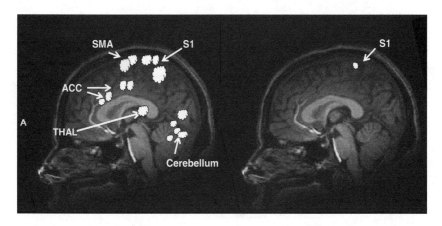

One heat pulse every 3 seconds   **One heat pulse every 6 seconds**

Figure 8.4
Areas of the human brain that showed temporal summation related to second pain: posterior thalamus (THAL), anterior cingulate cortex (ACC), supplementary motor area (SMA), first somatosensory cortex (S1), and cerebellum. Areas of significant elevations in neural activity are designated in white ($p < .001$). (Adapted from Staud et al., 2007.)

the pain (supplementary motor area and cerebellum), and higher order processing of meanings (frontal cortical areas) all show temporal summation in response to repeated C-fiber stimulation. Even areas involved in memory (temporal lobe) showed summation.

These observations suggest that the phenomenon of temporal summation applies to multiple aspects of the experience and behavior related to second pain. Experientially, the burning sensation of second pain becomes not only more intense but also more unpleasant (Price, 1972; Barrell and Price, 1977). Even extended pain-related emotions may become stronger with repeated C-fiber stimulation, given the summation found in prefrontal cortical areas (Staud et al., 2008). It also has been established that somatomotor and autonomic nervous system reflexes temporally summate in response to C-fiber stimulation (Price, 1972; 1988; 1999). Some evidence also suggests that the neural responses of at least some central nervous system structures just discussed are *causally* related to second pain summation. Electrical stimulation of axons originating from spinal nociceptive neurons induced burning pain sensations in human participants (Mayer et al., 1975) as did electrical stimulation of sites within pain-related regions of the thalamus (Lenz et al., 2004) and insular cortex (Ostrovsky et al.,

2002; see figures 8.4 and 8.5 for locations of these structures). The quality of "burning" is a salient characteristic of second pain.

Beyond temporal summation, other characteristics of pain evoked by C-nociceptor stimulation are that of spatial spread and referral. As this form of pain becomes more intense, it is often experienced as spreading into surrounding tissue and even into different types of tissue, termed referred pain. For example, painful angina (related to coronary disease or heart attack) is often referred to the inner part of the arm, and the area of this referred pain spreads as the pain becomes more intense. Again, except for the fact that nociceptors are being stimulated, these features cannot be explained by changes in the area of the stimulus because the stimulus itself is not necessarily spreading into surrounding or different tissues (such as the arm during angina). Instead, central neural activity spreads spatially as the magnitude of the peripheral impulse input from one site becomes stronger. Thus, central neural mechanisms help explain the spread of pain into areas not in direct contact with the stimulus. Not surprisingly, the first level in which the spread of neural activity occurs is the spinal cord dorsal horn (Coghill et al., 1991). Repeated heat stimulation causes a spread of dorsal horn neural activity into multiple segments of the spinal cord. When this happens, the perceived area of pain also radiates across wide areas of skin (Price et al., 1978).

Thus, temporal summation, painful aftersensations, spatial spread of pain, and referred pain are not predictable on the basis of physical characteristics of stimuli alone but can be explained by central nervous system mechanisms. Neural activity in widely distributed areas within the spinal cord and brain are the causes and correlates of different characteristics of second pain, characteristics partly identified using a first-person method. This explanation would not be possible without phenomenology and psychophysics. The latter includes self-reports of human participants who are not told about these phenomena beforehand and sometimes investigator–participants who directly confirm these phenomena in direct experience.

This account also has strong bearing on the issue of measurability of pain. If pain is not measurable because self-report of pain is untrustworthy, as some clinicians and scientists would claim, how would participants know to report temporal summation, aftersensations, and the spatial spread of pain, none of which are predictable or obvious prior to receiving the stimuli? And how would it turn out that these characteristics have the same information structure that can be found by recording from spinal cord neurons or recording activity within several areas of the brain? As we pointed out in chapter 2, even the individual variability in report of pain intensity can be accounted for by variability in brain responses and by genetic and environmental factors. When the same intensity of nociceptive stimulation is applied to a group of people, differences in ratings between individuals actually reflect differences in pain sensitivity more than the manner in which people use scales to rate pain (Coghill et al., 2003; Nielsen et al., 2005, 2007, 2009). This is not to say that people cannot sometimes lie or otherwise misrepresent their actual experiences when reporting pain, but one cannot easily make a prima facie case against pain ratings. Moreover, it is often difficult to disentangle biases and distortions from the pain itself because expectations and biases help shape the actual experience of pain. These modifying factors have associations with corresponding brain mechanisms, as discussed in chapter 9.

8.2   The Philosophical and Functional Implications of This Explanation of Second Pain

8.2.1   Ontological Identity?
The explanation just given relates to three questions. Is second pain the very same thing as neural activity (ontological identity) if neural correlates and causes of the characteristics of second pain are established? As pointed out by Velmans (2009) and our discussion of this general question in chapter 1, correlates and causes do not establish ontological identity but rather can be used against such a possibility. The properties of neural activities that correlate with second pain are not the same as those of second pain. Of course second pain and its related neural activity have a very similar information structure: They summate at the same frequency and to the same degree, outlast the stimuli, and spatially spread. However, this similar information structure is certainly not enough to establish ontological identity. Neural activity simply has a different appearance than the sensations and feelings of second pain, regardless of whether one is looking directly at neurons (presumably using a microscope), action potentials (using an oscilloscope), or a proxy measure of neural activity (using a brain scanner). Appearances are properties, and they matter a great deal because they are the only intrinsic properties for which we have direct access (Chalmers, 2003). Differences in appearance make neural responses and experiences ontologically irreducible to one another because not all of their properties are identical. Thus, we think characterization of neural mechanisms of second pain serves as a reductive explanation because it helps account for why second pain is experienced in a specific way. However, the reductive explanation is epistemological, not ontological.

8.2.2   Representation?

The second question is about representation. Do the characteristics of second pain *represent* features of the external environment or physiological conditions of the body? It is noteworthy that the explanation of second pain given so far makes a strong prima facie case against pure representationalist theories of pain. Some philosophers hold externalist perceptual theories of pain, according to which the phenomenal content of a pain experience is exhausted by its representational content (e.g., Dretske, 1995, 1999; Tye, 1995, 1997). Such a position requires the theorist to find a feature of the stimulus or its immediate effect on the body for every discernable phenomenological quality of pain as its representational content. As we have seen, however, the second pain summation phenomenon clearly does not correlate with any changes in stimulus property. This makes it hard to see what the phenomenology of second pain summation can have as its representational content (Price and Aydede, 2005). The same general argument can be made for the emotional dimension of pain, which can be modified in the absence of any change in the physical stimulus. External representationalist theories may be more applicable to some (but not all) aspects of visual experience that closely follow the properties of objects. Our perception of edges and contours, for example, can be shown to closely follow these features when they are independently verified by physical measurements of another observer. Pain, on the other hand, sometimes follows events in the central nervous system much more closely than events in the physical environment, second pain serving as a prime example. The subjective features of second pain closely follow responses of the central nervous system, starting with the dorsal horn of the spinal cord. The multiple subjective features, including sensation intensity, unpleasantness, arousal, and the urge to avoid or escape the pain, all have associations with neural activity that is widely distributed throughout the brain, yet none of these aspects of experience can be shown to represent features of stimuli.

8.2.3   Functional Significance

The third and final question is about the functional significance of characteristics of second pain. Clearly, one might suspect that temporal summation of second pain reflects critical biological and psychological functions because this phenomenon has unique sensory and affective characteristics that are paralleled by responses throughout the spinal cord and brain. Temporal summation may reflect an amplification mechanism generated by ongoing C-nociceptor activity, an amplification that serves to enhance pain. In fact, repeated C-nociceptor stimulation mimics a phenomenon that occurs naturally. Normally, C-nociceptors do not have ongoing impulse activity in the absence of intense stimulation (Li, Simone, and Larson, 1999; Price, 1999). However, when tissue inflammation occurs, they develop ongoing impulse activity whose frequency is often above one impulse every three seconds. Ongoing impulse frequency of C- nociceptors is likely to enhance the responsiveness of central neurons by the same mechanism that leads to temporal summation of second pain (Li, Simone, and Larson, 1999). It is conceivable that temporal summation of second pain represents a physiological condition of tissues of the body, such as inflammation, tissue damage, or injured and dysfunctional peripheral nerves. All of these conditions are often accompanied by persistent pain. The experiential features of second pain may simply reflect a functional mechanism, one that enhances ongoing pain and leads to behaviors that protect injured or dysfunctional tissues (Price, 1999).

8.3   Can We Build a More Refined Explanation of Second Pain, Relying on Improvements in First- and Third-Person Data?

In a general sense, neural activation within a network of distributed brain areas (figure 8.4) may be said to represent the different dimensions of second pain. This claim is supported by results of brain imaging and also results of specific stimulation or specific damage of these different areas. Damage to the somatosensory cortices produces deficits in ability to experience the location, quality, and intensity of pain (Kenshalo, Thomas, and Dubner, 1989). Damage to parts of the insular cortex has led to more controversial results (Berthier, Starkstein, and Leiquarda, 1988; Starr et al., 2010). If the lesion includes the anterior insula, it is more likely to result in selective deficits in the sense of intrusion or threat, consistent with the neuroimaging literature showing that perceived threat is associated with activation in the anterior insular cortex (Wiech et al., 2010). Damage to anterior cingulate and prefrontal cortical areas causes deficits in emotional aspects of pain with less effect on sensory aspects of pain (Foltz and White, 1962). This differential representation is similar to that found for sensory modalities such as vision, wherein damage to specific brains areas involved in visual processing results in a specific type of visual deficit, such as lack of perception of movement or lack of color perception (Velmans, 2009). Such neurological findings have led Zeki (2007) to suggest the idea of "essential nodes," each responsible for the perception of a given feature of a type of experience. In the case of pain, however, it is not clear that such sharp functional separations can be made. Thus, although the somatosensory cortices are likely to participate in pain-related sensations, they also have a role in pain-related emotions because of their serial connections to the rest of the "pain matrix." As mentioned in chapter 7, damage to somatosensory cortical areas produces deficits not only in pain but even in the ability to recognize emotions in others (Adolphs et al., 2000). The somatosensory cortex may participate not only in the direct experience of pain but also in recognizing pain in others and in *representing* the experience of pain in oneself. For example, somatosensory area 1 becomes activated during a brief actual pain and also afterwards when the participant is rating the pain after the stimulus terminates (Moulton et al., 2005).

In considering all of the relevant brain interactions during pain, including second pain, one cannot overemphasize the fact that neural activation in a given brain area does not occur in isolation—there is a vast interconnectivity within the brain. Even when an experimenter artificially activates a given brain region through electrical stimulation, the activated neurons send impulses to several other regions of the brain. Thus, Zeki's concept of essential node seems to have explanatory limitations. Given the spatial separation of pain-related areas of the brain (see figure 8.4), how does the brain "bind" the different aspects of pain into a unified *experience,* one that contains specific sensory qualities, the sense of threat, arousal, and unpleasantness? Chapter 7 reviewed the different areas in relation to aspects of pain experience, but we are still left with the problem of how these aspects of experience are bound together (the binding problem). One controversial yet intriguing possibility is the proposal that a mutual entrainment occurs between the different areas in the form of 40 Hz oscillations (Crick, 1994; Crick and Koch, 2007). This hypothesis has been around for some time, so we are not bringing up anything radically new. Yet regardless of whether or not this specific oscillatory mechanism accounts for functionally significant binding between pain-related areas, other evidence supports the idea that the different pain-related areas interact in functionally specific ways. Structural equation modeling, a form of path analysis, has been used to provide evidence for functional paths between pain-related areas. When this type of analysis was applied in the case of second pain, the established model contained the functional paths shown in figure 8.5. This model contains the pathways proposed in chapter 7 for pain in general as well as additional pathways. Pathways involved in sensory processing (somatosensory areas S1, S2, posterior insula; P-Ins), attention and cognitive evaluation (areas of ACC), and different stages of emotion (P-Ins, ACC) were shown to be significant parts of the overall model. Notably, both the P-Ins

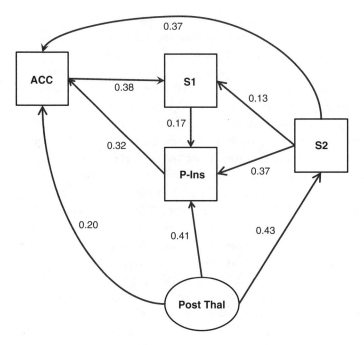

Figure 8.5
Functional pathways that positively interact during temporal summation of second pain. This figure is based on the same brain regions, participants, and stimuli as used in figure 8.4. The following functional connections were established: (1) posterior thalamus (Thal) → posterior insula (P-Ins), (2) posterior thalamus → second somatosensory area (S2), (3) posterior thalamus → dorsal region of mid-anterior cingulate cortex (dmACC), (4) S2 → posterior insula, (5) S2 → first somatosensory area S1, (6) S2 → mACC, (7) posterior insula → mACC, (8) mACC → S1, and (9) S1 → posterior insula. This analysis and figure (unpublished) were constructed by Dr. Jason Craggs of the University of Florida in collaboration with Drs. Michael Robinson, Roland Staud, William Perlstein, and Donald Price.

and dorsal region of the mid-anterior cingulate cortex (dmACC) have multiple input–output connections and are likely to be central hubs in interrelating sensory, cognitive-evaluative, and emotional dimensions of pain processing. In combination with the brain activations shown by the earlier experiments, this path analysis further demonstrates that temporal summation of second pain applies to all aspects of this type of experience, not just its qualitative sensory features.

There is a large potential for improving functional brain analysis, focusing not only on levels of neural activity in specific pain-related areas but also on how the areas interact under different experimental conditions. For example, the next chapter explains how pain experience is related to functional interactions between brain regions under baseline and placebo analgesic conditions. Improvements in third-person data and data analysis could help provide increasingly better explanations of a type of conscious experience. However, what may be more surprising is that advances in ability to collect high-quality first-person data would be equally important. To continue our example of second pain, results of numerous studies of this phenomenon point to several experiential features (e.g., burning sensation, arousal, unpleasantness, etc.), and many of these studies have presupposed that everyone experiences this phenomenon in the same way and as a unified experience. We have found that at least some features of second pain occur in all participants of a study, yet they can be highly modified by the nature of their experience prior to receiving the stimuli (Barrell and Price, 1975). When participants focused their attention on their hand, feeling it from the "inside," their experience of second pain had all the characteristics described so far, including temporal summation. However, when they focused their attention on the impending stimulus (focusing on the electrodes and impending shock) and not their hand, second pain was weak or absent and there was no temporal summation whatsoever. Thus, similar to pain in general, the experience of second pain is highly modifiable on a moment-to-moment basis, depending on attentional, emotional, and other psychological factors. All of these facets of experience can be captured in observers trained to notice details of their experience, using experiential methods. If that is the case, then variation can be induced in the experience of second pain. The experiential variation can then be linked to variation in levels of activity within multiple brain areas and in the functional connections between them (see, e.g., figure 8.5). It may then be possible to more rigorously test the relationships between neural activity and second pain, thereby providing a more refined way to explain and understand this type of conscious experience.

The same strategy could be applied to other types of conscious experiences.

9 Mysterious and Not-So-Mysterious Mechanisms of Placebo Responses

Placebo administration is one of the oldest health-care practices, dating back to antiquity. Its earliest conceptualization emphasized the intent to please the patient, leaving open the possibility as to whether this had any direct therapeutic effect on symptoms or diseases. Questions about whether placebo responses reflect actual attenuation of disease or biases to report reduced symptoms have extended over centuries, and estimates of efficacy of placebos range from almost negligible (Hrojartsson and Gøtzsche, 2001) to extremely powerful (Beecher, 1959). The complete absence of an experiential phenomenology of placebo responses has no doubt contributed to its mysterious nature for health-care professionals and patients alike. This chapter explores this mystery, beginning with questions about possible environmental and physical causes of placebo responses. Learning mechanisms, such as classical conditioning, are explored in relation to these environmental factors. We then move on to possible causes that exist *within* the experience of someone receiving a placebo, starting with dimensions such as "expectation," "desire for relief," and possible distortions in memory. The question of whether placebo responses can be at least partly explained by the desire–expectation model in preceding chapters is then raised. Although our ultimate intent in explaining placebo responses is to provide a parsimonious "first-person" experiential account of placebo responses, we don't begin with the phenomenology of placebo responses. This is because first-person experiential studies of placebo response have only recently been conducted (Kaptchuk et al., 2008; 2009; Vase et al., 2011), long after biological and psychological studies indirectly pointed to some experiential factors as mediators. However, results of these recent studies corroborate those based on psychophysical methods and neuroimaging. The integration of first- and third-person science is beginning to take place in placebo research.

Until recently, an unstated question in scientific research on placebo has been whether people have any experiences that are proximate causes of placebo responses, such as immediate expectations or a felt need for relief. After all, it is conceivable that placebo responses have unconscious mediators, and they just "go on in the dark." For example, one explanation invoked the idea that placebo responses could be explained by a stimulus substitution model of Pavlovian classical conditioning (Wickramasekera, 1985). Since this form of learning can be explained without using mentalistic concepts, there was no need to invoke conscious expectations of therapeutic effects, and in fact it was thought that no such expectations were present. However, experiential factors gradually entered into studies and explanations of placebo and consequently required consideration of the roles of conscious expectation, anticipation, and feelings about treatments. There are distinct advantages to knowing how placebo responses are enhanced or even generated by these factors. This knowledge could lead to ethical ways to enhance aspects of placebo responses within treatments because most treatments contain a placebo component. If so, then an experiential science of placebo offers a means to understand placebo mechanisms and to ultimately enhance this component of therapy.

9.1   Distinguishing Placebo Effects/Responses from Other Phenomena

9.1.1   Terminology

Before we begin this exploration, however, we need to precisely clarify what is meant by terms such as "physical placebo agent," "placebo response," and "placebo effect" and how these phenomena differ from changes due to "natural history," the natural progression of a medical condition such as pain. Although it is clear that the simulation of an active medical treatment, such as sham treatment, is sometimes followed by large reductions in symptoms in both individuals and groups of patients, it is usually not obvious whether the improvement is due to the effect of placebo. The reduction in symptoms may simply reflect the natural course of a disease or condition—that is, its natural history. Failure to appreciate this point has bedeviled and confused placebo research from its beginning. The physical placebo agent itself is a dummy treatment such as sham surgery, a sugar pill, magnets, and so forth. The placebo effect is the difference in mean treatment effect between sham and active treatment conditions across two groups of patients or at different times within the same group of patients (crossover studies). The placebo response refers to the improvement in symptoms in an individual which results from the experience of receiving a therapeutic intervention, regardless of whether the intervention is a "real" treatment or just a simulation of one. Placebo responses can be embedded in active treatments. The next time you take a medication for a symptom, such as pain, you may appreciate that part of the reason for reduction in pain is your expectation of relief, which is part of the placebo response,[1] From the standpoint of understanding mechanisms, it is the placebo response of the individual that is the most interesting and informative object of study because experiential understanding may be the key to learning how placebos work.

9.1.2   Common Confusion: The Importance of Natural History

The placebo response is widely misunderstood. This is due in part to modern clinical trials' methodology and in part to a failure of scientists and health-care professionals to come to terms with the actual proximate mediating causes of clinical improvement. In clinical trials the use of dummy treatment comparison groups is commonplace. The idea is to control for nonspecific factors related to administration of the treatment and to the patient's perception of the treatment. Optimal design often requires deception of both the subject and the person giving the treatment. It is common for participants in the placebo group to improve. The confusion often begins with the assumption that the reason they improved was because they received a placebo. This assumption is often unwarranted.

Despite the growth of interest in and study of the placebo effect, many early investigators made the error of assuming that the placebo manipulation was the cause of an observed change. Instead, changes in symptom magnitude over time without any intervention whatsoever could have easily accounted for a gradual decline in symptoms. This is likely to be the result of natural healing effects of the body or the decline in pathological factors that produce symptoms which are integral to natural history. It is frequently stated that a certain percentage of subjects or patients in a treatment trial are placebo responders. In most cases, this statement ignores the very real possibility that many of the patients would have improved with no treatment whatsoever (see figure 9.1).

To illustrate this problem, consider the hypothetical condition of a headache whose cause is not immediately known (called idiopathic headache). In most people, the headaches they experience will rise to a peak intensity and then gradually subside completely without treatment. Thus, both "any treatment" and "no treatment" given at the peak of headache severity will almost inevitably be followed by a decline in pain intensity (curve a in figure 9.1). This is true whether the treatment is a dummy

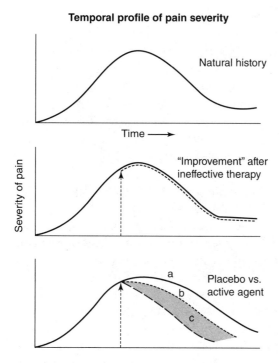

Figure 9.1

Temporal variation in pain intensity confounds the interpretation of placebo administration. Many painful clinical conditions show variations in intensity over time. The top panel illustrates a hypothetical painful episode such as an idiopathic headache, which starts at a low level and subsides in the absence of treatment. Giving a placebo (middle panel; vertical interrupted line with arrowhead indicates time) is followed by improvement, but this is no different than what would have happened in the absence of treatment. Lower panel: Under some circumstances, due to anticipation of pain relief, administration of a placebo results in a more rapid improvement than occurs with no treatment. The difference in pain levels between no treatment (a) and placebo (b) is the placebo analgesic effect. An active analgesic agent should produce an even more rapid or complete pain reduction (c) compared to placebo.

tablet, an active analgesic, or no treatment whatsoever. Chronic illnesses also are often relapsing and remitting, which leads to great variability in symptom intensity over time. Because of this variability in natural history, it is often difficult to know whether a treatment given at any point in time has had any effect. Clearly, the "response" to treatment is an inference, not a direct observation, and such an inference requires multiple measurements of a patient's treated and untreated medical condition. For example, under ideal circumstances, when highly reproducible and predictable levels of pain occur during natural history and these levels are consistently lower after placebo treatment, one could infer that a placebo response has occurred in an individual. This is most likely to occur under conditions of experimental pain, where the stimulus can be controlled. However, under typical clinical circumstances wherein *both* the natural history and the "effect" of a placebo treatment are highly variable, attributing relief to the placebo treatment is problematic.

Nevertheless, it is possible to measure placebo effects in studies that include both an untreated natural history and a placebo condition, especially when large groups of patients are studied. As shown by comparing curves a and b of figure 9.1, the difference in symptom magnitude between natural history (a) and placebo (b) conditions represents the placebo effect. It also can be measured in an individual patient but only with multiple trials of both natural history and placebo conditions. Finally, even when an active treatment is given (curve c of figure 9.1), the overall decrease in a symptom reflects the combination of changes due to natural history, placebo, and the active biological effect of the medication. In some instances, the last of these makes the least contribution to the overall effect. Antidepressants represent one of the best examples (Kirsch, 2009). Both natural history, which includes a host of unknown variables related to healing and natural progression of a disease, and placebo can be powerful agents.

9.2 Are There Environmental and Psychosocial Causes of the Placebo Effect?

9.2.1 Repeated Exposure to Effective Treatments: Conditioning

After patients are given repeated effective treatments, administration of a placebo treatment is often sufficient to produce a therapeutic effect in itself. To illustrate with an anecdote, a family member of one of us underwent knee surgery in our university hospital. Postoperatively, she received her pain medication through a "patient-controlled-analgesic pump"; pressing a button gave her an injection of an analgesic medication through an intravenous catheter. This device worked well throughout her three days of hospitalization. On the last day, as a hospital technician was removing the pump and the catheter, the patient smiled and commented that every time she pressed the button she would become sleepy and her pain would noticeably diminish. These responses occurred even an hour or so before the catheter removal. Immediately after her glowing comment about the analgesic pump, the technician remarked that the pump had contained no analgesic medication for the last day.

This anecdote is likely to be an example of both conditioning and a placebo response, wherein several environmental cues, such as the pump and the button controlling it, become strongly associated with pain relief after repeated button presses. Of course, there are several studies that demonstrate this phenomenon in a more formal manner. For example, perception of pain treatments is likely to be influenced by previous experiences with pain, the analgesic remedy, and the setting. Based on this common-sense idea and actual research, some investigators proposed the idea that placebo effects are based on Pavlovian conditioning. Wickramasekera (1985) suggests that when a patient receives an active biological agent (unconditioned stimulus; UCS) that reliably leads to analgesia (unconditioned response; UCR), contextual cues such as the hospital, the white coat, or the pill (conditioned stimuli; CSs) are likely to be associated with pain relief. These contextual factors which represent the CS come to elicit pain relief even in the absence of active agents. The stimulus-substitution model of classical conditioning posits that repeated exposure to a CS paired with a UCS is both necessary and sufficient for a conditioned response (CR). This model of learning emphasizes environmental "stimuli" and responses and does not require a conscious association between the CS and the UCS.

The first classic study of human patients that supports a conditioning model is that of Laska and Sunshine (1973). Several groups of patients with postoperative pain received two treatment medications on two subsequent days. On the first day, a given group would receive one of three doses of an analgesic medication called propoxyhene, and on the second day they received a placebo injection. The results showed convincing evidence of a dose–response relationship between the dose of the first medication and the analgesic response to placebo on the second day. Thus, consistent with classical conditioning, the CR (i.e., response to placebo) increased as a function of the strength of the CS (i.e., dose of drug) as well as the strength of the UCR (i.e., the magnitude of analgesia). Also, one of the groups in this study received placebo on the first day followed by placebo on the second day. On the second day the placebo had the same slight analgesic effect as the first administration, yet it was clearly less than in other groups that received active medication on the first day. Oddly enough, Laska and Sunshine did not interpret their results as supporting the classical conditioning model. Instead they proposed that the time course of the pain plus the *anticipation* of relief based on past experience probably combine in some complex and highly individualized subtle way to produce their patterns of results. Perhaps they were taking a more experiential perspective in interpreting their results. If so, it certainly was an implicit perspective.

Several studies have since demonstrated the effectiveness of conditioning in producing placebo effects on experimental pain. For example, Voudouris, Peck, and Coleman (1990) invented a conditioning procedure that combined repeated application of a topical cream with secretly lowered stimulus intensities. The baseline trials consisted of periods of painful iontopheretic stimulation of the skin, and stimulus strength was simply lowered during conditioning trials, unbeknownst to participants. Untreated baseline trials and conditioning trials were then followed by *placebo test* trials in which stimulus strength was raised back to that of the original baseline condition. A reduction in average pain ratings during placebo test trials as compared to original baseline trials reflects the placebo effect. Remember that the placebo effect is the difference in the magnitude of a symptom across natural history (or baseline) and placebo conditions (see figure 9.1). In finding a reliable placebo effect, this study was the first to establish a model of placebo by utilizing experimental pain. Studies have since demonstrated that conditioning is sufficient to produce placebo analgesia. A study by Amanzio and Benedetti (1999) conditioned participants with intravenous morphine on two successive days and then tested the placebo effect on a third day using intravenous saline. This experiment showed a moderate to large placebo analgesic effect on experimentally induced ischemic arm pain. However, this same study also conducted a second experiment that used only a verbal suggestion for pain relief ("A potent painkiller is being given"), again using ischemic arm pain. This suggestion alone produced a small but statistically significant placebo effect. Finally, a third variant of this same type of experiment combined conditioning with this verbal suggestion. The result was a placebo analgesic effect that was as large as the addition of effects of conditioning and suggestion. Thus, although conditioning may be sufficient for placebo effects, it can also be produced by verbal statements and by all of the psychosocial factors that are present in the context of the treatment.

9.2.2 Challenges to the Conditioning Hypothesis

Later in the twentieth century there were several challenges to explaining placebo effects on the basis of classical (Pavlovian) conditioning. In particular, Kirsch (1990) pointed out that various studies of placebo effects have failed several criteria that are used to decide whether a phenomenon can be attributed to classical conditioning: (1) Conditioning trials with tranquilizers weaken rather than produce the predicted strengthened placebo effect; (2) contrary to the criterion that the magnitude of the placebo effect should be directly proportionate to the strength of the active tranquilizer, it is *inversely related*; (3) the placebo effects are often not specific to the pharmacological properties of an active agent, such as caffeine or alcohol, but depend heavily on context and the type of suggestion; (4) placebo effects often stay the same size or get stronger with repeated placebo administration instead of getting progressively smaller, as would be predicted by the classical conditioning model (e.g., figure 9.3 shows increase in placebo effect over time); and (5) placebo effects can sometimes be as strong as or even stronger than the active medication, and we will provide examples of this later. On the other hand, nearly all of the criteria for classical conditioning were fulfilled by the Laska and Sunshine study just described. As well, Fedele et al. (1989) demonstrated a loss of analgesic effectiveness of placebo with repeated administration, thereby fulfilling an important criterion for classical conditioning. The exceptions cited by Kirsch may be unique to certain kinds of studies in which psychologically therapeutic effects are measured (for example, reductions in emotional aspects of pain, panic, or anxiety) or to instances where a drug induces arousal or sedation (e.g., caffeine or alcohol) depending on suggestions given or the way the context is framed. For example, sedation or arousal can occur after caffeine administration depending on the suggestions given (Kirsch, 1990). All of this demonstrates the limitations of trying to find causes of placebo responses by examining only variables related to the environment or to conditioning.

9.2.3 Do Placebo Effects Result from Simulation of Active Therapies?

Beyond the problems raised by Kirsch, one has to wonder what constitutes conditioned "stimuli," for which there are endless candidates. After all, when patients receive a treatment, there are many cues to which they can attend, and these cues are embedded in the behavior and appearance of the persons carrying out the treatment, the physical aspects of the treatment itself, and the overall environment. It might appear convenient to pick out the most salient cues and call them "conditioning stimuli," but this approach would always involve presuppositions and would ignore the enormous variability in the manner and degree to which people attend to specific cues. *Most critically, it would ignore the meanings patients give to the therapeutic context.* Benedetti's conceptualization is that a placebo manipulation reflects an overall *simulation* of an active treatment (Benedetti, 2002). In a very cleverly designed study, Amanzio and colleagues provide dramatic support for this idea of simulation (Amanzio et al., 2001). This study used human patients in the contexts of actual clinical treatments. The contribution of the placebo effect to the overall effectiveness of analgesic drugs was tested in clinical postoperative settings using *open* and *hidden* injections of traditional painkillers such as buprenorphine (Levine, Gordon, and Fields, 1978; Amanzio et al., 2001; Benedetti et al., 2003). The open–hidden paradigm represents a novel way of studying both placebo mechanisms and the specific effects of a drug. In this paradigm, the patient can receive an injection in one of two ways. The first is the standard clinical *open* manner, where the medication is given by the clinician and in full view of the patient. In the second method, the patient receives the treatment in a *hidden* manner, by means of a computer programmed drug infusion pump, where the clinician is not present and the patient is unaware that the treatment is being administered (Levine, Gordon, and Fields, 1984). Groups of patients of that receive medication in the open manner need less medication to reach postoperative analgesia in comparison to groups receiving hidden injections. The differences in medication needed for analgesia between open and hidden injections directly reflect placebo analgesic effects, as demonstrated for several types of analgesic medications shown in figure 9.2. There have been several analgesia studies using the open–hidden paradigm, and they all demonstrate that open administration of a drug is significantly more effective than hidden administration (Levine, Gordon, and Fields, 1978; Amanzio et al., 2001; Benedetti et al., 2003; Colloca et al., 2004).

In comparing open–hidden administration studies with those using conditioning or verbal suggestions, it becomes evident that even verbal suggestion is not a necessary condition for a placebo response because no verbal suggestions are given during open administration. There is just the appearance of a treatment in the open administration and its absence in the hidden condition. What is it about this simulation or appearance that contributes to the placebo effect, and how does this simulation cause its effect? Without an experiential perspective or method, we can only speculate about the answer to this question. Could it be, as suggested by Daniel

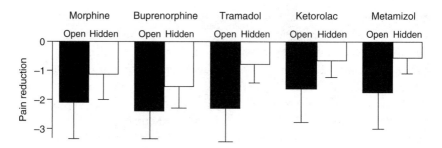

Figure 9.2
Comparison of analgesic effects of opioid (morphine, buprenorphine, tramadol) and nonopioid (ketorolac, metamizol) medications across hidden versus open intravenous injections in patients with postoperative pain. (Adapted from data from Amanzio et al., 2001.)

Moerman (2002), that the placebo response is shaped by the meanings within patients' experience of treatments?

9.3   Are There Experiential Causes of Placebo Responses: Roles of Expectation, Memory, Desire for Relief, and Emotional Feelings?

Even at this point in the history of placebo research, it is hard to envision an explanation of placebo responses without resorting to the use of terms that refer to human experience. After all, why would opposite effects occur for the same drug depending on context and types of suggestion—for example, sedation or arousal in the case of caffeine administration? And even if conditioning contributes to the placebo response, how do we know that it is not mediated by expectations? During the last decade of the twentieth century and continuing to the present, a gradual shift in emphasis occurred in how placebo phenomena were conceptualized. Emphasis on the nature of the external placebo manipulation and the environment has shifted to interest in the experienced factors in placebo phenomena. At first, the hypotheses were tested by manipulating the external context in a manner that the investigators *assumed* to increase expectations of symptom reduction. For example, investigators began to use "expectation" as a construct in explaining effects of placebo suggestion and conditioning despite the fact that they didn't directly measure expectation (e.g., Amanzio and Benedetti, 1999). Later, experiential factors hypothesized to mediate placebo responses were directly tested in experiments. This shift in emphasis was also related to the recognition that patients are likely to perceive environmental factors in different ways and these differences are likely to contribute to the magnitude, duration, and qualities of placebo responses. Cognitive and emotional factors that have been proposed to contribute to placebo effects include expected symptom intensity, desire for symptom change, changes in emotion, and distortions in memory.

9.3.1   Expectancy

As was explained in chapter 5, "expectancy" is the experienced likelihood of an outcome or an expected effect. For example, within the context of pain studies it can be measured by asking people about the level of pain they expect to experience. Montgomery and Kirsch (1997) conducted one of the first studies in which expected pain levels were manipulated and directly measured. They used a design very similar to that used in the Voudouris et al. (1990) study described earlier. As in the latter study, subjects were given cutaneous pain via iontopheretic stimuli. Once baseline stimuli were applied, subjects were secretly given stimuli with reduced intensities in the presence of an inert cream (i.e., conditioning trials). Then the stimulus strength was restored to its original baseline level, and several stimuli were then used in placebo test trials to test the effect of conditioning and determine whether there was a placebo effect. In addition, however, Montgomery and Kirsch had participants rate *expected* pain levels just before placebo test trials, and they were divided into two distinct groups. The first group did not know about the lowering of stimulus strength during the conditioning trials while the second group was told about the lowering of stimulus strength. A large placebo effect was found in the first uninformed group, and their expectation ratings strongly correlated with pain ratings during placebo test trials. In sharp contrast, no placebo effect occurred for the group that was informed about the lowering of stimulus strength, and their expectation ratings were not significantly correlated with their pain ratings during placebo test trials. It is important to recognize that the stimulus intensity was exactly the same across the baseline and placebo test trials, so that any reduction in ratings reflected psychological and physiological processes and not changes in characteristics of the stimulus. Clearly, informing one group of participants that stimulation was lowered during conditioning trials eliminated expectations of pain reduction and reversed effects of conditioning whereas expectations accounted for most of the variability in placebo responses in the uninformed group. For a stimulus substitution model of Pavlovian conditioning, none of this should matter because conscious knowledge of the reasons for the lowering of stimulus intensity is irrelevant to this form of learning. In the case of placebo analgesia, however, expectation appears to mediate placebo responses because (1) the correlation between expected reduction of pain and actual reduction of pain was high, accounting for 49% of the variability in placebo test trials, and (2) both expectations of reduced pain and the placebo effect were completely eliminated by informing participants about the lowering of stimulus strength during conditioning trials. Thus, conditioning can contribute to expectations, but conditioning only works if it affects expectations. The regression analysis and difference in results across groups show that conscious expectation is necessary for placebo analgesia. Some types of placebo effects, such as those involving conditioned autonomic nervous system responses, do not appear to require conscious awareness of the CSs.

Price and colleagues further tested the extent to which expectations of pain relief can be graded and related to specific areas of the body (Price et al., 1999). Using a similar paradigm involving secret lowering of stimulus strength during conditioning trials, they applied placebo creams and graded levels of heat stimulation on three adjacent areas of the subjects' forearm to give subjects expectations that cream A was a strong analgesic, cream B a weak analgesic, and cream C a control agent. Immediately after these conditioning trials, subjects rated their expected pain levels for the placebo test trials wherein the stimulus intensity was now *the same for all three areas*. The conditioning trials led to graded levels of expected pain (C > B > A) for the three creams as well as graded magnitudes of actual pain (C > B > A) when tested during placebo test trials. Thus, magnitudes of placebo analgesia could be graded across three adjacent skin areas, demonstrating a high degree of "somatotopic" specificity for placebo analgesia. Expected pain levels accounted for up to 36% of the variance in postmanipulation pain ratings.

9.3.2 Expectancy and Memory

The memory of previous experiences is also likely to influence the experience of pain. Price et al. assessed the placebo effect based on both concurrent ratings of pain during the placebo condition and on retrospective ratings of pain that were obtained approximately two minutes after the stimuli were applied (Price et al., 1999). The magnitude of placebo analgesic effects based on retrospective ratings was three to four times greater than those based on concurrent ratings. The main reason for this difference was that subjects remembered their baseline pain intensity as being much larger than it actually was. Similar to placebo analgesia effects assessed concurrently, the remembered placebo effects were strongly correlated with expected pain intensities (R = .5–.6). Thus, placebo analgesia effects may be enhanced by distorted memories of pretreatment levels of pain. Furthermore, as remembered pain and expected pain are closely related, these psychological factors seem to interact. These findings were replicated by De Pascalis et al. (2002).

9.3.3   Are Placebo Effects Related to a Desire–Expectation Emotion Model?

Although expectancy seems to be an important psychological mediator of placebo effects, it is unlikely to operate alone. Desire, which is the experiential dimension of wanting something to happen or wanting to avoid something happening, is also likely to be involved in placebo phenomena. As we discussed in chapters 2–4, desire and expectation also interact and underlie at least some human emotions, such as sadness, anxiety, and relief (Price and Barrell, 2000; Price et al., 1985; Price et al., 2001). It occurred to us that placebo responses might be generated as a consequence of emotional feelings about treatments or medications. If that is the case, then the emotion model discussed in earlier chapters might be used to test this simple hypothesis. In the context of analgesic studies, it is quite plausible that patients and participants of experiments have some degree of desire to avoid, terminate, or reduce evoked or ongoing pain. On the other hand, some placebo effects involve appetitive or approach goals, such as positive moods or increased arousal. In the following discussion, we provide an account of how *decreased* desire may contribute to placebo analgesia and *increased* desire may contribute to placebo effects during appetitive goals. We then propose that the roles of goals, expectation, desire, and emotional feelings all can be accommodated within the same explanatory model. It is possible that the emotion functions explained in chapters 2–5 can serve as a model for placebo effects and this model may have neurobiological underpinnings.

To further understand how desire and expectation influence placebo analgesia, Verne et al. (2003b) and Vase et al. (2003) conducted two similar studies. Patients with irritable bowel syndrome (IBS) were exposed to visceral distention by means of a balloon barostat, a type of stimulation that simulates their clinical pain. Patients were tested under the conditions of untreated natural history (baseline), visceral placebo, and visceral lidocaine. Pain was rated immediately after each of seven stimuli within each of these three conditions. Each condition lasted about an hour. The first study was conducted as a double blind clinical trial where patients were given an informed consent form, which stated that they "may receive an active pain reducing medication or an inert placebo agent" (Verne et al., 2003b). Each patient participated in all three conditions (natural history, placebo, and lidocaine). Exactly the same painful stimulus intensities were applied in all conditions, so that any statistical differences in average pain ratings found between them were the result of placebo or lidocaine. There was a significant pain-relieving effect of viscerally applied lidocaine gel as compared to placebo gel (p < .001), and there was a significant pain-relieving effect of placebo gel as compared to untreated natural history. In a second similarly designed study, IBS patients were told that "the agent you have just been given is known to significantly reduce pain in some patients" at the onset of each treatment condition, either visceral placebo or visceral lidocaine, but not during the natural history condition (Vase et al., 2003). A much larger placebo analgesic effect (about 33% larger) was found in the second study, as shown in figure 9.3, and it did not significantly differ from that of the lidocaine gel (the lidocaine effect is not

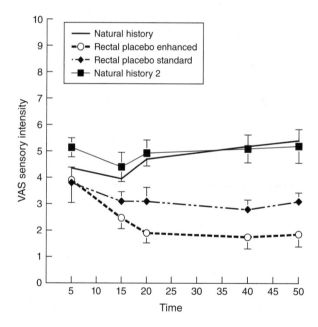

Figure 9.3

Comparison of natural history and rectal placebo scores on visceral pain intensity ratings (measured using a visual analog scale; VAS) during a fifty-minute session within a clinical trial design, where pain is assessed during natural history (NH, top 2 curves), a placebo condition wherein no suggestions for pain relief are given (middle curve) and within a placebo condition wherein verbal suggestions are given for pain relief (bottom curve). The x-axis refers to time in minutes. (Adapted from data from Verne et al., 2003b, and Vase et al., 2003.)

shown in figure 9.3). This second study shows that simply adding an overt suggestion for pain relief can result in a large increase in placebo analgesia, one that matches that of an active agent. Comparison of the placebo effect sizes of the two studies is shown in figure 9.3. The baseline pain ratings of the two groups were very similar, thus the difference in placebo effects across the two studies was not a result of different baselines.

In both studies, patients were asked to rate their expected pain level and desire for pain relief right after the agent was administered. Data from the two studies were pooled in order to determine whether changes in desire–expectancy ratings predicted changes in pain ratings across natural history and placebo conditions (i.e., placebo responses; Vase et al., 2004). The placebo response (natural history pain intensity minus placebo pain intensity), change in expected pain (natural history pain expectation minus placebo pain expectation), and change in desire for pain relief (desire for relief during natural history minus desire for relief during placebo) were all calculated for each of 23 subjects. The changes in expectation and desire were entered into a statistical analysis in which these factors and the multiplicative interaction between them (i.e., desire × expectation) served to predict placebo responses. As shown in table 9.1, this entire desire–expectation model accounted for 38% of the variability in placebo responses (corresponding to a correlation coefficient of .62). This analysis suggests that both desire for pain relief and expected pain intensity contribute to placebo analgesia, and a main factor is a multiplicative interaction between desire for pain reduction and expected pain intensity. This interaction is consistent with the desire–expectation model of emotions that shows that ratings of negative and positive emotional feelings are predicted by multiplicative interactions between ratings of desire and expectation (Price et al., 1985; Price and Barrell, 1984; Price et al., 2001), as shown in figure 9.4. Desire to reduce pain would be considered an avoidance goal, according to the desire–expectation model, and these results suggest that analgesia would be related to a reduction in desire for relief, a reduction in

Table 9.1
The contribution of changes in expectancy and desire to rectal placebo analgesia

Model	R^2 Change	p
Δ Expectancy + Δ desire	.16	.17
Δ Expectancy × Δ desire	.22	.02
Total model	.38	.02

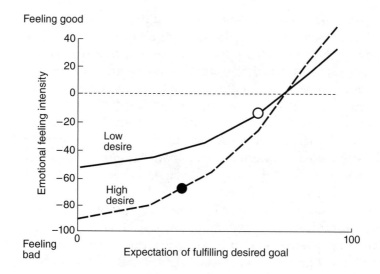

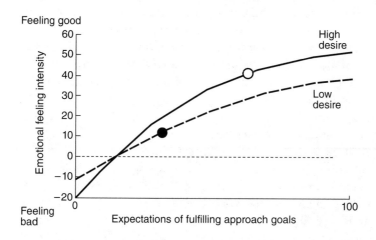

expected pain, and a consequent reduction in negative emotional feeling, as illustrated in the top panel of figure 9.4. This prediction also was supported by significant reductions in anxiety ratings in the two experiments (Vase et al., 2003; Verne et al., 2003b). It is further supported by a subsequent study showing that ratings of desire for pain reduction, expected pain, and anxiety all *decreased* during the same time that the placebo effect *increased* (Vase et al., 2005).

Interestingly, the desire–expectation model predicts that placebo responses in approach or appetitive goals would relate to *increased* levels of desire in the placebo condition, unlike avoidance goals (cf. top and lower panels in figure 9.4). The reason that this is so is that increased desire for a pleasant outcome is associated with increased positive emotional feelings throughout most of the range of expectation (see figure 9.4, lower panel). Support for this prediction was obtained in an experiment wherein participants were given placebo pills that were said to have a sedating effect (Jensen and Karoly, 1991). The desire to feel such effects was manipulated by telling one group of participants that individuals who become sedated by the pills tend to have negative personality characteristics. The second group was told that sedative effects were more common in participants

Figure 9.4
The desire–expectation model of emotions (Price and Barrell, 1984; Price et al., 1985; Price et al., 2001), showing hypothetical improvements in emotional states associated with a placebo response during an avoidance goal, such as wanting to be relieved of pain (top panel), and during an approach goal, such as wanting to feel energetic (bottom panel). These curves are similar to those empirically derived from ratings of desire, expectation, and positive/negative feelings (Price and Barrell, 1984; Price et al., 1985; Price et al., 2001) and show a multiplicative interaction between desire intensity and expectation with respect to their effects on positive and negative emotional feeling intensity (the curves intersect between 0 and 100). The closed circle in the top panel reflects a baseline negative feeling state. It is associated with a high desire for pain relief in combination with a low expectation of pain relief (or high levels of pain). After placebo administration, the postplacebo feeling state becomes less negative as a consequence of a lowering of desire (high desire to low desire) and an increased expectation of pain relief (or lower levels of pain). This change is represented by the upper open circle in the top panel. Likewise, the closed and open circles in the bottom panel reflect changes from the pre- to the postplacebo condition. In this case the placebo response (e.g., feeling more energetic) is accompanied by an increased desire for an effect, an increased expectation of an effect, and an increased positive feeling state. According to the model, placebo responses are driven by decreased negative or increased positive emotional feeling states for avoidance and approach goals, respectively.

who have positive personality traits. Not surprisingly, the authors found greater desire ratings for sedation and greater placebo sedation responses in the latter group.

Based on several interrelated experiments, Geers et al. (2005) argue that the placebo effect is most likely to occur when individuals have a goal that can be fulfilled by confirmation of the placebo expectation, consistent with the model just described. Their results demonstrated a role for desire for an effect across a variety of symptom domains, including those related to positive (approach or appetitive) and negative (avoidance) goals. For example, participants listened to a piece of music in one of their experiments. Two groups in the study were given a suggestion that the music would improve mood. One group was primed with a goal of independence, and another was primed with a goal of cooperation. Only the latter was compatible with the goal of improving mood. Placebo responses were calculated as differences in mood ratings across baseline and postplacebo conditions. The placebo effect was largest in the group given placebo suggestion coupled with the cooperation priming that was compatible with mood improvement. There were other groups in the study as well, but they had low to negligible placebo effects. Taken together, their results show the importance of desire for an effect across different types of placebo responses involving approach and avoidance goals.

9.4   Somatic Focus Moderates Effects of Goals and Expectancy

In addition to the roles of goals, desires, and expectations in placebo responding, there is evidence that the degree of somatic focus has a moderating influence on these psychological factors (Geers et al., 2006; Lundh, 1987). Somatic focus reflects the disposition to focus on body functions and to be vigilant to changes in them. In an experiment that induced expectations of unpleasant symptoms, individuals who expected they were taking a drug but given placebo tablets reported more placebo symptoms when they closely focused on their symptoms (Geers et al., 2006). This type of interaction also has been proposed for approach goals. Thus, Lundh (1987) proposes a cognitive–emotional model of the placebo effect in which positive placebo suggestions for improvements in physical health lead individuals to selectively attend to signs of improvement. When they closely notice these signs, they are said to take them as evidence that the placebo treatment has been effective.

If focusing on bodily symptoms or cues operates as a kind of feedback that supports factors underlying placebo responding, increasing the degree or frequency of somatic focusing could increase the magnitudes of placebo responses over time. This possibility is supported by observations showing that the growth of the placebo effect over time at least partly depends on the frequency of test stimuli. As discussed above, ratings of desire, expectation, and anxiety decrease over time along with the increase in placebo effect (Vase et al., 2005). As shown in figure 9.3, it took about twenty minutes for the placebo effect to increase to its maximum level in conditions wherein stimuli were applied at seven times per fifty minutes (Verne et al., 2003b; Vase et al., 2003). This same pattern of increase was found in a subsequent experiment that applied stimuli more rapidly, seven stimuli in ten minutes (Price et al., 2007). The placebo effect increased to its maximum level during the first three stimuli and over three to four minutes with this more rapid stimulus frequency, unlike the experiment that used less frequent stimulation. Taken together, the studies of Geers, Vase, Price, and their colleagues support a placebo mechanism wherein goals, desire, expectation, and consequent emotional feelings codetermine the placebo response. Somatic focus provides a self-confirming feedback that facilitates these factors over time, leading to less negative emotional feelings and higher expectations of avoiding aversive experiences or more positive feelings about obtaining pleasant consequences (see figure 9.3). The stimuli of the experiment help confirm that the treatment is working if someone is expecting it to work. Since the stimuli self-reinforce expectations and reduce desire for relief, the placebo effect increases more rapidly over time with higher frequencies of test stimulation. A similar dynamic may work for "nocebo" responses, the increase in symptoms over time as a result of catastrophic expectations.

If the desire–expectation model is accurate, then placebo phenomena occur within the context of emotional regulation and symptoms should be influenced by desire, expectation, and emotional feeling intensity regardless of whether or not these factors are evoked by placebo manipulations. A separate line of evidence for the role of expectancy in placebo analgesia includes studies that manipulate expectancy in nonplacebo contexts. Three studies found large reductions in pain from expectancy manipulations, and two of these studies found corresponding reductions in pain-related brain activity (Koyama et al., 2006; Keltner et al., 2006; Rainville et al., 2005). Desire and emotions also influence pain in nonplacebo contexts. Rainville et al. (2005) have shown that hypnotic inductions of changes in desire for relief as well as inductions of positive and negative emotional states modulate pain in directions they claim are consistent with the desire–expectation model.

Thus, to put it simply, placebo responses seem to relate to feeling good (or less bad) about prospects of relief (avoidance goal) or pleasure (approach goal) that are associated with treatments or medications. These feelings can be separately influenced by desire and expectation or by the combination of both variables. These variables change dynamically, leading to enhanced placebo response over time. What are needed are explanations that incorporate knowledge obtained from neuroscience. For example, do placebo-induced changes in expectations, desires, and emotions simply lead to subjective biases about symptoms/effects or do they affect their biological causes? These two alternatives would have somewhat different neurobiological explanations.

9.5   Is There a Potential Neurobiology of the Desire–Expectation–Emotion Model?

9.5.1   The Functional Role of Placebo-Related Decreases in Brain Activity

At least some types of placebo effects include reduction in biological causes. Several neurobiologists have found that placebo effects are accompanied by reductions in neural activity within brain areas known to process symptoms such as anxiety and pain. In two fMRI experiments published in a single report in *Science*, Wager et al. (2004) found that placebo analgesia was related to decreased neural activity in pain-processing areas of the brain. Pain-related neural activity was reduced within the thalamus, anterior insular cortex, and anterior cingulate cortex (ACC) during the placebo condition as compared with the untreated baseline condition. In addition, the magnitudes of these decreases were positively correlated with reductions in pain ratings. These reductions occurred in two experiments, one using painful electric shock and the other using painful heat stimuli to the skin.

A limitation of these experiments is that most of the decreases in neural activity occurred after the termination of the stimulus and during the time period that subjects rated pain, leaving open the possibility that placebo effects mainly reflected report biases. In a subsequent fMRI study, brain activity of IBS patients was measured in response to visceral stimulation, and the design of this experiment closely followed the experiments described earlier (e.g., figure 9.3; Price et al., 2007). As shown in figure 9.5 (plate 2), a large placebo effect was accompanied by large reductions in neural activity in known pain-related areas, such as thalamus, S-1, S-2, insula, and ACC (not shown in figure 9.5). Importantly, these reductions occurred *during the period of stimulation*, well before participants rated pain

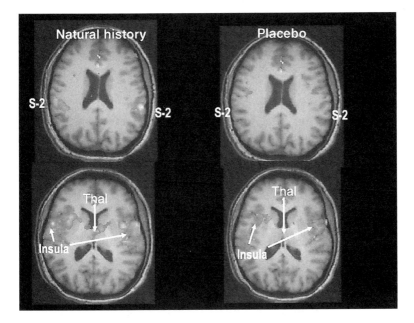

Figure 9.5 (plate 2)
Brain regions showing large reductions in pain-related brain activity, as represented by red–yellow regions, during the placebo condition (right horizontal brain slices) compared to untreated natural history or baseline condition (left horizontal brain slices). The thalamus (Thal), second somatosensory area (S-2), and insular cortical regions showed reduced activity. (These fMRI images are based on data from Price et al., 2007.)

intensity. Thus, the reductions in neural activity were unlikely to result only from report biases. Of course, there may well be other types of placebo phenomena that result mainly from biases or selective effects on experienced unpleasantness or disturbance. We know that this sometimes occurs in the case of hypnotic analgesia (see chapter 10).

9.5.2 Brain Mechanisms That Actively Generate the Placebo Response

Placebo responses are reflected by decreases in both symptoms and brain activities that are correlated with those symptoms. In the case of some symptoms, such as pain or anxiety, they also require activation of brain areas known to reduce pain and anxiety. Thus, in the case of pain, placebo analgesic responses are accompanied not only by decreases in activity in pain-related brain regions but also by increases in neural activity in several brain areas known to be involved in expectation, motivation, desire, reward, and emotions.

As a first example, an important aspect of Wager et al.'s study described above was that they imaged brain activity not only during evoked pain but also during the time that preceded the stimulus (heat or shock)—the period of anticipation. They hypothesized that, during anticipation, neural activity would increase in brain areas involved in generating placebo responses. In support of their hypothesis, increased activity occurred in the orbitofrontal cortex (OFC), dorsolateral prefrontal cortex (DLPFC), rostral ACC (rACC), and midbrain periaqueductal gray (PAG). The DLPFC is an area that has been consistently associated with the representation of and maintenance of information needed for cognitive control, consistent with a role in expectation (Miller and Cohen, 2001). This part of the prefrontal cortex is known for its role in working memory, a process that might be necessary to maintain a placebo response over time. On the other hand, the OFC is associated with evaluating reward information that is related to allocation of control, consistent with a role in motivational responses during anticipation of pain (Dias, Robbins, and Roberts, 1996). Such a role is consistent with desire for relief as a factor in placebo analgesia. The PAG is involved in emotional responses and descending modification of pain-related signals coming from the spinal cord. Thus, all of these activated areas of the central nervous system are likely to be involved in expectation, motivation, and emotion and yet are part of a pain-modifying system.

As a second example, a subsequent fMRI analysis of data in the study of IBS patients described above revealed areas of the brain that showed *increased* neural activity during placebo analgesia (Craggs et al., 2008), unlike areas that showed only *decreases* (i.e., figure 9.5). During the early part of the placebo condition, there was increased activity in areas of the temporal lobe (involved in memory), the precuneus (involved in associative thinking[2]; see figure 1.1), and the left and right amygdala (involved in emotions and in inhibition of pain). Activity in these three areas subsided somewhat during the late period of the placebo condition . Apparently, the greatest neurophysiological work in generating the placebo effect occurred during the early part of the placebo condition. This is a time when patients were likely to make associations between remembered suggestions about the placebo agent, internal cues that suggest whether or not the agent is working, and their expectations about pain reduction. The greatest "experiential work" also takes place during the early period, a time wherein the placebo effect is self-enhancing (cf. figure 9.3). Once the placebo effect is established, there is much less neurophysiological and experiential work required during the remainder of the experimental session. Clearly, this

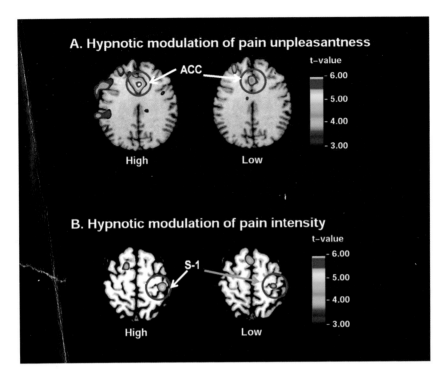

Plate 1 (figure 7.6)

The top pair of brain images shows results of a brain imaging study revealing selective modification of neural activity (measured by regional cerebral blood flow) in the anterior cingulate cortex (ACC) by hypnotic suggestions that targeted only pain unpleasantness (based on results from Rainville et al., 1997). Note the higher activity in the high pain unpleasantness condition (top left brain image, circled area) as compared to the low pain unpleasantness condition (top right brain image, circled area). In a second brain imaging experiment, activity within the S-1 somatosensory cortex was higher in the high pain sensation intensity condition (lower left image) as compared to the low pain sensation intensity condition (lower right image). (Based on results from Hofbauer et al., 2001.)

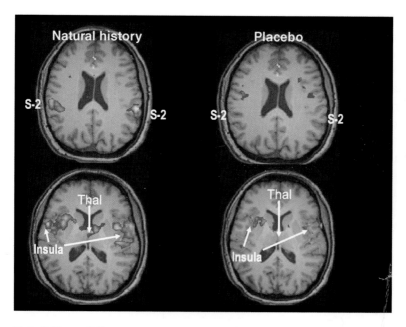

Plate 2 (figure 9.5)

Brain regions showing large reductions in pain-related brain activity, as represented by red–yellow regions, during the placebo condition (right horizontal brain slices) compared to untreated natural history or baseline condition (left horizontal brain slices). The thalamus (Thal), second somatosensory area (S-2), and insular cortical regions showed reduced activity. (These fMRI images are based on data from Price et al., 2007.)

explanation needs further testing and closer examination of the experiential and neural correlates of placebo analgesia. This will require more refined experiential and neuroimaging methods. The potential exists for using the descriptive experiential sampling (DES) method and other experiential methods in future studies.

For scientific and historical reasons, it is important to point out that the brain areas involved in generating placebo analgesia are known to be involved in reward/aversion, emotions, and the classical descending pain inhibitory pathway (Basbaum and Fields, 1978). The latter includes a core rACC–amygdala–PAG– rostroventral medulla–spinal cord connection, wherein pain-related signals are inhibited in the dorsal horn of the spinal cord (Mayer and Price, 1976; Basbaum and Fields, 1978). Direct evidence for the last step in this link is an fMRI study that has shown that placebo analgesia is accompanied by a reduced pain-related response in the spinal cord dorsal horn (Eippert et al., 2009).

However, the involvement of brain areas implicated both in emotions and in placebo responses is not restricted to pain modulation. Petrovic et al. (2005) demonstrated a placebo effect related to the reduction of anxiety associated with viewing unpleasant pictures. Reductions in experienced unpleasantness were accompanied by increases in activity within brain areas involved in reward/aversion and previously shown to be involved in placebo analgesia. These areas included those previously implicated in emotional modulation, such as the OFC and amygdala. They also included areas involved in treatment expectation, such as ventrolateral prefrontal cortex and rACC.

These neurobiological mechanisms of placebo extend an old observation that is pivotal in the scientific literature on placebo, and this observation has been repeated more recently. Some but not all forms of placebo analgesia require the activation of brain circuitry that utilizes the brain's own "morphine-like" compounds, well-known as endorphins and less well-known as endogenous opioids.[3] Fields and Levine (1984) first showed that the placebo effect could be reduced by giving an intravenous injection of naloxone, an antagonist to opioids. More recently it has been shown that if the placebo response is induced by means of strong expectation cues, it can be blocked by naloxone. Conversely, if the placebo response is induced by means of a prior conditioning with a nonopioid drug, it is not blocked by naloxone. Regional placebo analgesic responses can be obtained in different parts of the body (Montgomery and Kirsch, 1996; Price et al., 1999), and these responses are naloxone reversible (Benedetti et al., 1999). If four noxious stimuli are applied to the hands and feet and a placebo cream is applied to one hand only, pain is reduced only on the hand where the placebo cream had been applied. This effect is blocked by naloxone, which suggests that the placebo-activated endogenous opioids can act at specific body locations and not others depending on expectations of the participants (Benedetti et al., 1999).

9.6   Could the Desire–Expectation Model Apply to Other Medical Disorders?

We have emphasized analgesia as the main model used to study the placebo response because so much research has been conducted on pain over the last fifty years and placebo analgesia has been more extensively studied than placebo responses in other conditions. Opportunities exist for an application of an experiential perspective and methods for other medical conditions. Two phenomena, depression and Parkinson's disease, serve as interesting conditions which have been recently used to study placebo mechanisms. Could studies of placebo responses in these conditions benefit from an experiential approach?

Placebo effects in depression are common in clinical studies, and they are accompanied by biological changes (see Benedetti et al., 2003, for a review). For example, one study of unipolar depression found that placebo responses were accompanied by increases in brain glucose metabolism, measured using positron emission tomography (PET; Mayberg et al., 2002). In particular, placebo responses were associated with metabolic increases in the prefrontal, anterior cingulate, premotor, parietal, posterior insula, and posterior cingulate cortex. Metabolic activity is ordinarily low in many of these regions in depressed people. Metabolic decreases occurred in the subgenual cingulate cortex, parahippocampus, and thalamus.

However, what changes in desire and expectation accompany these placebo responses? Virtually nothing is known about how these dimensions of experience are changed, despite the fact that desire and expectation are integral to emotions of sadness and disappointment (see chapter 4) and are therefore almost certainly linked to the feelings of depression. It is natural to suspect that reduction in depressed feelings might occur as a result of more positive expectations or changes in desire. It is astounding how little attention has been given to this possibility.

Parkinson's disease also has emerged as an interesting model to understand the neurobiological mechanisms of the placebo response. Surprisingly, when Parkinson patients are given an inert substance (placebo) and are told that it is an anti-Parkinsonian drug that produces an improvement in their motor performance, they often respond quite well, both psychologically and biologically (Shetty et al., 1999; Goetz et al., 2000). Thus, a study that used PET to measure endogenous dopamine release showed that placebo-induced expectation of motor improvement activates dopamine in the basal ganglia (striatum) of Parkinsonian patients (de la Fuente-Fernandez et al., 2001). In addition, Pollo et al. (2002) showed that different and opposite placebo suggestions designed to elicit bad and good motor performance modulate the therapeutic effect of subthalamic nucleus stimulation in Parkinsonian patients who had undergone chronic implantation of electrodes for deep brain stimulation. By analyzing the effect of subthalamic stimulation on the velocity of movement of the right hand, they found the hand movement to be faster when the patients were given suggestions for a good motor performance (Pollo et al., 2002). All these effects occurred within minutes, suggesting that placebo responses are quickly accompanied by neural changes.

Yet despite the fact that the authors conclude that expectation mediates these changes in Parkinson patients, no direct measures of expectation were obtained. As is commonly the case, the authors assumed that their manipulations and suggestions led to expectations of good or poor performance. It seems very plausible that this is exactly what happened. However, assumptions like this have a notorious reputation for being overturned in psychology experiments, especially social psychology experiments where unsuspected variables seem to pop out of nowhere. The simple point is that if one claims that an experiential variable is a mediator of an effect, one should really directly measure that variable. In the case of placebo, as we have seen, there appear to be multiple experiential mediating variables.

9.7 An Experiential Phenomenology of Placebo Responses?

When participants rate variables on scales during placebo experiments, they provide first-person data. However, these data are truly meaningful only if they reflect what is actually taking place in experience. A more complete characterization of placebo mechanisms might utilize the experiential method outlined in chapters 4 and 5. Experiential factors that are commonly present during placebo responses would be identified in a study using an experiential–phenomenological method. Definitional and functional hypotheses would result from such a study (see chapter 4). These hypotheses would then be tested in subsequent studies using validated scales devised for each of the identified factors. This strategy was discussed in chapters 2 through 4. Clearly, this has not taken place in the case of placebo responses or effects. Instead, the variables that generate placebo effects have been identified and characterized in piecemeal fashion, similar to the progress in other fields of psychology and neuroscience. Yet an experiential–phenomenological study of placebo responses could be very illuminating and could help support or refute explanations of placebo mechanisms given thus far.

To determine whether reports of direct experience supported the quantitative data of the experiment on IBS patients discussed earlier, Lene Vase and her colleagues (2011) conducted in-depth structured interviews of 25 IBS patients who participated in the study wherein they were given either lidocaine or saline placebo gel (Vase et al., 2005). All patients were told "The agent you have been given is known to powerfully reduce pain in some patients" and were tested in both lidocaine and placebo sessions. The patients, investigators, and interviewer were all blind with respect to whether the patients had received placebo saline or lidocaine during the session in which they were interviewed. The interview followed the regular pain testing session. Following the experiential method, patients were asked to relive (i.e., reexperience) the session and describe their experience of the first part of the session wherein they were given the agent and then describe the later part of the forty-minute session (> twenty minutes).[4] They were instructed to try to describe their experiences as if they were taking place in the present. Their descriptions were taped and transcribed. The written accounts were analyzed using a template approach that establishes common categories of experience (Vase et al., 2011). The categories were formed on the basis of the descriptions themselves and consideration of common aspects associated with giving and receiving the treatment. They were framed by questions such as the following: (1) Do patients think they are getting an effective or ineffective treatment? (2) What are their focus of attention and emotional feelings (if any) during early and late parts of the session?

Using such questions as a template, the coauthors read and analyzed the descriptions. The results were generally similar across the 25 patients, consistent with large placebo responses in most of the patients. Reports of thoughts about the instructions and the agent they were receiving were much more prevalent in the beginning of the session than toward the end. These reports were often linked to statements about the "likeability," "credibility," or "competency" of the doctor who administered the treatment (e.g., "I feel he has more experience than others … he is an expert so he can help me"). Most patients (20/25) made statements suggesting that they were receiving an effective agent and no statements referred to receiving an ineffective agent. This is illustrated by a patient's saying "I believe it and also I am waiting to experience it." These 20 patients went along with the placebo suggestion ("This agent is known to powerfully reduce pain in some patients"). However, four patients appeared to be waiting to see if the agent worked, as implied by these two statements from different patients "I'm just waiting to see" and "I'm not convinced … I just go with the session … and that's how I evaluate how it's working." One patient just described her experience of the suggestion as "…something that he is supposed to say to me … as part of … the project…."

These patients referred to different types of bodily and/or emotional feelings such as comfort, ease, relief, excitement, relaxation, peace, calm, tired, drowsy, discomfort, apprehension, anxiety, and nervousness. The overall dimensions of calm and anxiety could be readily discerned among the variety of these feelings (e.g., ease, calm, peace, relief for *calm* and apprehension, anxiety, and nervousness for *anxiety*). Seventeen of the 25 patients were characterized as calm both in the early and late phase of the session. This is illustrated by a patient's saying "I'm feeling pretty calm … I'm not worried about anything … 'cause I'm given something to affect my pain" in the beginning of the session and in the later part of the session saying "Pretty relaxed … I'm pretty calm … pretty assured that it's gonna keep working…." The number of patients classified as calm increased from 17 to 21 in the last part of the session; four patients changed from anxiety to calm in the later part of the session. Two patients referred to anxious feelings, though perhaps not strong ones, as suggested by the sentence "I think I am a little bit more apprehensive…."

These qualitative results corroborate the rating scale data that were obtained from the same 25 patients (Vase et al., 2005) as well as the results of other similarly designed studies, including those which used brain imaging (Price et al., 2007). As shown by quantitative results in these patients, both expected levels of pain and desire for relief decreased as patients attended to the initial consequences of receiving a treatment. Further decreases likely resulted from attending to and "feeling" the results of initial changes. However, another qualitative study that was a randomized clinical trial of acupuncture for IBS did not appear to have patients with this same degree of optimism (Kaptchuk et al., 2009). Unlike the study by Vase et al. (2011), Kaptchuk claimed that patients in his study were concerned with whether they were receiving placebo or genuine treatment and they did not have expectations of relief but reported hope. There are possible reasons for the differences across the two studies. A randomized clinical trial may draw patients' attention to the possibility of receiving an inactive agent whereas explicit suggestions for pain relief may increase expectations, lower the experienced need for relief, and make patients feel better about the treatment. Another reason is that the expression of hope reflects a combination of desire and expectation, as stated in several definitions of this term (www.wordnik.com). In fact, patients in Vase et al.'s study used the word "hope" more often than the words "desire" and "expect." As pointed out in chapters 3–4, these dimensions of experience are often referred to implicitly.

9.8 Implications for Clinical Trials and Clinical Practice

9.8.1 Assessing Patients' Experience as a Means of Monitoring Placebo Factors within Clinical Practice and Clinical Trials

Advances in our understanding of placebo responses have interesting implications for clinical practice and clinical trials. Some of these implications center on the ethical enhancement of factors that generate placebo responses during administration of an active therapy. It is critical to point out that the clinical implications for placebo use involve exploitation of placebo factors and mechanisms when there is an active treatment being administered, not the deliberate use of a placebo when there is an active treatment available, which is unethical. Despite increases in the amount of studies of placebo mechanisms, there has been limited investigation of the ways in which these mechanisms can be harnessed to improve clinical trials and clinical practice.

A recent study illustrates the long-term clinical benefits of placebo factors when patients believe they have been given active treatments. In a double-blinded study of human fetal mesencephalic transplantation (an experimental treatment for Parkinson's disease), investigators studied the effect of this treatment compared with a placebo treatment for twelve months, using a standard randomized controlled trial design (McRae et al., 2004). They also assessed the patient's experienced assignment to either the placebo treatment (sham surgery) or active treatment (fetal tissue implant). There were no differences between the sham surgery and transplant groups on several physical and quality-of-life measures made by both medical staff and patients. Instead, the experienced assignment of treatment group had a beneficial impact on the overall outcome, and this difference was present at least twelve months after surgery. Patients who believed they received transplanted tissue had significant improvements in both psychological (quality-of-life) and physiological (motor function) outcomes, regardless of whether they received sham surgery or fetal tissue implantations. This study is unusual in providing evidence that the placebo effect can last a long time, quite possibly due to the elaborate and invasive nature of the placebo treatment. This outcome is astounding because it has serious implications for large clinical trials that are enormously expensive and which are used to obtain approval by the Food and Drug Administration for medical use. Although large clinical trials typically have large placebo groups, having a placebo group does not allow measurement of the placebo effect or placebo responses of individuals. Having a placebo group in a study only controls for the placebo effect—it does not measure it. Since these trials hardly ever measure anything like expected effects, desires for effects, and certainly not emotions, the trials miss an opportunity to assess the factors that drive placebo effects. As we have discussed, it is feasible to measure these factors that are predictive of the variability of placebo responses in all groups within a study. Importantly, the contribution of these factors can even be assessed in groups receiving the active treatment, not just the placebo group.

The approach we are suggesting was also used in two similar studies (Bausell et al., 2005; Linde et al., 2007) that compared real acupuncture to sham acupuncture for different painful conditions, such as migraine, tension-type headache, chronic osteoarthritis, and low back pain. These studies examined the effects of patients' expectations on the therapeutic outcome, regardless of group assignment of the patient. To do this, each patient was asked either which group he or she believed himself or herself to belong to (either placebo or real treatment; Bausell et al., 2005), and what he or she personally expected from the treatment (Linde et al., 2007). These studies found that patients who believed they belonged to the real treatment group experienced larger clinical improvement than those patients who believed they belonged to the placebo group (Bausell et al., 2005). Likewise, patients with higher expectations about acupuncture treatment experienced larger clinical benefits than patients with lower expectations, regardless of their allocation to real or sham acupuncture. Thus, it did not really matter whether the patients actually received the real or the sham procedure. What mattered was whether they expected a benefit from it and believed in acupuncture.

These studies are good examples of how simple experiential variables can be integrated into clinical trials, leading to a more exact understanding of why the results turn out the way they do. They underscore the necessity to consider clinical trials from an experiential perspective, in order to make their interpretations meaningful and more reliable. Some ambiguous out-comes of clinical trials could be clarified by some simple questions: "Which group do you believe you are assigned to? and "What do you expect from this treatment?" The questions could require verbal responses and also ratings on scales. This approach could help improve the understanding of results of clinical trials. Assessing variables that contribute to the placebo effect, such as perceived group assignment, expected changes, and desire for clinical benefits, could provide a means of assessing the contribution of placebo even when there is no natural history (i.e., untreated) condition. A secondary benefit would be a means of assessing the extent to which double-blind conditions are maintained.

9.8.2 Are There Ethical Ways to Produce or Enhance Placebo Responses?

To many who have studied this topic, the history of placebo research and the applications of placebos in health-care practice are replete with decep-tive attempts to please patients and reduce what is perceived as their unwarranted demands. Placebo administration has even been erroneously used to determine whether patients' conditions are "psychogenic" or not. Presumably, if patients respond positively to placebo, then the cause of their condition was in their mind all along. Even Carl Sagan, a former astrophysicist and popular scientist of the twentieth century, suggested that placebo effects may only occur for placebo diseases, indirectly sug-gesting that placebo responses reflect conditions that do not result from real pathological processes (Sagan and Druyan, 1995). The word placebo has been a pejorative term among health-care practitioners, patients, and clinical trial investigators. Yet, as discussed, placebo responses are already embedded in the overall response to active agents. They add benefits to existing therapies and in many instances, such as antidepressant therapy, constitute the major, if not exclusive, source of improvement (Kirsch, 2009). However, if a proven therapy is combined with the statement "The agent that has just been given is known to powerfully reduce pain in some people," this simple addition is not necessarily a deceptive manipulation because some agents have been shown to be efficacious (perhaps not anti-depressants, however). It could be a true statement and one that enhances the overall therapeutic effect. This type of enhancement of placebo responses could be applied in an ethical manner.

Another ethical issue surrounds the deceptive use of inert placebo agents. What happens to patients and participants in studies who receive a placebo treatment and then are told that they were given a placebo treat-ment and had a placebo response? Do they become disillusioned, resentful, disheartened, or otherwise psychologically harmed? Are their subsequent placebo responses diminished? Clearly, these questions raise ethical concerns about using only placebo agents in treatment. Two studies by Karen Chung and her colleagues directly addressed these questions in IBS patients and in pain-free undergraduate participants (Chung et al., 2007). Both the patients and the undergraduates were given placebos and then tested for placebo responses during experimentally induced pain. They were then told that they had placebo responses and were even shown graphs of the magnitudes of these responses. Neither the patients nor undergraduate participants changed their moods or attitudes toward the investigators. They liked and trusted the investigators just as much as before they learned about their placebo responses. When the undergraduates were tested for placebo responses a second time after learning about their first placebo responses, the magnitude of the second placebo response was about the same as their first exposure to placebo. Contrary to speculation that learning about your own placebo response may result in psychological harm, this study found that harm didn't occur. Nevertheless, since placebo responses can be enhanced and produced without having to administer inert agents, we think that nondeceptive use of placebo may provide the optimal strategy. The studies just discussed certainly may not be representative of all studies that include a placebo condition.

9.9   Future Directions in Relating Brain Activity to Psychological Variables Associated with Placebo

Large placebo effects that accompany corresponding decreases in activity within symptom-related areas of the brain underscore both the psychological and biological reality of the placebo response and support current models of mind–brain interactions (Schwartz et al., 2005).

However, elucidating the relationships between cognitive and emotional factors to placebo responses is an enormous challenge, as is determining their neurobiological underpinnings. Psychological studies of placebo responses have included progressively more variables, such as expectancy, desire, somatic focus, and type of goal. Measures of these variables can be potentially incorporated into brain imaging and other types of neurobiological studies, so that explicit mechanistic hypotheses about these factors can be tested at a level that is more refined both psychologically and neurobiologically. Such improvements should provide increasing potential for utilizing knowledge of these mechanisms in clinical research and practice. However, beyond this relatively straightforward approach, there remains a need to characterize placebo responses and effects in a much more refined manner. Thus, the following questions could serve as guidelines for studies of placebo responses: (1) How is the placebo suggestion experienced? (2) How do the suggestions, context, and feedback lead to increased expectations of relief? (3) How do expectations coupled with their desires lead to emotions that regulate the placebo response? (4) How do emotional feelings change the experience of symptoms such as pain and anxiety? (5) What are the neural causes and correlates of 1–4?

9.9.1 Experiences and Placebo-Related Brain Activation

A refined experiential account of placebo responses would also improve explanations of neurobiological mechanisms of placebo. This chapter provides two accounts of how placebo responses are generated. The first is about how dimensions of phenomenal experience interact with each other to result in the placebo response. This account results from experiments wherein reductions in desire for relief and expected decreases in pain mediate reductions in actual pain. Moreover, these changes increase over time as a result of feedback and somatic focus. The independent variables can be manipulated and measured using the same principles that operate in any good science. The observational arrangements of the study consist of applying suggestions/instructions, stimuli, and manipulations designed to induce changes or variation in both the independent and dependent variables, all of which are within participants' experience. The second account is based on observations of neural activity within brain regions that have causal interactions with each other as well as correlations with experiential variables of the first account. Neither of the two accounts is observer free, nor is one privileged over the other (Velmans, 2009). They differ according to their observational arrangements. It is just as appropriate to examine and verify causal interactions between dimensions of experience, such as those between intensities of desire, expectation, feeling, and pain intensity, as it is to verify interactions between brain regions. The approach and methods for the former type of verification have been spelled out in chapters 2 through 5.

We are making a large point about these two approaches to scientific investigation of placebo because we think there is an enormous bias in Western neuroscientific practice for the neural account and against the experiential account. An anecdote illustrates this bias. In 2001, one of us (DDP) attended and was a speaker at a conference on placebo at the National Institutes of Health. After my talk, someone from the audience asked me what I thought really *caused* the placebo response. My tentative answer was that I thought placebo responses were mediated by expectations of therapeutic benefit combined with changes in desires and emotions (my explanations were less elaborate and less certain then). This person looked puzzled and astonished at my answer. "No," he said, "What I really mean are the actual *causes* of the placebo response, such as the brain regions that are involved in the placebo response." When I stated that I thought dimensions of experience have causal interactions that can be studied using the scientific method and that they could potentially help explain the placebo response, he was not satisfied to say the least. Nothing other than a standard materialistic answer would be acceptable.

Although we don't think experiential variables within an account of placebo responses can be ontologically reduced to neural variables, we think analysis of the associative relationships between experiential variables and brain activity is enormously useful because they help refine explanations of placebo mechanisms. As Velmans (2009) has pointed out, explanations using mentalistic concepts and those that are about brain mechanisms are mutually irreducible to one another, yet both explanations benefit from each other. This approach also fulfills Varela's idea of a mutual circulation between phenomenological and neurobiological accounts of conscious phenomena (Varela, 1996).

10 Hypnotic and Other Background States of Consciousness

This chapter presents an example of how an experiential method can lead to both definitional and functional hypotheses about background conscious states and how these hypotheses can be further tested using the methods of natural science. The topic is about hypnotic and other background states of consciousness. Similar to some previous chapters, we begin with an account of how definitional and functional hypotheses were generated by the experiential method. We then describe studies in which these hypotheses were tested using direct scaling methods. Finally, we discuss brain imaging studies that help explain how an experiential model of hypnotic state can be at least partially integrated with a neurobiological model that conceives of a hypnotic state in terms of brain mechanisms that regulate consciousness. We think this sequence of scientific exploration and analysis has strong implications for understanding not only the hypnotic state but other background states of consciousness. This approach and method may even serve an empirical strategy for understanding consciousness in general. Of course, some of the more difficult philosophical issues will still be left open to question.

10.1 Some Historical Issues: Role Enactment and State Theories of Hypnosis

Before we launch into the story just outlined, we need to briefly describe the historical context in which the studies to be discussed were conducted. These studies occurred over a period extending between 1982 and the present. During that time and even several years before then, two major general theories proposed very different explanations for hypnotic phenomena. One theory proposed that participants cognitively relabel their reports of experiences such as pain, not because they really feel them to be different but simply to act in the role of someone who has less pain

(Spanos, 1986). This role-enactment theory was influenced by the closely related idea that demand characteristics of experiments exert a strong influence on participants' responses (Orne; 1962). The alternative view of hypnosis was that hypnotic inductions and suggestions produced different levels of an altered state of consciousness in people depending on their susceptibility or ability to experience this state (Hilgard, 1992; Hilgard and Hilgard, 1994). What was common to both views and the experiments conducted by investigators who held them was that almost no attempt was made to determine how participants directly experienced themselves during hypnosis. Hypnotic susceptibility tests have used many items that assess behavioral performance of some kind to determine hypnotic ability. An example of such an item on the Stanford Hypnotic Clinical Scale is that of having participants hold their hands straight out in front of themselves while imaging a force attracting their hands together (Hilgard and Hilgard, 1994). With repeated suggestions of a strong force between their hands, participants often exhibit the suggested behavior of moving their hands together. But what is their direct experience that accompanies this act? Is it that of role playing, complying with the demands of the hypnotist, or a feeling that the hands are responding by themselves without deliberation or effort? Behavioral measures alone cannot distinguish between these alternatives. Some hypnosis researchers do recognize the need to assess the phenomenal experiences of their participants, and some hypnotic susceptibility tests now include experiential items (Arendt-Nielsen, Zachariae, and Bjerring, 1990; Kosslyn et al., 2000; Szechtman, Woody, Bowers, and Nahmias, 1998). Experiential analysis has even become part of some hypnosis investigations. For example, Peter Sheehan (1992) contributed to understanding the hypnotic experience by use of the Experiential Analysis Technique. This technique involves videotaping the hypnotized person during an experiment. Immediately afterwards, the participant is then instructed to watch the videotape with the experimenter and to pause the tape at any point to comment on the experience. The experimenter might also pause the tape at some point to ask about the direct experience of the participant. Although this approach seems a bit unsystematic, it does enable some access to the experience of hypnotized participants.

Beginning in the 1990s and extending to the present, the hypothesis that hypnotic suggestions can actually modify phenomenal experience has received strong support from studies combining neuroscience methods, such as functional brain imaging, and experiential data in the form of self-ratings of dimensions of phenomenal experience (Szechtman et al.,

1998; Kosslyn et al., 2000; Arendt-Nielsen et al., 1990; De Pascalis, Magurano, and Bellusci, 1999; Hofbauer et al., 2001; Kropotov, Crawford, and Polyakov, 1997; Rainville et al., 1997; Wik et al., 1999; Willoch et al., 2000). However, most of these studies have examined the effect of hypnotic suggestions on various sensory modalities and perceptual dimensions (e.g., color vision, pain unpleasantness) and have not directly addressed the status of hypnotic *states*. The remainder of this chapter demonstrates how the use of both stages of the experiential method, in combination with natural science methods (e.g., neuroscience/brain imaging), establishes the hypnotic state as a unique background state of consciousness distinguishable from other background states. At least two criteria should be met in order to support a state theory of hypnosis. First, the induction of hypnosis should be shown to produce changes in aspects of phenomenal experience not restricted to specific domains or *contents* (i.e., objects) of experience, such as specific persons, places, or things. Second, it should engage specific neurophysiological mechanisms known to be involved in producing or maintaining conscious states. Meeting these criteria may be necessary to conclude that hypnosis is a "state" distinct from other forms of "normal" wakefulness.

10.2 Content-Specific and Background Dimensions of Consciousness

The distinction proposed here between *contents* and *states* of consciousness is consistent with David Chalmers's description of content-specific and background states of consciousness, respectively (Chalmers, 2000). The latter refers to the global state of an organism (e.g., attentive, awake, drowsy, asleep, dreaming,...) that constrains and regulates the content of consciousness but is *not* defined in terms of specific content or sensory modality. It provides a useful framework to investigate potentially separable neurobiological correlates for states of consciousness, including such states as hypnotic state, active attention, deep absorption, and even states of awareness. In a series of studies, we have adopted a relatively simple approach to the problem of hypnosis and consciousness. First, if hypnosis is an altered state of consciousness, then the phenomenal experience of being hypnotized should be characterized by changes in aspects of phenomenal experience that are essential to wakeful consciousness in general. In other words, hypnosis does not produce completely unique dimensions of experience but rather changes in experiential dimensions that already exist in conscious persons. Second, in order to conclude that hypnosis is an altered state of consciousness that involves brain systems associated with producing and maintaining states of consciousness, it would be useful to conduct brain imaging experiments that show how the neural activities of brain regions correlate with the experiential factors that have been already identified using experiential methods. In light of these considerations, the following two hypotheses can be formulated, the first by Rainville and colleagues (1999; 2002) and the second a modification of another one of his hypotheses:

1. Key phenomenal dimensions that characterize states of consciousness are significantly modified following the induction of hypnosis (Rainville et al., 1999; 2002).
2. These modifications in phenomenal experience produced by the induction of hypnosis accompany changes in neural activity within brain areas associated with the regulation of consciousness.

With this background and these general hypotheses in mind, the remainder of this chapter explains how these two hypotheses were tested using the two stages of the experiential method and then later integrated with brain imaging studies.

10.3   Experiential Characterization of a Hypnotic State

This story begins with a hypnosis project that took place within the context of a graduate course that I (DDP) taught at West Georgia University in the winter of 1982 (Price and Barrell, 1990). The course was attended by 21 psychology graduate students and psychology faculty members, and the class met weekly on Wednesday evenings for three hours. The major aim of this class was to understand the nature of a hypnotic state from a first-person perspective. Each class member was to answer the question "What is it like to experience a hypnotic state?" The beginning of this project was challenging because we assumed that some class members had read about or saw "hypnotic phenomena" and hypnotized people. For the first three weeks, class members were admonished not to read *anything* about hypnosis. Instead, they read articles about the experiential method and about how this method can be used to discover common factors and their relationships in phenomena such as emotions (Barrell and Barrell, 1975; Price and Barrell, 1980). They also practiced the steps of self-observation and experiential reporting described in chapter 3. Finally, they were instructed to suspend their preconceptions about hypnosis and the hypnotic state and to be open to the nature of their immediate experiences as much as possible. To practice the experiential method, they brought first-person reports of "ordinary" experiences to class and reported on them, excluding those that would be embarrassing or inappropriate for public discussion.

The issue of preconceptualizing the answer to this question was dealt with by instructing class members to attempt to put aside any previous ideas about hypnosis or their previous experiences of the hypnotic state and to simply notice and be open to the experiences that occurred after each induction, in keeping with the approach of the experiential method (see chapter 4). After several preliminary group inductions, class members noticed and agreed that a qualitative change in conscious state occurred after at least some inductions and, for some people, most of the hypnotic inductions.

After this preliminary stage, hypnotic inductions were carried out on an individual basis. Faculty offices and lounges were borrowed for these sessions, each lasting for about twenty to thirty minutes. As pointed out in chapter 4, the Psychology Department at West Georgia provided unusual opportunities for creative explorations into the nature of human consciousness (and no drugs were used to expedite anyone's changes in conscious state). Study group members were instructed to notice their own experiences during and describe them soon after each induction. Much of these data were immediate retrospective and included the reexperiencing of the preceding hypnotic state as if it were happening in the moment. Observations were to be made of members' experienced feelings, thoughts, sensations, actions, and meanings. In addition, they were to notice whether their experience contained many or few objects of attention. Most importantly, they were to be open to their experience, whatever its character. Each participant wrote a one paragraph description after each hypnotic session and collected three to five descriptions.

10.3.1 Representative Experiential Reports

The following reports are representative descriptions of experiences that were reported right after the end of hypnosis experiences (Price and Barrell, 1990):

Situation 1

As I sit and take deep breaths, I very quickly close my eyes and become deeply relaxed. I still see the crystal turning very slowly and find it easier to focus on the crystal than on his voice. I go more and more into the crystal and experience nothing but the crystal and light (Note: induction took place in a lighted room). When he [person doing the hypnosis] says something about energy, I immediately feel more alert and energized.... When he counts and reaches three, I feel my eyes jerk and realize that he had previously said to open my eyes at three. I open them feeling alert.

Situation 2

I become deeply relaxed and heavy at the suggestion of going back to the group induction in the other room. I don't feel that I'm deeply in a trance, but at the suggestion of my arm raising I feel like my arm occasionally jerks by itself, not under my control. As I open my eyes, I am surprised to see my arm suspended in front of me. I focus very intently but somehow easily on my hand and feel deeply comfortable. She [person doing the hypnosis] talks about the other classroom. I am aware that I have not been paying attention to the words and for several moments I don't know for sure where I am or what exactly she said. I come back to knowing where I am, still feeling comfortable and very relaxed.

Situation 3

I feel more and more relaxed as time goes by. I feel heaviness in my eyes as I watch her [the hypnotist]. I see her very clearly and notice very little else. As she speaks about my arm lifting, I notice that my arm makes a smooth arc all by itself and my finger touches my forehead. I am amazed by my experience. The room seems to be glowing and I feel a deep relaxation and quietness while everything takes place. I think momentarily that I must be in a deep trance.

Participants could not help but sometimes reflect on changes in their conscious state. This reflection often came at the end or beginning of the experience when suggestions were given to induce or terminate the period of hypnosis but could also occur during hypnosis as in situation 3 above. Participants were often surprised by the nature of their alteration in conscious experience. These features of experience are evident in the representative descriptions given above.

10.3.2 Identifying the Common Factors

Based on all of their descriptions, each class member made a list of factors that they saw as common to most or all of their experiential reports, such as the reports just described. Because hypnotic states are likely to vary in depth, we suspended the usual requirement that all of the factors had to be present in each description. Factors that were present in experiences of the most deeply altered states were given priority. We compiled a group list of common factors during group discussions. As in previous applications of the experiential method, the experiences themselves rather than beliefs or theories served as the arbiter in discussions of common factors. Class members often had different ways of stating these factors, which seemed to refer to a similar meaning. For example, factor 3 below was stated as "a feeling of ease" by some people, "relaxation" by others, and "letting go" by still other people. We made a tentative decision to consolidate these descriptors into a single factor or meaning. The following is a preliminary list that was made after six weeks of data collection:

1. An absorbed and sustained focus of attention on one or few targets (N = 20 of 21 members).
2. Narrow range of attention (N = 19 of 21 members).
3. A feeling of mental/physical ease or relaxation (N = 21 of 21 members).
4. One's responses experienced as automatic or without deliberation or effort (N = 18 of 21 members).
5. Suspension of usual orientation toward time, location of self, and/or sense of self (N = 11 of 21 members).
6. Relative absence of judging, monitoring, or censoring (N = 11 of 21 members).
7. Lethargy and heaviness (N = 9 of 21 members).
8. Strong orientation toward the present (N = 7 of 21 members).
9. Experience body as integrated whole (N = 8 of 21 members).
10. Focusing inwardly (N = 4 of 21 members).
11. Distinction between "inside" and "outside" less clear (N = 2 of 21 members).
12. Tingling and pulsing sensations (N = 1 of 21 members).

In accordance with experiential methods previously used, this preliminary list was subjected to extensive group analysis in which each factor was questioned as being present or absent in most if not all experiences after inductions and particularly during those experiences that were considered most different from "ordinary" experiencing. For example, the person who reported his experience in situation 3 above stated that his experience was that of a "deep trance." Each factor in the list above was then questioned for being necessary for this altered state. Finally, group consensus was reached about which combination of factors was sufficient for a hypnotic state.

Common factors 7–12 of the preliminary listing were eliminated because participants found that they were not necessary for the altered state they experienced and these factors were absent in most participants' experiences. In fact, opposite or contradictory experiences occurred. For example, some participants focused outwardly instead of inwardly (factor 10). Others did not closely attend to physical sensations such as tingling or pulsing (factor 12) or heaviness (factor 7). A strong present orientation (factor 8) was not noticed or was considered irrelevant by most participants.

Each of the remaining common factors (1–6) was unanimously agreed upon as being part of the unique altered state that occurred during hypnotic inductions. However, factors 1 and 2 were determined to be integral components of the same factor. The *sustained focus on one or few targets* (factor 1) automatically necessitates that the *range of attention becomes narrow* (factor 2). They are complementary parts of the same factor. There-fore, it was decided that factor 1 more precisely described the dimension of experience in question and that factor 2 was redundant. Thus, the final list of common factors is as follows:

1. An absorbed and sustained focus of attention on one or few targets.
2. A feeling of mental/physical ease or relaxation.
3. An absence of judging, monitoring, censoring.
4. Suspension of usual orientation toward time, location of self, and/or sense of self.
5. Own responses experienced as automatic/without deliberation or effort.

Factors 1, 2, and 5 were clearly and usually explicitly evident in the descriptions of participants because the descriptions contained words that conveyed this same type of meaning. The representative descriptions given earlier serve as examples. Factors 3 and 4 are different in that they were sometimes discerned only after reflecting on the experience that had just occurred. Thus, although 10 of 21 participants did not list factors 3 and 4, 7 out of these 10 participants agreed that factors 3 and 4 were present during their deepest levels of altered states. There were only 3 of 21 par-ticipants who reported not to have experienced all five factors during inductions. Noticing factors 3 and 4 often occurred in retrospect, and it is quite possible that it simply didn't occur to some participants to consider this part of their experience. Furthermore, ascertaining an *absence* of judging and monitoring may itself require monitoring. Similar to dreams, noticing the *absence* of usual self-orientation (factor 4) often occurs upon reflection. Each of the five factors listed above was considered necessary for a hypnotic state (hypothesis 1). Taken together, all five factors were considered sufficient for a hypnotic state (hypothesis 2). Eighteen of the 21 participants agreed upon these experienced factors. Because people vary considerably in hypnotic susceptibility, it is possible that at least some of the three participants who did not experience all five factors were not easily hypnotized.

It is important to determine which of these factors have been independ-ently discovered by others who use different methods. The common factors of nonvolition and effortless experiencing (Bowers, 1978; 1983) appear the same or very similar to *experiencing responses as automatic, without deliberation or effort* (factor 5). Pekula and Kumar (1984) used exten-sive statistical methods in combination with a phenomenology of con-sciousness inventory that was predictive of scores on hypnotic susceptibility tests. The most salient factors associated with hypnotic state were determined to be reduced volitional control, reduced self-awareness, reduced rationality, reduced memory, and increased inward absorbed attention. Pekula and Kumar's factor of reduced volitional control appears similar to factor 5 on the list above, *own responses experienced as automatic.* Their factors of reduced self-awareness and reduced rationality are comparable to *suspension of usual orientation toward time, location, and sense of self,* factor 4 of our analysis. A more obvious similarity is between the latter and Shor's (1965) description of a loss of a generalized reality orientation, a factor that also is relevant to dreams. Finally, Pekula and Kumar's factor of increased inward absorbed attention appears similar to our factor of *an absorbed sustained focus of attention on one or few targets* (factor 1 of our list). Thus, at least three of the five factors of the list presented above have been independently confirmed by Pekula and Kumar and other hypnosis researchers.

10.3.3 Comparisons to "Ordinary" States of Consciousness

In comparison to reports of "ordinary" conscious states, experiential descriptions of the hypnotic state were, surprisingly, much easier for most people to write. It was focused, and there were fewer targets of attention. Participants' experiential descriptions of ordinary waking states were considerably more "heterogeneous" than those occurring during hypnosis. In ordinary states, it was clear that some people were absorbed in fantasy, others were noticing sensory phenomena, and some people were just thinking. Although we didn't know what associative thinking was at the time, descriptions included associative thinking or "mind-wandering." Here is an example collected from one participant:

I was waiting in the classroom waiting for the class to start and realized that I hadn't provided any reports of experiences. I decided to meditate for a few minutes. At the end of my "meditation," here was what was going on:

Someone is talking in the next room. Howie? Is he going to be used in a class demonstration? Memory of last week's demonstration … image of arm levitation. I hear and feel my stomach growl. Are we going to have a break this evening? Maybe I need to drink some water.

Notice that, unlike the hypnotic state, there are multiple targets of attention and the thoughts are loosely associated and relatively unfocused. There is a sense of both the future and past and a present sense of at least part of the state of the body (stomach growl). Although this kind of associative thinking may be a common occurrence, it is difficult to conclude that it is representative of the "waking baseline condition," a term commonly used in studies of hypnosis. Multiple types of ordinary background states of consciousness exist, as shown by studies that sample experience on a random basis (e.g., Hurlburt's descriptive experiential sampling method).

10.4 Possible Interrelationships between Common Factors of a Hypnotic State

In keeping with the experiential method, we needed to formulate and test functional hypotheses about the interrelationships between the common factors within the hypnotic state. In examining participants' descriptions of experiences of the hypnotic state, it became evident that some of the factors were necessary for and supported other factors. Thus, factors 1 (*absorbed sustained focus*) and 2 (*relaxation, ease*) came first as a result of suggestions. These two factors appeared to result in factors 3 (*absence of judging, monitoring, and censoring*) and 4 (*suspension of usual orientation...*) because when the latter two factors appeared in the descriptions they usually followed factors 1 and 2. When mental/physical ease is coupled with absorbed attention, the movement of thought required for awareness of self-context (factor 4) as well as active detached reflection (factor 3) no longer occurs. Based on reports, self-context and assessment of current situation (i.e., monitoring, judging, etc.) become reduced during a hypnotic state. We reasoned that active detached reflection sustains awareness of self-context and supports the experience of deliberation or effort associated with one's responses. We then reasoned that without the experience of deliberation or effort, one's responses are experienced as originating from an external source and/or as automatic.

Based on results of this project, the work of others, and this reasoning, the following is a summary of the common factors within a hypnotic state and their interrelationships.

The experience of a hypnotic state begins with a relaxed condition of mental (and often physical) ease in combination with an absorbed and sustained focus on an object or objects of attention. Thus, initial suggestions for induction of those changes are commonly directed toward these two dimensions (mental ease and absorption). However, it can occur naturally during fascination, watching an absorbing movie, or watching ripples in a stream. It captures us. At first, it can be effortful but with time one proceeds from an active form of concentration to a relaxed passive form. There is often (though perhaps not necessarily) an inhibition or reduction in the peripheral range of experience. At the same time, this relaxation and/or reduction in range of active attention supports a lack of monitoring and censoring of that which is allowed into experience (altered self-regulation). Hence, inconsistencies are now more tolerable. Contradictory statements, which once arrested attention and caused confusion or disturbance, now no longer do so. The uncensored acceptance of what is being said by the hypnotist is not checked against one's associations. Consequently, one no longer chooses or validates the correctness of incoming statements. This allows thinking and meaning-in-itself that is disconnected from active reflection. From this way of experiencing, there emerges the sense of automaticity wherein thinking is no longer felt as preceding action but action is felt as preceding thought. Thus, if the hypnotist suggests a bodily action, a sensation, or a lack of sensation (e.g., pain), there is no experience of deliberation or effort. One simply and automatically identifies with the suggested action, sensation, or lack of sensation, as it is suggested. Changes in perception, mental activity, and behavior are simply felt as happening. Little, if any, consideration is given to the possibility of *not* carrying out the action or *not* experiencing the suggested changes in sensation. In this way, the changes experienced during hypnosis facilitate the incorporation of suggestions, such as analgesia, for example.

The results of experiential studies has led to a proposed characterization of a hypnotic state: *Changes in phenomenal experience induced by suggestions and characterized by mental ease, absorption, a focus on few targets, reduction in self-orientation, and automaticity.* This characterization approaches an experiential definition of a hypnotic state and is based on common experiential factors, similar to other phenomena such as emotions and pain (Rainville and Price, 2003). The hypnotic suggestions included in standardized procedures that induce a hypnotic state often target these five dimensions directly or indirectly. Typically, suggestions for mental ease and absorption are given explicitly and toward the beginning of hypnotic induction. The suggestions for reduced self-orientation and automaticity occur later and can be given directly or indirectly (e.g., suggestions expressed in the passive form). Automaticity corresponds to an altered sense of agency, as described earlier, and is pivotal for the relationship between hypnotic suggestions and targeted changes in experience (e.g., analgesia) or behavior (altered responses to motor challenges). Suggestions can be given by another person (heterohypnosis), or they can be self-generated (autohypnosis). Behavioral responses to standardized suggestions are often used to infer that the procedure induced a hypnotic state and to evaluate the subject's level of hypnotic susceptibility. However, self-report measures of subjective dimensions more directly assess whether someone experiences an altered sense of agency. Thus, reports and/or ratings of feelings of automaticity, effortlessness, or lack of control are useful in establishing the presence of a hypnotic state.

As with studies of other experienced phenomena, the purpose of the first phase of the experiential method in studies of hypnosis was to generate definitional and functional hypotheses that can then be explicitly tested in subsequent experiments wherein other groups of participants can rate these factors on scales. Thus, based on results of our hypnosis project and a consideration of the literature on hypnosis, a tentative model of interrelationships between common factors was formulated, as shown in figure 10.1. This model was subsequently tested in a study in which 62 participants rated their perceived magnitudes of these factors on visual analog scales during experimental conditions designed to produce "normal waking," mild, and deep hypnotic states (Price, 1996). As can be discerned from figure 10.1, path analysis (or structural equation modeling) provided at least a reasonable confirmation of this model. For example, the links (beta weights) between the factors in this model were stronger in comparison to alternative models that were tested. As discussed earlier, the experiential and conceptual basis for these common experiential dim-

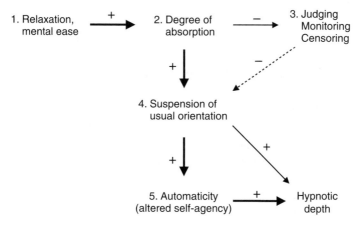

Figure 10.1
Experiential model of hypnosis. Hypnotic states are commonly felt and described using the multiple dimensions of subjective experience identified in the model. Positive (+) and negative (–) functional interactions are proposed in which changes in distinct experiential dimensions precede and facilitate changes in other dimensions. Full lines represent relations that were confirmed statistically in groups of naive subjects. (Adapted from Price, 1996.)

ensions and this model also is generally supported by the work of others who have independently arrived at many of these same common factors (Bowers, 1978; 1983; Pekula and Kumar, 1984). However, unlike previous accounts of factors within hypnotic states, we think the model of figure 10.1 is more inclusive and precisely specifies interactions between dimensions of experience. It also provides a basis for the increased responsiveness to suggestion that is unique and distinguishable from other types of psychologically mediated increases in responsiveness to suggestion, such as placebo, for example. This basis is directly evident in the phenomenology of the interrelationships between the common factors within this model and may be recognized by at least some readers' memories of hypnotic states.

10.5 Relating Hypnotic States to Brain Activity: Hypnotic Suggestions Activate Brain Mechanisms That Contribute to a Unique Background Conscious State

Pierre Rainville and his colleagues recognized the need to provide an experimental approach that relates self-reports of changes in phenomenal experience with changes in brain activity in order to investigate the neural correlates of hypnosis (Rainville et al., 1999; 2002; Rainville and Price, 2003). Although current functional brain imaging methods may not provide the fine-grain measurements of neurophysiological processes that are critically correlated with consciousness processes, Rainville has reasoned that if alterations in basic aspects of consciousness during hypnotic states really reflect altered states of consciousness, they should relate to corresponding changes in neural activity within brain regions involved in conscious states. The degree of spatial resolution of current methods used to measure brain activity should be at least sufficient to test this general hypothesis. This integrative approach could also lead to further identification of hypotheses about the neural underpinnings of hypnosis. If this approach can be made to work for hypnotic states, it might be applied to the characterization of other background states of consciousness within the more general framework of neurobiological theories of consciousness.

10.5.1 Patterns of Brain Activity Accompanying Hypnotic States
Based on this reasoning, Rainville and colleagues conducted two studies that related the experiential model of figure 10.1 to changes in brain activity during hypnotic states (Rainville et al., 1999; 2002). In the first study,

the approach was simple and consisted of identifying brain structures that were activated or deactivated during hypnotic states, using the "waking baseline" as a comparison condition. They examined the effects of hypnotic induction on the regional distribution of cerebral blood flow (rCBF), a proxy measure of neural activity, using positron emission tomography (PET). Brain scans were first acquired in a baseline condition; then, a standard hypnotic induction procedure was administered, and scans were acquired while subjects were in the hypnotic state (Rainville et al., 1999; 2002). Hypnosis-related changes were assessed by directly contrasting hypnosis and baseline conditions (using a paired t test applied to each volumetric sample). Those brain regions that changed their level of activity largely corresponded to those areas and mechanisms known to be involved in the regulation of consciousness.

Compared to the baseline condition, increases in neural activity occurred during hypnotic states for the following brain regions: (1) *the occipital cortex on both sides,* (2) *right frontal cortex,* (3) *right temporal gyrus,* (4) *left posterior insula,* and (5) *right anterior cingulate.* Areas 1, 2, and 5 are shown in figure 10.2 and will be discussed later in relation to functional connections between them. The increases in the occipital cortex were strongly correlated with increases in slow wave delta electroencephalogram (EEG) activity. These increases in occipital cortex neural activity and EEG delta waves reflect alteration of consciousness associated with possible facilitation of visual imagery and decreased arousal. Visual imagery was definitely present in one of us (DDP), who participated in the experiment in order to acquire a first-person account of the hypnotic state within this experimental context. One of the aims of the experiment was to alter the unpleasantness of pain evoked by a heated water bath. An example of a suggestion for reducing unpleasantness included imagining one's left hand being immersed in warm sand at the beach. As this suggestion was given, I had a visual image of my left hand dipping into the sand and a corresponding feeling of warmth in that hand. This image came automatically and there was no pain. At the time, I had no knowledge that a major result of the study would be increased delta wave activity in the visual (occipital) cortex. I also didn't know the temperature of the water bath was 49° C, a temperature that is distinctly painful for most people.

Frontal cortical activity and temporal cortex activity during hypnosis might reflect verbal mediation of the hypnotic suggestions, working memory (to maintain memory for suggestions), and top-down processes involved in reinterpretation of the participants' experience (i.e., as pleasant warmth instead of unpleasant pain). Insular cortex activity may be related

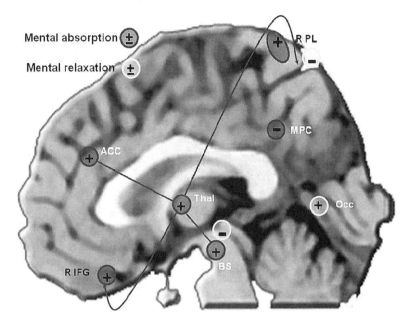

Figure 10.2

Associations between hypnotic relaxation and absorption with brain activity. Increases in hypnotic relaxation are associated with regional cerebral blood flow (rCBF) increases in the occipital cortex (Occ) and with decreases in the mesencephalic tegmentum of the brainstem (BS) and the right parietal lobule (R PL). In contrast, increases in self-reports of mental absorption during hypnosis are associated with increases (+) in rCBF within a coordinated network of brain structures (connected by lines) involved in attention and including the pontomesencephalic brainstem (BS), the medial thalamus (Thal), and the anterior cingulate cortex (ACC), as well as the inferior frontal (R IFG) and the parietal lobule (R PL) of the right hemisphere. Additional decreases in rCBF in the medial parietal cortex (MPC) are associated with absorption. (Adapted from Rainville et al., 2002, and Rainville and Price, 2003.)

to the altered feeling of somatic state and awareness (Craig, 2009), and anterior cingulate activity may be related to increased focus of attention during absorption, a critical aspect of the hypnotic state.

Equally important and revealing were decreases in brain activity associated with the hypnotic state. In comparison to the baseline waking condition, the following brain regions showed *decreases* in neural activity during the hypnotic state: (1) *right inferior parietal lobule*, (2) *posterior cingulate cortex*, (3) *medial parietal or precuneus cortex*, and (4) *medial prefrontal cortex*. Regions 2–4 are illustrated in figure 1.1 and comprise a network known to correlate with associative thinking. Thus, decreases in neural activity of this network during a hypnotic state may reflect the suspension of associative thinking. In contrast to a hypnotic state, associative thinking involves multiple targets and an expanded range of attention. It is not necessarily combined with relaxation or mental ease. To put it simply, associative thinking is a state of "mind-wandering" where one moves quickly from one object/thought to the next, often without focus. As pointed out in chapter 1, these brain regions are usually active during the "baseline" conditions of many brain imaging experiments wherein participants are told to quietly rest. Thus, in retrospect it not surprising that during the hypnosis condition these same regions decrease their activity relative to the baseline condition. After all, participants reduce the number of targets and range of attention and reduce their self-monitoring during hypnosis.

The decrease in activity within the inferior parietal lobule during hypnosis is especially noteworthy in the context of factor 5 of the experiential model of hypnotic state—automaticity. This region of the brain has been highly implicated in the experience of agency. The model shown in figure 10.1 predicts that increases in hypnotic relaxation/mental ease and absorption contribute to a suspension of usual self-orientation that further contributes to the sense of automaticity. Automaticity reflects an altered sense of self-agency. Although hypnotized individuals are the critical players in the responses to hypnotic suggestions, they often experience their own responses as happening by themselves. An active movement of their arm may be felt as happening by itself or under the influence of an imagined external cause (e.g., a lever pulling up the arm). Similarly, changes in sensory experience (e.g., hallucination or analgesia) may be experienced as simply happening automatically or as real properties of external objects rather than being generated as an act of one's deliberation or effort. Decreases in activity in the inferior parietal lobule during hypnosis is consistent with studies showing that this part of the brain is intimately involved in the experience of agency (Ruby and Decety, 2001; Chaminade and Decety, 2002; Farrer and Frith, 2002; Farrar et al., 2003). The inferior parietal lobule is active during experimental conditions wherein participants attribute their own intentions and efforts as the cause of their own responses, and it decreases its activity when they don't make this attribution, such as when they experience their responses as caused by an external source (Ruby and Decety, 2001; Chaminade and Decety, 2002). Thus, the idea that decreased activity in the inferior parietal lobule during hypnosis relates to a sense of automaticity is supported by independent evidence that this region shows decreased activity during similar experiences of automaticity, even within nonhypnotic contexts.

Another reason for proposing involvement of the inferior parietal lobule in the sense of agency and in hypnotic state is derived from a clinical case study of a man who had an abscess in his right inferior parietal cortex (Musulam, 1981). The patient experienced his body as being controlled by external forces. He also made statements such as "My head is empty," "I have no thoughts," and "I feel hypnotized." He experienced a loss of ability to sense his actions as coming from himself. This case study suggests an alteration in general consciousness, manifested by a radical change in sense of agency.

Other brain regions are also involved in the sense of agency. Functional brain imaging studies have explored how the anterior insula and posterior parietal cortex may be critical for alternative experiences of attributing the agency of action or response to oneself versus an external source (Ruby and Decety, 2001; Chaminade and Decety, 2002; Farrer and Frith, 2002; Farrer et al., 2003, 2003). One study has specifically examined the altered sense of agency in response to hypnotic suggestions for passive movement of the arm (Blakemore et al., 2003). In this study, the experimenter gave hypnotic suggestions to six highly hypnotizable participants to the effect that their left hand and forearm would be moved rhythmically by a pulley (*deluded passive movement*). Their brains were scanned during this condition, and results of this scanning were compared to those of two other conditions, one wherein participants voluntarily and deliberately made the same movements (*volitional movement*) and another in which their arms really were rhythmically moved by a pulley (*passive movement*). Both conditions of *deluded movement* and *passive movement* showed stronger activity in one region of the parietal cortex (parietal operculum) and cerebellum as compared to the *volitional movement*. These results are in a direction opposite to those found for the inferior parietal lobule discussed above.

Blakemore and Frith (2003) think that the experience of self-generated actions depends on a *match* between frontal control systems that provide intentions for motor commands with feedback from some of the sensory systems of the parietal cortex. Some areas of the parietal cortex, such as the parietal operculum just mentioned, and cerebellum can simultaneously receive input from both frontal control systems and sensory feedback, such as impulse input from muscles, skin, and joints that are stimulated during an active movement. When these impulse inputs are simultaneous, a *match* occurs both psychologically and neurophysiologically. The corresponding experience is that the source of the action is one's intentions, an experience that is associated with activity in the frontal cortex. In contrast, when there is robust parietal operculum activity and no input from frontal control systems, a feeling of self-agency is missing. In this case, the sensory feedback is perceived without the matching input from the frontal control systems. This mechanism can be imagined in the following way. When you reach to pick up a pencil, you feel your arm, hand, and fingers simultaneously move and you experience this all happening in proximity to your intention or urge to pick up the pencil. Your sensations of this act "match" something you intended and wanted to happen. Call this the "I'm doing it!" response. What if these sensations didn't occur, or what if you had the sensations without the experience of the intention? It should not be surprising that you would not feel yourself to be the agent of this act. There are parts of the parietal cortex that match neural activity related to these two aspects of your experience. These areas may monitor the degree of match, and once it occurs, their activity then diminishes when all is well. As discussed, other parietal areas such as the inferior parietal lobule provide a positive signal when one perceives himself or herself as agent and are deactivated during a feeling of automaticity. Thus, the sense of self-agency depends on a network of parietal cortical areas that monitor the match between signals that relate to intention and sensory feedback signals and other parietal areas that may directly signal the feeling of self-agency.

10.5.2 Hypnosis Activates Diffuse Brain Networks Involved in States of Consciousness

In the second experiment by Rainville and colleagues (2002), investigators asked participants to rate their levels of *mental relaxation* and *absorption* immediately after each brain scan in both the baseline and the hypnosis conditions. Relaxation and absorption were analyzed in relationship to changes in neural activity of the brain. Global changes observed in this study were reliable and similar to those found in an independent study by Maquet and coinvestigators (Maquet et al., 1999). Rainville's study demonstrated that the induction of hypnosis produced reliable changes in the relative level of neural activity of many brain regions, including increases in some areas and decreases in others. A brain network was characterized by using ratings of mental ease/relaxation and absorption as correlates of brain activities involved with the hypnotic state. This network is depicted in figure 10.2, wherein brain areas associated with ease/relaxation are represented by light grey circles with white outlines and brain areas associated with absorption are represented by dark grey circles. Increases and decreases in activity are represented by plus and minus signs, respectively. Strong associations with mental ease/relaxation ratings occurred in the lower brainstem, the thalamus, and the anterior cingulate cortex (ACC). Ratings of feelings of mental ease and relaxation were specifically associated with *lower* levels of neural activity in the midbrain of the lower brainstem, the thalamus, and the frontal part of the ACC. Relaxation-related *increases* in neural activity were observed in the midportion of the ACC, an area involved in attention and related functions.

In contrast with ease/relaxation, ratings of feelings of absorption were specifically associated with coordinated *increases* in the level of activity within the midbrain near the pons, the thalamus, and the frontal portion of the ACC (see figure 10.2). These increases of brain activity precisely map onto a distributed brain network underlying attention processes (Posner and Dehaene, 1994). This network reflects much of the brain's attention system. Several earlier EEG studies had proposed the involvement of brain attention processes in hypnosis. For example, activity in the EEG theta range (4–8 cycles per second) has been associated with both hypnosis and attention (Rainville et al., 2002).

The similarity between some effects of hypnotic relaxation observed in Rainville's study and the effects of slow wave sleep (e.g., Hofle et al., 1997) and decreased vigilance (Paus et al., 1997) are striking and may reflect the relative engagement of similar mechanisms. Paus (2000) has proposed that the coordinated pattern of changes in these brain areas reflects mechanisms regulating the brain's arousal level and the participants' level of vigilance. Consistent with this possibility, hypnotic relaxation may reflect a state of decreased vigilance and an attenuation of the state of readiness to engage or orient toward external sources of stimulation. Additional decreases observed in posterior parietal cortices within areas associated with orientation and attention to external visual, auditory, and somatosensory stimuli are consistent with this interpretation (Coull, Frackowiak, and Frith, 1998; Paus et al., 1997; Peyron et al., 1999). Similar to what has been proposed in previous cognitive studies, Rainville and Price (2003) suggest that these additional relaxation- and absorption-related *decreases* in rCBF in the right and left posterior parietal cortices may contribute to the hypnosis-induced disorientation toward space and time, and possibly sense of self (see figure 10.2; see also Gitelman et al., 1996; Coull and Nobre, 1998; Gitelman et al., 1999; Kim, Gitelman, and Nobre, 1999; Nobre et al., 1997).

The somewhat contrasting pattern of responses associated with hypnotic relaxation/mental ease and absorption may reflect either competing processes acting on the same populations of neurons or brain structures. One possibility is that the general increases in hypnosis-related ease/relaxation may reflect a reduction in arousal and vigilance that is coupled with high levels of absorption (focused attention). This coupling is in contrast to other background states of consciousness where arousal and vigilance are coupled with a lack of ease and/or lack of relaxation. Thus, the increases in absorption during hypnosis may require the activation of compensatory mechanisms to overcome the possible detrimental effect that the state of deep relaxation and decreases in vigilance–arousal would otherwise have on executive attention processes. Similar mechanisms have been suggested to account for the maintenance of the level of attention necessary to perform a visual discrimination task after sleep deprivation (e.g., Portas, et al., , 1998). This similarity is consistent with the overall idea that the state of attention in hypnosis is one of deep absorption (passive attention) that occurs within a background of decreased vigilance and increased ease/ relaxation.

In addition to the involvement of the brain's arousal and attention systems, somatosensory cortices displayed changes in neural activity. Hypnotic relaxation was associated with decreases in activity within primary and secondary somatosensory cortices and the posterior insular cortex mainly in the right hemisphere (Rainville et al., 2002). These areas are obviously of critical importance for the representation of the body, and these changes may contribute to an alteration of the overall feeling of one's body and closely related sense of self. These types of interactions are proposed by Damasio's theoretical model of consciousness (Damasio, 1999). A simple way of interpreting relaxation-related decreases in somatosensory cortical activity is that actual physical relaxation reduces sensory input to the somatosensory cortices, input that would normally occur from contracted muscles and other tissues. Diminished input to the primary somatosensory cortex would, in turn, result in diminished input from the latter to posterior parietal areas involved in higher order self-representations. It is plausible that all of these changes would be accompanied by a sense of ease and alterations in sense of self.

10.5.3   What Additional Studies Are Needed to Provide an Integrative Neurobiological and Experiential Explanation of the Hypnotic State?

The description of hypnosis as an altered state of consciousness implies that basic aspects of consciousness regulation are modified by the hypnosis procedure. Based on the results of studies discussed in this chapter, which can be interpreted in light of theories of consciousness, it has been shown that several dimensions of experience characterizing the background state of consciousness are modified by standard hypnotic procedures (see figure 10.1). Future studies investigating the neural correlates of all five of the common factors of the hypnotic state have to be conducted and related to their experiential counterparts. A similar strategy has been suggested for understanding emotional feelings, placebo responses, and pain (as discussed in chapters 2–9).

Technical improvements and additional methods are also needed. For one, more precise characterization of functional interactions between experiential factors in hypnotic states (e.g., absorption, automaticity) is needed, as is more precise characterization of neural interactions. Both require better temporal resolution. For example, moment-to-moment experiential measures of automaticity could be related to measures of brain activity that have high temporal resolution. Methods similar to those used to establish the connections shown in figure 10.1 need to be applied in brain imaging experiments, and this need reflects a real challenge. There should be at least some general correspondence between the experiential factors and the brain regions that serve them. Brain imaging methods that have better temporal resolution than PET, such as fMRI and MEG (magnetoencephalography), should be used to establish dynamic changes in brain activity and temporal interrelationships between brain areas associated with the establishment of the hypnotic state.

Despite the fact that this field of research is in its early stages, what has been established thus far is that the hypnotic state involves a unique combination of significant changes in basic aspects of conscious experience and in neural activity within specific networks of brain structures involved in body–self representation. Although much more remains to be investigated to explain the neural mechanisms underpinning the hypnotic state, we think that the investigation of hypnosis phenomena in the light of modern neurobiological and experiential theories of consciousness offers a great opportunity to improve our understanding of hypnosis. Could this approach and these methods be used to characterize other background states of consciousness?

We propose that the experiential factors that constitute a hypnotic state are clearly dimensions of consciousness in general. Each factor within the hypnotic state varies along a continuum. For example, attention can vary from a strong and sustained focus of attention on one or few targets to a weak and transient attention to multiple targets. The sense of one's mental/ physical state can vary from a deep feeling of ease/relaxation to an intense feeling of difficulty/tension. The degree of judging, monitoring, and censoring can vary from none to the most one can imagine. Similar continua occur for self-orientation and automaticity/deliberation.

It is plausible that different background states of consciousness could be specified by magnitudes along these five factors. For example, different types of associative thinking might be characterized by different profiles of magnitudes along these different factors.

10.6   Are There Other Similar Models of Consciousness?

10.6.1   Phenomenal Self-Model

Developments in the field of consciousness studies in philosophy have emphasized fundamental properties of the phenomenal experience of consciousness. The philosopher Thomas Metzinger has proposed a representational framework to capture some essential aspects of *what it feels like to be conscious* (Metzinger, 2000). The description of consciousness in terms of representations helps define properties that are more amenable to scientific inquiry. The study of consciousness can then be conducted by specifying the conditions in which those properties are brought into focus and/or modified. Metzinger's model recognizes the need for a representation of self for phenomenal experience to occur. The *phenomenal self-model* is a transiently activated representation of the system itself. According to his model, this phenomenal self-model is constantly reactivated when someone encounters a new object that enters consciousness (e.g., during an orienting response to a novel object). Three main target properties of the phenomenal first-person perspective are described in this model: *selfhood*, *perspectivalness*, and *mineness*.

Selfhood refers to the phenomenal experience of one's individual constancy and coherent wholeness (spatiotemporal stability). For example, as you are sitting somewhere reading this paragraph, you notice that *you* are the person sitting somewhere reading and not someone else, that you have been sitting in this place for some time, and that there is something stable about this state of affairs over space and time. Unless you are wildly psychotic, you don't suddenly experience yourself as a werewolf or someone with another gender and then reexperience your usual self again. It has been you sitting here reading all along. This felt stability of the phenomenal self-model has been suggested to depend on the relatively stable representation of the body and the neurobiological processes responsible for the regulation of homeostasis (Damasio, 1999). The phenomenal self constitutes the basic form of primitive (nonconceptual) self-awareness and is the essential reference allowing for subjectivity.

Perspectivalness reflects one's individual perspective, and it depicts the structure of phenomenal experience being centered on the phenomenal self, so that objects of consciousness are experienced in relation to a self-perspective. For example, the computer screen is in front of *me* right now. A telephone is to *my* left, and I know that there is a wallet that I feel against *my* behind, and on and on.

Finally, the sense of "mineness" describes a prereflective sense of ownership inherent to particular phenomenal contents. These contents could include those related to the body (e.g., "This is my arm, I am thirsty"), mental states (e.g., "I am absorbed"), affective states (e.g., "I am happy"), or intentions and voluntary actions (e.g., "I am speaking"). The feeling that all phenomenal properties of experience have internal or external referents is itself a basic phenomenal property. This duality of subject and object, or the self–world separation, may be described as *naive* realism, or *phenomenal* realism, because it is fostered by the phenomenal experience that some contents of experience pertain to the body–self while others reflect some external reality independent of the self. Indeed, this distinction not only reflects an important aspect of phenomenal experience but is integral to science and philosophy: Humans have a sense both of themselves and of a world external to themselves. An important aspect of the phenomenal property of "mineness" or "ownership" is the feeling of self-agency; the phenomenal experience that some intentions and actions are internally generated by *myself* (my phenomenal self) rather than by external objects or other individuals. Various clinical conditions can lead to a disruption of the sense of ownership such as the case study described earlier for the man with damage to his inferior parietal cortex and cases of schizophrenia (e.g., delusions of control or hallucinations). The phenomenal experience that something is internal or proximal (subject) versus external or distal (object) from self does not imply that this separation is epistemically valid but may rather reflect some unique properties of the organization of the neural systems underlying consciousness. The multiple aspects of self-representation may further depend on partly separate neural mechanisms and distinct brain structures (Damasio, 1999; Churchland, 2002).

10.6.2 Hypnosis and the Alteration of the Phenomenal Self-Model
The critical experiential dimensions identified in the West Georgia hypnosis study (Price and Barrell, 1990) can be translated into properties of the self-model proposed by Metzinger to describe consciousness phenomenology. First, it is clear that the experiential dimensions that describe the feeling of being hypnotized are not specific to a sensory domain. Rather, they pertain to the phenomenal self and relate to the (background) state of consciousness. Mental/physical relaxation and absorption, monitoring, orientation, and automaticity characterize the internal phenomenal self rather than properties of external objects. Those aspects of phenomenal experience felt as pertaining to the self are captured by the notion of "mineness." This observation is consistent with the hypothesis that hypnosis alters basic properties of phenomenal consciousness.

Each of those experiential changes induced by hypnosis may further reflect the modulation of separate aspects of the phenomenal self-model and their potentially specific neural correlates (Churchland, 2002). Relaxation and mental ease may relate biologically to the background state of the body and states of the brain that provide the substrates for the representation of self (Damasio, 1999) and for the property of selfhood (Metzinger, 2000). Mental ease characterizes the easy flow of thoughts and images experienced during hypnosis. This dimension of experience may reflect processes involved in orienting and shifting attention. Hypnosis may be typically associated with a reduction in the frequency of orienting responses and attentional shifts or with changes in the dynamics of these processes.

Mental absorption is the felt state of engagement of the self toward objects of consciousness. It is an experience that pertains to the self interacting with (or *being modified by*) objects. Mental absorption is likely to relate to focal, executive, attentional processes (e.g., Posner and Rothbart, 1998; Tellegen and Atkinson, 1974; Balthazard and Woody, 1992). However, the emphasis here is not on the information-processing analysis of attention mechanisms but rather on the phenomenal properties that are related to the activation of the underlying neurobiological systems. Accordingly, attention is conceived as a state of engagement of the embodied self in interaction with an object of consciousness. The magnitude of absorption then is the experienced *degree* of engagement of self toward object(s) of consciousness.

The disorientation reported by hypnotized subjects further suggests a suspension of the normally continuous and stable coherent whole that is subjectively felt during normal wakeful consciousness. Most of us at any given moment implicitly know where we are, approximately what time of day it is, and what distinguishes ourselves from other people. Finally, the feeling of automaticity is a critical factor in many independent accounts of hypnosis (Weitzenhoffer, 1980) and hypnotizabilty (Laurence, Slako, and Le Beau, 1998). As discussed above, hypnotic automaticity reflects an altered sense of self-agency consistent with a modification of the property of *mineness* normally associated with intention, voluntary action, and self-regulation of conscious mental activity. Taken together, these changes in experience are consistent with the view that hypnosis can be adequately described as an altered state of consciousness characterized by a modulation of basic properties of the phenomenal self-model.

10.7   Implications for a Neurophenomenology of Background States of Consciousness

We began by describing a hypnosis project in which graduate students and professors addressed a single question "What is it like to experience a hypnotic state?" Once the factors were discovered, functional interrelationships between them were then tested. Finally, using some of these factors as variables in brain imaging studies, brain regional activity associated with them was discovered and some functional interrelationships between them have been proposed. This strategic approach illustrates a phenomenon that is initially characterized by an experiential method, followed up by studies that explore the neural correlates and mechanisms of the hypnotic state. This same strategy could be applied to other background states of consciousness and to consciousness in general. For example, we can distinguish between the background states of *deep absorption*, *active vigilant attention*, and *awareness*. No doubt, these states involve the brain's attentional systems (e.g., brainstem reticular formation nuclei, midline thalamus, and ACC), brain regions involved in the present feeling of what is happening (e.g., anterior, mid-, and posterior insular cortex), and finally brain areas involved in self-representation (e.g., somatosensory cortices and posterior parietal cortex).

Background states of consciousness are critically important for *how* we experience ourselves and the world, independent of the specific contents or targets of experience. Recall that a main goal of the experiential method is to characterize how we experience phenomena rather than just the specific targets such as the person we are angry at or the specific outcome that we are anxious about. This principle applies not only to hypnotic states but to the different varieties of "ordinary" conscious states as well as to meditative states. Hurlburt's characterization of ordinary experiences of emotional feelings, sensory awareness, inner seeing, inner speech, and unsymbolized thinking (see chapter 4) are also categories of *how* someone is experiencing. Each of these categories has neural correlates, some of which are yet to be discovered and could be related to brain mechanisms involved in the regulation of consciousness.

Characterizing background states of consciousness and their relationship to brain activity and behavior has implications for deeper questions. One of them is whether humans have volition, a question addressed by philosophers for centuries and, more recently, by neuroscientists. Ancient teachings and practices describe background states of consciousness that are very different from those described in this chapter and relate to the question of volition. Like the hypnotic state, they may contain mental/ physical ease, but they are not likely to contain absorption and disorientation. They more likely include impartiality (vs. identification), sense of presence, and deliberateness/wakefulness. Similar states appear to exist in pathological conditions. For example, auras that precede certain types of epileptic seizures generated from the left anterior insula are often accompanied by heightened "sensed presence" or "self-awareness" in combination with positive feelings such as ecstasy (Landblom et al., 2010). In nonpathological conditions, an experience of presence combined with a sense of self-agency may serve as a background in the most conscious decisions. Thus, a certain kind of background state of consciousness may be critical for the experience of volition. It has many names—awareness, self-remembering, among others. If volition exists, it must include an experiential phenomenology. What if "volition" was characterized by the kinds of extended studies and analyses described in this chapter or the ones that we further propose in the next?

11 Using Experiential Paradigms to Extend Science and Help Solve Human Problems

In this century, human knowledge is extremely expanded and developed. But this is mainly knowledge of the external world. In the field of what we may call "inner science" there are many things, I think, that you do not know. You spend a large amount of the best human brain power looking outside—too much—and it seems you do not spend adequate effort looking within. Perhaps now that the western sciences have reached down into the atom and out into the cosmos finally to realize the extreme vulnerability of all life and value, it is becoming credible, even obvious, that the inner science is of supreme importance. Certainly physics designed the bombs, biology: the germ warfare, chemistry: the nerve gas, and so on, but it will be the unhealthy emotions of individuals that will trigger these horrors. These emotions can only be controlled, reshaped and re-channeled by technologies developed from successful inner science.

—Dalai Lama

Today the topic of consciousness is not implicitly forbidden among scientists as it was in the twentieth century, and there is a burgeoning emergence of the science of consciousness. There are even professional scientific and philosophical societies devoted to this topic. Given this state of affairs, we would certainly expect an integration of experiential science with the rest of the sciences, including social and natural sciences. However, as the Dalai Lama points out, we still do not spend adequate effort looking within. Nowhere is this more evident than the scientific topic agenda proposed for the 2011 interdisciplinary conference "Toward a Science of Consciousness." To illustrate this point, here is a list of the nine recent developments related to the understanding of consciousness. This list serves as a guideline for presentations at this conference:

1. Electromagnetic fields and massively coherent neuronal activities correlate with consciousness in the brain.
2. Transcranial therapies...

3. Neuronal activities: Will mapping the brain explain consciousness?

4. Anesthetic gases selectively erase consciousness and block coherent gamma activity...

5. Warm temperature biological quantum coherence...

6. Physics and cosmology are approaching the nature of reality...

7. Libet backward time referral ... perhaps accounted for by quantum physics...

8. Surprising end-of-life coherent brain activity ... and near death experiences

9. Eastern philosophy and secular spirituality accommodate quantum physics...

Most of these topics are fascinating, titillating, and inspire wonderment. Who among those interested in consciousness would not want to hear these presentations? Yet which of these presentations will explicitly discuss the merging of experiential science with the rest of the sciences or, for that matter, how to even develop a science of human experience? We think that a lot is at stake on this issue because without an experiential science it is hard to imagine that the most difficult human problems will be solved by brain science and technology alone. This chapter explains how experiential science can extend the efforts of science to understand consciousness and how it can be used to help solve difficult human problems.

11.1   A Strategy for Integrating an Experiential Science with Other Sciences

An experiential perspective and method can be applied to diverse phenomena such as emotions, motivations, background states of consciousness, choices, pain, and placebo responses. Given these applications, we can consider how some complex scientific and human problems can be addressed and perhaps even solved in a manner that is unique. In the remainder of this chapter, we first discuss a strategy for integrating an experiential science with other sciences, particularly neuroscience. We then provide some explanations as to how solutions to some human problems could be facilitated by experiential science. These problems include (1) the nature of decision making and volitional consciousness, (2) states of consciousness that undermine or facilitate decisions and other functions, and (3) complex negative emotions that are part of the basis for conflict. Entire books could easily be written about each of these topics.

Our purpose is to simply provide suggestions as to how a science of human experience could be beneficial in addressing solutions to problems associated with these topics.

The preceding chapters of this book suggest a strategy for integrating experiential science and the natural sciences. This integration seems to be useful in scientific explanations and understanding of conscious phenomena. For some of these phenomena, the strategy begins with questions posed to experience, such as "What is it like to experience pain?" or "What is it like to experience a type of background state of consciousness such as a hypnotic state? " The questions are simple and unfettered by complex theoretical issues and tend to avoid presuppositions. The approach and methods are also simple, despite being very challenging. Ideally, they begin with a group of coinvestigator–participants who learn to notice and describe experiences of a given kind with as little influence from preexisting presuppositions and theories as is possible. The common factors in a given type of experience—such as a type of emotion, for example—are identified and subjected to an analysis that determines which factors are necessary and, taken together, sufficient for this experience. Definitional and functional hypotheses emerge from this approach, hypotheses that can then be tested in studies that use qualitative and quantitative methods and research participants that are unfamiliar with the experiential hypotheses. Finally, both types of studies can be combined with neuroscience, as in the case of pain and hypnotic state. In this chapter we reflect on the advantages of this strategy and the implications this paradigm has for science and for some major practical problems.

11.1.1   What Are the Advantages of This Strategy?

At the outset, we think there are at least five distinct advantages that this strategy holds for scientific studies of conscious phenomena: (1) Scientific experiments would be guided less by presuppositions and theories and more by experiential phenomenology; (2) both the results and the interpretations of scientific studies would be more transparent and better understood by scientists and nonscientists; (3) the process of scientific exploration would require awareness in the case of an experiential science and would have intrinsic value; (4) the results of scientific studies could achieve a higher level of reliability and veracity than those of the past; and (5) using this strategy, the results and interpretations of studies may be more directly applicable to critical human problems.

11.1.2   Scientific Experiments Guided by Experiential Phenomenology

Scientific research in psychology and neuroscience has been claimed to be heavily guided by theories, as is the case for most sciences (Velmans, 2009). If one of the aims of these sciences is that of understanding consciousness, we need to question the necessity of designing experiments based on theory alone. The strategy that we have outlined begins with questions posed to phenomenal experience rather than theories. Of course, one can always maintain the skeptical position that such an approach is not possible and that everyone has preconceptions, if not actual theories, about the phenomena he or she sets out to investigate. One could further claim that these preconceptions and theories help shape what is actually experienced in experiential–phenomenological studies. In conducting some of the studies discussed in this book, we found that participants often do have preconceptions and presuppositions about the phenomena they are beginning to observe. For example, we found that prior to experiencing it, some students in our classes claimed that hypnosis is nothing more than compliance with authority, others claimed that it is simply relaxation, and still others claimed that the mind is completely controlled by someone else during hypnosis. Wide variation in viewpoints about hypnosis has even been found among people who study this topic.

However, it is not inevitable that these "views" or presuppositions guide experiential research on hypnotic states of consciousness or, for that matter, any experiential phenomenon. Just as some people can be trained to be sensitive psychophysical observers, they can also be encouraged and trained to have awareness of their phenomenal experiences and to bracket presuppositions (chapter 4). For similar reasons, it is not inevitable that we have to begin with a preexisting theory. For example, participants of our experiential study of the hypnotic state engaged in hypnosis sessions and were instructed to simply notice what took place in their experience (see chapter 10). We found that there was considerable consensus about the common factors of a hypnotic state only *after* engaging in several hypnotic inductions, a consensus that was found to be in agreement with previous and subsequent studies (Pekula and Kumar, 1984; Rainville et al., 1999; 2002; Shor, 1965). Thus, we think that progress in the understanding of consciousness has to begin with experiential–phenomenological studies that *generate* testable hypotheses. Theories would eventually result from studies that test alternative hypotheses yet would include testing those generated in experiential studies. Interfacing results of such studies with social and natural science designs could mitigate the influence of preconception and bias in directing scientific research.

11.1.3 A Scientific and Practical Way of Understanding Consciousness Phenomena

Understanding consciousness is ultimately derived from a personal perspective even when there is intersubjective consensus about a phenomenon of interest. If this is the case, then the most trustworthy way of knowing that an explanation or a theory of a conscious phenomenon optimally accounts for the observations would be that of engaging in direct observation of the phenomenon in question followed by evaluating results of scientific studies. For example, understanding states of consciousness in various forms of meditation, hypnosis, and associative thinking requires actual direct noticing of what these states are like. Reading everything that has been written about them will be helpful but will not lead to an understanding of their nature. This complementary way of knowing is related to the common-sense notion that it is helpful to understand any conscious phenomenon in terms of our own direct experience. Is it possible to provide experientially transparent explanations of conscious phenomena? If so, an advantage of this kind of understanding is that scientific explanations about conscious phenomena could be more accessible to a much broader audience, including people who are not scientists. Throughout this book, we have provided topics that are familiar in most people's experiences, and we have occasionally invited the reader to engage in thoughts and explorations of what it is like to experience several conscious phenomena. Simple examples include (1) the experience of light intensity with equal increments of stimulus intensity (if a three-way light bulb is available; chapter 2), (2) spatial summation of warmth (if a bathtub or sink is available; chapter 2), and (3) imagined happy or unhappy emotional feelings in response to different probabilities of gaining a large prize or losing someone or something of great value (chapter 3). More complex examples include (4) noticing the common factors in some basic emotions, such as anger and anxiety, as well as emotions that apply to specific situations such as performance anxiety (chapters 4 and 5); (5) considering what is common in all experiences of pain (which almost everyone has experienced), despite the extreme diversity of types of pain (chapter 7); (6) noticing what different background states of consciousness are like (chapter 10); and (7) distinguishing between our responses/actions that feel automatic as compared to those accompanied by a feeling of self-agency (chapter 10). We think these phenomena are "recognizable" when engaging in the suggested exercises or noticing them when they occur (e.g., pain). These suggested explorations were interwoven with the rest of the explanations in such a manner that the explorations were helpful in understanding the experiences being explained, including the factors that constitute a type of experience and their interrelationships. The results of scientific studies could be greatly facilitated by this kind of recognition.

11.1.4 Confirming Scientific Truths about Consciousness: Cause–Effect Relationships

Science is largely about confirming cause–effect relationships, and some relationships are easier to verify than others. Classical Newtonian physical interactions are relatively straightforward and very different in this respect than quantum mechanics. Cause–effect relationships also occur *within* conscious phenomena and *between* the latter and the brain and vice versa. Establishing causal relationships with certainty is often thought to be scientifically and/or philosophically problematic. Velmans (2009) has outlined four types of causal relationships: brain–brain, brain–mind, mind–brain, and mind–mind. We have alluded to all four of types of causation in preceding chapters. Attempts to demonstrate brain–brain causation are common in neuroscience. Studies of how neural activity that occurs in one brain area (or spinal cord) affects neural activity in other parts of the central nervous system abound. Brain–mind causation is exemplified in studies in which sites within the central nervous system are artificially stimulated and experiences are then reported by individuals (e.g., electrical stimulation of a particular thalamic area elicits burning pain). Mind–brain causation is illustrated in experiments wherein participants are told that "the agent you have been given powerfully reduces pain." Experienced expectations of pain reductions and a lowered concern (i.e., reduced desire), which are both experiential variables, lead to actual reduction in pain-related signals within the brain. Finally, mind–mind causation occurs, for example, when positive emotional feeling intensity increases as a function of increased expectation of acquiring what one wants or increased expectation of avoiding an unwanted outcome. All of these variables are within experience. Examples of mind–mind causation were provided in chapters 5 and 6 in the cases of emotions/decisions and chapter 7 for pain.

The observational arrangements of experiments designed to establish causation differ across all four types of causation. Brain–brain experiments are arranged by using established methods to observe and record neural activity in two or more sites within the brain as well as methods of stimulation and correlation. Both the independent and dependent variables are about events that take place in the nervous system. It is noteworthy that they depend on conscious observations. In this sense even an external viewpoint is still experienced within the framework of an inner perspective. Although differentiated, the inner viewpoint contains the outer viewpoint.

It is inevitable that the dependent variables of brain–*mind* experiments and independent variables of *mind*–brain experiments require participants' observations (noticing) of what is present in their direct experience and reporting these observations to the person(s) in charge of the study. As explained in chapters 2 through 5, the participant is a critical observer of at least one set of variables. Sometimes scientists may not notice this state of affairs and would rather think of themselves as objective observers. In one sense they are right because someone has to provide methods for presenting the data in a form that is accessible to those in charge of the experiment and eventually to the readers of scientific reports. *Mind–mind* experiments of the kind described in chapters 5 and 6 may be the most challenging because experiential variables are both the independent and dependent variables of the experiments and because the experimenter often has no direct control over the independent variables. The experimenter can provide manipulations or conditions that would provide variation in magnitude of the independent variables and measure the magnitudes of experiential variables (the "subjective responses") once the conditions or manipulations are established. This approach is used in some hypnotic analgesia experiments, wherein inductions and suggestions are given to induce variation in experiential variables that cause reduction in pain, variables such as automaticity, absorption, and mental relaxation (chapter 10). Relationships between experiential variables and pain reduction are then established. This kind of naturalistic approach is also used in other sciences wherein one has no direct control over the independent variables. Astronomy and astrophysics serve as examples.

Regardless of the type of causation one is attempting to establish, it can be based on using as many of the following lines of evidence as is feasible: (1) establishing correlations between A and B, recognizing that correlation is necessary but not sufficient to establish causation; (2) inducing B by selectively activating A; (3) reducing or eliminating B by eliminating or reducing A; and (4) demonstrating a physical connection between A and B in the case of brain–brain relationships. These lines of evidence are commonly used in neuroscience. As an example, these lines of evidence were used to establish that impulse activity in a type of spinal cord neuron is a cause of pain (Price and Dubner, 1977). This type of neuron responds with an increasing impulse frequency as the stimulus intensity to the skin increases over a very wide range, extending from a low-frequency response to gentle stimulation to a high-frequency response to nociceptive stimulation. It is appropriately termed a "wide dynamic range" (WDR) neuron. Multiple experiments over the years have shown that (1) the magnitudes of neural response and changes of neural responses of WDR neurons to controlled nociceptive stimulation are highly correlated with psychophysical responses, such as experienced magnitudes of pain and differences in pain intensity; (2) selective stimulation of WDR neurons elicit pain; (3) reduction in neural responses of WDR neurons to nociceptive stimuli leads to reduction in pain responses; and (4) WDR neurons are anatomically connected with brain regions involved in pain. This combination of evidence has been used to establish that a high level of neural activity of WDR neurons is both a cause and correlate of pain experience (Price, 1999).

The same strategy can be used in other types of causation outlined above, except that establishing physical connections is not presently possible for mind–mind causation. Experiments are conducted to either correlate activity between experiential and neural variables or induce changes in one set of these variables while measuring the other set. Sometimes the procedures are devised to induce a set of variables, but the procedures themselves are not the independent variables. This strategy is sometimes used in physical, biological, and social sciences. For example, suggestions may be given to induce a placebo effect, but the suggestions themselves don't have to be the independent variables of the experiment. Instead, experienced magnitudes of desire for symptom change and expectation levels can be the main factors of investigation (chapter 9).

Mind–mind causation requires careful consideration because much less work has been done to establish this kind of relationship and because one cannot demonstrate a physical connection between the independent and dependent variables. As discussed in chapters 4 and 5, relationships between desire, expectation, and emotional valence (degree of happiness unhappiness, feeling good or bad) were mainly based on cross-sectional samples of experience, and these relationships were in agreement with those derived from hypothetical scenarios with stated probabilities. Although these results help confirm possible psychological relationships, much more work is needed. Thus, experiments are needed in which conditions are provided to systematically *induce* increases or decreases in desire or expectation or to systematically vary these variables over time.

However, once the observational arrangements are made and the experiment is conducted, the data of *mind–mind* experiments can be subjected to the same kinds of tests and interpreted using the same inferential methods and deductive reasoning as are used in all of the sciences. Only the method of observation is different. Otherwise, the same epistemological principles that apply to the natural sciences could be applied to experiential phenomenological studies.

11.1.5   Accepting and Integrating Inner and Outer Viewpoints

It is important to emphasize at this point that the term "mind" in three of the four forms of causation outlined above refers to phenomenal consciousness, not concepts related to functions. Functionalist theories redefine consciousness to be a form of processing such as "limited capacity channel" or a "global workspace" (Baars, 2003). These terms are theoretically based and conceptualize conscious phenomena in terms of the functions they perform. Most critically, these constructs are from a third-person or external viewpoint. In contrast, we are claiming that aspects of conscious experiences themselves have causal influences on other conscious experiences and on brain states and body functions. In the case of the placebo analgesic response, for example, it is possible to demonstrate that *decreased* desire for pain reduction, *increased* expectation of pain reduction, and associated *decreased* negative emotions mediate reductions in pain, the placebo analgesic responses. All of these variables, including both the independent variables and dependent variable (pain), are within experience. They can be described and rated on scales from a first-person perspective. Experimental observational arrangements can be constructed so as to test how changes in one set of experiential variables (desire, expectation, emotional feeling intensity) causally influence another set (e.g., pain, anxiety, depression, etc.). These dimensions of experience are not the same as theoretical constructs such as "global workspace" or "limited capacity channel" because they have distinct phenomenal appearances that can be directly experienced by trained observers (chapters 2–5).

Once one accepts phenomenal consciousness on its own terms without redefining it in functionalist frameworks, the realization that conscious experiences causally interact with each other and with activities of the brain/body is profound. This realization is at odds with some materialist views that such experiences are nothing more than brain states or some dualist views that such experiences are completely separate from yet interact with brain states. A third position is that of reflexive monism, a view put forth by Velmans (2009). According to his view, brain states can be causes and correlates of conscious experiences but they are not ontologically identical to them (Velmans, 2009). According to reflexive monism, experiences and physical matter are two reflexive sides of the same underlying reality. As discussed earlier, causal relationships extend across both sides, yet neither side can be reduced to the other. In other words, the world is psychophysical. As pointed out in chapter 1, demonstrations of causation and correlation do not establish ontological identity. Experiments whose observational arrangements consist of obtaining observations of direct experience can establish causal relationships *within* experience, whereas experiments that contain both experiential and neurophysiological observations can establish causal relationships *between* experience and brain states. The latter require observations of brain activity from an external perspective (recognizing that any perspective is in at least someone's experience). Examination of these causal relationships does not provide a basis for reducing one type of phenomenon (or variable) to the other. Both the first-person and third-person accounts are mutually irreducible to each other. Neither account is observer free, yet knowledge of the existence of a phenomenon is always contingent upon observation of some kind even when the observation is very indirect.

When we acknowledge this status of affairs, we are left with a paradox. If one examines neural information processing exclusively from the third-person perspective of an external observer, consciousness does not seem necessary for any form of processing. The operations of brains and their functional outputs seem to be explainable entirely in functional or physical terms that make no direct reference to what we experience. Indeed, this is a very common viewpoint in modern neuroscience. An example taken from chapter 2 is the multisensory integration that mediates a cat's motoric orientation toward a novel stimulus such as a chirping bird in a tree. Superior collicular neurons of the midbrain collect and integrate auditory and visual impulse inputs in a manner that exceeds the additive effects of the auditory and visual stimuli taken alone. Thus, the interaction between the two types of input is synergistic—more than the sum of both inputs. As a result of this synergistic interaction, the cat tends to orients toward the chirping bird *if* the origin of the chirp and the actual bird exist in the *same* physical location. Alternatively, the cat is inhibited from doing so *if* the auditory and visual inputs originate from *different* spatial locations. The neural basis of these interactions has been well characterized not only for superior collicular neurons but for cerebral cortical areas (Stein and Meredith, 1993). This account of multisensory integration explains the presence or absence of an overt orienting behavior, and it requires no explanation of how conscious recognition enables this behavior. It avoids any reference to consciousness, despite the difficulty of imagining how motor orientation could take place in an unconscious cat! The point here is that experiential phenomenological description is not considered necessary to explain functions of this type. As in this example, once the processing within the nervous system required to carry out a given function (e.g., behavioral orientation) is specified in biological terms, one does not have to add an "inner conscious life" to make the function work (Velmans, 2009). A similar argument can be made about observing brain activity in general. If one studies neural activity using advanced neuroscience technology, no subjective experience can be directly observed.

On the other hand, and here is the paradox, viewed from a *first-person* perspective, it seems absurd to deny the role of phenomenal experience in mental life and in the initiation of behaviors, and it seems just as absurd to deny its role in science and scientific explanation (Velmans, 2009). Examples from previous chapters abound. If the intensity of someone's desire, level of expectation, and magnitude of happy/unhappy feelings are shown to reliably interact in both qualitative and quantitative ways, how could these dimensions of experience be left out of an overall explanation of human emotions? If emotional feelings, which *are* phenomenal experiences, contribute to our experiences of decisions, pains, and some types of placebo responses, how could they be eliminated or ignored in scientific explanations? What would a purely third-person neural account of the placebo analgesic response look like? For at least some types of placebo analgesic responses, they begin with suggestions to the person receiving them. People receiving a placebo must understand the suggestion and its meaning (e.g., "This agent produces strong pain relief in some people"), retain a working memory of that meaning, and develop expectations and feelings associated with it. Even investigators who analyze placebo analgesia from neurochemical and neuroimaging perspectives appreciate that the placebo response is initiated or regulated by emotions and neural structures involved in emotions (Zubieta et al., 2006). What is needed is an integration of first- and third-person science in explanations of phenomena such as placebo responses.

Neuroscientists appear to prefer third-person explanations of even the most subjective phenomena. Yet would a purely neural account of the placebo analgesic response resemble something like the following: Neural auditory activity in the primary auditory cortex is sent to language processing areas and to the hippocampus and temporal lobes and from there to structures involved in emotional regulation and then to the periaqueductal gray, rostroventral medulla, and finally the dorsal horn where nociceptive transmission is reduced? This account is ultimately nothing more than a "thigh bone connected to the knee bone" type of explanation with no coherent integration of meanings that underpin the experience of pain reduction. Although this is a hypothetical example, classical and current explanations of placebo responses are predominantly framed in concepts of classical conditioning (Wickramasekera, 1985), psychosocial interactions (Harrington, 1997), or functions that are served by specific neural connections and/or neurochemical mechanisms (Zubieta et al., 2001; 2005). Experiential factors in explanations of placebo responses have only recently been included (Montgomery and Kirsch, 1996; Price, Finniss, and Benedetti, 2008; Vase et al., 2011).

It is partly understandable that investigators avoid experiential terms and explanations because they are unaware of or do not trust experiential methods. Furthermore, the semantic content of words, their relationship to memory and emotions, and the role of specific emotions in inhibiting or facilitating pain may have a complexity that may appear to exceed our grasp at this time in neuroscience and psychology. Nevertheless, if a first-person account of the placebo response can be developed, then experiential variables can be configured in the overall explanation of placebo responses. After all, these variables are causes of each other. For example, simple manipulations that increase or decrease expectations can cause pain to increase or decrease in intensity (Koyama et al., 2005). Neurophysiological variables also are causally interrelated with each other and with experiences. Neural activity within forebrain, midbrain, and medullary structures causes inhibition in the spinal cord dorsal horn and consequently pain reduction. If all these interactions occur, an ideal strategy in studying placebo responses would include correlating experiential and neural variables. It would, of course, include more than just correlation. For example, temporarily deactivating prefrontal cortical areas by transcranial magnetic stimulation has been shown to suppress the placebo response (Krummenacher et al., 2010), suggesting that even higher order cognitive processing involving executive functions is necessary for placebo responses. If so, some placebo responses may have an experientially rich phenomenology.

Given the distinctions between first- and third-person accounts of phenomena, the causal paradox arises because one cannot arrive at explanations of first-person phenomena using only results obtained from an external viewpoint (Velmans, 2009). Yet viewed from a first-person perspective, consciousness appears to be necessary for most forms of complex processing of meaning. At the very least, it seems extremely difficult to proceed without a first-person perspective. After all, how would one explain the semantic integration of a placebo suggestion and its ultimate effect on expectations, desires, and emotions without obtaining first-person data? However, viewed from a third-person perspective, consciousness does not appear to be necessary for any form of processing that leads to a behavioral outcome (e.g., multisensory integration). As Velmans puts it, it makes no sense to reject either perspective:

An adequate theory of consciousness needs to resolve the Causal Paradox in a way that violates *neither* our intuitions about our own experiences, *nor* the findings of science. (Velmans, 2009)

11.1.6   Can Conscious Phenomena Be Reductively Explained?

The same epistemology and principles of science apply to all four forms of causation. As far as we can discern, none of them entail ontological reduction. Consistent with Velmans, the independent and dependent variables are mutually irreducible to each other in all cases. When neural activity in one brain area induces neural activity in another, the two sets of neural activity are obviously different. Phenomenal experiences and brains states are also different from each other, as are different dimensions of experience (desire and expectation are not the same dimensions). Some causal relationships seem deeply mysterious. For example, we don't know exactly how distributed responses throughout the brain bind in a way that leads to a unified experience of a type of pain even though we are learning which areas are necessary and sufficient for such an experience and how the different areas interact during pain. The relationships between activity in networks of brain structures and even simple experiences, such as temporal summation of second pain (chapter 8), remain extremely challenging. Explanations that result from such efforts are reductive because they show how neuronal activity in different brain regions serves the different dimensions of pain. Thus, higher order phenomena such as pain are explained at a fundamental neurobiological level. However, for reasons discussed throughout this book, we think that these reductive explanations are epistemological, not ontological.

11.1.7   The Importance of Correctly Identifying the Type of Causation

Presently there is considerable debate and some confusion about which of the four types of causation are present in results of scientific experiments, clinical trials, and other studies of medical treatments. The debate occurs across philosophical and scientific lines. Some researchers have attempted to replace *mind–brain* causal explanations with materialistic ones or to emphasize the latter at the expense of the former. Examples include debates on the influence of placebo factors on pain and depression. At the turn of the twenty-first century, several claims were made to the effect that placebo effects were weak or absent in most clinical trials of medical treatments and that small but statistically significant effects occurred only for "subjective" phenomena such as pain and depression (Hróbjartsson and Gøtzsche, 2001; Kienle and Kiene, 1999). These claims were soon followed by a resurgence of interest in placebo mechanisms among clinicians, neuroscientists, and psychologists (see chapter 9 and references therein). Results of the last decade have unequivocally demonstrated that placebo effects on pain are biologically and psychologically real events and that the sizes of placebo effects can be made to be small, medium, or large depending on the number of factors used to induce them (Price, Finniss, and Benedetti, 2008, and references therein). These effects critically depend on actual experiences of those who receive placebo suggestions (or conditioning) and thereby reflect *mind–mind* and *mind–brain* causality. Attributing these effects to statistical artifacts or to mindless brain interactions (*brain–brain*) alone no longer suffices to explain placebo analgesia and placebo effects for other conditions.

A generally similar evolution has taken place in understanding the role of placebo factors in antidepressant therapy. Several meta-analyses, particularly those led by Irving Kirsch (Kirsch, 2010; Kirsch et al., 2008), have shown that the placebo effect makes by far the largest contribution to the overall reduction in depression by antidepressants. In one meta-analysis involving thirty-eight studies and over 3,000 patients, 75% of the overall therapeutic effect was the placebo effect, not the contribution of the active agent (in Kirsch, 2010). However, even the remaining 25% of the effect likely included placebo effects related to active cues from side effects of antidepressants. The contribution of the placebo effect was even higher, 82%, in a meta-analysis of studies submitted to the Food and Drug Administration (Kirsch et al., 2008). Again, even this figure likely overestimates the contribution of the active agent because side effects are likely to serve as additional contributions to placebo effects. In this study, the contribution of the active agent was relatively small even for severely depressed patients. Thus, the medical profession, pharmaceutical industry, and even many depressed patients have attributed the wrong type of causation to mechanisms of antidepressant therapy. It has been mainly *mind–brain* causation (i.e., placebo effect) all along.

This misattribution has not just been a scientific or philosophical error—it may have led to devastating consequences. Based on numerous studies, several types of antidepressants have been shown to put children, adolescents, and young adults at risk for mania, psychosis, violence, and suicide (Breggin, 2008, and references therein). On the basis of this information, the Food and Drug Administration now requires that these risks be put on the label of containers of antidepressants. One has to seriously wonder about the risk–benefit relationship of this form of therapy and the extent to which the rationale for using antidepressants has been grounded in materialistic psychiatry and philosophy.

11.2 Experiential Science and Volition

We now turn to direct applications of the experiential–natural science combination in addressing complex human phenomena that relate to practical problems. The problems posed by the question of "free will" or volition have perpetuated reflection and debate among philosophers for centuries, and much of ethical and legal decision making is critically linked to societal views of volition. There is a critical need to understand the nature of volition because assumptions about this phenomenon permeate considerable aspects of our personal and social life as well as legal decisions. More recently, neuroscientists, psychologists, and philosophers have attempted to deal with potential empirical resolution of these problems by combining brain recording with self-reported experiences of intentions to act or by examining the relationships between experiences of self-agency and neural activity. Examples of the latter were given in chapter 10. In the following discussion, we provide a succinct example of how scientists have dealt with this problem and then show how an experiential science could help characterize the nature of volition and its meaning in human life.

11.2.1 Volition from an External Viewpoint: A View Proposed by Libet

The work of Benjamin Libet has promoted extensive discussion and controversy about the relationships between brain activity and the decision to act. Based on his work, Libet expressed the view that "a freely voluntary act" is generated in the brain unconsciously before someone becomes consciously aware of the desire to perform that very action. His view is based on experiments which showed the presence of brain activity, in the form of a "readiness potential" (RP), that consistently occurred *before* the conscious intention to flex one's wrist. In his first experiment, Libet and his coinvestigators asked participants to decide to flick or flex their wrist whenever they chose (Libet, Wright, and Gleason, 1982). Electrodes on the scalp and computer averaging of several trials detected the RP that marks neuronal events associated with the preparation for movement. On average, the RP began about 550 milliseconds before activation of the muscles moving the wrist. What is this cerebral signal that acts as a sort of advance process that begins the path to a motor command? How does it relate to the conscious decision to act?

In Libet's next experiments, he attempted to establish when the decision to move occurred in relation to the RP and to the movement itself. Using an electronic clock with a fast "second hand," a rotating spot on an oscilloscope, participants reported where the rotating spot was located when they first became aware of the intention to move. (They had practiced using this clock and type of reporting in other tasks.) Consciousness of the intention to move occurred, on average, about 350 milliseconds after the onset of the RP and 100 to 200 milliseconds before the muscles were activated.

These experiments led Libet and others to the conclusion that if free will exists at all, it can only exist after the occurrence of neural activity that precedes a conscious intention or urge (Libet, 1985). To some, this result seemed to deal a serious blow to the idea of free will. Nevertheless, Libet's experiments did lead him to the possibility that free will could occur after the neurologically determined intention to perform a certain action: It could *veto* the original intention to carry out some action. His reason why a veto is possible is that 100–200 milliseconds remain before the time of wrist flexing, a time that is known to be sufficient for a conscious event such as "vetoing." In his words,

We were ... able to show that subjects could veto an act planned for performance at a prearranged time. They were able to exert the veto within the interval of 100–200 msec. before the pre-set time to act. A large RP preceded the veto, signifying that the subject was indeed preparing to act, even though the action was aborted by the subject. (Libet, Wright, and Gleason, 1982)

11.2.2 Do These Experiments Based on "Timing" Really Support or Refute Volition?

The types of experiments conducted by Libet appear to support a kind of timing between neural events and conscious intentions to perform an act, and for that matter, the intention to veto an act. If the RP reflects neural events that *lead to* an intention and occurs *prior* to a conscious intention to act to act now, it would be difficult to conclude that the intention when to act is chosen consciously. One must keep in mind, however, that it has never been directly demonstrated that this RP reflects the neural events that lead to an intention to act. What if the RP reflects something else, such as the memory of the instructions or even the preparation to have an intention (e.g., I must decide to act now!)? The latter could be related to maintenance of a mind-set that was initiated by the instructions.

These questions relate to several fatal flaws in both the design and the interpretations of these types of experiments, mainly because of an inadequate account of the participants' experience while participating in the experiment. If the experiment is about volition, then it seems entirely inappropriate to ignore the detailed experience of the participant. Libet's experiments seem to propose an alternating sequence: (1) neurological activity that precedes a conscious intention to "flex now," (2) a neurological preparation for a veto of this intention, (3) the conscious decision to veto the original intention, and (4) neural inhibition of the circuitry that initiates muscular activity. As best any neuroscientist has determined, conscious experiences are accompanied by corresponding neural activity and do not take place in an alternating sequence. A rise and fall of a type of pain, for example, is accompanied simultaneously by a rise and fall of somatosensory cortical activity. Thus, to make the above sequence coherent, the onset of the RP precedes a conscious intention, but even a conscious intention must be accompanied by neural activity somewhere in the brain. If a veto is installed into the trial, it too must be accompanied by corresponding neural activity somewhere in the brain. Finally, there is central inhibition. A large mystery in this entire sequence is what the RP represents. The question is complicated by the fact that the RP is based on computer averages of several trials. It is interesting and ironic that neuroscience has no real answer here except for the past claim that the RP reflects an unconscious neural process that instantiates the intention to act.

However, is that necessarily the case? Let us examine a possible first-person experiential account of what it might be like to be a participant in Libet's experiment. The instructions to Libet's participants were "...let the urge to act appear on its own at any time without preplanning or concentrating on when to act ... that is, try to be spontaneous in deciding when to perform" (Libet, Wright, and Gleason, 1982). The instruction was designed to evoke actions that were freely capricious in origin.

At this point, we invite the reader to follow the above instructions and select a motor act (e.g., eyeblink, wrist movement) that is feasible to perform. Then make it capriciously and spontaneously, as suggested by the authors of Libet's study. What is the experience of carrying out this act? In carrying out this exercise ourselves and asking several people to perform it, we found that the experience varies widely and corresponds roughly to some of the types of experiential categories of Hurlburt and Heavy discussed in chapter 4. Thus, an urge or intention to move may be accompanied by inner seeing (image of hand moving), inner speech ("I am going to move right NOW!"), emotional feeling (want to get this done!), and unsymbolized thinking (wordless equivalent of "move real soon"). Some of our colleagues' and our own experiences were sometimes simply approximate to "I had no idea what was going on" or "I was completely surprised by my hand moving." This latter result also constituted a minority of responses found by Libet's group. It seems hardly surprising that when you instruct someone to make a freely capricious and spontaneous movement, you obtain a large variety of experiences, not just ones that indicate a feeling of self-agency or conscious effort. Given these instructions, responses seem to occur that are unlikely to entail deliberate intentional action, and it is entirely unclear as to where to distinguish the "desire to move" from the "intention to move soon" and from the latter to "intention to move immediately." Moreover, the entire experience of moving the hand might closely approximate the experience of automaticity described in chapter 10 in which case the possibility of feeling self-agency or conscious intention would certainly be eliminated.

Why, then, is this study and studies like it presumed to investigate models of volition or "free will," and why has so much discussion and debate arisen from their results and interpretations? The studies and the debates that follow them seem to presume that a decision to act is encapsulated entirely in a narrow window of time just before the action. To us, this approach may make experiments on volitional action appear more feasible and easier to interpret, but do they represent the extended temporal phenomenology of choosing?

When examined from a first-person perspective, the relationships between deliberations of alternative acts, the conscious choosing of which act to follow, and the actual conduct of an action have an enormously rich and extended phenomenology. Nahmias (2005) has distinguished between proximal and distal intentions. In his view,

distal intentions are intentions to perform an action at some future time, with varying degrees of specificity regarding the time to perform the action and how exactly to carry it out. And sometimes the intention is to perform an action in response to some predicted situation. (Nahmias, 2005)

He gives as an example the intention to offer a particular answer to a question a student would ask in class. Nahmias claims that distal intentions are often formed with conscious deliberation and we can be conscious of them when we form them. When we plan the number of concerts to go to in a season, we deliberately weigh the values and expectations of enjoyment of each event and then calculate the costs of attending them. This process is followed by even more proximal intentions such as checking off the boxes in the brochure and then driving to the concert events on appropriate dates. The phenomenal distinction between distal and proximal intentions could even have been made in the contexts of Libet's experiments and those which followed them. For example, did the participants have a planned strategy when they were first instructed in the experiment?

11.2.3 Adding an Inner Viewpoint: An Experiential Approach to Analysis of Volition?

Suppose Libet's experiments had been done differently and in the following manner. Instead of telling participants to "respond capriciously," they could have been told to deliberately choose one option over the other and notice what that choice is like. And instead of using wrist flexion, one could use cooking a pizza with two alternative cooking methods as the experimental paradigm. The first method might consist of using a regular oven for three minutes followed by three minutes of microwaving. The second method might consist of simply microwaving the pizza for five minutes. The experience of choosing between the two cooking methods might vary enormously across participants, and that is good because such an approach could more optimally reveal the experiential factors that underpin choice. For example, desire and expectation of optimum taste might be a priority for some people and desire to avoid the effort of a more complex task might be a factor for others. Yet regardless of which choice is made, the choice itself is likely to be influenced by desires and expectations associated with the outcome and/or the anticipated effort related to each cooking method (i.e., option). Importantly, all of these factors can be noticed *within* one's experience of choosing between the two options.

This approach was described in chapter 6 in relation to a study of choice responses (Price, Riley, and Barrell, 2001). Results from that study provide evidence that, at least part of the time, people choose options based on how good or how bad they feel or imagine feeling about the prospects associated with each option. These feelings can be explicit or just in the background of experience. Choices are interdependent with emotional feelings, however subtle they may be. However, there are other potential conscious dimensions that shape choice. One may or may not notice how one's values and present level of information influence desires and expectations associated with each option. It is also possible to have a broad and relaxed perspective on the options and not be "caught up" with a single option. Although the consequent feeling states resulting from desire and expectation may ultimately have a large influence on the choice that is made, one's background state of awareness and attention determine how these feeling states relate to information and one's values. Thus, a complex choice may require deliberation and awareness, in contrast to a capricious or impulsive choice that may focus more immediately on the range of the moment, a single feeling, or on one option. The nature of the choice experience would be related to one's background state of consciousness at the time of choosing. Thus, one can "mindlessly" or "mindfully" plan the preparation of a meal. It would be possible to characterize background states of consciousness during both mindful and capricious choosing, using experiential methods and direct scaling methods.

Consideration of proximal and distal intentions and background states of consciousness in volitional choice extends to large sections of our personal life experiences. It also appeals to common sense. We may develop distal intentions to go to college, plan a well-constructed lecture, or attend a series of musical performances. These distal intentions surely influence our subsequent behaviors, which become more focused and specific as time goes on. Choices occur at each juncture, yet they are influenced by a myriad of distal intensions. Had the motor act chosen in Libet's experiment actually counted for something meaningful to participants, there might have been personal histories that preceded and causally related to the choice that was made. For example, suppose you are immediately presented with two music CDs to listen to and you must choose one within 0.5 seconds. You may experience your choice as immediate. Your immediate decision is likely to be preceded by a long history of listening to different types of music, your mood at the time of decision, and various other factors. If your choice is preceded by 300 milliseconds by a "readiness potential" or any other measure of neural activity, isn't it possible even that neural activity is influenced by prior *conscious* reflection? Although a particular choice of CD_1 versus CD_2 in a given situation might occur as a result of unconscious neural mechanisms, those neural mechanisms would be associated with prior experiences that reflect *conscious* activities. That relevant unconscious neural activities immediately precede the choice that is made is not really a refutation of volition.

11.2.4 Are Voluntary Actions Caused by Conscious Intentions to Perform Them?

Daniel Wegner focuses on exceptions to the ostensible rule that voluntary actions are caused by conscious intentions to perform them (Wegner, 2002). He cites instances wherein people perform an action that looks voluntary but the performers of the action do not experience themselves to be the cause of the action. His examples include automatisms and a schizophrenic's sense of alien control. Conversely, he cites other instances in which people experience relevant thoughts about performing an action but the action is shown not to be caused by those thoughts. In his "helping hands" experiment, participants look into a mirror at the movements produced by confederate's arms which are placed underneath the participants' arms (Wegner, 2002). When participants hear a verbal command for an arm movement (e.g., make the okay sign) that occurs just before their seeing the movements made by the confederates' arms, they report an increased sense of controlling or willing the action in comparison to conditions wherein the verbal command does *not* match the movements they see in the mirror. Thus, some increased sense of agency can be induced for actions that participants clearly did not perform. Thus, experiences of voluntarily guided acts can *sometimes* be an illusion.

Wegner discusses several examples, similar to those just given, that he claims are exceptions to behavioral actions caused by feelings of voluntary control. He then uses them to conclude that our experience of consciously willing our actions is an illusion (Wegner, 2002). Nahmias, 2005) gives reasons to doubt that Wegner has adequately supported his case against volition. Among them is one that is most directly relevant to one of the main points made in this book, that science from an external viewpoint often neglects the experience of the subject. According to Nehmias, a person's experience of X is illusory if the content of that experience includes that X has various features, but X does not in fact include those features. For example, our visual experience of Muller–Lyer lines (see figure 11.1) includes the feature that the line with the inward-pointing arrowheads (lower line) appears longer than the line with the outward pointing arrows, but the lines do not have this feature if measured with a ruler.

So, in the case of the experience of voluntarily performing an act, what features of this voluntary act appear to occur but do not in fact occur? According to Nehmias, understanding the relevant experiential phenomenology is as important as understanding all of the other relevant psychological and neurobiological facts (Nahmias, 2005). And as he points out,

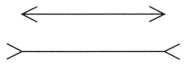

Figure 11.1
Muller–Lyer illusion that the lower line is longer than the upper line.

the relevant phenomenology has not been adequately explored by the studies of Wegner (2002) just discussed, by Libet's studies of brain potentials preceding a capricious movement, or by anyone else. For this reason and others, virtually all studies that attempt to characterize or refute volition from an external viewpoint ultimately fail to make a general case against all experiences of volition. And when illusions are demonstrated by science, these demonstrations are from an external viewpoint.

Certainly, there are instances of disconnections between our experience of intending an action and the action itself, and we may commonly misattribute our actions to prior intentions. We also may sometimes erroneously believe that the most proximate causes of our actions are conscious when they are more likely to arise from unconscious processing. Giving a well-planned speech is an example. While speaking, one does not really know what one is going to say until one has said it. Yet the speech can reflect well-reasoned and well-planned points of an explanation, one that has been given careful consideration and thought. Even a strict deterministic relationship between neural processes immediately preceding a voluntary act and the act itself would not rule out conscious causes of one's action.

It is also important to recognize that we may spend much of our life *not* practicing volition. Perhaps volition is not an all-or-none phenomenon but may be a capacity that requires practice and development. Through awareness and perspective, we may learn to be more volitional.

Velmans makes the critical point that volition and related phenomena are as much experiences as anything else (Velmans, 2009). Thus, our conscious feelings of authorship, self-agency, responsibility, and volition are all experiences that serve us in representing what is going on in our bodies, the world, and ourselves. He points out that

...when we feel that we are free to choose or refuse an act, within the constraints of biology and social circumstances imposed on us, we usually *are* free to choose or refuse (having calculated the odds in light of inner needs and goals, likely consequences, and so on) [see also chapter 6]. When this occurs, experienced free will is an *accurate* (albeit rough and ready) representation of what is going on in our own minds, and in this sense, it is *not* an illusion. (Velmans, 2002)

As pointed out several times so far, explanation of volition is largely a first-person account even though it may relate to fundamental neural causes and correlates. It is also important to emphasize that the experience of volition is by no means rigidly linked to whether a given choice results in the intended result, nor is it rigidly linked to the right choice. However, we act on the assumption that, at least for some types of decisions, volitional choices more often lead to right choices than capricious or impulsive choices.

11.2.5   A Potential Experiential Approach to the Science of Volition

If the foregoing reasoning is correct, then an experiential science is exactly what is needed to characterize the nature of volition. In chapter 10 we used the hypnotic state and other background states of consciousness as examples of conscious phenomena that could be analyzed and character-ized in experiential–phenomenological studies and then related to neural mechanisms in subsequent brain imaging studies. Recall that the hypnotic state was found to contain the following common factors:

1. An absorbed and sustained focus of attention on one or few targets.
2. A feeling of mental/physical ease or relaxation.
3. An absence of judging, monitoring, censoring.
4. Suspension of usual orientation toward time, location of self, and/or sense of self.
5. One's own responses experienced as automatic/without deliberation or effort.

Structural equation modeling analysis provided at least a preliminary view as to how these factors were interrelated, and two brain imaging studies have begun to relate these experiential factors with neural activities in brain structures known to be involved in the regulation of consciousness (e.g., inferior parietal cortex, anterior cingulate, midbrain pontine area; Rainville et al., 1999; 2002).

What if a similar approach were taken in the case of volition? We pro-posed a model of choice in chapter 6 that was similar to decision affect theory (Mellers, 2000) and incorporated experiential factors of desire, expectation, and positive/negative feeling intensity. The overall hypothesis of this model was that choosing one option over another largely involves comparing sets of these factors across two or more options. Chapter 10 compared background states of consciousness that involved a feeling of being the agent of one's actions versus automaticity. It also compared states that included self-orientation versus those which do not include this factor. Unlike hypnotic states, volitional states of consciousness may include "presence"/awareness. The difference between volitional and non-volitional choice may be related to differences in background states of consciousness that optimize or reduce awareness of one's values and infor-mation that would lead to expectations. Consider then the possibility that a mind-set that characterizes volitional choice might include some or all of the following common factors:

1. Lack of identification and attachment (Ouspensky, 1971).
2. Awareness of *relevant information*, values, meanings and feelings (desires, expectations, etc.) associated with the different options (chapters 4–6).
3. Based on 2, a conscious weighing of feelings associated with each option, leading to a deliberate choice (chapter 6).
4. A feeling of being the agent of one's choice (chapter 10).

This list is not meant to be a definitive characterization of conscious choice but merely suggested possible factors, based on discussions in chapters 6 and 10. Some of the factors, such as "lack of attachment," may be present in both hypnotic states and in "mindful" choice. On the other hand, other factors, such as feeling oneself to be the agent of one's choice versus the automaticity that occurs during hypnosis, appear to be at opposite ends of a continuum. The list is also based on a consideration of "mindfulness," a subject that has gained considerable attention in psychology and neuroscience (Bohdi, 2005; Grant, Courtenmanche, and Rainville, 2011; Ives-Deliperi, Solms, and Meintjes, 2011; Zeiden et al., 2011). Mindfulness also follows Eastern psychological traditions, most particularly Buddhism. However, it may not be necessary to practice Buddhism or any other ancient teaching to arrive at an understanding of the structure of volitional action. Nevertheless, to the extent to which such teachings foster the practice of awareness, the practice of meditation would likely facilitate the process of understanding. The experiential approach and methods described in chapters 3 and 4 could be used to arrive at the common factors and test interrelationships between them, just as this approach was used to characterize the hypnotic state and distinguish it from other background states of consciousness, such as associative thinking.

Regardless of the exact experiential method used to study it, volition seems to require awareness. Awareness means the experience of feeling present to the moment, being embedded in the experience yet remaining impartial. Awareness contrasts with absorption, where one is lost in the moment, and forms of attention where one lacks presence. Put another way, it contrasts with "identification," which is losing one's sense of presence (Ouspensky, 1971; Givot, 1998), and "attachment," which is an inability to let go of what one is identified with (Bohdi, 2005; Ouspensky, 1971).

An experiential approach to this problem may help distinguish what does and does not constitute volition, a phenomenon that has been debated and redefined for centuries. A dictionary definition of volition is *an act of making a choice or decision.* This definition refers only to a behavior and does not differentiate between the conscious experience of choosing and unconsciously making choices. The experience of choosing must include the feeling that "I am choosing" (self-agency), which is based in part on knowing that "I can choose" (chapter 10). Knowing that one can choose is constrained by external conditions but may not be fully determined by them. Clearly, there are physical, social, and political circumstances under which individuals experience their ability to choose as severely limited or, alternatively, greatly enhanced. Knowing that one can choose is required for the feeling that one is choosing and is a measure of relative freedom. It is relative since we have no absolute control over external circumstances or the outcomes of our choices. That our choices are influenced by our values and hence our genes and learning history does not negate the possibility that we can choose with perspective and awareness.

11.2.6   Can Neuroscience Help Us Understand Volition?

Neuroimaging studies of meditation and "mindfulness" are beginning to proliferate in the cognitive neuroscience literature, and this topic is highly relevant to the issue of volitional consciousness. According to at least one set of authors, "Mindfulness is a capacity for heightened present-moment awareness that we all possess to a greater or lesser extent" (Ives-Deliperi et al., 2011). A considerable number of studies have shown that "mindfulness" reduces negative emotions and hence alleviates "stress" and it promotes physical and mental well-being in general. Ives-Deliperi and colleagues (2011) recently employed fMRI to identify brain regions involved in the state of mindfulness and to elucidate their associated neural mechanisms of action. During mindfulness, they found significant *decreases* in neural activity in midline cortical areas associated with interoception, including bilateral insular areas, left ventral anterior cingulate cortex, right medial prefrontal cortex, and bilateral precuneus. Most of these areas are the very ones that show *increased* neural activity during associative thinking Mindfulness and mind-wandering appear to have approximately opposite neural representations in brain structures involved in the regulation of consciousness.

One can anticipate at this point that an experiential science combined with the methods of neuroscience can help clarify the experiential and neurophysiological distinctions between background states of consciousness that support volitional action versus those that support nonvolitional actions and states of consciousness that reflect "attachment" and "identification." The latter are more likely to be associated with negative emotions and mind-sets that are detrimental not only to individuals having them but also to everyone around them.

11.3   Applying Experiential Science to Problems Posed by Negative Emotions

The possibilities discussed so far have far-reaching implications for problems possessed by individual human beings, groups, and even entire countries, problems that result from negative emotions. Chronic negative emotions such as hatred, jealousy, and resentment give rise to enormous amounts of conflict and violence. How do such emotions arise, and why do they support such violent actions and conflict? If science could achieve a deep understanding of the experiential basis for complex negative emotions and combine this understanding with neurobiology, this approach might greatly facilitate solutions to problems generated by negative emotions. These problems are by no means new. For several centuries, complex negative emotions have been considered to pose enormous problems for humanity. They have even been called the seven deadly sins: lust, gluttony, greed, sloth, wrath, envy, and pride (Schimmel, 1997). They have been the topic of extensive debate and many publications. Could an experiential perspective and method be used to characterize the qualitative nature of emotional states such as jealousy and envy or provide insight into the nature of greed? Some preliminary studies suggest the feasibility of such an approach.

11.3.1   Jealousy and Envy
Using the experiential method outlined in chapter 4, a study by Barrell and Richards (1982) identified the common factors of jealousy. The study was guided by the following question: "What is it like to be *in* the experience of jealousy toward someone?" The group, constituted from volunteers solicited from undergraduates at a state university and staff members of a county mental health facility, was structured with a diverse composition to satisfy the need for generality of its findings. As in the study of performance anxiety, the experiential method was used and group meetings provided opportunities for sharing descriptions and reaching a consensus about the common factors in the experience of jealousy. Many of the group members were having problems with jealousy in their lives, and so there were considerable opportunities to generate descriptions prior to and in some cases even during group meetings.

The following representative description was submitted by one group member:

I am sitting alone at the beach. My wife has gone down to the seaside and is playing in the water. Suddenly, another man appears alongside her. He appears big and good-looking. They begin to play and splash water on each other.

He does not suspect my presence and is enjoying himself with my wife. All I have is my wife. I imagine he is free and has other women. How can he enjoy my wife too? How can she be enjoying another man when I have blocked myself from other women? This is not right! I want to put a stop to their pleasure. I can't do it without making a scene.

Similar to other studies using the experiential method, this study in combination with follow-up analyses arrived at the following common factors of jealousy:

1. I perceive or imagine someone having an experience with an object, event or person that we both desire.
2. I expect it to be difficult or impossible for me to have this experience.
3. I don't feel that the other person deserves this experience.
4. I have a desire for the other person *not* to have the experience (this can include both a sense of unfairness and a feeling of anger or resentment).

All four factors are evident in the representative example, and it appears that the participant is jealous of *both* the other man and his wife's enjoyable time, an experience that he finds difficult to have. Neither the other man nor his wife is experienced as deserving. He would like to put a stop to their good time but finds it difficult. We can imagine that the presence of factors 1 and 2 without factors 3 and 4 would more likely be associated with the experience of envy, not jealousy. In envy, someone can have something we want and we can feel it to be difficult or impossible to have. Yet we don't begrudge the person's good fortune because we don't feel that they are undeserving and we have no desire to take anything away. In experiencing envy and jealousy, we can notice that the two emotions feel different. Whereas envy may contain sadness, regret, or even despair, jealousy more likely entails anger or resentment. Factor 4 includes a desire to acquire the experience held by the other person and/or a desire to take it away from that person.

Historically, the distinction between jealousy and envy is one that has not been easily made, despite consideration of these phenomena across several centuries. We suggest that an experiential characterization of this phenomenon may be a useful beginning in understanding both jealousy and envy and the distinction between them. Moreover, at least some of the factors listed above may be scaled using the methods we have outlined earlier and functional relationships between them could be tested. It is probably even possible to neuroimage jealousy since it mainly requires an active imagination and the common circumstances that evoke this phenomenon.

The problems posed by jealousy and envy apply to cultures and nations, not just individuals. The disposition to acquire what the other has or to remove it from them forms part of the basis of international conflict and is an impetus for war. This disposition is fueled by the collective emotions of a country or culture, emotions that are poorly understood from an experiential perspective. If we could learn the nature of these emotions, our resulting understanding may help mitigate conflicts that arise between nations as well as individuals.

11.3.2 Experiencing Greed in Others and in Oneself

Another example of a complex but common phenomenon is greed. Barrell and Lueders applied the experiential method to a study of the experience of greed in others as well as the experience of greed in oneself (Barrell and Lueders, 1990). Clearly, this topic has relevance to the social and economic problems presently faced throughout the world. A study group comprised of 32 undergraduate students initially collected descriptions of experiencing greed in other people from an outside perspective.

To provide a sense of the nature of descriptions of the perception of greed in others, the following description is representative:

While I was waiting to talk to a professor I noticed a young male student reading from a note on the bulletin board. I watched as he pulled it from the board and stuffed it in his books. I had the following experience:

What a jerk! He could just as easily have written down the information he needed. That information is for everyone—not just him. He begins to walk away. I can't believe it. I feel myself getting tense. I want to confront him.

The young male student is perceived as follows:

1. *Keeping others from having their part of a limited supply.* The person is seen as hoarding or consuming more than his entitlement to a portion of a finite supply. For example, the message taken from the board represents a fixed quantity—to be made available to all in an equitable manner.

2. *Being no more deserving than self or others.* How deserving of the item is this person? We make an immediate value judgment. Clearly, other people deserve the message on the board as much or more than the person who takes it. "That information is for everyone—not just him."

3. *Ignoring the perspectives of others.*   Greedy behavior is readily recognized in others. Thus, we presume this person must be aware of this behavior and know what he is doing. We can easily imagine his lack of empathy and a deliberate ignoring of the viewpoints of others as he persists in greedy behavior.

4. *Being preoccupied with one's own wants and needs.*   This greedy person is seen as unable or unwilling to see beyond the target of his desire (e.g., tunnel vision).

Since perceiving greed in ourselves requires that we experience our behavior from the perspective of another person, then the same four factors of the "outer" perspective must be present in the experience of greed from one's own viewpoint. Barrell and Lueders found this to be the case. But what would the experience of engaging in greedy behavior be like prior to our recognizing ourselves as greedy, such as *before* someone points it out to us or just before we recognize it in ourselves? The same method to determine the common factors was used in a second part of the study of experiences *just before* recognizing greed in oneself. A simple example illustrates this type of experience:

There was a group of ten people sitting in a circle and cookies were being passed around. I did not count the cookies. I took two cookies and the following experience occurred:

"Wow! They look so good. One is not enough. I can already taste them. Mouth watering. I am glad I went first."

This description is based on this person's experience that only appears "greedy" in retrospect (i.e., upon finding out there were ten people and ten cookies!). The descriptions of the other participants' similar experiences corroborated this representative sample. Consensus was reached on the following common factors:

1. I am preoccupied with fulfilling my desires and needs.

There is simply an unawareness of context. The world has shrunk around the target of my need or desire.

2. I do not consider myself undeserving or the issue of deserving is not part of my experience.

One can justify greedy behavior through feeling one has worked hard to earn it, is a good person, or has suffered in the past. Therefore, one does not feel the need to justify the behavior. Additional common factors relate to motivation:

3. I expect I can fulfill the goal.
4. I have more to gain than lose by acting.

These last two factors are required for greedy behavior. There is a final type of experience of greed that was not directly addressed in this study. It is entirely possible that individuals can engage in greedy behavior, know that they are engaging in greedy behavior, and thoroughly enjoy their own greediness.

The common factors of experiencing greed in others and in oneself prior to noticing oneself as greedy, like other experiences, are similar in terms of *how* a type of experience occurs. Are there different types of greed that are dependent upon what the greed is about? There are innumerable numbers of objects of greed, and often greed is embedded in enormous situational complexity which obscures the presence of greed itself. Nevertheless, there may be common factors in how we experience greed in others and in ourselves. Thus, it may not matter whether greed is about cookies or acquiring large profits from an insider trading deal at the expense of other investors. In either case, there is unawareness of one's overall context and a world that has collapsed around the target of a need or desire. It is fostered by values that are learned (e.g., "Greed is good"?).

11.3.3 Background States of Consciousness and Emotions

There are relationships between background states of consciousness and emotional feelings. As an example, we have shown that hypnotic states have dimensions of absorption, mental and/or physical relaxation, reduction in self-orientation, and automaticity. They tend to be associated with somewhat positive emotional states because they dispose one to positive feelings that are often suggested by the hypnotist. Thus, if the suggestions are about being in a pleasant place with "nothing to be concerned about and no one to please," one could easily feel deeply absorbed and relaxed, feel unconcerned with time, place, or even sense of self, and experience the flow of events as happening automatically. However, we suggested that the same dimensions that characterize hypnotic states are ones that vary in magnitude across a variety of background states of consciousness.

What kind of background states of consciousness accompany and support complex positive and negative emotions? In the example of jealousy given above, absorption might be high whereas mental and/or physical relaxation may be low. During greed, one may have a strong focus on a desire and lose contact with social and even physical contexts. Both jealousy and greed may be accompanied by identification and attachment. All of these possibilities are testable. The question of how background states of consciousness support complex and destructive negative emotional states is a timely one.

11.4 Using Experiential Science to Understand and Help Solve Human Problems

11.4.1 A Summary of an Experiential Strategy and Its Integration with Neuroscience

We began this book by showing that psychophysical science provides knowledge of fundamental principles of sensory experience and that psychophysics relies on simple forms of introspection. This approach can be taken a step further to study rudimentary forms of human meaning. When these scaling methods are integrated with qualitative paradigms, it is possible to improve understanding of distinct types of human experience such as specific emotions, choices, and motivation. This strategy can be merged with neuroscience to investigate the neural basis of emotions, choosing, pain and suffering, and background states of consciousness. Increased knowledge of these phenomena necessarily includes an understanding of how they can be modified qualitatively and quantitatively. For example, simple and complex forms of pain can be modified by changes in desire, expectation, and emotions brought about by placebo factors within treatments. These modifications are accompanied by corresponding changes in the brain and spinal cord. As another example, background states of consciousness can be characterized along several dimensions, including absorption, self-agency, and automaticity, dimensions that have corresponding brain activations and interactions.

11.4.2 The Process of Experiential Understanding and Solutions

Can this strategy adequately address complex problems such as jealousy, greed, and the distinction between volitional and nonvolitional choice? A deep and personal understanding of common experiential factors that constitute choice, greed, or jealousy may lead to a higher knowledge of such experiences. For example, through awareness it is possible to step back and see that our present experience of choosing includes a sense of self-agency or, alternatively, that our choosing is experienced as capricious, impulsive, or deliberate. Thus, we can come to notice and learn *how* we are choosing. This is so despite the fact that our choices may be strongly influenced by levels of desire and expectation. As with other types of experience, characterizing the common factors within volition, including their interrelationships, can promote the induction and maintenance of volition itself. If common factors are necessary and sufficient for volition, then efforts to include their presence helps instantiate it. It may take a lot of hard work and practice.

A similar approach could be taken to deal with the problems posed by intense and complex negative emotions. Again, seeing and understanding the common factors helps with a solution. For example, we saw in chapter 4 that several factors were necessary and, taken together, sufficient for performance anxiety. Reducing or eliminating any one of the factors (e.g., believe there are important people who can judge you) would be sufficient to greatly reduce and perhaps eliminate performance anxiety. Using the same reasoning and strategy, eliminating one or more of the common factors in jealousy or greed could be used to reduce the magnitudes of the complex negative emotions. This approach is not a coping method but is based instead on understanding of the structures of these experiences. Sometimes becoming aware of *how* our mind/brain "creates" these negative states is enough to reduce their power over us. Experiential understanding becomes part of the solution.

11.4.3 The Results of an Experiential Science

There are two types of results of the experiential paradigms discussed in this book, direct personal results and their application to societal problems. Both make potentially valuable contributions to psychological understanding and other sciences. This psychological understanding would be self-understanding to a major extent because coinvestigators would be trained to notice the contents and dynamics of their own experience, just as well-trained psychophysical observers become adept at noticing quantitative and qualitative aspects of their sensory experiences. For example, we may find the causes of emotions, such as jealousy and anger, are more understandable when the perceived meanings of situations are understood, meanings that may be common across individuals. These meanings are not exclusively "outside" of us but depend on factors within our own experience of situations. Once we have a clear understanding of this, as in the examples of jealousy or greed, we can begin to take more responsibility for our reactions to situations and not attribute the causes of our complex emotions to others or the environment. This understanding could facilitate people's becoming more responsible for their actions instead of relying on the authority of others. Understanding the common factors within the experience of volitional action could accomplish the same thing. An additional realization is that our choices are influenced by basic positive human values such as achievement, intimacy, and self-esteem as well as negative values such as avoiding helplessness, loneliness, and emptiness. These common values underscore our connectedness as human beings.

11.4.4   A Final Perspective

A science of human experience cannot take place by "traditional" psychological experiments alone or by substituting neuroscience for experiential science. Rather, a deeper understanding can take place through integration of experiential science with the rest of science. If it takes place, this approach could result in merging the exploratory, confirmatory, and applied dimensions of science. Furthermore, both the liberal arts and sciences of higher education could be revitalized. As pointed out by Edward O. Wilson, students seeking a "higher" education would be helped to see that in the twenty-first century the world will not be run only by people with the most information. Information of all kinds is available on computers, mobile devices, and television screens. Beyond the ordinary information that exists in the world, what principle can be used to achieve deep understanding? Clearly, the answer is synthesis, or to use Edward Wilson's book title, consilience, the unification of human knowledge. As he points out, "We are drowning in information, while starving for wisdom" (Wilson, 1998). The integration of a science of human experience with the rest of science could provide understanding that is both deeply personal and widely public. It could provide a basis for making the most important choices wisely.

Notes

Chapter 1

1. The experiential method originated from a combined interest in several disciplines and sciences: psychophysics, neuroscience, phenomenology, meditative practices, and cognitive psychology. An interest common to most of these disciplines is self-observation and awareness of what is taking place in moments of experience. For example, Buddhist and Yoga meditative practices offer a method for observing what one's mind is doing as it does it, to be present with one's mind. As Varela, Thompson, and Rosch (1991) point out, "The purpose of the mind in Buddhism is not to become absorbed but to render the mind able to be present with itself long enough to gain insight into its own nature and functioning." The meditative training in these traditions typically requires the ability to quiet the mind, including slowing down or even stopping thoughts. Inevitably, thoughts, feelings, and images reemerge despite these efforts, and it is at these moments that they can be observed. Another practice of some teachings is that of deliberately placing oneself in situations wherein experiences of a given kind tend to take place, including those wherein positive or negative emotions are likely to emerge. The purpose of these teachings is to facilitate awareness of these experiences (Ouspensky, 1971). Awareness is the practice of noticing whatever is taking place in one's experience. From this noticing, in combination with later reflection and analysis, comes understanding of beliefs, thoughts, feelings, and their underlying meanings. This approach is indispensable for a science of experience.

Chapter 3

1. Participants responded by producing line lengths to desire and emotional feeling (feeling good or feeling bad). Thus, a standard psychophysical procedure of line production was used, a form of cross-modality matching.

Chapter 4

1. In an expositional interview described by Hurlburt and Akhter (2006), a participant Ahmed said, "I was saying to myself, 'my girlfriend should buy some bananas.'" The interviewer then noted that people don't generally say to themselves, "My girlfriend should…" Instead, they say the much more natural "Jessica should…" The interviewer considered Ahmed to probably not be quoting himself accurately and pressed him two more times with the questions "Exactly what were you saying?" and "Yes, but exactly what words, if any, were you saying?" Ahmed's replies consistently reflected his wanting Jessica/girlfriend to bring bananas. Nevertheless, all of his responses seemed unsatisfactory to the interviewer. Ahmed said he was talking to himself, but he was unable to say exactly what the words were. He became frustrated for reasons that are ambiguous to us. Was he frustrated because he couldn't remember the words or because he knew he was right and felt unable to convince the interviewer? Hurlburt and Akhter (2006) go on to claim that "DES interviewers see this particular kind of interchange with its attendant frustration frequently, and it often means that at the moment of the beep the subject was experiencing thinking that was occurring without words, images, or any other symbols (a phenomenon DES calls unsymbolized thinking; Hurlburt, 1990, 1993,1997; Hurlburt & Heavey, 2006). Ahmed (incorrectly) assumed that all thinking is in words…, so if he's thinking, he must be talking to himself. When he couldn't remember the words that he must have been saying, he became frustrated." So the interviewer, based on a notion of what was really going on in Ahmed's experience, suggests to Ahmed that he may have been thinking without words. So then "The interviewer reassured Ahmed by saying, 'Sometimes words are present during thinking, sometimes not; either way is OK. We don't have to worry too much about this particular sample—if this phenomenon is important, we'll see it on subsequent sampling days and we can figure it out then.' That aimed to relax Ahmed's defenses and to help him truly describe his subsequent experience." Is the interviewer leading and/or biasing Ahmed in this interview? The interviewer appears to suggest to Ahmed that he was wrong about his description of his experience and that if he was really thinking without words "we'll see it on subsequent sampling days and we can figure it out then…" Hopefully, DES has ways of clarifying the distinction between inner speech and nonsymbolized thinking without leading participants. Moreover, Ahmed may not have been wrong at all about the essential meaning of his experience: He wanted some bananas and he wanted Jessica (his girlfriend at the time) to bring them!

2. *Working groups and their aim*   Our studies that utilized the qualitative stage of the experiential method were conducted with "working groups" that either included one or both authors and other coinvestigators, either students or faculty members. We would meet regularly at a class on campus or at our home. Some of our qualitative studies were combined with quantitative procedures, the second stage of the experiential method, and some of these studies are described in some of the remaining chapters.

3. An anecdote from a public speaker that we know further illustrates the type of noticing used in the experiential method. He has told us that sometimes when he is giving a lecture, he is also quietly watching and listening to himself give the lecture as if he was another person watching the speaker. According to his experience, this parallel witnessing in no way compromises the content of the lecture, the words of the lecture, or even the emotional feelings that are associated with the content.

4. *Inner and outer viewpoints*   Once investigators are able to participate in this type of experiential inquiry, another issue becomes evident. That is, for any given situation, two viewpoints are possible (Barrell and Barrell, 1975; Giorgi, 1970). An "outside viewpoint" refers to experiencing from the point of view of our cognition or imagination. For example, I can imagine how I am being seen from the outside or I can think about my behavior as if I were another person observing myself (e.g., "I must look upset and people must be noticing how loud my voice is right now"). In contrast, the "inside viewpoint" refers to experiencing from our own embodied viewpoint (Gendlin, 1962; Price and Barrell, 1980). Thus, in noticing our experience of anger we would likely find ourselves experiencing feelings and thoughts within ourselves rather than how we see or imagine ourselves from the outside. For example, an experience of anger might include thoughts and feelings that refer to "inner" feelings in combination with meanings about someone else. When we experience anger, we feel resistance to setting things right and feel body tension.

The distinction between inside and outside viewpoints also can be made if someone were to write a lower case "b" on your forehead. From an inside viewpoint you would report a "d" being written. From an outside viewpoint you would report a "b" as seen from someone else's position. Both inside and outside viewpoints can be noticed. However, some experiences may be more related to the outside viewpoint and others may be more related to the inside viewpoint. The outside viewpoint is taken in the initial phases of embarrassment: "I think that I am being observed by another person. I imagine or think about how this person is viewing and judging me. I then judge myself as if I were that person." Other experiences, like anxiety, are most often related to an inside viewpoint: "I really want to avoid these negative results and feel uncertain about whether I will avoid them. I feel tension build in myself as I become preoccupied with thoughts about these negative consequences."

5. *Awareness and attention*   When we decide to observe our experiences (thoughts, feelings etc.), a specific kind of observation is necessary. We all understand what it means to pay attention to something. However, when we attempt to strongly focus on and pay active attention to such targets as thoughts and feelings, the data are often unavailable (a problem for classic introspectionists). This is because when we pay attention, we actively "move out" to the object of interest. There is a distance between the observer and the observed. Such active attending (outputting) impacts the observation so that input is unavailable. We cannot input and output at the

same time. What is needed is a form of observation that has been referred to as passive attending and better described as *awareness*. Unlike attention, awareness means *allowing* the targets or objects to "come to you." It is passive in this sense. There is no distance between the observer and observed. The observer is simply parallel to and *with* the experience, but the experience itself contains only the observing and the observed. There is an awareness of being present to the situation where both observing and observed is happening. Without an observer standing apart from the experience, all the richness of the experience becomes available to the observer.

6. The sentences in the description may or may not have started with the use of the word "I." When participants become trained in experiential reporting, they make less use of the word "I" and also use more incomplete sentences. In early studies, we encouraged use of I-statements and now no longer do so. Another change has been to encourage the statement "The following experience occurred" so as to distinguish description of the setting and context of the experience from the moment-by-moment experience itself.

Chapter 5

1. On the scales we used for expectation, 0 means that we feel that it is impossible to fulfill the goal and 100 means that it is completely certain that it will be fulfilled. The numbers in between reflect varying degrees of likelihood. The data were analyzed after transforming 0–100 scales into 0–1.0 scales because of greater ease of computation. Some behaviorists tend to avoid using words such as "expectations" and instead refer to concepts such as "perceived degree of reinforcement." These concepts are often applied to situations wherein impending rewards and punishments can be assumed to be perceived by but not yet delivered to the organism.

2. On scales we used for emotional feeling intensity (sometimes referred to as "valence" by psychologists), separate VASs were used for positive feeling and negative feeling. The scales were anchored at the left end by 0 (feeling neither good nor bad) and at the right end by "the most positive feeling imaginable" (+100) and "the most negative feeling imaginable" (–100) for positive and negative emotional feelings, respectively.

3. This same issue is critical for understanding patterns of psychophysiological responses during several types of emotional feelings. In this regard, it is noteworthy that over a century of research on emotion has not completely resolved the question of whether the experience of specific emotions is related to specific and unique patterns of somatovisceral responses (James, 1890; Damasio; 1994) or results from the experience of specific cognitions during a generalized autonomic arousal, as proposed by Schacter and Singer (1962; see also review by Barrett, 2007). It is easy to see why this controversy remains for two reasons. Characterizing patterns of somatic and visceral activity requires multiple physiological measures (ideally more

than one or two!), and in-depth experiential characterization of emotional feelings has been almost nonexistent throughout the history of emotion research.

Chapter 6

1. We asked 40 people to choose between two options that each combined a stated probability and money amount, as in the examples given so far. Several choice scenarios were presented. In this analysis, the correlation between the percentage of people choosing the higher value (e.g., $9,000, F_1) over the lower value ($1,000, F_2) option and $F_1 - F_2$ was .74. This result means that about 55% of the variability in choice responses can be accounted for by this $F_1 - F_2$ model. F_1 and F_2 were each computed from the emotion model formula ($F = -0.3D + 1.3DE^{1/2}$), wherein F is magnitude of emotional feeling, E is stated probability (assumed in this simplified scenario to be similar to subjective probability), and D is desire intensity as rated by the participants. Using this same strategy, we also asked the same people to choose between options related to durations of continuous rain. In this case, the correlation between the percentage of people choosing the option with least unpleasant outcome (ten days' rain) and $F_1 - F_2$ was .93. The overall point is that the functions that we had previously derived in emotion studies were good predictors of choices when hypothetical scenarios were presented.

2. To satisfy our curiosity about anticipated "regret" or risk, we then added a small risk factor to both approach and avoidance goal choice models and found correlations between choice models and percent choice of the options to be very high (.96 and .97). It seemed reasonable to think that this risk or regret factor was proportional to F_2 itself, the more certain but lower gain outcome. Thus, two formulas closely predicted choices of the F_1 option. The formula that predicted choice for the approach goal of gaining money was *percent choice of* $F_1 = -F_2 + 2(F_1 - F_2)$ ($r = .96$) and for avoiding rain it predicted that *percent choice of* $F_1 = +F_2 + 2.4(F_1 - F_2)$ ($r = .97$). F_1 and F_2 were computed differently for approach and avoidance goals and based on emotion formulas described in chapter 5.

Chapter 7

1. Thus, when an investigator or clinician asks someone to rate pain, exactly what is he or she asking the person to rate and how is this study participant or patient instructed? Our approach to teaching people the distinction between the dimensions of pain is to provide an analogy with listening to unpleasant music from a radio. Our instructions include the following statements:

Pain is like listening to unpleasant music from a radio. As I turn up the volume, I can ask you to rate either "loudness" or "how unpleasant it is to hear the music." If it is the wrong kind of music, it may be unpleasant even if it is just loud enough to hear, but it will grow more unpleasant as the volume increases. Similar to listening to unpleasant music, the unpleasantness of pain is influenced by its sensory intensity as well as other things that may affect you, such as the meaning of the pain.

We have found this analogy to be very useful in teaching patients and study participants the distinction between the two pain dimensions (Price et al., 1983).

2. This study by Zeiden et al. (2011) is one of many whose results show that a psychological phenomenon, in this case mindful meditation, can actually reduce the unpleasantness of pain (by 57%) and its sensory intensity (by 40%). Similar to other psychological methods of pain control, such as placebo and hypnosis, the effects on pain can be powerful and are accompanied by corresponding reductions in pain-related activity within the brain. What makes this study so unique is that the authors characterized not only the effects on pain but also the patterns of brain activity associated with the meditative state and their interaction with pain processing. This particular meditative state, termed *Shamatha* (Sanskrit: calm abiding detachment) differs from other types of pain-reducing methods in that it is a volitionally induced nonjudgmental state of awareness of the present moment. Remarkably, the study shows that participants can acquire enough skill in four days of brief practice (twenty minutes a day) to substantially reduce experimental pain. What else can this practice accomplish?

Chapter 9

1. Years ago I (DDP) had mild headaches from time to time for which I took one or two aspirins. They nearly always worked. One day I noticed that the headache disappeared within five minutes after taking one aspirin. This was not enough time for the medication to be absorbed. I have noted this same brief latency effect several times since then. Aspirin still works within five minutes even though thoughts of placebo response come to mind.

2. Associative thinking was described in chapter 1 as a conscious background state wherein subjects make unconstrained associations that are unrelated to the immediate external environment. Images and thoughts are linked together quickly in associative thinking. If associative thinking is involved in generating the placebo response, we might suspect that brain areas involved in this type of thinking would be most active during the early part of the experimental session when the placebo response is being generated (see figure 1.1). Brain areas known to be involved in associative thinking were more highly active during the early part of the session as compared to the later part. These areas included right posterior cingulate, left precuneus/postcingulate, left middle frontal gyrus, and parts of the posterior temporal lobe (temporoparietal junction; Bar et al., 2007). Their greater activation during the early part of the placebo condition means that the brain and the mind are doing the most work in producing the placebo effect soon after the placebo suggestion is given. This pattern may help explain the dynamics of placebo analgesia. During the early part of the placebo analgesia condition, participants were likely to be making

associations between prior suggestions about the placebo agent, internal cues that suggest whether or not the agent is working, and their expectations about future pain experience. These associations require memory, somatic focus, and comparison of present experience to expectation of pain following placebo suggestion, as we discussed earlier. This conceptualization is consistent with a self-enhancing feedback mechanism (Price, Finniss, and Benedetti, 2008; Vase et al., 2003, 2004, 2005).

3. This hypothesis is also supported by a brain imaging study that found similar regions in the cerebral cortex and in the brainstem affected by both a placebo and the rapidly acting opioid remifentanil. This suggests a related mechanism in pla-cebo-induced and opioid-induced analgesia (Petrovic et al., 2002). The direct dem-onstration of placebo-induced release of endogenous opioids has been obtained by using in vivo receptor binding with positron emission tomography (PET) by Zubieta et al. (2005). By using an experimental model of pain in healthy volunteers, these authors found an increase of mu-opioid receptor neurotransmission in different brain regions, such as the ACC, the OFC, the insula, and the nucleus accumbens. All of these areas are known to have pivotal roles in the generation of emotions, consistent with the idea that some types of placebo responses occur in the context of emotional responses.

4. The 25 IBS patients were not trained in using the experiential method described in chapter 4. They were encouraged, as much as feasible, to reconstruct their experi-ences of the forty-minute experimental session and to report their experiences as if they were taking place in the present. The interviewer used "markers" of time points indicated by introductory phrases such as "The time at which the agent was being applied…," "The first few minutes after the treatment…," and "Toward the end of the session…" Not all participants were equally comfortable reporting in this way, and the method was not forced on anyone. The interviewer simply repeatedly encouraged confining the reports to just what the participants had been experienc-ing and gently discouraged interpretations and information that was irrelevant to their experiences.

References

Adair, E. E., Stevens, J. C., and Marks, L. E. (1968). Thermally induced pain: The dol scale and the psychophysical power law. *American Journal of Psychology, 81,* 147–164.

Ader, R., and Cohen, N. (1982). Behaviorally conditioned immunosuppression and murine systemic lupus erythematosus. *Science, 215,* 1534–1536.

Ader, R., Kelly, K., Moynihan, J. A., Grota, L. J., and Cohen, N. (1993). Conditioned enhancement of antibody production using a antigen as the unconditioned stimulus. *Brain, Behavior, and Immunity, 7,* 334–343.

Adler, M. (1971). *A Parents' Manual.* Springfield, IL: Charles C. Thomas.

Adolphs, R., Damasio, H., Tranel, D., Cooper, G., and Damasio, A. R. (2000). A role for somatosensory cortices in the visual recognition of emotion as revealed by three-dimensional lesion mapping. *Journal of Neuroscience, 20,* 2683–2690.

Amanzio, M., and Benedetti, F. (1999). Neuropharmacological dissection of placebo analgesia: Expectation activated opioid systems versus conditioning-activated specific subsystems. *Journal of Neuroscience, 19,* 484–494.

Amanzio, M., Pollo, A., Maggi, G., and Benedetti, F. (2001). Response variability to analgesics: A role for non-specific activation of endogenous opioids. *Pain, 90,* 205–215.

Anderson, A. K., Christoff, K., Stappen, J., Panitz, D., Ghahremani, D. G., and Glover, G. (2003). Dissociated neural representation of intensity and valence in human olfaction. *Nature Neuroscience, 6,* 196–202.

Arendt-Nielsen, L., Zachariae, R., and Bjerring, P. (1990). Quantitative evaluation of hypnotically suggested hyperaesthesia and analgesia by painful laser stimulation. *Pain, 42,* 243–251.

Armstrong, D. (1968). *A Materialist Theory of the Mind.* London: Routledge and Kegan Paul.

Arnold, M. B. (1970). *Feelings and Emotions*. New York: Academic Press

Averill, J., and Rosen, M. (1972). Vigilant and nonvigilant coping strategies and psychophysiological stress reactions during the anticipation of stress. *Journal of Personality and Social Psychology*, *23*, 128–141.

Aydede, M. (2001). Naturalism, introspection, and direct realism about pain. *Consciousness and Emotion*, *2*(1), 29–73.

Aydede, M. (2005). *Pain: New Essays on Its Nature and the Methodology of Its Study*. Cambridge, MA: MIT Press.

Baars, B. J. (2003). How brain reveals mind: Neural studies support the fundamental role of conscious experience. *Journal of Consciousness Studies*, *10*(9–10): 100–114.

Bakan, D. (1967). *On Method*. San Francisco: Jossey-Bass.

Bakan, D. (1968). *Disease, Pain, and Sacrifice*. Chicago: University of Chicago Press.

Balthazard, C. G., and Woody, E. Z. (1992). The spectral analysis of hypnotic performance with respect to "absorption." *International Journal of Clinical and Experimental Hypnosis*, *40*, 21–43.

Bar, M. E., Aminoff, M., Mason, J., and Fenske, M. (2007). The units of thought. *Hippocampus*, *17*(6), 420–428.

Barrell, J. J., and Barrell, J. E. (1975). A self-directed approach for a science of human experience. *Journal of Phenomenological Psychology*, *6*(1), 63–73.

Barrell, J. J., and Jourard, S. (1976). Being honest with persons we like. *Journal of Individual Psychology*, *32*(2), 185–193.

Barrell, J. J., and Lueders, P. W. (1990). Greed is destroying our world: A human science study. In J. J. Barrell, D. C. Medeiros, & K. L. Foley (Eds.), *The Experiential Method: Exploring the Human Experience* (pp. 45–58). Acton, MA: Copley Publishing Company.

Barrell, J. J., and Neimeyer, R. (1986). A mathematical formula for the psychological control of suffering. In J. J. Barrell (Ed.), *A Science of Human Experience* (pp. 181–188). Acton, MA: Copely Publishing Company.

Barrell, J. J., and Price, D. D. (1975). The perception of first and second pain as a function of psychological set. *Perception & Psychophysics*, *17*(2), 163–166.

Barrell, J. J., and Price, D. D. (1977). Two experiential orientations toward a stressful situation and their related somatic and visceral responses. *Psychophysiology*, *8*(6), 517–521.

Barrell, J. J., and Richards, A. C. (1982). Overcoming jealousy—An experiential analysis of common factors. *Personnel and Guidance Journal*, *61*(1), 40–47.

Barrell, J. J., & Ryback, D. (2008). *The Psychology of Champions*. Westport, CT: Praeger.

Barrell, J. J., Medieros, D., Barrell, J. E., and Price, D. D. (1985). Anxiety: An obstacle to performance. *Journal of Humanistic Psychology, 25*, 106–122.

Barrett, L. F. (2004). Feelings or words? Understanding the content in self-report of experienced emotion. *Journal of Personality and Social Psychology, 87*(2), 266–281.

Barrett, L. F. (2007). The experience of emotion. *Annual Review of Psychology, 136*(1), 23–42.

Barrett, L. F., and Wager, T. D. (2006). The structure of emotion—Evidence from neuroimaging studies. *Current Directions in Psychological Science, 15*(2), 79–83.

Basbaum, A. I., and Fields, H. L. (1978). Endogenous pain control mechanisms: Review and hypothesis. *Annals of Neurology, 4*(5), 451–462.

Bausell, R. B., Lao, L., Bergman, S., Lee, W. L., and Berman, B. M. (2005). Is acupuncture analgesia an expectancy effect? Preliminary evidence based on participants' perceived assignments in two placebo-controlled trials. *Evaluation & the Health Professions, 28*, 9–26.

Bechara, A., Damasio, H., Tranel, D., and Damasio, A. R. (1997). Deciding advantageously before knowing the advantageous strategy. *Science, 275*, 1293–1295.

Bechara, A., Damasio, H., Damasio, A. R., and Lee, G. P. (1999). Different contributions of the human amygdala and ventromedial prefrontal cortex to decision-making. *Journal of Neuroscience, 19*, 5473–5481.

Beecher, H. K. (1959). *Measurement of Subjective Responses: Quantitative Effects of Drugs*. New York: Oxford University Press.

Benedetti, F. (2002). How the doctor's words affect the patient's brain. *Evaluation & the Health Professions, 25*(4), 369–386.

Benedetti, F., Arduino, C., & Amanzio, M. (1999). Somatotopic activation of opioid systems by target-directed expectations of analgesia. *Journal of Neuroscience, 9*, 3639–3648.

Benedetti, F., Pollo, A., Lopiano, L., Lanotte, M., and Vighetti, S. (2003). Conscious expectation and unconscious conditioning in analgesic, motor and hormonal placebo/nocebo responses. *Journal of Neuroscience, 23*, 4315–4323.

Benedetti, F., Colloca, L., Torre, E., Lanotte, M., and Melcarne, A. (2004). Placebo-responsive Parkinson patients show decreased activity in single neurons of subthalamic nucleus. *Nature Neuroscience, 7*, 587–588.

Benedetti, F., Arduino, C., Costa, S., Vighetti, S., and Tarenzi, L. (2006). Loss of expectation-related mechanisms in Alzheimer's disease makes analgesic therapies less effective. *Pain, 121*, 133–144.

Bernard, J. F., and Besson, J. M. (1990). The spino(trigemino)pontoamygdaloid pathway: Electrophysiological evidence for an involvement in pain processes. *Journal of Neurophysiology, 63,* 473–490.

Bernoulli, D. (1954). Exposition of a new theory on the measurement of risk. Originally published in Latin in 1738. *Translation in Econometrica, 22,* 23–35.

Berthier, M., Starkstein, S., and Leiquarda, R. (1988). Asymbolia for pain: A sensory–limbic disconnection syndrome. *Annals of Neurology, 24*(1), 41–49.

Birnbaum, M. (2008). New paradoxes of risky decision making. *Psychological Review, 115*(2), 463–501.

Blair, K., Marsh, A. A., Morton, J., Vythilingham, M., Jones, M., and Mondillo, K. (2006). Choosing the lesser of two evils, the better of two goods: Specifying the roles of ventromedial prefrontal cortex and dorsal anterior cingulate in object choice. *Journal of Neuroscience, 26*(44), 11379–11386.

Blakemore, S. J., and Frith, C. (2003). Self-awareness and action. *Current Opinion in Neurobiology, 13,* 219–224.

Blakemore, S. J., Oakley, D. A., and Frith, C. D. (2003). Delusions of alien control in the normal brain. *Neuropsychologia, 41,* 1058–1067.

Bogen, J. E. (1995). On the neurophysiology of consciousness: I. An overview. *Consciousness and Cognition, 4,* 52–62.

Bohdi, B. (2005). *In the Buddha's Words: An Anthology of Discourses from the Pali Canon.* Boston: Wisdom Publications.

Borg, G. H., Diament, L., Strom, B., and Zotterman, Y. (1967). The relation between neural and perceptual intensity: A comparative study on the neural and psychophysical response to taste stimuli. *Journal of Physiology, 192,* 13–20.

Boring, E. G. (1957). *A History of Experimental Psychology.* New York: Appleton Century Crofts.

Bowers, K. S. (1978). Responsivity, creativity, and the role of effortless experiencing. *International Journal of Clinical and Experimental Psychology, 26,* 184–202.

Bowers, K. S. (1983). *Hypnosis for the Seriously Curious.* New York: Norton.

Brandt, L. W. (1970). Control or reduction of variables? An experimenter inclusive model. *Psychological Reports, 27,* 80–82.

Breggin, P. (1991). *Toxic Psychiatry.* New York: St. Martins.

Breggin, P. (2008). *Brain Disabling Treatments in Psychiatry: Drugs, Electroshock, and the Role of the Food and Drug Administration.* New York: Springer.

Breiter, H. C., Aharon, I., Kahneman, D., Dale, A., and Shizgal, P. (2001). Functional imaging of neural responses of expectancy and experience of monetary gains and losses. *Neuron, 30,* 619–639.

Bruce, V., Green, P. R., and Georgeson, M. A. (1996). *Visual Perception* (3rd ed.). New York: Psychology Press.

Burstein, R., Cliffer, K. D., and Giesler, G. J. (1987). Direct somatosensory projections from the spinal cord to the hypothalamus and telencephalon. *Journal of Neuroscience, 7,* 4159–4164.

Bush, F. M., Harkins, S. W., Harrington, W. G., and Price, D. D. (1993). Analysis of gender effects on pain perception and symptom presentation in temporomandibular pain. *Pain, 53,* 73–80.

Bushnell, M. C., Duncan, G. H., Dubner, R., and He, L. F. (1984). Activity of trigeminothalamic neurons in medullary dorsal horn of awake monkeys trained in a thermal discrimination task. *Journal of Neurophysiology, 52,* 170–187.

Buytendyck, F. J. J. (1961). *Pain.* London: Hutchinson.

Cacioppo, J. T., von Hippel, W., and Ernst, J. M. (1997). Mapping cognitive structures and processes through verbal content: The thought-listing technique. *Journal of Consulting and Clinical Psychology, 65*(6), 928–940.

Calhoun, J. B. (1971). *How the Social Organization of Animal Communities Can Lead to a Population Crisis Which Destroys Them. Reported by M. Pines, Mental Health Program Reports, No.5 (DHEW) Publication No. (HSM) 72–9042.* Chevy Chase, MD: National Institute of Mental Health.

Casey, K. L., and Bushnell, M. C. (Eds.). (2000). *Pain Imaging: Progress in Pain Research and Management* (Vol. 18). Seattle: IASP Press.

Casey, K. L., and Morrow, T. J. (1983). Ventral posterior thalamic neurons differentially responsive to noxious stimulation in the awake monkey. *Science, 221,* 675–677.

Chalmers, D. J. (1996). *The Conscious Mind: In Search of a Fundamental Theory.* New York: Oxford University Press.

Chalmers, D. J. (2000). What is a neural correlate of consciousness? In T. Metzinger (Ed.), *Neural Correlates of Consciousness: Empirical and Conceptual Questions* (pp. 17–39). Cambridge, MA: MIT Press.

Chalmers, D. J. (2003). Consciousness and its place in nature. In S. Stich & F. Warfield (Eds.), *Blackwell Guide to the Philosophy of Mind* (pp. 1–37). Malden, MA: Blackwell.

Chalmers, D. J. (2004). How can we construct a science of consciousness? In M. Gazzaniga (Ed.), *The Cognitive Neurosciences III* (pp. 1–19). Cambridge, MA: MIT Press.

Chaminade, T., and Decety, J. (2002). Leader or follower? Involvement of the inferior parietal lobule in agency. *Neuroreport, 13*, 1975–1978.

Chung, J. M., Kenshalo, D. R., Jr., Gerhart, K. D., and Willis, W. D. (1979). Excitation of primate spinothalamic neurons by cutaneous C-fiber volleys. *Journal of Neurophysiology, 42*, 1354–1369.

Chung, J. M., Lee, K. H., and Surmeier, D. J. (1986). Response characteristics of neurons in the ventral posterior lateral nucleus of the monkey thalamus. *Journal of Neurophysiology, 56*, 370–390.

Chung, S. K., Price, D. D., Verne, G. N., and Robinson, M. E. (2007). Revelation of a personal placebo response: Its effects on mood, attitudes, and future placebo responding. *Pain, 32*(3), 281–288.

Churchland, P. S. (2002). Self-representation in nervous systems. *Science, 296*, 308–310.

Coghill, R. C., Price, D. D., and Hayes, R. (1991). Spatial distribution of nociceptive processing in the rat spinal cord. *Journal of Neurophysiology, 65*, 133–140.

Coghill, R. C., Mayer, D. J., and Price, D. D. (1993). Wide dynamic range but not nociceptive specific neurons encode multidimensional features of prolonged repetitive heat pain. *Journal of Neurophysiology, 69*(3), 703–716.

Coghill, R. C., McHaffie, J. G., and Yen, Y. F. (2003). Neural correlates of individual differences in the subjective experience of pain. *Proceedings of the National Academy of Sciences of the United States of America, 100*(14), 8538–8542.

Cohen, J., and Cohen, P. (1983). *Applied Multiple Regression/Correlation Analysis for the Behavioral Sciences* (2nd ed.). New York: Lawrence Erlbaum.

Colloca, L., and Benedetti, F. (2004). The placebo in clinical studies and in medical practice. In D. D. Price & M. C. Bushnell (Eds.), *Psychological Modulation of Pain* (pp. 187–206). Seattle: IASP Press.

Colloca, L., and Benedetti, F. (2005). Placebos and painkillers: Is mind as real as matter? *Nature Reviews. Neuroscience, 6*(7), 545–552.

Colloca, L., and Benedetti, F. (2006). How prior experience shapes placebo analgesia. *Pain, 124*, 126–133.

Colloca, L., Lopiano, L., Lanotte, M., and Benedetti, F. (2004). Overt versus covert treatment for pain, anxiety, and Parkinson's disease. *Lancet Neurology, 3*, 679–684.

Coricelli, G., Dolan, R. J., and Sirigu, A. (2007). Brain, emotion, and decision making: The paradigmatic example of regret. *Trends in Cognitive Sciences, 11*(6), 258–265.

Coull, J. T., and Nobre, A. C. (1998). Where and when to pay attention: The neural systems for directing attention to spatial locations and to time intervals as revealed by both PET and fMRI. *Journal of Neuroscience, 18*, 7426–7435.

Coull, J. T., Frackowiak, R. S., and Frith, C. D. (1998). Monitoring for target objects: Activation of right frontal and parietal cortices with increasing time on task. *Neuropsychologia, 36*, 1325–1334.

Costa, P. T., and McCrae, R. R. (1985). *The NEO Personality Inventory Manual*. Odessa, FL: Psychological Assessment Resources.

Craggs, J. G., Price, D. D., Verne, G. N., Perlstein, W. M., and Robinson, M. E. (2007). Functional interactions within brain areas serving cognitive-affective processing during pain and placebo conditions. *NeuroImage, 38*(4), 720–729.

Craggs, J. G., Price, D. D., Perlstein, W. R., and Robinson, M. E. (2008). The dynamic mechanisms of placebo induced analgesia: Evidence of sustained and transient regional involvement. *Pain, 139*(3), 660–669.

Craggs, J. G., Price, D. D., Perlstein, W. R., Verne, G. N., and Robinson, M. E. (2008). The dynamic mechanisms of placebo induced analgesia: Evidence of sustained and transient regional involvement. *Pain, 139*(3), 660–669.

Craig, A. D. (2009). How do you feel—now? The anterior insula and human awareness. *Nature Reviews. Neuroscience, 10*(1), 59–70.

Cramer, G., (1728). Letter to Nicholas Bernoulli, 1732. [Quote in note appended to Bernoulli 1738.]

Crawford, H. J., Knebel, T., Kaplan, L., Vendemia, J. M. C., Xie, M., and Jamison, S. (1998). Hypnotic analgesia: I. Somatosensory event-related potential changes to noxious stimuli, and II. Transfer learning to reduce chronic low back pain. *International Journal of Clinical and Experimental Hypnosis, 46*, 92–132.

Crick, F. (1994). *The Astonishing Hypothesis: The Scientific Search for the Soul*. London: Simon and Schuster.

Crick, F., and Koch, C. (2007). A neurobiological framework for consciousness. In M. Velmans & S. Schneider (Eds.), *The Blackwell Companion to Consciousness* (pp. 567–579). Malden, MA: Blackwell.

Dado, R. J., Katter, J. T., and Giesler, G. J., Jr. (1994). Spinothalamic and spinohypothalamic tract neurons in the cervical enlargement in rats: II. Responses to innocuous and noxious mechanical thermal stimuli. *Journal of Neurophysiology, 71*, 981–1002.

Damasio, A. (1994). *Descartes' Error*. New York: Avon Books.

Damasio, A. (1999). *The Feeling of What Happens*. New York: Avon Books.

Damasio, A. R. (1996). The somatic marker hypothesis and the possible functions of the prefrontal cortex. *Philosophical Transactions of the Royal Society of London. Series B, Biological Sciences, 351*, 1413–1420.

deCharms, R. C., Maeda, F., Glover, G. H. and Mackey, S. (2005). Control over brain activation and pain learned by using real-time functional MRI. *Proceedings of the National Academy of Sciences of the United States of America, 102*(51), 18626–18631.

de Craen, A. J., Kaptchuk, T. J., Tijssen, J. G., and Kleijnen, J. (1999). Placebos and placebo effects in medicine: Historical overview. *Journal of the Royal Society of Medicine, 92*(10), 511–515.

de la Fuente-Fernandez, R., Ruth, T. J., Sossi, V., Schulzer, M., and Calne, D. B. (2001). Expectation and dopamine release: Mechanism of the placebo effect in Parkinson's disease. *Science, 293,* 1164–1166.

De Pascalis, V., Magurano, M. R., and Bellusci, A. (1999). Pain perception, somatosensory event-related potentials and skin conductance responses to painful stimuli in high, mid, and low hypnotizable subjects: Effects of differential pain reduction strategies. *Pain, 83,* 499–508.

De Pascalis, V., Chiaradia, C., and Carotenuto, E. (2002). The contribution of suggestibility and expectation to placebo analgesia phenomenon in an experimental settings. *Pain, 96,* 393–402.

Dennett, D. C. (1991). *Consciousness Explained.* London: Allen Lane.

Derogatis, L. R. (1987). The Derogatis Stress Profile (DSP): Quantification of psychological distress. *Advances in Psychosomatic Medicine, 17,* 30–54. (Revised in 1994).

Devinsky, O., Morrell, M. J., and Vogt, B. A. (1995). Contributions of anterior cingulate cortex to behavior. *Brain, 118*(Pt 1), 279–306.

Dias, R., Robbins, T. W., & Roberts, A. C. (1996). Dissociation in prefrontal cortex of affective and attentional shifts. *Nature, 380*(6569), 69–72.

Douglass, D. K., Carstens, E., and Watkins, L. R. (1992). Spatial summation in human pain perception: Comparison within and between dermatomes. *Pain, 50,* 197–202.

Dretske, F. (1995). *Naturalizing the Mind.* Cambridge, MA: MIT Press.

Dretske, F. (1999). The mind's awareness of itself. *Philosophical Studies, 95,* 103–124.

Duncan, G., Bushnell, M. C., and Levigne, G. (1989). Comparison of verbal and visual analogue scales for measuring the intensity and unpleasantness of experimental pain. *Pain, 37,* 295–303.

Edwards, W. (1992). *Utility Theories: Measurement and Applications.* Boston: Kluwer.

Eippert, F., Finsterbusch, J., and Bingel, U. (2009). Direct evidence for spinal cord involvement in placebo analgesia. *Science, 326*(5951), 404.

Ekman, G. (1962). Measurement of moral judgment: A comparison of scaling methods. *Perceptual and Motor Skills, 15,* 3–9.

Ekman, P. (1993). Facial expression and emotion. *American Psychologist, 48,* 384–392.

Ekman, G., and Sjoberg, L. (1965). Scaling. *Annual Review of Psychology, 16,* 451–474.

Eysenk, H. J., and Eysenk, S. B. G. (1975). *The Manual of Eysenk Personality Questionnaire.* London: Hodder and Stoughton.

Farrer, C., and Frith, C. D. (2002). Experiencing oneself vs. another person as being the cause of an action: the neural correlates of the experience of agency. *Neuroimage, 15,* 596–603.

Farrer, C., Frank, N., and Georgieff, N. (2003). Modulating the experience of agency: a positron emission tomography study. *Neuroimage, 18,* 324–333.

Fechner, G. T. (1860). *Elemente der Psychophysik.* Elements of Psychophysics.

Fedele, L. M., Marchinin, B., Acaia, U., Garagiola, V., and Tiengo, M. (1989). Dynamics and significance of placebo response in primary dysmenorrhea. *Pain, 36,* 43–47.

Fields, H. State-dependent opioid control of pain. (2004). *Nature Reviews of Neuroscience, 5,* 565–575.

Fields, H. L., and Basbaum, A. I. (1999). Central nervous system mechanisms of pain modulation. In P. D. Wall & R. Melzack (Eds.), *Textbook of Pain* (pp. 309–329). Edinburgh: Churchill Livingstone.

Fields, H. L., and Levine, J. D. (1981). Biology of placebo analgesia. *American Journal of Medicine, 70,* 745–746.

Fields, H. L., and Levine, J. D. (1984). Placebo analgesia—A role for endorphins? *Trends in Neurosciences, 7,* 271–273.

Fields, H. L., and Price, D. D. (1997). Toward a neurobiology of placebo analgesia. In A. Harrington (Ed.), *The Placebo Effect: An Interdisciplinary Exploration* (pp. 93–116). Cambridge, MA: Harvard University Press.

Flanagan, O. (1992). *Consciousness Reconsidered.* Cambridge, MA: MIT Press.

Foltz, E. L., and White, L. E. (1962). Pain "relief" by frontal cingulumotomy. *Journal of Neurosurgery, 19,* 89–100.

Friedman, D. P., Murray, E. A., and O'Neill, T. (1986). Cortical connections of the somatosensory fields of the lateral sulcus of macaques: Evidence for a corticolimbic pathway for touch. *Journal of Comparative Neurology, 252*(3), 323–347.

Galanter, E. (1962). The direct measurement of utility and subjective probability. *American Journal of Psychology, 75,* 208–220.

Gallagher, S. (2008). Interview with Jaak Panskepp. *Journal of Consciousness Studies,* *15*(2), 89.

Gallagher, S., and Overgaard, M. (2005). Introspections without introspeculations. In M. Aydede (Ed.), *Pain: New Essays on Its Nature and the Methodology of Its Study* (pp. 277–290). Cambridge, MA: MIT Press.

Geers, A. L., Weiland, P. E., Kosbab, K., Landry, S. J., and Helfer, S. G. (2005). Goal activation, expectations, and the placebo effect. *Journal of Personality and Social Psychology, 89*(2), 143–159.

Geers, A. L., Helfer, S. G., Weiland, P. E., and Kosbab, K. (2006). Expectations and placebo response: A laboratory investigation into the role of somatic focus. *Journal of Behavioral Medicine, 29*(2), 171–178.

Gendlin, E. T. (1962). *Experiencing and the Creation of Meaning; A Philosophical and Psychological Approach to the Subjective.* New York: Free Press.

Gendlin, E. T. (1978). *Focusing.* New York: Bantam Books.

George, M. S., Ketter, T. A., Parekh, P. I., Horwitz, B., Herscovitch, P., and Post, R. M. (1995). Brain activity during transient sadness and happiness in healthy women. *American Journal of Psychiatry, 152,* 341–351.

Gescheider, G. (1997). *Psychophysics: The Fundamentals* (3rd ed.). Mahwah, NJ: Lawrence Erlbaum.

Giang, D. W., Goodman, A. D., Schiffer, R. B., Mattson, D. H., and Petrie, M., (1996). Conditioning of cyclophosphamide-induced leukopenia in humans. *Journal of Neuropsychiatry and Clinical Neurosciences, 8,* 194–201.

Giesler, G. J., Jr., Yezierski, R. P., Gerhart, K. D., and Willis, W. D. (1981). Spinothalamic tract neurons that project to medial and/or lateral thalamic nuclei: Evidence for a physiologically novel population of spinal cord neurons. *Journal of Neurophysiology, 46*(6), 1285–1308.

Giorgi, A. (1970). *Psychology as a Human Science.* New York: Harper and Row.

Gitelman, D. R., Alpert, N. M., Kosslyn, S., Daffner, K., Scinto, L., and Thompson, W. (1996). Functional imaging of human right hemispheric activation for exploratory movements. *Annals of Neurology, 39,* 174–179.

Gitelman, D. R., Nobre, A. C., Parrish, T. B., LaBar, K. S., Kim, Y. H., and Meyer, J. R. (1999). A large-scale distributed network for covert spatial attention: Further anatomical delineation based on stringent behavioural and cognitive controls. *Brain, 122,* 1093–1106.

Givot, I. (1998). *Seven Aspects of Self-Observation.* Aurora, OR: Two Rivers Press.

Goebel, M. U., Trebst, A. E., Steiner, J., Xie, Y. F., and Exton, M. S. (2002). Behavioral conditioning of immunosuppression is possible in humans. *FASEB Journal, 16,* 1869–1873.

Goetz, C. G., Leurgans, S., Raman, R., and Stebbins, G. T. (2000). Objective changes in motor function during placebo treatment in PD. *Neurology, 54,* 710–714.

Gracely, R. H., Dubner, R., Wolskee, P. J., and Deeter, W. R. (1983). Placebo and naloxone can alter post-surgical pain by separate mechanisms. *Nature, 306,* 264–265.

Grant, J. A., Courtemanche, J., and Rainville, P. (2011). A non-elaborative mental stance and decoupling of executive and pain-related cortices predicts low pain sensitivity in Zen meditators. *Pain, 152,* 150–156.

Greene, L. C., and Hardy, J. D. (1958). Spatial summation of pain. *Journal of Applied Physiology, 13,* 457–464.

Gregory, R. L. (1966). *Eye and Brain: The Psychology of Seeing.* London: Weidenfeld & Nicholson.

Grevert, P., Albert, L. H., and Goldstein, A. (1983). Partial antagonism of placebo analgesia by naloxone. *Pain, 16,* 129–143.

Guilford, J. P. (1954). *Psychometric Methods.* New York: McGraw-Hill.

Gustafson, D. (2005). Categorizing pain. In M. Aydede (Ed.), *Pain: New Essays on Its Nature and the Methodology of Its Study* (pp. 219–242). Cambridge, MA: MIT Press.

Hahn, R. A. (1985). A sociocultural model of illness and healing. In L. White, B. Tursky, and G. E. Schwartz (Eds.), *Placebo: Theory, Research, and Mechanisms* (pp. 167–195). New York: Guilford Press.

Hahn, R. A. (1997). The nocebo phenomenon: Scope and foundations. In A. Harrington (Ed.), *The Placebo Effect: An Interdisciplinary Exploration* (pp. 56–76). Cambridge, MA: Harvard University Press.

Hardy, J. D., Wolff, H. G., and Goodell, H. (1940). Studies on pain. A new method for measuring pain threshold: Observations on spatial summation of pain. *Journal of Clinical Investigation, 19,* 649–657.

Hardy, J. D., Wolff, H. G., and Goodell, H. (1952). *Pain Sensations and Reactions.* Baltimore: Williams and Wilkins.

Harkins, S. W., Price, D. D., & Braith, J. (1989). Effects of extraversion and neuroticism on experimental pain, clinical pain, and illness behavior. *Pain, 36,* 209–218.

Harrington, A. (1997). Introduction. In A. Harrington (Ed.), *The Placebo Effect: An Interdisciplinary Exploration* (pp. 1–11). Boston: Boston University Press.

Harrison, N. A., Gray, M. A., Gianaros, P. J., and Critchley, H. D. (2010). The embodiment of emotional feelings in the brain. *Journal of Neuroscience*, *30*(38), 12878–12884.

Head, H. (1920). *Studies in Neurology*. London: Oxford University Press.

Head, H., and Holmes, G. (1911). Sensory disturbances from cerebral lesions. *Brain*, *34*, 102–154.

Heavey, C. L., and Hurlburt, R. T. (2008). The phenomena of inner experience. *Consciousness and Cognition*, *12*, 110–126.

Hilgard, E. R. (1992). Dissociation and theories of hypnosis. In E. Fromm & M. R. Nash (Eds.), *Contemporary Hypnosis Research* (pp. 69–101). New York: Guilford Press.

Hilgard, E. R., and Hilgard, J. R. (1994). *Hypnosis in the Relief of Pain* (Revised edition). New York: Brunner/Mazel.

Hofbauer, R. K., Rainville, P., Duncan, G. H., and Bushnell, M. C. (2001). Cognitive modulation of pain sensation alters activity in human cerebral cortex. *Journal of Neurophysiology*, *86*(1), 402–411.

Hofle, N., Paus, T., Reutens, D., Fiset, P., Gotman, J., and Evans, A. C. (1997). Regional cerebral blood flow changes as a function of delta and spindle activity during slow wave sleep in humans. *Journal of Neuroscience*, *17*, 4800–4808.

Hróbjartsson, A., and Gøtzsche, P. C. (2001). Is the placebo effect powerless? An analysis of clinical trials comparing placebo with no treatment. *New England Journal of Medicine*, *344*, 1594–1602.

Hurlburt, R. (1992). *Sampling Normal and Schizophrenic Inner Experience*. New York: Plenum Press.

Hurlburt, R. T. (1997). Randomly sampling thinking in the natural environment. *Journal of Consulting and Clinical Psychology*, *65*, 941–949.

Hurlburt, R., and Heavey, C. L. (2006). *Descriptive Experience Sampling Codebook, Manual of Terminology*. Las Vegas: University of Nevada.

Hurlburt, R. T., and Akhter, S. A. (2006). The descriptive experience sampling method. *Phenomenological Cognitive Science*, *5*, 271–301.

Hurlburt, R. T., and Akhter, S. A. (2008). Unsymbolized thinking. *Consciousness and Cognition*, *17*, 1364–1374.

Hurlburt, R. T., and Heavey, C. L. (2001). Telling what we know: Describing inner experience. *Trends in Cognitive Sciences*, *5*, 400–403.

Hurlburt, R. T., and Heavey, C. L. (2002). Interobserver reliability of descriptive experience sampling. *Cognitive Therapy and Research*, *26*, 135–142.

Hurlburt, R. T., and Heavey, C. L. (2004). To beep or not to beep: Obtaining accurate reports about awareness. *Journal of Consciousness Studies*, *11*, 113–128.

Hurlburt, R. T., and Knapp, T. K. (2006). Muensterberg in 1898, not Allport in 1937, introduced the terms "idiographic" and "nomothetic" to American psychology. *Theory & Psychology*, *16*, 287–293.

Hurlburt, R. T., and Schwitzgebel, E. (2007). *Describing Inner Experience? Proponent Meets Skeptic*. Cambridge MA: MIT Press.

Hurlburt, R. T., Happe, F., and Frith, U. (1994). Sampling the form of inner experience in three adults with Asperger syndrome. *Psychological Medicine*, *24*, 385–395.

Hurlburt, R. T., Koch, M., and Heavey, C. L. (2002). Descriptive Experience Sampling demostrates the connection of thinking to externally observable behavior. *Cognitive Therapy and Research*, *26*, 117–134.

Husserl, E. (1952). *Ideas: General Introduction to Pure Phenomenology*. New York: MacMillan.

Isen, A. M. (1993). Positive affect in decision making. In M. Lewis & J. M. Haviland (Eds.), *Handbook of Emotions* (pp. 234–251). New York: The Free Press.

Isen, A. M., Nygren, T. E., and Ashby, F. G. (1988). Influence of positive affect on the subjective utility of gains and losses: It is just not worth the risk. *Journal of Personality and Social Psychology*, *55*, 710–717.

Ives-Deliperi, V. L., Solms, M., and Meintjes, E. M. (2011). The neural substrates of mindfulness: An fMRI investigation. *Social Neuroscience*, *6*(3), 231–242.

Jackson, F. (1986). What Mary Didn't Know. *Journal of Philosophy*, *83*(5), 291–295.

James, W. (1890). *The Principles of Psychology*. New York: Dover.

Jensen, M. P., and Karoly, P. (1991). Motivation and expectancy factors in symptom perception: A laboratory study of the placebo effect. *Psychosomatic Medicine*, *53*, 144–152.

Johnson, E., and Tversky, A. (1983). Affect, generalization, and the perception of risk. *Journal of Personality and Social Psychology*, *45*, 20–31.

Kahneman, D., and Tversky, A. (1979). Prospect theory. *Econometrica*, *47*, 263–292.

Kahneman, D., and Tversky, A. (1982). The psychology of preferences. *Scientific American*, *246*, 160–173.

Kaptchuk, T. J. et al. (2008). Components of placebo effect: Randomised controlled trial in patients with irritable bowel syndrome. *BMJ (Clinical Research Ed.)*, *336*(7651), 999–1003.

Kaptchuk, T. J., Shaw, J., Kerr, C. E., Conboy, L. A., Kelley, J. M., Csordas, T. J., Lambo, A. J., and Jacobson. (2009). "Maybe I made up the whole thing": Placebos and patients' experiences in a randomized controlled trial. *Culture, Medicine and Psychiatry, 33*(3), 382–411.

Keltner, J. R., Furst, A., Fan, C., Redfern, R., and Inglis, R.. (2006). Isolating the modulatory effect of expectation on pain transmission: A functional magnetic resonance imaging study. *Journal of Neuroscience, 26*(16), 4437–4443.

Kenshalo, D. R., Decker, T., and Hamilton, A. (1967). Spatial summation on the forehead, forearm, and back produced by radiant and conducted heat. *Journal of Comparative and Physiological Psychology, 63*, 510–515.

Kenshalo, D. R., Thomas, D. A., and Dubner, R. (1989). Somatosensory cortical lesions change the monkeys' reaction to noxious stimulation. *Journal of Dental Research, 68*, 897.

Kienle, G. S., and Kiene, H. (1999). Placebo effects and placebo concepts: A critical methodological and conceptual analysis of reports on the magnitude of the placebo effect. *Alternative Therapies in Health and Medicine, 2*, 39–54.

Kiernan, B. D., Dane, J. R., Philips, L. H., and Price, D. D. (1995). Hypnotic analgesia reduces R-III nociceptive reflex: Further evidence concerning the multifactorial nature of hypnotic analgesia. *Pain, 60*, 39–47.

Kim, Y. H., Gitelman, D. R., and Nobre, A. C. (1999). The large scale neural network for spatial attention displays multifactorial overlays but differential asymmetry. *Neuroimage, 9*, 269–277.

Kirsch, I. (1990). *Changing Expectations: A Key to Effective Psychotherapy*. Pacific Grove, CA.: Brooks/Cole.

Kirsch, I. (Ed.). (1999). *How Expectancy Shapes Experience*. Washington, DC: APA Books.

Kirsch, I. (2009). *The Emperor's New Drugs: Exploring the Antidepressant Myth*. London: The Bodley Head.

Kirsch, I. (2010). *The Emperor's New Drugs: Exploding the Antidepressant Myth*. New York: Basic Books.

Kirsch, I., Deacon, B. J., Huedo-Medina, T. B., Scoboria, A., Moore, T. J., and Johnson, B. T. (2008). Initial severity and anti-depressant benefits: A meta-analysis of data submitted to the Food and Drug Administration. *PLoS Medicine, 5*(2), 260–268.

Klein, G. (2002). *Intuition at Work*. New York: Doubleday.

Kordes, U. (2009). The phenomenology of decision making. *Interdisciplinary Description of Complex Systems, 7*(2), 65–77.

Kosslyn, S. M., Thompson, W. L., Costantini-Ferrando, M. F., Alpert, N. M., and Spiegel, D. (2000). Hypnotic visual illusion alters color processing in the brain. *American Journal of Psychiatry*, *157*, 1279–1284.

Koyama, T., McHaffie, J. G., Laurienti, P. J., and Coghill, R. C. (2005). The subjective experience of pain: Where expectations become reality. *Proceedings of the National Academy of Sciences of the United States of America*, *102*(36), 12950–12955.

Krishnamurti, K. (1967). *Talks in Europe*. Wassenaar, The Netherlands: Servire.

Kropotov, J. D., Crawford, H. J., and Polyakov, Y. I. (1997). Somatosensory event-related potential changes to painful stimuli during hypnotic analgesia: Anterior cingulate cortex and anterior temporal cortex intracranial recordings. *International Journal of Psychophysiology*, *27*, 1–8.

Krummenacher, P., Candia, V., Folkers, M., Schedlowski, P., and Schonbachler, G. (2010). Prefrontal cortex modulates placebo analgesia. *Pain*, *148*(3), 368–374.

Lackner, J. M., Jaccard, J., and Blanchard, E. B. (2005). Testing the sequential model of pain processing in irritable bowel syndrome: A structural equation modeling analysis. *European Journal of Pain (London, England)*, *9*, 207–218.

Landau, W., and Bishop, G. H. (1953). Pain from dermal, periosteal, and fascial endings and from inflammation. *Archives of Neurology and Psychiatry*, *69*, 490–504.

Landblom, A. M., Lindehammer, H., Karlsson, H., and Craig, A. D. (2010). Insular cortex activation in a patient with "sensed presence"/ecstatic feelings. *Epilepsy & Behavior*, *20*(4), 714–718.

Lane, R. D., Reiman, E. M., Bradely, M. M., Lang, P. J., Ahern, G. L., and Davidson, R. J. (1997). Neuroanatomical correlates of pleasant and unpleasant emotion. *Neuropsychologia*, *35*, 1437–1444.

Laurence, J. R., Slako, F., and Le Beau, M. (1998). Automaticity, Hypnotizability and the Creation of Anomalous Experiences: Neuro-physiological Indicators. *Presented at INABIS '98–5th Internet World Congress on Biomedical Sciences at McMaster University, Canada, Dec 7–16th. Invited Symposium.* Reference Type: Internet Communication.

Laska, E., and Sunshine, A. (1973). Anticipation of analgesia. A placebo effect. *Headache*, *13*(1), 1–11.

Lenz, F. A., Seike, M., Lin, Y. C., Baker, F. H., Rowland, L. H., and Gracely, R. H. (1993). Neurons in the area of human thalamic nucleus ventralis caudalis respond to painful heat stimuli. *Journal of Neurophysiology*, *70*(1), 200–212.

Lenz, F. A., Ohara, S., Gracely, R. H., and Dougherty, P. M. (2004). Pain encoding in the human forebrain: Binary and analogue exteroceptive channels. *Journal of Neuroscience*, *24*(29), 6540–6544.

Leuchter, A. F., Cook, I. A., Witte, E. A., Morgan, M., & Abrams, M. (2002). Changes in brain function of depressed subjects during treatment with placebo. *American Journal of Psychiatry*, *159*, 122–129.

Leuchter, A. F., Morgan, M., Cook, I. A., Dunkin, J., Abrams, M., and Wittle, E. (2004). Pretreatment neurophysiological and clinical characteristics of placebo responders in treatment trials for major depression. *Psychopharmacology*, *177*, 15–22.

Levin, D. T., and Simon, D. J. (1997). Failure to detect changes to attended objects in motion pictures. *Psychonomic Bulletin & Review*, *4*, 501–506.

Levin, D. T., Momen, N., and Drisdahl, S. B. (2000). Change blindness blindness: The metacognitive error of overestimating change detection ability. *Visual Cognition*, *7*(1/2/3), 397–412.

Levine, J. D., Gordon, N. C., and Fields, H. L. (1978). The mechanisms of placebo analgesia. *Lancet*, *2*, 654–657.

Lewin, K. (1943). Defining the field at a given time. *Psychological Review*, *50*, 292–310.

Lewin, W., and Phillips, C. G. (1952). Observations on partial removal of the post-central gyrus for pain. *Journal of Neurology, Neurosurgery, and Psychiatry*, *15*, 143–147.

Lewis, T., and Pochin, E. E. (1938). The double response of the human skin to a single stimulus. *Clinical Science*, *3*, 67–76.

Li, J., Simone, D. A., and Larson, A. A. (1999). Windup leads to characteristics of central sensitization. *Pain*, *79*, 75–82.

Libet, B. (1985). Unconscious cerebral initiative and the role of conscious will in voluntary action. *Behavioral and Brain Sciences*, *8*, 529–566.

Libet, B. (2002). The timing of mental events: Libet's experimental findings and their implications. *Consciousness and Cognition*, *11*(2), 291–299.

Libet, B., Wright, E. W., Jr., and Gleason, C. A. (1982). Readiness-potentials preceding unrestricted "spontaneous" vs. pre-planned voluntary acts. *Electroencephalography and Clinical Neurophysiology*, *54*, 322–335.

Linde, K., Witt, C. M., Streng, A., Weidenhammer, W., Wagenpfeil, S., Brinkhaus, B., Willich, S. N., and Melchart, D. (2007). The impact of patient expectations on outcomes in four randomized controlled trials of acupuncture in patients with chronic pain. *Pain*, *128*(3), 264–271.

Lipman, J. J., Miller, B. E., Mays, K. S., Miller, M. N., North, W. C., and Byrne, W. L. (1990). Peak B endorphin concentration in cerebrospinal fluid: Reduced in chronic pain patients and increased during the placebo response. *Psychopharmology*, *102*, 112–116.

Lundh, L. G. (1987). Placebo, belief, and health. A cognitive-emotional model. *Scandinavian Journal of Psychology*, *28*(2), 128–143.

Lycan, W. G. (1996). *Consciousness and Experience*. Cambridge, MA: MIT Press.

Lyons, J. (1973). *Experience*. New York: Harper and Row.

Maquet, P., and Phillips, C. (1998). Functional brain imaging of human sleep. *Journal of Sleep Research*, *7*(Suppl 1), 42–47.

Maquet, P., Faymonville, M. E., Degueldre, C., Delfiore, G., Franck, G., Luxen, A., and Laureys, S. (1999). Functional neuroanatomy of hypnotic state. *Biological Psychiatry*, *45*, 327–333.

Marcel, A. (2003). Introspective report: Trust, self-knowledge, and science. *Journal of Consciousness Studies*, *10*, 167–186.

Marks, L. W. (1974). *Sensory Processes: The New Psychophysics*. New York: Academic Press.

Marsh, A. A., Blair, K. S., Vythilingham, M., Busis, S., and Blair, R. J. (2007). Response options and expectations of reward in decision-making: The differential roles of dorsal and rostral anterior cingulated cortex. *NeuroImage*, *35*(2), 979–988.

Mason, C. J., and Brady, F. (2009). The psychomimetic effects of short-term sensory deprivation. *Journal of Nervous and Mental Disease*, *197*(10), 783–785.

Mayberg, H. S., Silva, A. J., Brannan, S. K., Tekell, J. L., Mahurin, R. K., McGinnis, S., and Jarebok, J. M. . (2002). The functional neuroanatomy of the placebo effect. *American Journal of Psychiatry*, *159*, 728–737.

Mayer, D. J., and Price, D. D. (1976). Central nervous system mechanisms of analgesia. *Pain*, *2*, 379–404.

Mayer, D. J., Price, D. D., and Becker, D. P. (1975). Neurophysiological characteristics of the anterolateral spinal cord neurons contributing to pain perception in man. *Pain*, *1*, 51–58.

McRae, C., Cherin, E., Yamazaki, G., Diem, G., Vo, A. H., et al. (2004). Effects of perceived treatment on quality of life and medical outcomes in a double-blind placebo surgery trial. *Archives of General Psychiatry*, *61*, 412–420.

Mellers, B. A. (2000). Choice and the relative pleasure of consequences. *Psychological Bulletin*, *126*, 910–924.

Mellers, B., Schwartz, A., Ho, K., and Ritov, I. (1997). Elation and disappointment: Emotional responses to risky options. *Psychological Science*, *8*, 423–429.

Mellers, B. A., Schwartz, A., and Ritov, I. (1999). Emotion-based choice. *Journal of Experimental Psychology. General, 128,* 1–14.

Melzack, R., and Casey, K. L. (1968). Sensory, motivational, and central control of determinants of pain. In D. R. Kenshalo (Ed.), *The Skin Senses* (pp. 423–439). Springfield, IL: Charles C. Thomas.

Melzack, R., and Torgerson, W. S. (1971). On the language of pain. *Anesthesiology, 34,* 50–59.

Melzack, R., and Wall, P. D. (1965). Pain mechanisms: A new theory. *Science, 150,* 971–979.

Melzack, R., and Wall, P. D. (1983). *The Challenge of Pain.* New York: Basic Books.

Mendell, L. M., and Wall, P. D. (1965). Responses of single dorsal cord cells to peripheral cutaneous unmyelinated fibres. *Nature, 206,* 97–99.

Merleau-Ponty, M. (1962). *The Phenomenology of Perception.* New York: Humanities Press.

Mersky, H., and Bogduk, N. (1994). *Classification of Chronic Pain.* Seattle: IASP Press.

Metzinger, T. (2000). The subjectivity of subjective experience: A representationalist analysis of the first-person perspective. In T. Metzinger (Ed.), *Neural Correlates of Consciousness: Empirical and Conceptual Questions* (pp. 285–306). Cambridge, MA: MIT Press.

Miller, E. K., and Cohen, J. D. (2001). An integrative theory of prefrontal cortex function. *Annual Review of Neuroscience, 24,* 167–202.

Moerman, D. E. (2002). *Meaning, Medicine and the Placebo Effect.* Cambridge: Cambridge University Press.

Mogil, J. S. (2009). Animal models of pain: Progress and challenges. *Nature Reviews. Neuroscience, 10*(4), 283–294.

Monson, C. K., and Hurlburt, R. T. (1993). A comment to suspend the introspection controversy: Introspecting subjects did agree about imageless thought. In R. T. Hurlburt (Ed.), Sampling Inner Experience in Disturbed Affect. New York: Plenum.

Montgomery, G. H., and Kirsch, I. (1996). Mechanisms of placebo pain reduction: An empirical investigation. *Psychological Science, 7,* 174–176.

Montgomery, G., and Kirsch, I. (1997). Classical conditioning and the placebo effect. *Pain, 72,* 107–113.

Morris, D. B. (1994). *The Culture of Pain* (pp. 1–342). Berkeley: University of California Press.

Moulton, E. A., Keaser, M. L., Gullapalli, R. P., and Greenspan, J. D. (2005). Regional intensive and temporal patterns of functional MRI activation distinguishing noxious and innocuous contact heat. *Journal of Neurophysiology*, *93*(4), 2183–2193.

Mountcastle, V. B. (1974). Pain and temperature sensibilities. In V. B. Mountcastle (Ed.), *Medical Physiology* (13th ed., Vol. 1, pp. 348–381) Saint Louis: Mosby.

Mountcastle, V. B., Talbot, W. H., and Werner, G. (1962). The neural transformation of the sensory stimulus at the cortical input level of the somatic afferent system. In R. W. Gerard and J. W. Duyff (Eds.), *Information Processing in the Nervous System* (pp. 196–217). Amsterdam: Excerpta Medica Foundation.

Mountcastle, V. B., Talbot, W. H., and Kornhuber, H. H. (1966). The neural transformation of the mechanical stimuli delivered to the monkey's hand. In Ciba Foundation Symposium: *Touch, Heat, and Pain* (pp. 325–345). London: Churchill.

Murphy, F. C., Nimmo-Smith, J., and Lawrence, A. D. (2003). Functional anatomy of emotions—A meta-analysis. *Cognitive, Affective & Behavioral Neuroscience*, *3*(3), 207–233.

Musulam, M. M. (1981). Dissociative states with abnormal temporal lobe EEG: Multiple personality and the illusion of possession. *Archives of Neurology*, *36*, 176–181.

Nahmias, E. (2005). Agency, authorship, and illusion. *Consciousness and Cognition*, *14*, 771–785.

Nielsen, C. S., Price, D. D., Vassend, O., Stubhaug, A., and Harris, J. R. (2005). Characterizing individual differences in heat-pain sensitivity. *Pain*, *119*(1–3), 65–74.

Nielsen, C. S., Staubhaug, A., Price, D. D., Vassesend, O., Czajkowski, N., and Harris, J. R. (2007). Individual differences in pain sensitivity: Genetic and environmental contributions. *Pain*, *136*(1–2), 21–29.

Nielsen, C. S., Staud, R., and Price, D. D. (2009). Individual differences in pain sensitivity: Measurement, causation, and consequences. *Journal of Pain*, *10*(3), 231–237.

Nobre, A. C., Sebestyen, G. N., Gitelman, D. R., Mesulam, M. M., Frackowiak, R. S., and Frith, C. D. (1997). Functional localization of the system for visuospatial attention using positron emission tomography. *Brain*, *120*, 515–533.

Nogrady, H., McConkey, K. M., Laurence, J. R., and Perry, C. (1983). Dissociation, duality, and demand characteristics in hypnosis. *Journal of Abnormal Psychology*, *92*, 223–235.

Nygren, T. E., Isen, A. M., Taylor, P. J., and Dulin, J. (1996). The influence of positive affect on the decision rule in risk situations. *Organizational Behavior and Human Decision Processes*, *66*, 59–72.

O'Doherty, J., Kringelbach, M. L., Rolls, E. T., Hornak, J., and Andrews, C. (2001). Abstract reward and punishment representations in the human orbitofrontal cortex. *Nature Neuroscience, 4*, 95–102.

Olness, K., and Ader, R. (1992). Conditioning as an adjunct in the pharmacotherapy of lupus erythematosus. *Journal of Developmental and Behavioral Pediatrics, 13*, 124–125.

Orne, M. T. (1962). On the social psychology of the psychological experiment: With particular reference to demand characteristics and their implications. *American Psychologist, 17*, 776–783.

Ostrowsky, K., Magnin, M., Ryvlin, P., Isnard, J., Guenot, M., and Mauguiére, F. (2002). Representation of pain and somatic sensation in the human insula: A study of responses to direct electrical cortical stimulation. *Cerebral Cortex, 12*, 376–385.

Ouspensky, P. D. (1971). *The Fourth Way*. New York: Vintage Books.

Oxford Dictionary of Philosophy (Introspection). (2008). Oxford: Oxford University Press.

Panskepp, J. (2008). Interview with Jaak Panskepp. *Journal of Consciousness Studies, 15*(2), 89.

Paus, T. (2000). Functional anatomy of arousal and attention systems in the human brain. *Progress in Brain Research, 126*, 65–77.

Paus, T., Zatorre, R. J., Hofle, N., Caramanos, Z., Gotman, J., Petrides, M., and Evens, A. C. (1997). Time-related changes in neural systems underlying attention and arousal during the performance of an auditory vigilance task. *Journal of Cognitive Neuroscience, 9*, 392–408.

Pekula, R. J., and Kumar, V. K. (1984). Predicting hypnotic responsivity by a self-report phenomenological instrument. *American Journal of Clinical Hypnosis, 27*, 114–121.

Perls, F. (1969). *Gestalt Therapv Verbatim*. Lafayette, CA: Real People Press.

Perls, F., Heffereline, R. F., and Goodman, P. (1951). *Gestalt Therapy*. New York: Harper & Row.

Petrovic, P., Kalso, E., Petersson, K. M., and Ingvar, M. (2002). Placebo and opioid analgesia—Imaging a shared neuronal network. *Science, 295*, 1737–1740.

Petrovic, P., Dietrich, T., Fransson, P., Andersson, J., and Carlsson, K. (2005). Placebo in emotional processing-induced expectations of anxiety relief activate a generalized modulatory network. *Neuron, 46*(6), 957–969.

Peyron, R., Garcia-Larrea, L., Gregoire, M. C., Costes, N., Convers, P., Lavenne, F., Mauguire, F., Michel, D. and Laurent, B., (1999). Haemodynamic brain responses to acute pain in humans—Sensory and attentional networks. *Brain, 122,* 1765–1779.

Place, U. (1956). Is consciousness a brain process? *British Journal of Psychology, 47,* 44–50.

Ploner, M., Gross, J., Timmermann, L., and Schnitzler, A. (2002). Cortical representation of first and second pain sensation in humans. *Proceedings of the National Academy of Sciences of the United States of America, 99,* 12444–12448.

Polanyi, M. (1969). *Knowing and Being.* Chicago: University of Chicago Press.

Pollo, A., Amanzio, M., Arslanian, A., Casadio, C., and Maggi, G., (2001). Response expectancies in placebo analgesia and their clinical relevance. *Pain, 93,* 77–84.

Pollo, A., Torre, E., Lopiano, L., Rizzone, M., Lanotte, M., Cavanna, A., Bergamasso, B., and Benedetti, F.. (2002). Expectation modulates the response to subthalamic nucleus stimulation in Parkinsonian patients. *Neuroreport, 13,* 1383–1386.

Pollo, A., Vighetti, S., Rainero, I., and Benedetti, F. (2003). Placebo analgesia and the heart. *Pain, 102,* 125–133.

Pons, T. P., Garraghty, P. E., and Friedman, D. P. (1987). Physiological evidence for serial processing in somatosensory cortex. *Science, 237*(4813), 417–420.

Portas, C. M., Howseman, A. M., Josephs, O., Turner, R., and Frith, C. D. (1998). A specific role for the thalamus in mediating the interaction of attention and arousal in humans. *Journal of Neuroscience, 18,* 8979–8989.

Posner, M. I., and Dehaene, S. (1994). Attentional networks. *Trends in Neurosciences, 17,* 75–79.

Posner, M. I., and Rothbart, M. K. (1998). Attention, self-regulation and consciousness. *Philosophical Transactions of the Royal Society of London. Series B, Biological Sciences, 353,* 1915–1927.

Powers, R. J., and Kutash, I. L. (1980). Alcohol abuse and anxiety. In I. L. Kutash and L. B. Sehleslinger (Eds.), *Handbook on Stress and Anxietv* (pp. 461–482). San Francisco: Jossey-Bass.

Price, D. D. (1972). Characteristics of second pain and flexion reflexes indicative of prolonged central summation. *Experimental Neurology, 37,* 371–387.

Price, D. D. (1988). *Psychological and Neural Mechanisms of Pain.* New York: Raven Press.

Price, D. D. (1996). Hypnotic analgesia: Psychological and neural mechanisms. In J. Barber (Ed.), *Hypnosis and Suggestions in the Treatment of Pain* (pp. 67–84). New York: Norton.

Price, D. D. (1999). *Psychological Mechanisms of Pain and Analgesia*. Seattle: IASP Press.

Price, D. D. (2000). Psychological and neural mechanisms of the affective dimension of pain. *Science, 288*, 1769–1772.

Price, D. D. (2001). Assessing placebo effects without placebo groups: An untapped possibility? *Pain, 90*, 201–203.

Price, D. D., & Aydede, M. (2005). Experiential–phenomenological paradigms for pain and consciousness. In M. Aydede (Ed.), *Pain—New Essays on its Nature and the Methodology of its Study* (pp. 145–168). Cambridge, MA: MIT Press.

Price, D. D., and Barber, J. (1987). An analysis of factors that contribute to the efficacy of hypnotic analgesia. *Journal of Abnormal Psychology, 96*, 46–51.

Price, D. D., and Barrell, J. J. (1980). An experiential approach with quantitative methods: A research paradigm. *Journal of Humanistic Psychology, 20*(3), 75–95.

Price, D. D., and Barrell, J. J. (1984). Some general laws of human emotion: Interrelationships between intensities of desire, expectations, and emotional feeling. *Journal of Personality, 52*, 389–409.

Price, D. D., and Barrell, J. J. (1990). The structure of the hypnotic state: A self-directed experiential study. In J. J. Barrell (Ed.), *The Experiential Method: Exploring the Human Experience* (pp. 85–97). Acton, MA: Copely Publishing Group.

Price, D. D., and Barrell, J. J. (1999). Expectancy and desire in pain and pain relief. In I. Kirsch (Ed.), *Expectancy, Experience, and Behavior* (pp. 341–367). Washington, DC: APA Books.

Price, D. D., and Barrell, J. J. (2000). Mechanisms of analgesia produced by hypnosis and placebo suggestions. *Progress in Brain Research, 122*, 255–271.

Price, D. D., and Dubner, R. (1977). Neurons that subserve the sensory discriminative aspects of pain. *Pain, 3*, 307–388.

Price, D. D., and Mayer, D. J. (1975). Neurophysiological characteristics of the anterolateral quadrant neurons subserving pain in M. mulatta. *Pain, 1*, 59–72.

Price, D. D., Hu, J. W., Dubner, R., and Gracely, R. H. (1977). Peripheral suppression of first pain and central summation of second pain evoked by noxious heat pulses. *Pain, 3*, 57–68.

Price, D. D., Hayes, R. L., Ruda, M. A., and Dubner, R. (1978). Spatial and temporal transformations of input to spinothalamic tract neurons and their relation to somatic sensation. *Journal of Neurophysiology, 41*, 933–947.

Price, D. D., McGrath, P. A., Rafii, A., and Buckingham, B. (1983). The validation of visual analogue scales as ratio scale measures for chronic and experimental pain. *Pain, 17*, 45–56.

Price, D. D., Barrell, J. E., and Barrell, J. J. (1985). A quantitative experiential analysis of human emotions. *Motivation and Emotion, 9,* 19–38.

Price, D. D., Harkins, S. W., and Baker, C. (1987). Sensory affective relationships among different types of clinical and experimental pain. *Pain, 28*(3), 291–299.

Price, D. D., McHaffie, J. G., and Larson, M. A. (1989). Spatial summation of heat induced pain: Influence of stimulus area and spatial separation of stimuli on perceived pain sensation intensity and unpleasantness. *Journal of Neurophysiology, 62,* 1270–1279.

Price, D. D., McHaffie, J. G., and Stein, B. E. (1992). The psychophysical attributes of heat induced pain and their relationships to neural mechanisms. *Journal of Cognitive Neuroscience, 4,* 1–14.

Price, D. D., Mao, J., Frenk, H., and Mayer, D. J. (1994). The N-methyl-D-aspartate receptor antagonist dextromethorphan selectively reduces temporal summation of second pain in man. *Pain, 59,* 165–174.

Price, D. D., Bush, F. M., Long, S., and Harkins, S. W. (1996). A comparison of pain measurement characteristics of mechanical visual analogue and simple numerical rating scales. *Pain, 56,* 217–226.

Price, D. D., Milling, L. S., Kirsch, I., Duff, A., & Montgomery, G. H. (1999). An analysis of factors that contribute to the magnitude of placebo analgesia in an experimental paradigm. *Pain, 83,* 147–156.

Price, D. D., Riley J., and Barrell, J. J. (2001). Are lived choices based on emotional processes? *Cognition and Emotion, 15*(3), 365–379.

Price, D. D., Craggs, J., Verne, G. N., Perlstein, W. M., and Robinson, M. E. (2007). Placebo analgesia is accompanied by large reductions in pain-related brain activity in irritable bowel syndrome patients. *Pain, 127,* 63–72.

Price, D. D., Finniss, D. G., and Benedetti, F. (2008a). A comprehensive review of the placebo effect: Recent advances and current thought. *Annual Review of Psychology, 59,* 565–590.

Price, D. D., Patel, R., Robinson, M. E., and Staud, R. (2008b). Characteristics of electronic visual analogue and numerical scales for ratings of experimental pain in healthy subjects and fibromyalgia patients. *Pain, 140*(1), 158–166.

Price, D. D., Craggs, J. G., Zhou, Q. Q., Verne, G. N., Perlstein, W. R., and Robinson, M. E. (2009). Widespread hyperalgesia in irritable bowel syndrome is dynamically maintained by tonic visceral impulse input and placebo/nocebo factors: Evidence from human psychophysics, animal models, and neuroimaging. *NeuroImage, 47*(3), 995–1001.

Radtke, H. L., and Stam, H. J. (1991). The relationship between absorption, openness to experience, anhedonia, and susceptibility. *International Journal of Clinical and Experimental Hypnosis*, *39*, 39–56.

Rainville, P., and Price, D. D. (2003). Hypnosis phenomenology and the neurobiology of consciousness. *International Journal of Clinical and Experimental Hypnosis*, *51*, 105–129.

Rainville, P., Duncan, G. H., Price, D. D., Carrier, B., and Bushnell, M. C. (1997). Pain affect encoded in human anterior cingulate but not somatosensory cortex. *Science*, *277*, 968–971.

Rainville, P., Carrier, B., Hofbauer, R. K., Duncan, G. H., and Bushnell, M. C. (1999). Dissociation of sensory and affective dimensions of pain using hypnotic modulation. *Pain*, *82*(2), 159–171.

Rainville, P., Hofbauer, R. K., Paus, T., Duncan, G. H., Bushnell, M. C., and Price, D. D. (1999). Cerebral mechanisms of hypnotic induction and suggestion. *Journal of Cognitive Neuroscience*, *11*, 110–125.

Rainville, P., Hofbauer, R. K., Bushnell, M. C., Duncan, G. H., and Price, D. D. (2002). Hypnosis modulates activity in brain structures involved in the regulation of consciousness. *Journal of Cognitive Neuroscience*, *14*, 887–901.

Rainville, P., Bao, Q. V., and Chetrien, P. (2005). Pain-related emotions modulate experimental pain perception and autonomic responses. *Pain*, *118*(3), 306–318.

Rakover, S. S. (2002). Scientific rules of the game and the mind/body: A critique based on the theory of measurement. *Journal of Consciousness Studies*, *9*(11), 52–57.

Reason, P., and Rowan, J. (1981). *Human Inquiry: A Sourcebook of New Paradigm Research*. New York: Wiley.

Riley, J. L., Wade, J. B., Myers, C. D., Sheffield, D., Papas, R., and Price, D. D. (2002). Ethnic differences in the experience of chronic pain. *Pain*, *100*(3), 291–298.

Riley, J. R., III, Wade, J. B., Robinson, M. E., and Price, D. D. (2000). The stages of pain processing across the adult lifespan. *Journal of Pain*, *1*(2), 162–170.

Rogers, C. R. (1951). *Client-Centered Therapy: Its Current Practice, Implications, and Theory*. Boston: Houghton Mifflin.

Rogers, R. D., Ramnani, N., Mackay, C., Wilson, J. L., Jezzard, P., Carter, C. S., and Smith, S. M. (2004). Distinct portions of anterior cingulate cortex and medial prefrontal cortex are activated by reward processing in separable phases of decision-making cognition. *Biological Psychiatry*, *55*(6), 594–602.

Rotter, J. B. (1972). *Applications of Social Learning Theory of Personality*. New York: Holt, Rinehart, and Winston.

Rubins, J. L., and Friedman, E. D. (1948). Asymbolia for pain. *Neurologie et Psychiatrie, 60*, 554–560.

Ruby, P., and Decety, J. (2001). Effect of subjective perspective taking during simulation of action: A PET investigation of agency. *Nature Neuroscience, 4*, 546–550.

Rushworth, M. F., and Behrens, T. E. (2008). Choice, uncertainty, and value in prefrontal and cingulate cortex. *Nature Neuroscience, 11*(4), 389–397.

Sagan, C., and Druyan, A. (1995). *The Demon-Haunted World: Science as a Candle in the Dark*. New York: Ballantine Books.

Sardello, R. (1971). The role of direct experience in contemporary psychology—A critical review. *Duquesne Studies in Phenomenological Psychology, 1*, 30–49.

Savage, L. J. (1954). *The Foundations of Statistics*. New York: Wiley.

Schacter, S., and Singer, J. (1962). Cognitive, social, and psychological determinants of the emotional state. *Psychological Review, 69*(5), 379–399.

Schimmel, S. (1997). *The Seven Deadly Sins: Jewish, Christian, and Classic Reflections on Human Psychology*. Oxford: Oxford University Press.

Schwartz, J. M., and Begley, S. (2002). *The Mind and the Brain: Neuroplasticity and the Power of Mental Force*. New York: Harper Collins.

Schwartz, J. M., Stapp, H. P., and Beauregard, M. (2005). Quantum physics in neuroscience and psychology: A neurophysical model of mind–brain interaction. *Philosophical Transactions of the Royal Society of London. Series B, Biological Sciences, 360*, 1309–1327.

Searle, J. (1996). *The Rediscovery of the Mind*. Cambridge, MA: MIT Press.

Shackman, A. J., Salomons, T. V., Slagter, H. A., Fox, A. S., Winter, J. J., and Davidson, R. J. (2011). The integration of negative affect, pain, and cognitive control in the cingulate cortex. *Nature Reviews. Neuroscience, 12*(3), 154–167.

Shah, J., and Higgins, E. T. (1997). Expectancy × value effects: Regulatory focus as determinant of magnitude and direction. *Journal of Personality and Social Psychology, 73*(3), 447–458.

Shapiro, A. K., and Morris, L. A. (1978). The placebo effect in medical and psychological therapies. In S. L. Garfield and A. E. Bergin (Eds.), *Handbook of Psychotherapy and Behavior Change: An Empirical Analysis* (2nd ed., pp. 369–409). New York: Wiley.

Sheehan, P. W. (1992). The phenomenology of hypnosis and the Experiential Analysis Technique. In E. Fromm & M. R. Nash (Eds.), *Contemporary Hypnosis Research* (pp. 364–389). New York: Guilford Press.

Shetty, N., Friedman, J. H., Kieburtz, K., Marshall, F. J., and Oakes, D. (1999). The placebo response in Parkinson's disease. Parkinson study group. *Clinical Neuropharmacology, 22*, 207–212.

Shinn, A. M., Jr. (1969). An application of psychophysical scaling techniques to the measurement of national power. *Journal of Political Measurement, 31*, 932–951.

Shor, R. E. (1965). Hypnosis and the concept of generalized reality orientation. In R. Shor & M. Orne (Eds.), *The Nature of Hypnosis: Selected Basic Readings* (pp. 288–305). New York: Holt, Rinehart, and Winston.

Siminov, P. (1970). Information theory of emotions. In M. Arnold (Ed.), *Feelings and Emotions* (pp. 145–149). New York: Academic Press.

Skinner, B. F. (1957). *Verbal Behavior.* New York: Appleton-Century-Crofts.

Snodgrass, J. G. (1975). Psychophysics. In B. Scharf (Ed.), *Experimental Sensory Psychology* (pp. 17–67). Glenview, IL: Scott, Foresman.

Solomon, R. L., and Corbit, J. D. (1974). An opponent process theory of motivation: I. Temporal dynamics of affect. *Psychological Review, 81*, 119–145.

Spanos, N. P. (1986). Hypnotic behaviour: A social-psychological interpretation of amnesia, analgesia, and "trance logic." *Behavioral and Brain Sciences, 9*, 440–467.

Starr, C. J., Sawaki, L., Wittenberg, G. F., Burdette, J. H., Oshiro, Y., Quevedo, A. S., and Coghill, R. C. (2010). Role of the insular cortex in the modulation of pain. *Journal of Neuroscience, 29*(9), 2684–2694.

Staud, R., Vierck, C. J., Cannon, R. L., Mauderli, A. P., and Price, D. D. (2001). Abnormal sensitization and temporal summation of second pain (wind-up) in patients with fibromyalgia syndrome. *Pain, 91*, 165–175.

Staud, R., Price, D. D., Robinson, M. E., Mauderli, A. P., and Vierck, C. J. (2004). Maintenance of windup of second pain requires less frequent stimulation in fibromyalgia patients compared to normal controls. *Pain, 110*, 689–696.

Staud, R. M., Robinson, M. E., Vierck, C. J., and Price, D. D. (2005). The n-methyl-d-aspartate receptor antagonist dextromethorphan attenuates second pain summation in fibromyalgia patients and normal control subject. *Journal of Pain, 6*(5), 323–332.

Staud, R. M., Craggs J. G., Robinson, M. E., Perlstein, W. M., and Price, D. D. (2007). Brain activity related to temporal summation of C-fiber evoked pain. *Pain, 129*(1,2), 130–142.

Staud, R., Craggs, J. G., Perlstein, W. M., Robinson, M. E., and Price, D. D. (2008). Brain activity associated with slow temporal summation of C-fiber evoked pain in fibromyalgia patients and healthy controls. *European Journal of Pain, (London, England), 12*(8), 1078–1089.

Stein, B. E., and Meredith, M. A. (1993). *The Merging of the Senses.* Cambridge, MA: MIT Press.

Stein, B. E., London, N., Wilkenson, L. K. & Price, D. D. (1996). Enhancement of perceived visual intensity by auditory stimuli: A psychophysical analysis. *Journal of Cognitive Neuroscience, 8*(6), 497–506.

Sternbach, R. A. (1968). *Pain: A Psychophysiological Analysis*. New York: Academic Press.

Stevens, J. C., & Marks, L. E. (1971). Spatial summation and the dynamics of warmth sensation. *Perception & Psychophysics, 9*, 291–298.

Stevens, S. S. (1966). Quantifying the sensory experience. In P. K. Feyeraband and G. Maxwell (Eds.), *Mind, Matter, and Method: Essays in Philosophy of Science in Honour of Herbert Fiegl* (pp. 215–233). Minneapolis: University of Minnesota Press.

Stevens, S. S. (1975). *Psychophysics—Introduction to Its Perceptual, Neural, and Social Prospects*. New York: Wiley.

Stevens, S. S., Guirao, M., and Slawson, A. W. (1965). Loudness, a product of volume times density. *Journal of Experimental Psychology, 69*, 503–510.

Szechtman, H., Woody, E., Bowers, K. S., and Nahmias, C. (1998). Where the imaginal appears real: A positron emission tomography study of auditory hallucinations. *Proceedings of the National Academy of Sciences of the United States of America, 95*, 1956–1960.

Tellegen, A., and Atkinson, G. (1974). Openness to absorbing and self-altering experiences ("absorption"), a trait related to hypnotic susceptibility. *Journal of Abnormal Psychology, 83*, 268–277.

Thompson, S. W., and Woolf, C. J. (1990). Primary afferent-evoked prolonged potentials in the spinal cord and their central summation: Role of the NMDA receptor. In M. R. Bond & C. J. Woolf (Eds.), *Proceedings of the VI. World Congress of Pain* (pp. 291–298). Amsterdam: Elsevier.

Thurston, L. L. (1959). *The Measurement of Values*. Chicago: University of Chicago Press.

Titchener, E. B. (1908). *Experimental Psychology of the Thought Processes*. New York: MacMillan.

Titchener., E. B. (1924). *The Psychology of Feeling and Attention*. New York: MacMillan.

Tolman, E. C. (1955). Principles of performance. *Psychological Review, 62*, 315–326.

Tommerdahl, M., Delemos, K. A., Vierck, C. J., Favorov, O. V., and Whitsel, B. L. (1996). Anterior parietal cortical response to tactile and skin-heating stimuli applied to the same skin site. *Journal of Neurophysiology, 75*, 2662–2670.

Turner, J. A., Deyo, R. A., Loeser, J. D., Von Korf, M., and Fordyce, W. E. (1994). The importance of placebo effects in pain treatment and research. *Journal of the American Medical Association*, *271*, 1609–1614.

Tversky, A., and Kahneman, D. (1981). The framing of decisions and the psychology of choice. *Science*, *211*(4481), 453–458.

Tye, M. (1995). *Ten Problems of Consciousness*. Cambridge, MA: MIT Press.

Tye, M. (1997). A representational theory of pains and their phenomenal character. In N. Block, O. Flanagan, and G. Güzeldere (Eds.), *The Nature of Consciousness: Philosophical Debates*. Cambridge, MA: MIT Press.

Tye, M. (1999). Phenomenal consciousness: The explanatory gap as a cognitive illusion. *Mind*, *108*, 705–725.

Van Kaam, A. L. (1959). Phenomenal analysis: Exemplified by a study of the experience of really feeling understood. *Journal of Individual Psychology*, *5*, 66–72.

Van Manen, M. (1990). *Researching Lived Experience*. New York: SUNY.

Varela, F. (1996). Neurophenomenology: A methodological remedy for the hard problem. *Journal of Consciousness Studies*, *3*, 34–56.

Varela, F. J., and Shear, J. (1999). First-person methodologies: What, why, and how? *Journal of Consciousness Studies*, *6*, 1–14.

Varela, F., Thompson, E., and Rosch, E. (1991). *The Embodied Mind: Cognitive Science and Human Experience*. Cambridge, MA: MIT Press.

Vase, L., Riley, J. L., and Price, D. D. (2002). A comparison of placebo effects in clinical analgesic trials versus studies of placebo analgesia. *Pain*, *99*, 443–452.

Vase, L., Robinson, M. E., Verne, G. N., and Price, D. D. (2003). The contributions of suggestion, desire, and expectation to placebo effects in irritable bowel syndrome patients. *Pain*, *105*(1–2), 17–25.

Vase, L., Price, D. D., Verne, G. N., and Robinson, M. E. (2004). The contribution of changes in expected pain levels and desire for pain relief to placebo analgesia. In D. D. Price & M. Catherine Bushnell (Eds.), *Psychological Modulation of Pain* (pp. 207–234). Seattle: IASP Press.

Vase, L., Robinson, M. E., Verne, G. N., and Price, D. D. (2005). Increased placebo analgesia over time in irritable bowel syndrome (IBS) patients is associated with desire and expectation but not endogenous opioid mechanisms. *Pain*, *115*(3), 338–347.

Vase, L., Norskov, K. N., Peterson, G. L., and Price, D. D. (2011). Patients' direct experiences as central elements of placebo analgesia. *Philosophical Transactions of the Royal Society of London. Series B, Biological Sciences*, *366*(1512), 1913–1921.

Velmans, M. (2002). How could conscious experiences affect brains? *Journal of Consciousness Studies*, *9*(11), 3–29.

Velmans, M. (2004). Why conscious free will both is and isn't an illusion. *Behavioral and Brain Sciences, 27*, 677–678.

Velmans, M. (2009). *Understanding Consciousness* (2nd ed.). London and New York: Routledge.

Vermersch, P. (1999). Introspection as practice. *Journal of Consciousness Studies, 6*, 17–42.

Verne, G. N., Himes, N. C., Robinson, M. E., Gopinath, K. S., Briggs, R. W., Crosson, B., and Price, D. D. (2003a). Central representation of visceral and cutaneous hypersensitivity in the irritable bowel syndrome. *Pain, 103*(1–2), 99–110.

Verne, G. N., Robinson, M. E., Vase, L., and Price, D. D. (2003b). Reversal of visceral and cutaneous hyperalgesia by local rectal anesthesia in irritable bowel syndrome (IBS) patients. *Pain, 105*, 223–230.

Vierck, C. J., Cannon, R. L., Fry, G., Maixner, W., and Whitsel, B. L. (1997). Characteristics of temporal summation of second pain sensations elicited by brief contact of glabrous skin by a preheated thermode. *Journal of Neurophysiology, 78*, 992–1002.

Von Neumann, J., and Morgenstern, O. (1947). *Theory of Games and Economic Behavior*. Princeton, NJ: Princeton University Press.

Voudouris, N. J., Peck, C. L., and Coleman, G. (1990). The role of conditioning and expectancy in the placebo response. *Pain, 43*, 121–128.

Wade, J. B., Dougherty, L. M., Hart, R. P., Rafii, A., and Price, D. D. (1992). A canonical correlation analysis of the influence of neuroticism and extraversion on chronic pain, suffering, and pain behavior. *Pain, 51*, 67–74.

Wade, J. B., Dougherty, L. M., Archer, C. R., and Price, D. D. (1996). Assessing the stages of pain processing: A multivariate approach. *Pain, 68*, 157–168.

Wade, J. B., Riddle, D. L., Price, D. D., and Dumenci, L. (2011). Role of pain catastrophizing during pain processing in a cohort of patients with chronic and severe arthritic knee pain. *Pain, 152*(2), 314–319.

Wager, T., Rilling, J. K., Smith, E. E., Sokolik, A., Casey, K. L., Davidson, R. J., Kosslyn, S. M., Rose, R. M., and Cohen, J. D. (2004). Placebo-induced changes in fMRI in the anticipation and experience of pain. *Science, 303*(5661), 1162–1167.

Wegner, D. (2002). *The Illusion of Conscious Will*. Cambridge, MA: MIT Press.

Weich, J. K., Yau, W. Y., Scott, D. J., and Stohler, C. S. (2006). Belief or need? Accounting for individual variations in neurochemistry of the placebo effect. *Brain, Behavior, and Immunity, 20*(1), 15–26.

Weinstein, E. A., Kahn, R. L., and Slate, W. H. (1955). Withdrawal, inattention, and pain asymbolia. *Archives of Neurology and Psychiatry, 74*, 235–240.

Weitzenhoffer, A. M. (1980). Hypnotic susceptibility revisited. *American Journal of Clinical Hypnosis*, *22*, 130–146.

White, J. C., and Sweet, W. H. (1966). *Pain and the Neurosurgeon*. Springfield, IL: Charles C. Thomas.

Wickramasekera, I. (1985). A conditioned response model of the placebo effect: Predictions of the model. In L. White, B. Tursky, & G. E. Schwartz (Eds.), *Placebo: Theory, Research and Mechanisms* (pp. 206–213). New York: Guilford Press.

Wiech, K., Lin, C. S., Broderson, K. H., Bingel, U., Ploner, M., and Tracey, I. (2010). Anterior insular transforms information about salience into perceptual decisions about pain. *Journal of Neuroscience*, *30*(48), 16324–16331.

Wik, G., Fisher, H., Bragée, B., Finer, B., and Fredrikson, M. (1999). Functional anatomy of hypnotic analgesia: A PET study of patients with fibromyalgia. *European Journal of Pain (London, England)*, *3*, 7–12.

Willoch, F., Rosen, G., Tölle, T. R., Øye, I., Wester, H. J., Berner, N.,Schwainger, M., and Bartenstein, P. (2000). Phantom limb pain in the human brain: Unravelling neural circuitries of phantom limb pain sensations using positron emission tomography. *Annals of Neurology*, *48*, 842–849.

Wilson, E. O. (1998). *Consilience: The Unity of Knowledge*. New York: Vintage Books.

Woolf, C. J., and Thompson, S. W. (1991). The induction and maintenance of central sensitization is dependent on N-methyl-D-aspartic acid receptor activation; implications for the treatment of post-injury pain hypersensitivity states. *Pain*, *44*, 293–299.

Zeiden, F., Martucci, K., Kraft, R., Gordon, N., McHaffie, J., and Coghill, R. (2011). Brain mechanisms supporting the modulation of pain by mindfulness meditation. *Journal of Neuroscience*, *61*(14), 5540–5548.

Zeki, S. (2007). A theory of microconsciousness. In M. Velmans & S. Schneider (Eds.), *The Blackwell Companion to Consciousness* (pp. 580–588). Malden, MA: Blackwell.

Zubieta, J. K., Smith, Y. R., Bueller, J. A., Xu, Y., Kilbourn, M. R., Jewett, D. M., Meyer, C. R., Koeppe, R. A., and Stohler, C. S. (2001). Regional mu opioid receptor regulation of sensory and affective dimensions of pain. *Science*, *293*(5528), 311–315.

Zubieta, J. K., Bueller, J. A., Jackson, L. R., Scott, D. J., Xu, Y., Koeppe, R. A., Nichols, E., and Stohler, C. C.. (2005). Placebo effects mediated by endogenous opioid activity on µ-opioid receptors. *Journal of Neuroscience*, *25*, 7754–7762.

Zubieta, J. K., Beuller, J. A., Xu W. Y., Kilbourne, M. R., Jewett, M., Meyer, C. R., Koeppe, R. A., and Stohler, C. S. (2006). Belief or need: Are there individual variations in neurochemistry of the placebo effect? *Brain, Behavior, and Immunity*, *20*(1), 15–26.

Index